THE WILDER HOUSE SERIES IN POLITICS, HISTORY, AND CULTURE

The Wilder House Series is published in association with the Wilder House Board of Editors and the University of Chicago.

David Laitin, *Editor*
Leora Auslander, *Assistant Editor*
George Steinmetz, *Assistant Editor*

A list of titles in the series appears at the end of the book.

ALSO BY WILLIAM F. S. MILES:

Elections and Ethnicity in French Martinique: A Paradox in Paradise

Elections in Nigeria: A Grassroots Perspective

De la politique à la Martinique: Paradoxe au Paradis

Imperial Burdens: Countercolonialism in Former French India

HAUSALAND DIVIDED

On the borderline: Lawal Nuhu (right) stands on the outskirts of Yardaji, Nigeria, while his friend stands in Niger.

HAUSALAND DIVIDED

Colonialism and Independence in Nigeria and Niger

WILLIAM F. S. MILES

Cornell University Press

Ithaca and London

First published 1994 by Cornell University Press.

The following materials are reproduced by permission: Figure 2 and data for Tables 5 and 6
and the accompanying text first appeared as "Nationalism versus Ethnic Identity in Sub-
Saharan Africa," by William F. S. Miles and David A. Rochefort, in *American Political
Science Review* 85, no. 2 (1991). Map 7, based on *African Boundaries,* by Ian Brownlie
(copyright © 1979 by the Royal Institute of International Affairs), and Map 8, from *Affairs of
Daura: History and Change in a Hausa State, 1800–1958,* by Michael Smith (copyright © 1978
by The Regents of the University of California), appear by courtesy of University of
California Press. "The Tale of Alhaji Mallam H." first appeared as "Islam and Development
in the Western Sahel: Engine or Brake," by William F. S. Miles, in *Journal of the Institute of
Muslim Minority Affairs* 7, no. 2 (1986).
    All translations of archival materials and all photographs are the author's.

Printed in the United States of America

⊗ The paper in this book meets the minimum requirements
of the American National Standard for Information Sciences—
Permanence of Paper for Printed Library Materials, ANSI Z39.48-1984.

Library of Congress Cataloging-in-Publication Data

Miles, William F. S.
    Hausaland divided : colonialism and independence in Nigeria and Niger / William F. S.
Miles.
        p.   cm. — (The Wilder House series in politics, history, and culture)
    Includes bibliographical references and index.
    ISBN 0-8014-2855-6
    1. Hausa (African people)—Ethnic identity.   2. Hausa (African people)—Government
relations.   3. Niger—Colonial influence.   4. Nigeria—Colonial influence.   5. Assimilation
(Sociology)—Niger.   6. Assimilation (Sociology)—Nigeria.   I. Title.   II. Series.
DT515.45.H38M55   1994
966.26'004937—dc20   93-31669

This book is dedicated to two Samuel Mileses:
to the father who came to Hausaland and
to the son whom I yearn to bring

Contents

ix

Illustrations, Maps, Tables, and Figures

Illustrations

Maps

Tables

Figures

Preface

This book began with a theft. In 1979, as my two-year stint as a Peace Corps high school teacher in south-central Niger was drawing to a close, my home was broken into and my precious JVC shortwave radio/cassette recorder-player—a gift from my father—was stolen. Although there was a suspect, the prospects of recovering the radio were, according to the town's police chief, virtually nil: the suspect's movements immediately after the break-in were traced to a village across the border in Nigeria. Presumably the radio had been hidden or sold there, in Nigerian territory. Even if the radio could be traced, the police chief went on, its recovery would necessitate foreign diplomacy and the invocation of international law: Nigérien authorities in Niamey (Niger's capital) would have to contact their counterparts in Lagos, who would then need to follow the administrative chain of command down to the small, rather insignificant border village. I was made to understand that even in the unlikely event that the appropriate government officials were to take an interest in my pilfered radio—hardly a matter of consequence in the larger scheme of Nigérien-Nigerian relations—the process would be inordinately time-consuming and that in all probability I would be long gone from the country by the time the affair was resolved.

As it turned out, I did get my radio back, though its recovery had little to do with Nigérien-Nigerian diplomatic intervention at the national level. My radio was returned thanks to the successful invocation of local Hausa norms. The chief of the Nigérien district where I resided sent messengers to the nearby Nigerian village to inform the chief there of the problem. The village chief summoned the fishmonger who had bought my purloined radio and prevailed upon him to sell it back to my chief's messengers. In the end, then, though it had been smuggled across an international boundary, I was able to buy back and retrieve my property from a foreign country.

The theft of my radio and the circumstances of its return whetted my curiosity about the partition of the Hausa into Niger and Nigeria and the consequences of that partition for frontier life in Hausaland today. It also planted the seeds for a research agenda that entailed four subsequent trips to Hausaland (of seventeen months' cumulative duration) and culminated in my participation in the Nigeria-Niger Transborder Cooperation Workshop, held under the auspices of the National Boundary Commission of Nigeria in July 1989.

I initiated my fieldwork with a null hypothesis: that the partition made little difference in the lives of Hausa who lived in villages along the boundary. I assumed that, as independent-minded as African agriculturalists generally are, they would prefer to have as little to do with government as possible and would tend to ignore external impositions upon their conduct and lifestyle. I expected to enhance my understanding of Hausa culture, language, and society during my nine sponsored months in the borderlands, but in the end to emerge from the bush without much to report in the way of political transformation or development. In fact, I was so smitten by the impact of the colonial boundary (and other invisible lines of separation) that I not only prolonged my research in Hausaland but have extended this line of inquiry to South Asia (Pondicherry) and the South Seas (Vanuatu).

But to return to the *causa causans:* though *kumya* (discretion) prevents me from naming the radio filcher, let it be known that we have long since been reconciled and that I now accept his attribution of his proprietary lapse to involuntary *bori*—a possession trance.

My initial fieldwork was accomplished between February 1983 and January 1984. My surveys, alas, were lost in the diplomatic pouch, and I returned during the summer of 1986 to redo them, thanks to the intercession of Senator Edward Kennedy and the commiseration of the Fulbright Program. Unless I specify otherwise, the ethnographic present is 1983–1986.

Whether fieldwork is a science or an art is an ongoing debate in anthropological and sociological circles. My colleagues in political science are usually removed from such controversies. But here the issue cannot be avoided. In this book I have tried to integrate the two approaches, applying strict random sampling techniques in surveys on self-identity and ethnic affinity (Chapter 3) and extracting research insights while avoiding arrest as I stumbled upon a government investiture ceremony during a chance horseback ride along the border (Chapter 7). In like manner, I gleaned oral testimony both from scheduled formal interviews (during which I took written notes) and from spontaneous utterances during long marches and cold-season bonfire chats (which I noted in my field diaries as soon as circumstances allowed). To be honest, I am not sure which method is the more reliable: the standardized note-taking and tape-recorded sit-down interview—which academic colleagues abjure—or the spontaneous, uncontrived causerie—a more culturally appropriate means of information exchange.

Since I have gathered information by both methods, I must exercise more caution than usual in identifying informants by name: circumstances did not always lend themselves to determining whether comments were for attribution. Political sensitivity, moreover, prevents me from identifying the source of each quotation, even when anonymity was not explicitly re-quested: in expressing criticism of government or authority, village friends placed in me a trust that still weighs heavily. At the risk of failure to adhere to strict canons of methodological disclosure, I have chosen to err on the side of discretion.

Gaining acceptance within an African village requires one to fashion a new persona. Achieving credibility within the society of scholars demands another kind of projection altogether. Despite the inherent contradiction, I have tried in these pages to be faithful to both of these profiles. To the extent that I have succeeded in bringing together the communities of scholarship and borderline life, I am satisfied that my efforts have been worthwhile. May both groups forgive whatever errors they detect.

My inquiry into life along the Niger-Nigeria boundary has been im-mensely facilitated by those first-generation scholars who built an early foundation for Hausa studies, as well as those who subsequently reconnoi-tered the border in doctoral quest. In the first category I pay homage to Polly Hill, Guy Nicolas, the late M. G. Smith, and C. S. Whitaker, Jr.; in the second I salute John Collins and Derrick Thom. Scholars whose vast ex-perience and knowledge have contributed enormously, through both pub-lication and conversation, to my own understanding of Hausaland include Barbara Callaway, Bob Charlick, Michael Horowitz, Michael Mortimore, John Paden, and Pearl Robinson. Development practitioners—cultural as well as economic—whom I acknowledge for the same reasons are Andy Cook (with special thanks for currency and cattle bailouts), Jeff Metzel, and Connie Stephens. I especially acknowledge Professor Horace Miner for providing me with my first fieldwork research opportunity in Hausaland.

Some scholars who are not Hausa specialists have nevertheless had a considerable influence on my Africanist thinking and writing. A. I. Asi-waju, the dean of partitioned Africans, has imparted a new respectability to the rest of us "borderline scholars." Naomi Chazan, *grande dame* of Afri-can politics, stuck up for my "grassroots perspective" on Nigerian Hausa elections and launched me on my way. Larry Diamond, my patron scholar-saint, rescued me in Kano and has kept at it ever since. Lenny Markovitz, *tsaddek* for generations of summer (and lifetime!) senior students of Africa, volunteered to read my draft and patiently nudged me to whip it into shape. And to *APSR*-collaborator Dave Rochefort, who never dreamed of being included within the family of Africanists, I can only cite a Hausa proverb: "Duniya mace da ciki ce": The world is a pregnant woman (one never knows what it will produce next).

Other scholar-friends based in Kano fortified me for my longer stints in the bush. They include Abdel Muta'al zein el Abdin Ahmed, M. K. Bashir, Momodou Darboe ("Not again, Mallam Bill!"), Ali Farbood, Martin Fisher, Shahina Ghazanfar, and Gerry Kleis. Also in Kano, Jeffrey Lite acted as cultural affairs attaché par excellence.

For sustenance in Magaria—spiritual as well as physical—I thank Mallam Souleymane Abdou dan Tata and Mamman Alassane. My debt to Sarkin Harou, chief of Magaria, is also acknowledged.

Alhaji Bashar Muhammadu Bashar, Sarkin Daura, blessed my efforts within his emirate. Others in Daura town who unstintingly assisted me were Alhaji Lawal, Alhaji Galadima, Alhaji Sani, Yahaya Yusufu, Alhaji Idi Salihu, Ubandawaki, and all the other palace guards. In nearby Zango, Gambo Mai Mai kept me moving on my motorcycle as well as on my psycholinguistic nerve paths.

Among the institutions to which I am grateful are the Fulbright Research Program, Bayero University (Department of Sociology), the National Archives of Kaduna, the Prefecture of Magaria, the Institut de Recherche en Sciences Humaines (Niger), and Northeastern University (Research and Scholarship Development Fund). Eliza McClennan, artist-cartographer, did a magnificent job preparing the maps and figures from my crude sketches. At Northeastern University, Terry Beadle also assisted in preparing tables and graphics; Fred Anang, research assistant, helped with glossary and index; and Karyn Harvey, departmental secretary, retyped some of the most inscrutable passages. But for the enthusiastic editorial support of David Laitin, director of the Wilder House Series in Politics, History, and Culture, none of these good people would be acknowledged in print now. Similar thanks to Roger Haydon of Cornell University Press.

How can I sufficiently convey my gratitude to my friends and neighbors of Yardaji and Yekuwa? Without your hospitality and generosity this research would have been impossible. As it was, you made everything possible. This book, therefore, belongs to you.

In Yardaji, I again thank the Sarkin Fulani Alhaji Harou and his sons

Hassan (Sarkin Aiki) and Ibrahim (Sarkin Wayo). My neighbors Alhaji Lassan, Malam Ja, Ilu (Sarkin Shayi), Amadu Shawagi, Azimi, and Uma made the village my home. So did Alhaji Usman Kongo, Alhaji Musa Tela and Ali, and Ousseini, Sidi (Sarkin Allura), Moutari, Issoufou, and Issaka (Sarkin Rawa). Taigaza (Makogaro) remains my broadcast system and Mamman my ever-loyal groom. Sani Dauda helped with interviews. But it remains to Lawal Nuhu, Yardaji's first university graduate and premier English speaker, to translate and convey these thanks.

In Yekuwa, first thanks go to chiefs Sule of Kofai and Alhaji Adamu Danjuma of Hamada. *Godiya,* too, go to Alhaji Aminu, Kaiga, Alhaji Mallam Harou, Issoufou (Sarkin Wasa), and Alhaji Mamman. Faralu helped with the horse, Yerima cared for the house, and Mansour kept us all in tea. I am especially grateful to my census takers and interview helpers, Abdurazaki and 'Dan Subdu.

"A good wife, who can find? She is precious far beyond rubies." Without the sufferance, support, and, yes, patience of Loïza Nellec-Miles, I could never manage both to write *and* to live. Long ago you came to me, *jusqu'au fin fond de la brousse africaine.* Here, *enfin,* is your M.O.

WILLIAM F. S. MILES

Boston, Massachusetts

A Note on Hausa Orthography

The Hausa language contains three glottalized consonants that are represented by hooked letters: 6, ɗ, and ƙ (Ɓ, Ɗ, Ƙ in the upper case). Although all three are explosive glottals, the 6 and ɗ sounds are also often formed implosively (i.e., with the airstream pulled into the mouth). The ƙ is a click sound. Appendix F contains a glossary of Hausa terms used in the book.

HAUSALAND DIVIDED

I

Introduction:
Rehabilitating the Borderline

Kama da wane ba wane ba ne.

Similarity is not the same thing as identity.

—Hausa proverb

Incongruously, provocatively, it towers on high: a fifteen-foot metal pole, springing out of the dirty brown Sahelian sand. No other human artifact is to be seen in this vast, barren, flat savanna; only an occasional bush, a tenacious shrub, a spindly tree break up the monotonous, infinite landscape. One stares and wonders how, by beast and porter, such a huge totem could have been lugged here and erected in this desolate bush. But there it stands: a marker of an international boundary, a monument to the splitting of a people, a symbol of colonialism, an idol of "national sovereignty." Local people refer to it as *tangaraho*.

"Tangaraho" literally means "telegraph pole." Between 1906 and 1908, sixty-three of these thick metal rods were placed on or near the thirteenth and fourteenth northern parallels, between the fourth and the fourteenth eastern longitudinal marks in West Africa. The exact placement of these poles had been determined far away, in London, by British and French diplomats who had never set foot in the territory. Nor would they ever visit here. Yet for the people who live in the areas where the poles were erected the consequences have been far-reaching.

The poles would determine the identity, fate, and life possibilities of the people along and behind them. First under European colonial rule and then under independent African governments the tangaraho has come to identify the spot where one alien power ends and the next one begins.

The tangaraho symbolizes what the local inhabitants call *yanken ƙasa*. The noun "ƙasa" means country or homeland; "yanke," a verb, means to

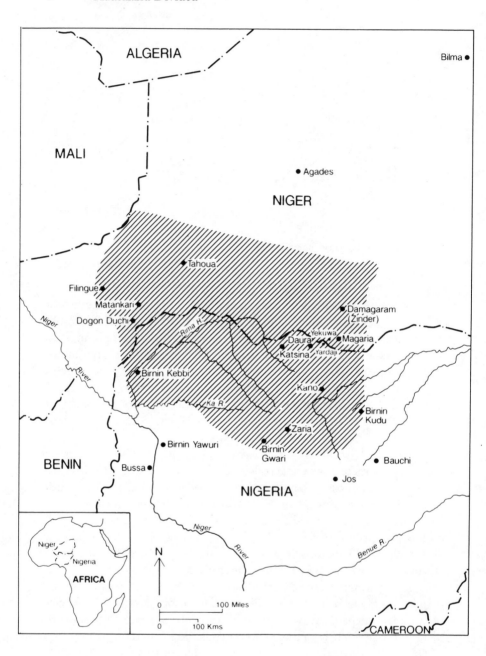

Map 1. Hausaland

split, to cut, to rip, as with a knife. "Yanken ƙasa" may thus be rendered "the splitting of the country." The country is called Hausaland, but don't look for it on any map of the world. Hausaland may exist for the Hausas and for their ethnographic and historical chroniclers (Map 1), but as a political entity it ceased to exist shortly after the turn of the century.

To stand on one side of the pole is to be, in common parlance, in Faranshi (France); to step across it is to enter Inglishi or, more commonly, Nijeriya. For the people who live here, these designations have not changed for well over eighty years. Westerners and "educated" Africans, though, distinguish thus: from 1890 to 1960, the territory was divided into two colonies, under British and French rule. One is remembered as the Colonie du Niger, which was part of Afrique Occidentale Française (AOF), or French West Africa. The other was the Colony and Protectorate of Nigeria.[1] After 1960, the former became the République du Niger; the latter is now the Federal Republic of Nigeria (see Map 2). Around the tangaraho, people also know they are either 'yan Nijeriya or 'yan Faranshi—that is, people of Nigeria or people of Niger. But though they are split into two sovereign states, they still live in Hausaland. They are still Hausa.

Does it matter on which side of the tangaraho the Hausa people live, here in the remote, outer fringes of Niger and Nigeria? Do those heady global phenomena of "European colonialism" and "Third World national liberation" actually make a difference in the lives of humble Hausa peasants, eking out survival from the sandy Sahelian soil? These are the immediate questions that this book aims to explore. An overarching consideration is the contribution of "borderline" studies for inquiries into nation building, national consciousness, and ethnic identity, particularly in an era when so many states are unstable.

---

[1] Both colonies underwent considerable transformation both in name and in territory before assuming their more familiar forms. Niger was originally part of the French Sudan before becoming its own Military Territory of Niger in 1911. (From 1901 until 1911 it was classified as an "autonomous military territory.") In 1922 it was renamed Colony of Niger. From 1900 until 1914 the Protectorate of Northern Nigeria was administered separately from the Colony and Protectorate of Southern Nigeria (which, before having Lagos added to it in 1906, was merely the Protectorate of Southern Nigeria). Amalgamation into the single Colony and Protectorate of Nigeria occurred in 1914. Until 1900, trading rights were exercised by the Royal Niger Company (Henige 1970:31, 149; Donaint & Lancrenon 1972:55). Although the British and French pressed territorial claims before 1890, that year is a convenient benchmark for discussion of partition, for that was the year the first Anglo-French treaty governing the region was signed.

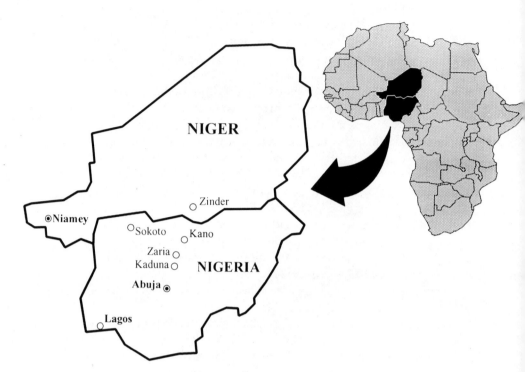

Map 2. Niger and Nigeria in Africa

Comparative Borderline Studies

A revealing, if unfortunate, meaning of the term "borderline" is marginal: not important, nonessential, dispensable, not quite standard. Social scientists, no less than government officials, have generally dismissed borderland communities as "borderline" in this pejorative sense and thus peripheral to mainstream concerns. Yet an immense amount can be learned if we pay greater attention to the interstices of states, particularly when they bisect members of a single ethnic group.

The partition of colonial Africa provides a textbook case of ethnic divisions along seemingly artificial boundaries. But ethnic partition is not unique to Africa. Indeed, Europe is replete with such cases. Two particularly compelling borderlands that have commanded the attention of scholars are the Basque country and Catalonia, both spanning the boundaries of France and Spain.

Thomas Lancaster's (1987) survey research reveals that, despite a higher degree of ethnic consciousness among the Basques of Spain than among those of France, in general both groups accept the legitimacy of state sovereignty and their own identification as French and Spanish citizens. These findings parallel to a remarkable extent the situation that prevails along the Nigeria-Niger boundary with respect to the Hausa.

Peter Sahlins's (1989) examination of the Cerdanya Valley, which straddles France and Spain in the Pyrenees (Catalonia), is more historical in approach and more comprehensive in scope. Yet Sahlins's conclusions replicate Lancaster's and foreshadow developments in Hausaland. "Frontier regions are privileged sites for the articulation of national distinctions," Sahlins writes. "In many ways the sense of difference is strongest where some historical sense of cooperation and relatedness remains" (271). A particularly interesting observation, and one that anticipates challenges to European-African borderland comparability, is that this sense of intra-ethnic cross-border differentiation antedated material development and differentiation along the frontier. Long before French Cerdagne began to enjoy an infrastructure superior to Spanish Cerdaña's (a development that Sahlins places in the 1880s, coincidentally when the European division of Hausaland was just beginning), an unmistakable sense of national (in contrast to ethnic) identity had developed. "Cerdans came to identify themselves as French or Spanish, localizing a national difference and nationalizing local ones, long before such differences were imposed from above" (286).

Can the experiences of the Catalan and Basque borderlands be regarded as prototypes for an analysis of the division of Hausaland? If so, these histories can indeed help us to understand the partitioned borderland phenomenon today, in Africa as well as Europe. They would also shed light on the processes by which partitioned border communities deal with externally introduced levels of identity and the development of national consciousness in new states.

Or does the prototype paradigm undermine the singularity of the African experience? Do the conquest, partition, and colonization of Africans by Europeans not irremediably qualify the comparison? Despite the "parallels between the means French rulers employed to gain the loyalty of a subject population abroad and the cultural apparatus of induced loyalty at home," observes Herman Lebovics (1992:132), "we should not automatically assume that the growth of Parisian power in the provinces should be understood as the same process as the ascendancy of France over distant colonies" (126). Indeed, such assumptions must be subjected to analysis, particularly comparative analysis.

Assimilation and the Colonial Enterprise

To be sure, the racial dimension to colony building in Africa cannot be dismissed. There prevailed throughout the colonial enterprise a general belief in the superiority of lighter over darker peoples. Moreover, the implantation of an intermediate level of government (the local colonial administration) between the metropolitan sovereign and the overseas population complicated the relationship between indigenous communities and "national" society: a dual allegiance, to the colonial capital and to the "mother country," was imposed.

But aside from these qualifications, how novel actually was the enterprise of European hegemony building? The colonization of Africa represented the extension of a process that characterized nation building in Europe. The strategy of assimilation—of incorporating the colonized into the colonizer—developed in Europe for Europeans. Indeed, as Eugen Weber brilliantly documents in *Peasants into Frenchmen* (1976), France became France in the first place through an internal process of assimilation that was "akin to colonization" (486). For Weber, not until World War I was the peasantry of France transformed into truly French peasants. "[U]ncivilized, that is unintegrated into, unassimilated to French civilization: poor, backward, ignorant, savage, barbarous, wild, living like beasts with their beasts" (Weber 1976:5): these were terms employed by Gallic Frenchmen not to denigrate colonials of color but to designate racially similar but no less disdained countryfolk. It is all the more striking that such attitudes prevailed during an era when France was colonizing overseas. Or perhaps one should say, when France was colonizing *also* overseas.

For colonization and its attendant rationalizations persisted in the metropole as well. Landes, certainly no hinterland outpost, came in for particular approbation. Populated by a "people alien to civilization," it was often compared to a cultural and physical desert: "our African Sahara: a desert where the Gallic cock could only sharpen his spurs." But Landes was by no means alone: well into the twentieth century, parts of Arcachon were likened to "some African land, a gathering of huts grouped in the shadow of the Republic's flag." Or Sologne: "clearly a question of colonization." Brittany complained of state efforts in "faraway lands [i.e., Africa] to cultivate the desert [when] the desert is here." Limousin bitterly noted that "they are building railway lines in Africa" and demanded comparable treatment. Perhaps more illustrative of the colonial parallel was the argument for use of the same French-language teaching method employed in Brittany (i.e., target language immersion) in Africa. The proposal was defended "as applicable to little Flemings, little Basques, little Bretons, as to little Arabs and little Berbers" (contemporary sources quoted in Weber 1976:488–90).

Long after Gallic assimilation had proceeded to create more epigrammatic "black Frenchmen" throughout the empire (see Murch 1971), metropolitan assimilation was still laboring to create white Frenchmen. Though the process was certainly more pronounced in France than in Great Britain, even there the task of turning English, Scots, and Welsh into people with a British identity entailed a recognizable strategy of cultural assimilation. (The mitigated success of British assimilation in Northern Ireland, another example of metropolitan colonialism, helps explain the persistence of severe conflict there.) As Linda Colley (1992) demonstrates, however, the underpinnings of "Britishness" are external and transient, casting doubts on the solidity of British national identity.

Religion, warfare, and colonization are the three factors that combined to "invent Britain," says Colley. But now that Britain can no longer boast about defending Protestantism, no longer needs to defend itself against France, and no longer reigns over an august (and profitable) overseas empire, it is not only less Great but less British. Defining Britain as "an invented nation superimposed, if only for a while, onto much older alignments and loyalties" (1992:5), Colley traces the process by which three culturally and politically distinct peoples, the English, Welsh, and Scots, were amalgamated into one.

Overseas colonization, with its assimilationist subtext, was not sui generis. It was the continuation of a core imperialism—sometimes brutal, sometimes subtle—that originated in and was originally applied within the metropole itself.

Both Weber and Colley describe "modern" (i.e., eighteenth- and nineteenth-century) processes of nation building that evoke familiar variations in assimilationist strategy. Early metropolitan imperialism in Europe, however, belies the oft-invoked dichotomy between Gallic and Anglo-Saxon colonization policies. James Given (1990) finds that in the thirteenth century greater local autonomy was retained (and tolerated) in an area of French domination (Languedoc) than in English-conquered Wales. Given's medieval comparison serves as wise caution regarding the transience of so-called core elements of culture as well as the historical limitations of our own time-bound theories.

Herman Lebovics's (1992) historical inquiry into the battle over French cultural identity in the first half of the twentieth century also tempers the image of a unidirectional French assimilationist project. As his ironically titled chapter on the French colonial enterprise in Vietnam ("Frenchmen into Peasants") elucidates, there have been even recent contexts and circumstances in which "assimilation" could be promoted by a return to the native language, arts, history—but always in ways conceptualized and molded by (so as to buttress the overall interests of) the colonizer. Lebovics is skeptical that any wall (high or otherwise) categorically separated assimilation from association (a more tolerant colonial cultural policy that ostensibly allowed for the coexistence of indigenous norms along with French sovereignty). Lebovics's skepticism is justified: French colonial association never approached the degree of cultural, not to mention political, autonomy of modern British rule.

Borderlands, National Integration, and Decolonization

Revolution, secession, and fragmentation in Eastern Europe, Czechoslovakia, and the former Soviet Union in the last decade of the twentieth century should remind us that even the mightiest of empires can be brittle constructs. Such developments should also serve as reminders that national integration of plural societies is far from irreversible—a point that Colley can make only prophetically for her fellow Britons. The end of the experiment in communist and Soviet-style nationalism provides stronger evidence that assimilation needs to be rooted in a core culture that is both relevant and functional: ideology alone does not provide the necessary glue.

Of course, one could claim that it was the material failure of Soviet communism that doomed Soviet nationalism, not the insufficient ideological basis of its assimilating mission. Yet analyses of nationalities immediately before the breakup bear out the observation that ethnic cleavages along territorial lines persisted throughout the Soviet era, and that these regional-ethnic disparities were only indirectly linked to unequal levels of economic prosperity. In particular, different types of *cultural* integration of peripheral elites within the Slavic-dominated Soviet center seem to have fostered nationalist movements of varying intensities and distinct consequences (see Laitin 1991). Contradictions between imperfect, differential Russification and universal assimilationist Marxism undermined Soviet union and turned the Soviet republics into sovereign states. An even more patent lesson from Soviet fragmentation is that territorial boundaries *are* mutable and that under certain circumstances borderland regions can be rapidly dissolved.

How will the structural and psychological divisions that separated communities along and behind the now defunct East-West German frontier be erased? How will the thousands of centrally located Soviet towns and villages cope, now that they suddenly find themselves on the margins of newly independent republics? And what kind of transborder relations will emerge in the constitutent parts of the old Yugoslavia, once the fratricide there recedes?

A long-held presumption in the permanence of international boundaries crumbled with the Berlin Wall. So did traditional expectations regarding nationalism and interstate alliances. Instability and uncertainty, even for the enlarged European Economic Community of Western Europe, run rife. Today's core is tomorrow's periphery; today's periphery may be tomorrow's reality.

With a prescience unusual in academe, in the late 1980s the University of Durham established an International Boundary Research Unit. The IBRU is a testament to the growing relevance of boundary studies, not only for scholarship but for policy making. However nascent, a new science of boundaries is beginning to emerge. But the development of such a science still depends on a storehouse of case studies firmly rooted in the ground and in history. My concern here, then, is not merely to reexamine previously covered terrain in the historiography of colonial Africa or to forecast boundary instability in West Africa. It is to place the division of Hausaland within the larger story of partitioned peoples and colonized societies, and the perennial process of the construction of group identity.

Comparative Colonialism in West Africa

To conduct a comparison of British and French colonialism in West Africa is hardly a novel idea. One might even think the topic thoroughly exhausted by this time. A full century after the Berlin Conference first initiated the scramble for pieces of the continent and a generation since independence came to the region, hundreds, perhaps thousands of books, articles, and conference papers have been devoted to the subject. An impish but irrepressible thought arises: If the trees felled to provide pulp for the colonial historian's mill had instead been transplanted to the Sahel, would not a greater service to the parched reality of modern-day Africa have been done?

But the clock of the publishing industry cannot be turned back, any more than the colonial era can be undone. Printed pages can no longer trees become, nor can the legacies of colonialism be erased. (Is there no connection, in fact, between the occupation and division of Africa by Europeans in the 1890s and early 1900s and the famines that afflict the continent in the 1980s and 1990s?) The trauma of colonialism is irrefutable; the extent and significance of different "styles" of colonialism are more subject to debate.

There are two schools of thought concerning this issue. The classical or "contrast" school agrees that Britain and France displayed different colonial philosophies, policies, and practices in administering their respective colonies. Britain, governing through indirect rule, molded and adapted traditional African institutions of government only gradually. They were to promote British values and goals, but cautiously, so as not to discredit or destroy indigenous ways and customs. Thus the chieftaincy was retained as a legitimate means of governance, and it served as an intermediate layer between British colonizers and African colonized. Lord Frederick Lugard is regarded as the architect of indirect rule.

The French, for their part, reputedly displayed little tolerance, admiration, or respect for indigenous institutions or leaders. Practicing direct rule, they set aside African law and administration in favor of French procedures and norms. The criterion for the selection of chiefs was not customary legitimacy but mastery of the French language. Direct rule entailed the radical transformation of African political, administrative, legal, and social institutions to a French model. Furthermore, the philosophy of assimilation encouraged the adoption of French norms, values, language, education, and thought in place of the "backward" or "traditional" indigenous analogues. The contrast school accepts the stark difference between these two approaches to colonial rule, and highlights them by detail and example.

With Hubert Deschamps's seminal article in 1963 ("Et Maintenant, Lord Lugard?"), the similarity school was launched. Deschamps agreed that the British and French may at one point have intended to run their colonial shows in their own ways, according to their own principles and methods. In practice, however, the reality of the colonial situation transcended such neat categories as direct and indirect rule—a distinction Deschamps refers to as "limpid manicheism" (294). Both French and British needed and used traditional chiefs as their agents. More than official colonial policy, what the man on the spot—that is, the local-level colonial administrator—felt and did was what prevailed.[2] As a result, uniform colonial policy tended to give way to idiosyncratic colonial practice. In the end, the similarities of the colonial situations faced by the French and the British—European administrators ruling alien peoples for the benefit of the mother metropole—by far outweighed the supposed differences.

More recently African scholars have taken this line of argument one step further. They argue that discussions or analyses of the differences between French and British colonialism tend to obfuscate the more important reality: the evil of the colonial system.[3] British or French, colonialism was economic exploitation based on racial domination: this more than any minor differences between direct and indirect rule is what counts. How archaic—and amoral—to quibble over colonial "styles"! This argument is sometimes advanced with such indignation that the very idea of discussing British and French colonial differences is scorned as downright reactionary. Is it not futile and misleading to debate "objectively" whether Hitler was worse than Pol Pot? Do such discussions not detract from the more significant issue, the horror of genocide?

The second generation of the similarity school may overstate its case in passionate condemnation of colonialism.[4] Yet it is still possible that there is validity in rejecting the direct-versus-indirect approach to British and French colonialism. Not that the differences between the British and French were not real, but these terms—"direct" and "indirect rule"—may glibly oversimplify the colonial reality. The task, therefore, is not to bury the notion of contrast in West African colonial historiography but to replace these dialectical categories with more suitable concepts and terms. Perhaps we can find them by listening to those people most directly concerned: a partitioned African people.

2 This point is made more directly by Pierre Alexandre (1970b:8) and John Smith (1970:18–20).

3 Although I have not yet found a good published representation of this position, it was forcefully argued at the Hausa International Studies Conference in Sokoto, 1983, and at the faculty–graduate student seminar at Bayero University, Kano, where I presented some of my findings in January 1984.

4 Richard Hodder-Williams (1984:2) interestingly observes that the younger generation of postcolonial-born African intellectuals are generally more vitriolic in their condemnation of colonialism than the elites and intelligentsia who lived through the colonial era and may actually have fought against colonial rule.

The Empirical Challenge

The problem with most comparisons of British and French colonialism is that they take a general, theoretical, un-"scientific" approach to the subject. Vast chunks of culturally dissimilar areas are lumped together to constitute "Anglophone" or "Francophone" units, which are then compared with each other.[5] This singularly Eurocentric perspective on colonialism results more in unconfirmable statements of political and historical philosophy than in verifiable hypotheses in social science. An understanding of European cultural, political, administrative, and philosophical differences is gained, but at the expense of an understanding of African cultures, politics, administrations, and philosophies. When one rides slipshod over vastly different African cultures and ethnic groups, an entire dimension of the "culture contact" aspect of colonialism is lost.[6] The challenge, then, is to conduct detailed case studies in areas where single ethnic groups have been partitioned by alien powers. However compelling the task, it is surprising how few such case studies have actually been conducted in Africa. Those few that have been done shine for the effort. Two worth considering are Claude Welch's (1966) treatment of the Ewe in Togo and Ghana and A. I. Asiwaju's (1976b) study of the Yoruba in (British) Nigeria and (French) Dahomey.[7]

The Ewe case is particularly significant because it represents "the first nationalist movement in West Africa to achieve widespread popular support in favor of self-government" (Welch 1966:41). The Ewe, a noncentralized, politically fragmented people historically divided into numerous subgroups (*dukowo*), were initially partitioned into German and British colonies. The former was known as German Togoland, the latter the Gold Coast. As a result of Germany's defeat in World War I, Togoland was repartitioned into French and British zones of occupation. Under the influence of traditional chiefs, modernizing elites, and the Ewe Presbyterian church, Ewe irredentism took the form first of a desire to unite Eweland and then of a movement to reconstitute the original Togoland. Neither dream of unity, however, ultimately succeeded: British Togoland was eventually in-

[5] This point is also made by A. I. Asiwaju (1976b:4). Contemporary comparative analyses of French and British decolonization—many of them excellent on their own terms—follow this tradition. See, e.g., Fieldhouse 1988, Low 1988, Panter-Brick 1988, and Tony Smith 1978.

[6] On the subject of culture contact in colonialism, see Balandier 1955, esp. chap. 1.

[7] Asiwaju has edited a fine collection of essays that also analyze the partition from a variety of indigenous African cultural perspectives. See Asiwaju, ed., 1985.

corporated into the Gold Coast (at independence renamed Ghana), and the French mandate eventually achieved independence as Togo.

It is significant that although "German administration in Togo was strict" (especially in its reliance on compulsory labor), some Togolanders considered French rule even harsher. In 1921 a letter addressed to President Warren G. Harding offered the following cross-colonial comparison:

> Please allow us to say the French method of administration as we see it is worse than that of the Germans. . . . During the German regime there were some methods of administration which we disliked and protested against; now they are being recalled into the colony, such as the poll-tax, market-tax, forced labour, oppression, etc. (Welch 1966:52, 56)

French administrative parsimony, British colonial prosperity, and a flourishing transborder Ewe commercial network all encouraged a flow of workers and economic aspirations from the French to British areas of Eweland. Educational philosophies and possibilities also favored the Ewe in British zones: education in British Togoland was more extensive than in French Togoland, and instruction in the local language was permitted. "The thirst for education brought many young Ewe from the French-administered area into British Togoland and the Gold Coast, and helped implant a favorable attitude toward British rule among many French Togolese" (Welch 1966:51). The harshness of Vichy rule during World War II (compulsory labor, deprivations, movement restrictions) exacerbated Ewe discontent with French rule and favored a postwar indigenous movement for Ewe unification under British administration. In the end, though, "self-determination in Togoland" ultimately perpetuated the partition of the Ewe people according to Togolese and Ghanaian citizenship.

Asiwaju (1976b) has conducted an admirable study of the partition of Western Yorubaland into French and British zones of colonial rule. His period covers the early European occupation until the end of World War II (1889–1945), because "after that date the effective phase of colonial rule gradually drew to a close" (6). Professor Asiwaju comes down firmly on the side of the contrast school in West African colonial historiography:

> The gulf between French and British rule over the Western Yoruba is unmistakable. . . . [T]he differences in the various aspects of the two colonial administrations stemmed largely from similar differences in the metropolitan traditions. Colonial exigency, as a factor making for comparable diversity of practice within each colonial area, is acknowledged; but its role has not been

found to cancel out the significance of the basic cultural predilections of the two rival European powers. (Asiwaju 1976b:257)

Asiwaju comes to this conclusion after comparing the differential changes in Yorubaland resulting from the French and British approaches to administrative boundaries, chieftaincy institutions, civil obligations (forced labor, taxation, conscription), economic incentives (in agriculture and trade), "cultural change" (including religion, architecture, family solidarity), and education and language. In each case, he highlights the differences in effect that resulted from contrasting European policies in these domains (taking for granted the contrasting intentions).

Without considering whether there might be an alternative way of characterizing these differences, Asiwaju accepts—and thereby legitimizes—the paradigm of direct and indirect rule. Neither does Asiwaju go much beyond his role as scholar to pass any moral judgment on the two systems (though when he discusses such phenomena as the eastward Yoruba migrations out of [French] Dahomey to [British] Nigeria, a certain preference cannot be hidden). And he considers the postcolonial implications of his findings only obliquely.[8]

The Next Step: Partition's Legacies at the Grassroots

This book responds to Asiwaju's call for more case studies to provide empirical evidence in the contrast-similarity debate on French and British colonialism. Beyond this historical perspective, I hope to provide a springboard for others who are grappling with the long-term problematics of decolonization, for those who are also asking: What is the ultimate impact of the colonizing society on the colonized? For how long, and in what forms, does the colonial influence persist after independence?

Like Asiwaju, I compare a partitioned people in terms of chieftaincy, education, religion, economics, civil obligations, and the rest. I stand with Asiwaju in presenting evidence that the contrasts between French and British rule in Hausaland far outweigh the similarities. (In fact, I am hard-

[8] "[T]oday in Africa, and particularly in West Africa, when serious moves are being made by the various independent states (mostly former colonies of France and Britain) to establish common institutions aimed at achieving political, cultural and economic harmonisation, comparative studies of European colonialism in Africa along the lines suggested should assist government policy makers and planning authorities to arrive at more detailed appreciation of the historical framework and problems involved" (Asiwaju 1976b:7).

pressed to pinpoint the similarities.) Yet I part company with him in two important respects.

First, whereas Asiwaju's (and to a great extent Welch's) study pertains above all to the implication of the partitioned Yorubas (and Ewes) in the colonial era, I am even more concerned with the implications of this split in the independence era. We should not forget that the partitioning of Africans not only was a colonial phenomenon but has been maintained by every African government since independence. (Until its own civil breakdown, the irredentism of Somalia served as the classic exception to this rule.) I will, then, be concentrating on how Nigérien Hausa society differs from Nigerian Hausa society *today*. The differences established in the colonial era by colonial institutions are of course crucial. Only through them can we understand the present-day ramifications of the yanken ƙasa. Nevertheless, when we do analyze British and French colonial doctrine and practice in Hausaland, it is with the ulterior purposes of understanding Hausa life in the independent states of Niger and Nigeria.

I am fully conscious of the hazards of this approach. I know I am eschewing the safety of historical distance that scholars of African colonial history and European metropolitan imperialism enjoy. European colonialism in Hausaland endured for seventy years; Niger and Nigeria have been independent for roughly half that time. A fairer assessment of decolonization in Niger and Nigeria (indeed, in most of Africa) should perhaps wait until the year 2030, when these two countries will have been independent as long as they were under colonial rule. By that time subtle, embryonic, and future processes in both these countries may very well mitigate or negate the major thesis of this book, which is the *continuity of colonial institutional norms in the postcolonial state*.[9] An ancillary theme is the power of boundaries to endure long after their imperial demarcators have gone.

The temptation to retreat into historical objectivity is strong but must be resisted. Transepochal understanding is always imperfect to some degree, and to renounce analysis today in the hope of greater objectivity tomorrow

[9] A similar thesis has been argued in the case of India, in the cultural as well as the administrative realm. Ashis Nandy (1983:2) maintains that "thirty-five years after the formal ending of the Raj, the ideology of colonialism is still triumphant in many sectors of life." David Potter (1986:3) agrees that "colonial administrative tradition persisted without major change after the departure of the colonialists." Just as scholars of India have been "mesmerized" (Potter 1986:8) by 1947, India's year of independence, Africanists have endowed 1960 with almost mystical qualities. Hopes were high that, as Basil Davidson (1989:131) put it, Kwame Nkrumah would be joined by other "new Africans" who would be similarly successful in seeking the "political kingdom" and making a "fresh start." But decolonization is a process, not an event: Africa is not exceptional in this respect.

is to flee before the imperative at hand. That imperative is to understand, however imperfectly, the past that has shaped the present, and the present that will give us our future. The first step is to make Africa part of our present.

The second way in which my approach differs from Asiwaju's relates to scale, or level of analysis. Like Welch with the Ewes in Togo and Ghana, Asiwaju has done a comprehensive analysis of Western Yorubaland divided into the larger colonies of French Dahomey and British Nigeria. Although I have until now cast this investigation as an analagous comparison of Nigérien and Nigerian Hausaland, it is not quite that. In the narrowest sense, it is a comparative analysis of two neighboring Hausa villages on opposite sides of the Niger-Nigeria border. Although I will have recourse to local archival records and the scholarly literature on Nigérien and Nigerian Hausaland, I mainly adopt a bottom-up perspective at the grassroots level rather than the broader territorial method followed by Asiwaju, Welch, and Sahlins. I aim to extrapolate my findings to the level of rural Hausaland,[10] but the inherent vulnerability of extrapolation from microlevel analysis to macrolevel hypothesis is so obvious that I make no claim to absolute certainty in my generalizations. Nevertheless, I shall attempt to legitimize this "right to extrapolation."[11]

There is no question of arguing that my two Hausa villages are "typical." Anyone who has lived for any time at all in a rural African community knows how patronizing and even condescending such an assertion would be.[12] Every Hausa village has its own character, its own personality. A village's people appreciate its distinctiveness more than any outsider can. The two villages differ in many ways, not only from each other but from every other village in Hausaland.

Nevertheless, even if I do not argue that my villages are typical, I can and do claim that they are representative. There is nothing about the village on the Nigérien side of the boundary that makes it fundamentally unlike other Hausa villages in Niger; likewise for the Nigerian village. What does distinguish them from most Hausa villages in Niger and Nigeria is their proximity to the border. It is precisely the border difference

---

[10] The need to study rural Hausaland, as opposed to its more widely known urban centers, has been argued by Polly Hill (1972:xii) and John Wiseman (1979:1).

[11] The choice of specific villagers is explained in chap. 1 and app. A. It is heartening to read even in an essay as monumental as Charles Tilly's *Big Structures, Large Processes, Huge Comparison:* "A concrete, historical program of inquiry must include work at the small scale and can well include our own time" (1984:14).

[12] Hill makes a similar point in her description of Batagarawa (1972:4).

that I wish to highlight. While the findings cannot be transposed undiscriminatingly from village to wider society, experience with life in other contexts throughout Hausaland tends to validate the general trends and observations found within the villages.[13]

After the colonial partition, differences in the evolution of urban Hausa life are to be expected. Both the British and the French established headquarters in towns and cities, and the sites they chose for their administrative centers soon mushroomed into capital importance. The best example of this development in (or on the fringes of) Hausaland is Kaduna, a "new city" that sprang up in the 1900s when the British decided to establish their capital for Northern Nigeria there. In Niger, Niamey (in Zarma territory) became the new capital in 1927, and it is by far the most Western city in the country.

The Europeans stamped their images on African urban centers in the colonial era, and those images have not faded in the independence era. That Hausa society in Zinder (Niger) is different from that in Kano (Nigeria) should come as no surprise. The differences that prevail in rural Hausaland, however, are particularly interesting. One expects relatively little penetration by the state and its agents in the countryside, at least in comparison with urban areas and centers. Yet the differences between Nigérien and Nigerian Hausaland at the village level are considerable.

Perhaps the most cogent justification for conducting this case study of a partitioned African people at the village level is that it permits a more intimate and hence more powerful presentation of the reality of the border split. To the extent that my own unavoidable historical and intellectual baggage will allow, I shall leave behind classical, a priori notions of how the issue of French versus British colonialism should be conceptualized and concentrate instead on the way it actually is perceived by the inheritors of the partition. Rather than employ exclusively Western terminology and categories, such as direct and indirect rule, I shall particularly elicit a direct, relatively unfiltered perspective on the *mulkin Inglishi* and *mulkin Faranshi* (English and French rule) by Hausa villagers on both sides of the Niger-Nigeria border.[14]

---

[13] In addition to my village fieldwork, I have lived and worked in larger towns and cities in both Niger and Nigeria (Magaria and Zinder in Niger, Kano and Kaduna in Nigeria), and have traveled extensively throughout both countries.

[14] Such an approach is consistent with Mary Smith's *Baba of Karo* (1954/1981), an autobiographical record of a Hausa woman's life. Oral history always runs the risk of distortion, as Jan Vansina (1961:76) elaborates: "A testimony is no more than a mirage of the reality it describes." But as one method among several, oral history constitutes a valuable and in some

In Chapter 2 I explain why I chose the particular villages I did. (Readers interested in a more detailed discussion of the methodology of village selection may refer to Appendix A.) I also relate the villages' histories.

In Chapter 3 I examine the nature of Hausa identity, a group identity that is more problematic than it may appear at first blush. I then review one attempt to measure and compare levels of identity among the partitioned Hausa. Quantitative methods, however, are ancillary to my overall approach.

The creation and impact of the boundary between Niger and Nigeria are the subjects of Chapter 4. Chapter 5 examines how different colonial policies in Niger and Nigeria differentially affected the local regions of Zinder and Daura and how these policies are recalled by borderline villagers today. Chapter 6 provides archival documentation of these policy differences and their cross-border effects.

Chapter 7 contrasts the traditional rulers in Nigérien and Nigerian villages, revealing significant disparities in the status, prestige, and influence of their chiefs. Chapter 8 contrasts the villages in economic terms, highlighting the more robust activity on the Nigerian side of the boundary.

Chapters 9 and 10 deal with social evolution in rural Hausaland, the former through the prism of education and the latter through the lens of religion. Chapter 11 contrasts the two communities in respect to village culture. Chapter 12 revisits questions of decolonization, boundary persistence, group consciousness, and national identity in light of the earlier findings. Six general hypotheses (including one middle-level one) are tentatively offered to account for colonial continuity in postcolonial society.

Although I have not devoted a separate chapter to the gender implications of partition, gender-derivative effects indeed surface in the domains of economy, education, religion, and village culture. Future investigators of Hausa women may wish to integrate the partition factor in their analyses of female evolution in rural Hausaland,[15] just as those who conduct follow-up borderline studies will need to examine the differential impact of boundary superimposition on partitioned women.

---

circumstances indispensable source of knowledge. What Vansina asserts for history and the historian should be considered by the social scientist at large: "[T]here is no such thing as 'absolute historical truth.' . . . The truth always remains beyond our grasp. . . . [B]y using calculations of probability, by interpreting the facts and by evaluating them in an attempt to recreate for himself the circumstances which existed at certain given moments of the past, . . . the historian can . . . arrive at some approximation to the ultimate historical truth" (185–86).

15 Recent books on Hausa women have focused mostly on town dwellers (see Callaway 1987b and Coles & Mack, eds., 1991). Though excellent in their own right, they do tend to reinforce the urban bias in Hausa studies noted in n. 10.

Boundary Abidance

In contrast to newspaper headlines that cry unceasingly of Third World civil strife; in opposition to political science that forecasts the demise of the African state; and in respectful dissent from neo-anticolonialists who prophesy the inexorable dismantling of "artificial boundaries," I maintain that the colonial partition, though external in origin, has become an internalized, commonplace reality for millions of borderline villagers throughout Africa. Since independence, furthermore, colonial-era divisions have been not only maintained but reinforced, though in ways that often deviate from the colonizers' original intent. We shall see how effectively national differences can be superimposed upon antecedent ethnic identities and how powerfully boundaries function to reinforce this process.

Challenges to "paper independence," in Africa as elsewhere throughout the Third World, have generally employed a neocolonial paradigm that relies heavily on the retention of economic relationships favorable to Western interests. But other, arguably more firmly rooted influences in thought, action, and culture serve to prolong the colonial era beyond its formal demise. To dwell on the transcendent impact of colonialism is not to extoll it. To the contrary, only consciousness of these persisting legacies can lead to their uprooting.

By focusing on only two villages, I received greater feedback on these questions from the villagers themselves. To the maximum extent, *they* will speak, they will compare, they will judge. For the best way to evaluate the long-term impact of colonial rule and its ultimate reversal is to go to the people who were split, who *are* split, and ask them. Go to Hausaland and let the people speak. Find the tangaraho and listen.

2

The Setting

Kowane tsuntsu ya yi kukan gidansa

Every bird has the note peculiar to its own kind.

—Hausa proverb

The villagers upon whom European sovereignty intruded had their own worldview, and when a boundary was drawn between neighboring communities, it had the contradictory effect of widening the scale of group consciousness along colonial lines. But partition does not explain everything in borderline communities. Even here partition is but one component of social life.

Questions of Comparability

Most of Niger's population is found along its southern latitudes, and a great many villages are quite close to the border. Economically, they profit considerably from their proximity to "wealthy" Nigeria. On the Nigerian side, many villages nestled along the country's northern border have also served as refuge and supply stations for their poorer Hausa cousins in Niger. Thus pairs of Hausa villages along the Niger-Nigeria border number in the hundreds. Before I could choose an appropriate pair, five initial criteria—administrative, demographic, institutional, economic, and spatial—had to be satisfied. Two villages that satisfied these criteria were Yekuwa, in the Magaria district of Niger, and Yardaji, in the Daura district of Nigeria.[1] (Appendix A explains the process of village selection in more detail.)

[1] The spelling used in this book for the two villages follows M. G. Smith 1978. In Niger itself, which follows French orthographical style, Yekuwa is written "Yékoua." Yardaji was apparently first rendered in English as "Herdaji" (in the "Agreement between the United Kingdom and France Respecting the Delimitation of the Frontier between the British and

Administrative and Hierarchical Comparability

Nigérien and Nigerian administrative and chieftaincy structures (basically the same as those inherited from French and British rule) are not identical. An exact one-to-one correspondence, therefore, cannot be made. Nevertheless, within their respective countries and local government groupings, Yardaji (Nigeria) and Yekuwa (Niger) do occupy equivalent positions in respect to their administrative and chiefly status.

In each village the chief bears the title of *mai gari* (literally, "holder of the village"). He is responsible to two people above him in the chieftaincy hierarchy. In Yekuwa the chief is responsible first to the canton chief (*sarki*) of Magaria and then to the sultan (sarki) of Zinder; in Yardaji, it is first to the district head (*hakimi*) in Zango and then to the emir (sarki) of Daura. The chiefs of both Yardaji and Yekuwa have authority over smaller settlements in their surrounding area, though the Yardaji chief's authority is more official because he also holds the title of village area head (*dagaci*). (See Figure 1.)

Yardaji is thus both an individual village (*gari*) and the seat of a village area (*gunduma*). (In Niger, where village areas do not exist, Yekuwa is only a village; were such an administrative unit to exist, however, it is certain that Yekuwa's relative demographic, economic, and institutional importance would make it a Nigérien "village area.") There are three higher administrative units into which both Yardaji and Yekuwa fit in their respective countries. In Nigeria, Yardaji area is part of (*a*) the Zango local government, which is part of (*b*) Daura emirate, which in 1986 was part of (*c*) Kaduna state. Yekuwa is part of (*a*) the canton of Magaria, which falls within (*b*) the arrondissement (county) of Magaria, which is part of (*c*) the department of Zinder. (See Map 3.) (When I conducted my research, there were nineteen states in Nigeria and seven departments in Niger.) Thus Yekuwa and Yardaji occupy parallel rungs in their respective countries in respect to their administrative positions and the title and status of their respective chiefs.

Population

Africa in general and Nigeria in particular are notorious for the unreliability of their censuses. The need for caution is usually mentioned when

---

French Possessions East of the Niger," 1910; see Thom 1970:284–301, esp. 293). Villagers literate in Roman script today usually write their village as "Yardaje." Given the Hausa etymology of the village's name (discussed below), however, "Yardaji" will be retained here.

Chief Executive	Organizational Unit			Organizational Unit	Chief Executive
President	Federal Republic	**NIGERIA**	**NIGER**	Republic	Supreme Milita Council Preside
Governor	19 States	**KADUNA**	**ZINDER**	7 Departments	Prefect
Emir	7 Emirates	DAURA	MAGARIA	5 Arrondissements	Subprefect
District Head	5 Local Gov't Areas	ZANGO	MAGARIA	7 Cantons	Canton Chie
Village Head	7 Village Areas	YARDAJI	YEKUWA	148 Villages	Village Chief
Village Chief	9 Villages	Yardaji	Kofai Hamada	2 Villages	Village Chief

Figure 1. The places of Yardaji and Yekuwa in the administrative structures of Nigeria and Niger, 1986

national figures are cited, but the cautious ones often overlook the fact that the aggregate distortion is only an accumulation of distortions at the local level. The "local level" can as easily be a village as a region or a province. When I compared the official figures on the villages' populations, I discovered that apparently the phenomenon had struck again.

Undoubtedly, Yekuwa is spatially larger than Yardaji. 'Yan Yekuwa insist that their village is larger in population as well; 'yan Yardaji protest the opposite. It is conceivable that population density is greater in Yardaji than in Yekuwa, but not so much so that Yardaji has over twice as many inhabitants as Yekuwa, as official records indicate.

According to 1979 census figures in the Zango local government headquarters, Yardaji had 6,820 inhabitants. The figures for Yekuwa at the subprefecture of Magaria indicated a total population of 3,022 in 1982. My own census, conducted in the summer (when most itinerant men have returned for the agricultural season) of 1986, determined that there were fewer than 3,500 residents of Yardaji and over 4,000 in Yekuwa (see Table 1). The discrepancies arise, I am certain, from incentives to underreport the official population in Yekuwa (so as to avoid susceptibility to taxation and military conscription) and to exaggerate the size of Yardaji (to buttress demands for public works and social services).

An objection to the comparability of the two villages could be made on grounds of scale. How can one hope to compare a village of 4,000 in a country of 5 million with an even smaller village within a country of over 80 million? Will not the significance of the former greatly exceed that of the

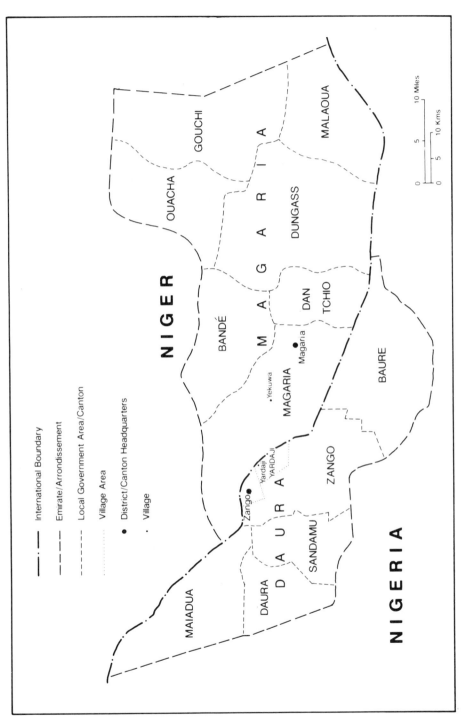

Map 3. Local government areas of Daura and Magaria

Table 1. Populations of Yardaji and Yekuwa, by status in household, 1986

	Heads of household				Wives		Unmarried children				Other relatives[a]		Workers		All residents	
	Male		Female				Boys		Girls							
	No.	%	No.	%	No.	%	No.	%	No.	%	No.	%	No.	%	No.	%
Yardaji	637	18.2%	50	1.4%	820	23.5%	999	28.6%	899	25.7%	54	1.5%	33	0.9%	3,492[b]	99.8 %
Yekuwa																
Kofai	457	19.2	12	0.5	614	25.7	650	27.2	566	23.7	43	1.8	44	1.8	2,386	99.9
Hamada	224	13.6	1	0.1	346	21.0	539	32.7	517	31.4	18	1.1	4	0.2	1,649	100.1
All Yekuwa	681	16.9	13	0.3	960	23.8	1,189	29.5	1,083	26.8	61	1.5	48	1.2	4,035[c]	100.0

[a] Usually the male householder's mother.
[b] At the time of enumeration, 24 of these people were away from the village (16 in Mecca).
[c] At the time of enumeration, 52 of these people were away from the village (45 in Mecca).

Table 2. Number and size of Yardaji and Yekuwa households

	Individual households	"Big houses"/ family units	Average household size
Yardaji	687	380	5.1
Yekuwa			
Kofai	469	253	5.1
Hamada	225	154	7.3
All Yekuwa	694	407	5.8

latter, drowned in the national demography? But recall that I am not comparing Nigeria with Niger, or even all Nigerian Hausaland with Nigérien Hausaland. The focus here is rather on a specific territory in Daura Hausaland and the changes within village society since the turn of the century. For this reason chieftaincy, administrative, and institutional parallels are even more important than demographic similarity. In any case, the objection implies that, for reasons of scale, Yekuwa must be more significant in Niger than Yardaji is in Nigeria. In fact, not only do the institutional parallels work as effective equalizers, but differences in the respective administrative structures have given Yardaji even greater influence in its area than Yekuwa has in its own.

Closer inspection highlights the demographic similarities of the villages. They are composed of virtually equal numbers of household units (see Table 2) and have the same proportional profile of male and female householders, boys, girls, other relatives, and unrelated but resident workers (see Table 1). Two secondary differences are that families are larger in Yekuwa (an average of 5.8 persons) than in Yardaji (5.1) and, conversely, Yardaji has four times more small and single-member households headed by women (usually widows), though the village's overall population is 13 percent smaller than Yekuwa's.

Institutional Comparability

If separate rural communities in different states are to be compared, it is essential that their levels of state penetration be roughly equivalent. Unless it can be shown that the villages' exposure to agents and representatives of their respective governments is similar, their comparability will be severely challenged.

Yardaji and Yekuwa pass this test, in that both do have the same two state-built and -run institutions: a primary school and medical dispensary.

The medical dispensary in Yardaji.

Both villages have resident state-trained schoolteachers and medical practitioners. (Although these practitioners are called doctors [*likita*], they are more accurately described as paramedics.) The existence of these two institutions places each village a cut above the smaller villages surrounding them, thereby reinforcing their local socioeconomic equivalence. Yekuwa also has a guesthouse where border patrol personnel and custom agents stay from time to time. Although Yardaji does not have any such boarding facilities, it is also visited from time to time by agents from the nearby Zango immigration and customs station.

Economic Importance

In Hausa society, no other institutional activity assumes such social and economic significance as the market. Many Hausa compare their settlements primarily in terms of market size. Marketplaces are important not solely for their economic role but because they attract people from nearby communities. In addition to the buying and selling that go on, news is exchanged, friendships are maintained, and even marriages have their be-

The medical dispensary in Yekuwa.

ginnings in the market. A lack of a market—and many small villages have none—is truly a mark of socioeconomic inferiority.

Both Yardaji and Yekuwa do have weekly markets. Each draws traders and visitors from the other. Because Yardaji's market is in Nigerian territory, it is larger, busier, and more diversified than Yekuwa's, but it is still a typical "bush market."

Proximity

Yardaji and Yekuwa are approximately 8 miles (12 kilometers) from each other (see Map 4). Only sand tracks link the two, and all travel between them is done either by foot (most common) or by beast (donkey or horse).[2] It thus takes approximately one and a half to two hours to complete the trip in each direction. Such a distance presents no obstacle to Hausa peasants. A constant stream of villagers trade and visit back and forth, and intervillage marriages are common: at one point I counted sixteen Yekuwa women married to Yardaji men. Although many pairs of villages in the region are closer to each other than Yardaji and Yekuwa, and a good number of villages are closer to Yardaji and Yekuwa than the two are to each other, no other pair are as similar in economic, demographic, institutional, and administrative and chiefly considerations.

[2] When I returned to the area in 1986, a Land Rover owned by a local businessman was beginning to serve as an inter-village market-day shuttle.

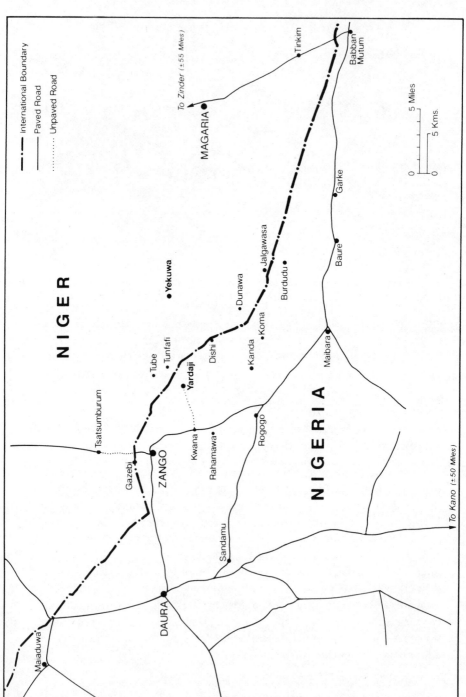

Map 4. The Niger-Nigeria border region

Table 3. Number of Yardaji and Yekuwa husbands and wives born outside village of residence

	Husbands	Wives	Total	Percent of all spouses[a]
Yardaji				
Elsewhere in Nigeria	26	145	171	12%
Niger (incl. Yekuwa)	19	76	95	7
Yekuwa	6	18	24	
Yekuwa				
Elsewhere in Niger	20	96	116	7
Nigeria (incl. Yardaji)	8	38	46	3
Yardaji	2	1	3	

[a]N = 1,457 in Yardaji, 1,641 in Yekuwa.

Table 4. Number of handicapped persons in Yardaji and Yekuwa

	Yardaji	Yekuwa
Blind	10	5
Deaf	9	7
"Insane"	8	1
Crippled	8	5
Lepers	6	1
Total	41	19

The level of interaction between the two villages parallels the economic imbalance between Niger and Nigeria. Yardaji is more important to Yekuwa than Yekuwa is to Yardaji. Yardaji not only is the major outlet for and supplier of material goods to Yekuwa but the link between Yekuwa and the outside world: most people traveling far from Yekuwa (whether to Kano or Mecca) stop first at Yardaji. Yardaji looks to Zango and then to Daura for its most important contacts; Yekuwa looks to Yardaji. It is therefore not surprising to find twice as many Nigérien-born persons (including twenty-four from Yekuwa) settled in Yardaji as Nigerian-born persons living in Yekuwa (see Table 3).

No other village in Niger has as many ties with Yardaji as Yekuwa. Even if Yardaji does tend to look down on Yekuwa as "backward" (as Nigerians close to the border generally tend to look down on Nigériens), only Yardaji's intimate knowledge of its Nigérien counterpart allows it to make such judgments. (Were 'yan Yardaji concerned with the relative number of handicapped persons in each village [see Table 4], their vanity might be tempered somewhat.) 'Yan Yardaji may well be puffed up by Yekuwa's dependence on them, but given the two villages' proximity, they also know, on some level, that there but for the grace of Allah—and colonial happenstance—go they.

Village Histories

Each of the villages has its own historical reckoning or variations thereon. Precolonial and local historical recollections of the people of Yardaji and Yekuwa provide truly local perspectives on their communities today.[3]

Yekuwa

Yekuwa is known as one of the settlements where Sarkin Gwari Abdu, king of Daura until he ws chased out by the Fulani in the first half of the nineteenth century, established a capital in exile. It is also his final resting place. But Yekuwa neither began with Sarkin Gwari's presence nor ended with his death.

Yekuwa is said to have been founded by a certain hunter, Mahalbi, also called Takwalkwalo. He had come from Tsamia, near Sassambouroum, in quest of game. At that time the area was true bush, inhabited by elephants, lions, and roan antelope but not by people.

Having hunted some animals, Mahalbi sought shade under a thorn tree at the site of what is now the eastern side of Yekuwa. He stored the meat he had caught and returned home to tell his brothers what a rich land he had discovered. When his brothers came and saw, they agreed to stay and live there. Each one built his own house.

Once one of the brothers went out into the bush and got lost. Mahalbi

---

[3] The following accounts are syntheses of various versions that I gathered during my fieldwork in the villages. Some of the versions vary in details. I have therefore relied on the criteria of plausibility and consistency in constructing the present version. My sources for Yekuwa's history were Mai Gari Hamada, Alhaji Moussa Makaho, Alhaji Allasane, Sagiur (recalling from the deceased Archai), Alhaji Harou Bachirou, Mallam Kobo, Hajiya Kunya (granddaughter of Sarkin Harou), Habou Cha'aibou (recalling Mai Gari Nalalu's version), and Mallam Ibra Gwadagwama (of Komo village). My sources in Yardaji were Mai Gari Yardaji, Alhaji Kosso, Alhaji Mallam Maman, Moussa dan Yardaji, and Musa Tela. In addition, I have availed myself of a handwritten document from the Kaduna National Archives (KAT-PROF [Katsina Province] 549, dated 1922 or 1927—the handwriting is unclear) and a somewhat tantalizing printed record of major events in the village's history which came my way unfortunately without cover or title. I have intentionally preserved, to the extent possible, the village narrational voice.

went out to search, shouting for his lost brother. He not only found his brother but in the process gave the new settlement its name. *Ya kuwa* ("he called" or "he shouted") became Yekuwa.[4]

Gradually more people came to settle at Yekuwa. News reached Sarkin Gwari Abdu that a new town was being settled, and Gwari, who had been routed from his throne in Daura, came to see for himself. He had originally intended to look and move on, but the people prevailed upon him to stay, saying, "You will become our sarki [chief, king] here." Gwari Abdu agreed and instructed the people to fell trees and construct a more permanent habitation. Thus did Yekuwa acquire its original defensive stockade.

Sarkin Gwari and his family and retinue lived on the eastern edge of Yekuwa, now called Hamada (abundance) for the plentiful well there. Another name for the well was Uwar Ruwa, Mother of Water. Commoners lived on the western edge of town, called Kofai.

Takwalkwalo, the original founder, left Yekuwa after six years. He went to Bande (at that time also a clan of hunters) and dwelt among the people there.

Sarkin Gwari Abdu fell ill and died in Yekuwa. His burial place, an unmarked spot near the Hamada well, is still visited periodically by his descendants, the restored ruling family of Daura.[5] After Gwari's death, Hamada was abandoned. The common folk (*talakawa*), however, continued to inhabit Kofai.

It appears that the first man to become chief of Kofai after Gwari died was one Kalo (he may also have been called Galadima dan Baduku), but he lost the confidence of the people and was deposed. Sarkin Gabas Goto was the next village chief. It was during his tenure that Mai Tumbi, a white man, arrived.[6] Mai Tumbi asked if Sarkin Gabas Goto wanted to become a veritable sarki—that is, chief over the surrounding countryside as well. Goto, fearful of possible recriminations from Damagram, demurred, claiming he was a mere farmer. He did recommend a certain Nababa, in Magaria, who was a true prince. Nababa was gambling when he was approached with the offer. Nababa was made Sarkin Magaria, and his family has ruled there

[4] This is but one of several explanations for the town's name. Others are that Mahalbi, to assert his authority, later issued a proclamation (*yekuwa*) that men were to carry timber to Magaria; that Sarkin Gwari Abdu put out a proclamation commanding people to gather in Yekuwa; and that a great proclamation followed Sarkin Gwari's death.

[5] In 1979 the emir of Daura (of Nigeria) paid homage, in Yekuwa, to his ancestor Sarkin Gwari Abdu.

[6] "Big Belly." This was Capt. H. C. Phillips, a British officer, whose arrival at the turn of the century presaged the partition of Hausaland.

ever since. Thus was Yekuwa removed from the suzereinty of Dawambey to that of Magaria.[7]

After his death, Sarkin Gabas Goto, who had been chief for ten years, was succeeded by his younger brother Yaroro. During Yaroro's time Yekuwa flourished: *Maguzawa* (pagans, but excellent farmers) settled from Kolfao, butchers came from Danbadada, and blacksmiths and hunters arrived from Dogo. It was also during Yaroro's reign, however, that Yekuwa split in two.

A dispute broke out between Chief Yaroro and one Nakada (or Nasada). (The origin of the dispute is today shrouded in mystery. One old man, however, claims that a murder committed by a man of Damagaram was blamed on a certain Sarkin Baka in an effort to extort blood money.) So Sarkin Baka left Kofai to settle in Hamada, site of Sarkin Gwari Abdu's old settlement.

When Nakada left Kofai for Hamada, he took eight families with him, at that time a significant portion of the community, thus effectively splitting Yekuwa into two villages, Yekuwa-Kofai and Yekuwa-Hamada. Over the years, however, the two Yekuwas expanded until they merged. Today Yekuwa appears to be a single village with no visible barrier (see Map 5). Geographic contiguity should not be mistaken for political uniformity, however: not only does each Yekuwa retain its own chief, but the people themselves identify with only one or the other Yekuwa.[8]

Kofai was thus under Yaroro, while Hamada followed Nakada. After about thirty years, Nakada was discharged by the French and succeeded by Nagalabu (said to have held office for fifty-three years). Nagalabu was succeeded by Sule, the current mai gari of Yekuwa-Hamada. Sule was chosen chief in 1973.

Back in Kofai, Yaroro was succeeded by his son Nalalu (each may have been mai gari for about four decades). Nalalu died in 1979, reputedly at the age of ninety-nine. He was succeeded by his own son Adamu Danjuma, the current village chief of Yekuwa-Kofai.

There are eight wards (*unguwoyi*) in Kofai: Tadeta, Kurna-modé, Sabon Gari, Limam, Maguzawa, Alhajiya, Mahauta, and Makera.

---

[7] Actually, the French dissolved the Dawambey dynasty, establishing Magaria as their administrative headquarters.

[8] There are several cases, in fact, of homesteads that lie physically within Hamada but whose families actually "follow" (i.e., are under the authority of) the chief of Kofai.

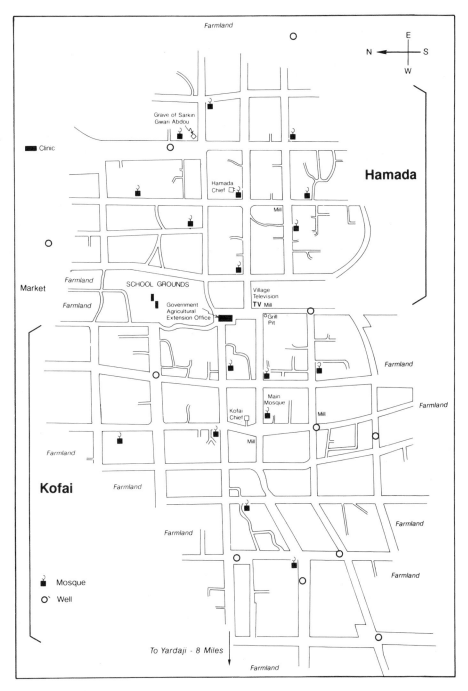

Map 5. Yekuwa

Yardaji

Just as Yekuwa is associated historically with Sarkin Gwari Abdu, Yardaji is remembered as the sometime dwelling place of his son and successor, Lukudi. Yet even before Lukudi arrived, a small group of hunters were living in the nearby (and still extant) village of Bulungudu.

Lukudi established his capital in exile around the well called Kwatang-wam; the site is known as Kuroni. Only frequent and eventually successful attacks on Lukudi by Sarkin Ibram of Damagaram forced him to leave Yardaji.[9] The village's name stems from the circumstances that followed his defeat and departure:

Sarkin Ibram ordered the commoners (Lukudi's own people having left with him) to abandon the site built up by Lukudi and to resettle a bit to the south (by the site of the present-day dispensary). The way he put it, the people were to abandon Lukudi's settlement (Tsohon Birni, or "Old Town") and to "agree with [living in] this bush[land]" (*ku yarda da nan daji.*)[10]

Yardaji may have been completely abandoned shortly thereafter or it may have struggled on as a marginal settlement. In either event, it required the intervention of a Fulani named Kemfo (or Magaji, great-grandfather of Yardaji's present chief), from Mamani, for its partial resurrection. Kemfo dug (or restored) the wells of Sabuwa and Kwatangwam and founded the ward (unguwa) of Yardaji Galadima, on the west side of today's Yardaji. Since Kemfo was Fulani, Yardaji Galadima too was basically a Fulani community. Kemfo was succeeded as ward head (mai unguwa) by Dalli.

Parallel to Yardaji Galadima's development, a Haɓe (that is, un-Fulanized Hausa) ward grew up. This unguwa, at first also under Kemfo's oversight, was called Yardaji Jaji. It was demarcated from Yardaji Galadima at a spot known as Dankafo (near the well in front of the present-day palace of the chief). The first mai unguwa of Yardaji Jaji was Wadai, who ruled for twelve years. Then Kudai took over as village chief (mai gari) for nine years; and then Mato, for thirteen years.

In or shortly before 1911, a dispute broke out between the two wards of Yardaji. One proffered origin of the conflict contends that "a young

[9] One poignant twist to the story, not to my knowledge recounted in other histories of Daura, is that Lukudi, out of anger and sadness because of these travails, went blind. Another detail is that Lukudi's forces lost because they had only muskets and swords while Ibra's had Arab guns.

[10] One informant places Ibram's ultimatum as occurring one year after Lukudi's defeat, when the Damagaram chief returned to see if Lukudi had perhaps come back. He reputedly told the people to evacuate Tsohon Birni because it was "poisonous."

woman from Jaji brought *rumaci* [senseless drivel] upon her boyfriend of [the other ward]." The dispute escalated into fistfights, first among the young and then even among the old. Another version recalls dissatisfaction with a certain Sarkin Dawaki, a member of the royal Kaurawa family of Zango, who settled in Yardaji Galadima and oppressed the commoners of Jaji. In any event, people were so upset by the system that had given rise to such interward conflict that they wished to be rid of both their ward heads. Suntali, a fiefholder from Zango, officially deposed the two.

In the outlying Fulani settlement of Yamachin Gida there was a respected leader known as Hardo Daji. As a neutral and venerated outsider, Hardo Daji was asked to become the first mai gari over both sections of Yardaji.[11] Hardo Daji accepted, thereby initiating the present lineage of Yardaji rulers.

Hardo Daji (also known as Sarkin Fulani Muhammadu) appointed new men as heads of the wards: Galadima Labaran for Yardaji Galadima (succeeded by Tsahiro and then Alhaji Galadima) and Sarkin Gabas Wale for Yardaji Jaji (succeeded by Kari, Moussa Nalatu, 'Dan Gata, and finally 'Dan Dabo). Every chief of Yardaji has since been titled Sarkin (King of the) Fulani. In addition, Yardaji's chief carries the titles of mai gari (village chief), mai gunduma (village area head), and dagaci (another term for village area head).

Sarkin Fulani Muhammadu remained chief for twenty-one years. In 1932 his son Tumbi (who had also been born outside of the village, in Yamachin Gida) was turbaned chief and ruled for thirty years as Sarkin Fulani Ahmadu. It was during Ahmadu's time that a community over the border came to Yardaji to escape repression in "Faranshi." These refugees from Niger founded Tube Baƙi (Strangers, or Guests' Settlement), which is known today also as Sabon Gari (New Town). Tube Baƙi originally was organically separate from Yardaji proper, but both the satellite and central villages expanded until they became physically contiguous.[12] Yardaji

[11] There had been masu unguwoyi (ward heads) and even a sarki or chief (Lukudi), but never a ruler in the intermediate category of village chief (mai gari). This local version of Yardaji's history ignores the possibility that the installation of a Fulani outsider to rule over a consolidated village (with subsequent jurisdiction over outlying settlements) may have been an undertaking of the British administration. This would not be the first time that steps taken by colonial powers have been incorporated in indigenous accounts. Even the partition of Hausaland itself, some Hausa believe, was an initiative of local potentates.

[12] The theoretical question whether to regard Sabon Gari as part of Yardaji (villagers generally do not) is similar to that for Yekuwa's Kofai and Hamada (discussed shortly). The situation is less problematic in Yardaji's case, for Sabon Gari is substantially smaller than Yardaji proper.

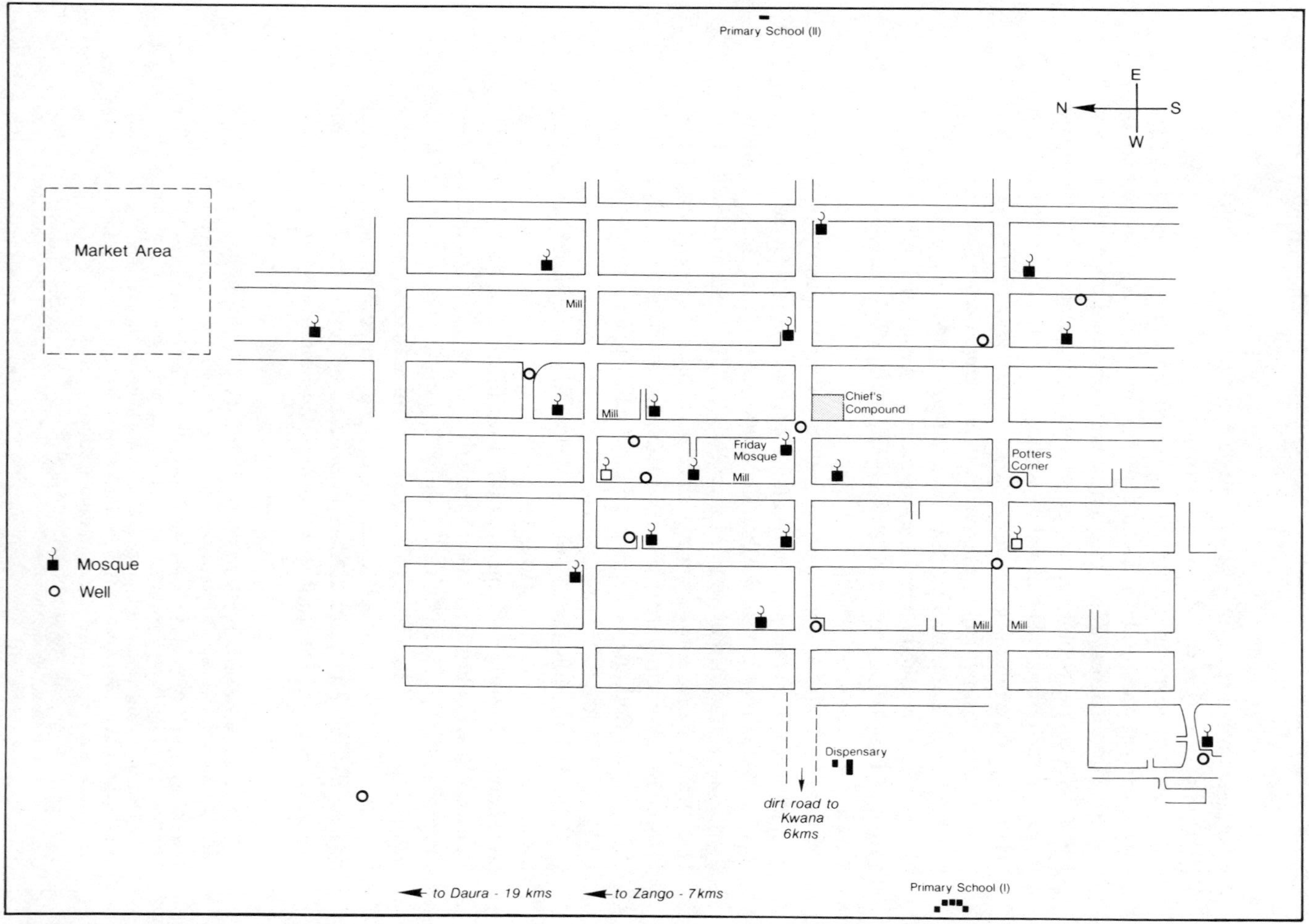

Map 6 Yardaji

N
E + W
S

Primary School (II)

Market Area

Chief's Compound

Potters Corner

Friday Mosque

Mill

Mill

Mill

Mill

Mill

Dispensary

dirt road to Kwana 6kms

← to Daura - 19 kms

← to Zango - 7kms

Primary School (I)

Mosque

Well

itself saw two more wards emerging out of the original two: Labaran and Kwaki. Bulungudu, the primordial settlement in the vicinity ("a place of hunters, where there were lions, gazelles, elephants, hyenas") still survive within eyeshot of Yardaji.

The present mai gari (and thus dagaci) of Yardaji, Sarkin Fulani Haruna, was the first to be born within the village. (His father and grandfather, it will be recalled, were born in an outlying Fulani camp.) Sarkin Fulani Haruna (also referred to more familiarly simply as Alhaji) was turbaned in 1948. He was the first native of Yardaji to receive a governmental education (at a Daura primary school) and to serve in the Daura emirate local council. As Yardaji chief, he also witnessed the transition from British to Nigerian sovereignty. In 1964 Haruna traveled to Mecca to perform the hajj (Muslim pilgrimage).

Sarkin Fulani Haruna today presides over a relatively unified village (see Map 6). It is difficult to imagine that fifty years ago the two wards Jaji and Galadima were separated by a large, empty space, and that tension between the two even inhibited intermarriage. Indeed, the first such wedding occurred only in the 1930s, when Alkassam, a Jaji man, took Jaru of Galadima to be his bride.

Factionalization

Local accounts of both villages highlight the presence of factions. Major splits in the community have been resolved in a variety of ways, but such ancient divisions temper the image of an insouciant, unified, precolonial sense of polity within single rural communities of Hausaland. By separating neighboring villages and joining distant territories, partition and colony formation may have forced local communities to look outward and redefine themselves. But internal divisions persist.

The friction between the Galadima and Jaji sections of Yardaji resulted in the ouster of the ward heads and the choice of an outsider—a Fulani—to be the ruler of the entire settlement. (Perhaps it was the Fulanis' general distinction of ruling Hausaland after the early nineteenth-century jihad that prompted the choice.)

In Yekuwa, disagreement within a single community led to the creation of two separate settlements, Kofai and Hamada. Despite physical merger, each Yekuwa has continued its separate corporate existence. This was borne home by a complaint lodged to the chief of Kofai during my stay. The complainant was from Kofai, as were his son and grandson. After weaning, however, the grandson was taken to his maternal grandparents' home (in accordance with Hausa custom) in Hamada. Now the grandson had been enrolled in school, and had been registered as a resident of Hamada. This was an outrage the complainant could not countenance. Why should the boy be recorded as belonging to Hamada when he had been born in Kofai to a family of Kofai elders?

Relations between the two village chiefs of Yekuwa are nevertheless cordial, and I know of no major disagreement arising in the recent past between the two Yekuwas. It is true that of the two, Kofai considers itself to be the "true" Yekuwa. Inhabitants of Kofai refer to their village as Yekuwa proper, but never use "Yekuwa" in reference to the Hamada section. (They use "Kofai" only in contexts in which they *have* to distinguish themselves from Hamada.) Hamada residents do not appropriate the same nominal privilege: they refer to their own part of the extended community indiscriminately as "Hamada," "Yekuwa," or "Yekuwa-Hamada." The Nigérien administration, for its part, does not discriminate—it hyphenates both sections of the community.

Though the existence of two Yekuwas makes little difference now in the daily lives of most villagers, it poses a theoretical problem for the researcher. Should the two factions be treated as two separate communities, Kofai and Hamada, or as a single Yekuwa? Should only Kofai (the "true" Yekuwa) serve as the counterpart to Yardaji?

Arguments can surely be marshaled for considering them separately, or even in disregarding Hamada. For one thing, the people perceive themselves as belonging to one or the other "village." Kofai adults know all the minutiae about all other Kofai residents, and their ignorance about the internal affairs of Hamada is taken for granted. For another thing, activities and decision-making processes may follow separate courses. The mechanical water pumps installed in Kofai in 1986 were paid for out of the chief's own pocket, for instance, but in Hamada the chief organized a general collection among Hamada households to pay for the pumps in his part of the village.

Nevertheless, I shall consider Yekuwa as a single community, encompassing both Kofai and Hamada. It is not merely out of methodological expedience that I do so. If this were a simple study of a single village, the imperatives of anthropology, sociology, and political science would mandate a more explicit treatment of the implications of factionalization for life in Yekuwa. But for a comparison of Nigerian and Nigérien societies, the internal factional dimension is less critical. Moreover, economically Kofai and Hamada function as a single unit.

Perfect units for social-scientific comparison are virtually impossible to come by. Rather than detract from the validity of the comparison, the factionalization of Yekuwa should be viewed as a further instance of the individuality of the "typical" African village. An appreciation of such idiosyncrasies should enrich one's understanding of rural Hausa society. For the sake of comprehensiveness, separate data are presented, wherever possible, for Kofai and Hamada.

Famines

No account of life in the Sahel should neglect what is for its inhabitants the most important feature of life there: the struggle for sheer survival. Life is tenuous in this region, and local versions of historical reckoning invariably use times of famine as benchmarks. It is common, for instance, for elders to state their age according to the famines they recall. Ultimately, the absence or presence of food transcends all other considerations of social life. It is not surprising, therefore, that famines have entered folklore in a personalistic way, with their own names and remembered peculiarities.

The oldest famine that any living villager can recall is Kaƙalaba, which occurred "seventy years ago," according to my informant in 1983.[13] Kaƙalaba lasted six months, and forced people to eat fig trees (*cediya*) without fruit, prickly burrs from grass (*karangiya*), certain weeds (*tsaidau*), coarse flour gruel (*yanburu*), and a resin-yielding shrub (*dashi*). Hungry villagers scavenged in anthills for grains of millet stored away by the black ant *tururuwa*. In Hausa, Ƙaƙalab is synonymous with *babu*—"none" or "nothing."

Four years later, Nothing's younger sister (Kanwa Kaƙalaba) arrived. People survived by eating the root of a lily plant (*kinciya*), which made them itch. This famine is thus humorously recalled as a time when villagers went around scratching their throats and buttocks. It lasted three months.

Shell (a deformation of *sam,* or "none at all") came eight years after

[13] The major sources for these local recollections of famines are Alhaji Issoufou of Yardaji and Mallam Ibra Gwadagwama of Komo. Calendar dates and years are not generally used in rural Hausaland, and details supplied by informants are at times at variance with one another. I have therefore been obliged to combine information, and when I encounter discrepancies, I favor the version that appears most credible. For instance, the dating for Kaƙalaba provided by Gwadagwama in 1983 ("seventy years ago") appears more accurate than Issoufou's "seventy-seven years," for it parallels R. C. Abraham (1958:457), who identifies Kaƙalaba as "the Great Famine of 1913–14." I have also been aided by Michael John Watts's (1983b) account of famines in Northern Nigeria. Localization of famine names may cause some confusion; for example, Watts's informants have named Kaƙalaba both Gyallare and Malali (285). In general, to avoid giving a spurious impression of dating accuracy, I have refrained from merely counting backward (as the informants did) to arrive at a specific year in the Gregorian calendar.

Kaƙalaba. (In Yekuwa it is also referred to as Karyen Damina—the rainy season's lie.) It, too, lasted three months, and it was accompanied by ƙaɗababai, a fearful insect that devoured plants before they could grow. Shell was followed two years later by Mai Buhu, so called because millet was brought from the north in large sacks (buhu). It sold for 10 kobo (cents) a tiya (the traditional measure), a considerable sum in those days.

Yediko came seven years later and lasted five months. Yardaji at first had sufficient millet to sell to Daura, whence it was then resold in Katsina. (Katsina was then under Emir Diko—hence the name of the famine.) When Yardaji's own supply ran out, villagers resorted to smuggling millet, at night, from Niger. Yekuwa was not severely affected by Yediko.

Kwajaja, sixteen years later, spelled death for people in Yekuwa.[14] Millet and cassava flour had to be brought from as far away as Yola, and even then it was scarce. Kwajaja endured for four months. The word kwajaja has at least two meanings. R. C. Abraham (1958:577) renders it as "thin [person] with pot-belly"; villagers use it to describe the hay cram-cram, which in times of need was pounded and eaten.

Seven years later Uwar Sani ("Sani's Mother") struck. During this time a woman complained of hunger after giving birth to a son, named Sani. Her mother-in-law told her there was no food to be had. When she wailed in anguish ("Wayyo, yunwa!") the famine was named after her.

Five years later came Mai Amaro, the "groundnut famine." This time, as one can guess, people survived by selling and eating groundnuts. Locally, Mai Amaro is recalled as the last of the great famines, more catastrophic than the Sahelian droughts of the early 1970s (Kaƙuɗuba) and mid-1980s (Taƙaƙabwa). "After Mai Amaro, nobody has starved. If anyone is without, his brother can give him, and he will pay it back during the next harvest."[15]

Also recalled is Marisuwa (the influenza epidemic of 1913) and Balati (thirteen years after Marisuwa). At the time of Marisuwa, "if you caught the illness, two days later you were dead. But if you lasted three days, you would recover." Balati wiped out entire families; "the emir prohibited marriages until the next rainy season."

[14] Kwajaja probably corresponds to the great famine of 1942–43, which Watts (1983b:516) alternately refers to as 'Yar Balange, 'Yar Gusau, 'Yar Dikko, and Sanho.

[15] This observation fits Yardaji better than Yekuwa, where severe grain shortfalls have also been offset by foreign aid. It is not my intention to minimize the gravity of these more recent famines or to challenge Robert Charlick's assertion (1991:99–100) that "in the past, hunger in Niger had largely been a matter of well-documented periodic droughts and famines. Since the late 1960's, however, hunger and terrible poverty have become chronic and endemic characteristics." It is important, however, to appreciate the variations in the local experiences of regional phenomena. Since rainfall patterns can vary considerably even within small areas, a few miles' difference can mean the difference between survival and disaster.

Michael Watts (1983b) has argued that the famines of British Hausaland were caused largely by exploitive colonial economic policies that invalidated traditional strategies for coping with drought. This is a perspective that the farmers of Yardaji and Yekuwa, more used to attributing natural calamity to divine will, are unlikely to share. Famine is one phenomenon that Yardaji and Yekuwa have shared in the past, and whose psychological specter still is a common denominator. As international disaster relief becomes more organized and politicized, however, even drought and famine become linked to arbitrary colonial divisions. In 1984–85 Yekuwa, as part of Niger, received extensive gifts of food through the U.S. Agency for International Development, whereas nearby Yardaji, lying within Nigeria, received nothing.

Scaling Up

An underlying problem in comparative social science is the tendency to foist upon the human subjects of research the concerns, theses, and intellectual predilections of the investigator.[16] My primary concern is the effect of the colonial partition on the consciousness and prospects of villagers along such a boundary. By first acknowledging the precolonial foundations of the villages, their internal political dynamics, and their material preoccupations (particularly food security), I hope to reduce the hermeneutic danger of a *reductio ad partitionem*.

Now that we have a nodding acquaintance with two Hausa villages in particular, we can step back a moment and take a broader tack: What does it mean to be Hausa?

[16] See Miles 1989a for a broader discussion of this issue.

3

Ethnic Identity and National Consciousness: Who Are the Hausa?

Bahaushe mai ban haushi. Ka so mutum ka rasa abin da zaka bashi.

The Hausa is a frustrated man. Though he likes his fellow, poverty obliges him to give less than he would like.

—Hausa proverb

To colonize is to alter identity. Among its other transformative consequences, colonialism entails the superimposition of the colonizer's sovereignty and, to varying degrees, its very self upon the colonized. As a result, the colonized society can no longer define itself independently of the hegemon.

The disruptive psychological and cultural impact of colonialism is familiar ground for students of Frantz Fanon (1967) and Dominique Mannoni (1964). Less recognized is the contradiction between "national liberation" as the outcome of decolonization and "national identity," which in most cases is an inheritance of colonial territorial reconfiguration. It is difficult to celebrate Nigérien independence when one considers that "Nigérien" is a French construct, just as "Nigerian" owes its meaning to British empire builders. Indeed, reconciling ethnic aspirations with nation building has proved difficult enough, even without rethinking the existential legitimacy of African nation-statehood.

Discussions of the impact of colonialism on indigenous peoples too often assume consensus regarding the primordial identity of the colonized. Yet not only is ethnic identity ordinarily evolving and situational, colonialism itself shapes group identity. For Nigeria, this is a point usually made with reference to the Igbo, but, as Frank Salamone (1992) has shown, it is relevant to the Yoruba and Hausa as well.

The partition of the Hausa also requires their contemporary chroniclers to recognize that ethnic Hausa identity and culture can no longer be considered apart from the superimposed national identities of "Nigerianhood" and "Nigérienhood."[1] It is never easy to separate components of a group's or individual's identity, and an attempt to measure the ethnic components may seem a dubious enterprise; the palpable intervillage contrast in survey results should alleviate some of those doubts.

The Nature of Hausa Identity

Twenty million strong, based principally in Northern Nigeria and Niger, the Hausa constitute the largest group in West Africa. But what kind of group are they? Although most Hausa scholars agree on who their subjects are, there seems to be less agreement on what they are. This issue increases in importance when we examine the relationship between national consciousness and self-identity among Hausa villagers in Niger and Nigeria.

Traditionally, Hausa scholars have divided into two basic camps on the issue of Hausa identity. On the one hand are those for whom "Hausa" is primarily a linguistic designation and who minimize it as a cultural or ethnic category. They point to the substantial historical and religious diversity among the various Hausa-speaking peoples, seeing only language as a common point of reference. Thus M. G. Smith says that "Hausa is a linguistic term" and that "it is misleading in other contexts" (1959:239–40), and Polly Hill asserts that "Hausa is a linguistic not an ethnic term, and refers to those who speak the Hausa language by birth" (1972:3).

On the other hand are those scholars who, despite variations, perceive an underlying common ethnic denominator among those people whose native language happens to be Hausa. Here we may place Guy Nicolas ("The term 'Hausa' designates one of the most important ethnic groups of Africa . . . not all Hausa speakers are Hausa" [1975:399]) and Abner Cohen ("One of the best-known ethnic groups [in] West Africa is the Hausa" [1968:8]).

Other anthropologists avoid this language/ethnicity dichotomy by claiming that Hausa is both—or neither. Thus Jerome Barkow (1973:186) writes: "Hausa [is] a term with two referents: first, Hausa is a language . . . second, it is a civilization encompassing kingdoms, conquests, walled cities, an an-

---

[1] Throughout this book I deliberately use "national" to designate Nigérien and Nigerian referents and "ethnic" for Hausa ones. I recognize that this simple distinction may be inappropriate in other contexts, particularly when "nationalism" refers to an ethnic group's aspirations for political sovereignty. Distinguishing "ethnic" from "national" in this treatment of Hausaland obviates a long theoretical digression into the relationship between ethnicity and nationalism, such as I have undertaken in Miles 1986a:161–86.

cient literate tradition . . . ." Frank Salamone (1971:337), wishing to avoid the standard definitional choice, claims that "many problems disappear if one regards 'Hausa' as a cultural term and uses other terms for various ethnic groups who share . . . in that culture. . . . [The use of] 'Hausa' [as] a linguistic term . . . presents one immediately with the problem of being misunderstood."

Even if they do not settle the definitional issue, Barkow and Salamone do agree on an important point: the situational nature of Hausa ethnicity. So do John Paden (1967, 1970b) and Abner Cohen (1969). All would agree with Barkow that "whether or not a person is described as 'Hausa' often depends on social context since, as an ethnic category, the term covers a multiplicity of individuals and groups" (1973:186).

Barkow comes to this conclusion after contrasting Muslim Hausas of "Wurinsalla" with the Maguzawa (non-Muslim Hausa) surrounding them. Although both originated from a common Haɓe (that is, pre-Fulani jihad) race and culture, one adopted an "urban-Islamic subculture," whereas the other (the Maguzawa) retained the older, "pagan" rites, religion, and culture. Inasmuch as both groups came consciously to accept these differences, Barkow concludes that "an incipient ethnic split" has occurred: the two communities have emerged as separate ethnic groups.

In his study of Yauri, Salamone (1975) also demonstrates the situational nature of ethnicity, but in reverse order. Here, by adopting the (advantageous) identity of Islam, the native Gungawa have become Hausafied. As a result, the Hausa population, once a minority in Yauri, has grown considerably not only in number but in status and power. Religious conversion, undertaken in anticipation of material benefit, has led the Gungawa to "become Hausa."

Paden (1967, 1970b, 1973), through colonial censuses and other documentation, also demonstrates how Hausa identity has extended to areas outside of traditional Hausaland and to non-Hausa ethnic groups. He cites three processes responsible: acculturation and assimilation, travel and migration patterns, and the widespread use of Hausa as a lingua franca. He implicitly rejects the colonial definition, as expressed in the 1952 census, that "the Hausa are simply a linguistic group consisting of those who speak the Hausa language as their mother tongue and do not claim Fulani descent, and including a wide variety of stocks and physical types." Paden argues instead that "Hausa ethnicity has become largely affiliational. By an act of will, a person can choose to speak Hausa, become a Muslim (perhaps nominal), and claim to be a Hausa" (1973:380).

Cohen's (1969) extensive analysis of the immigrant Hausa community in

Ibadan (Sabo) reveals the various processes that diaspora Hausa may exploit to maintain their ethnic exclusiveness (for the purposes of maintaining commercial hegemony). The complexity and evolution of these processes attest to their necessity and bespeak a certain danger: Sabo Hausa acknowledge, if by default, that without effort and vigilance, they might lose their distinctiveness and cohesiveness amid their surrounding Yoruba competition. They can claim a twofold distinctiveness, in fact, for they distinguish themselves not only from their Yoruba neighbors but from Hausa communities elsewhere. "Hausa culture in Sabo is not an extension of Northern Hausa culture. In fact there is no uniform, homogeneous, Hausa culture" (Cohen 1969:47).

The question of Hausa ethnicity is complicated by the existence in Hausaland itself of two competing standards of what constitutes Hausa identity. Traditionally, according to Hausa folklore and cosmogeny, there are seven separate Hausa nations or "families," distinguished by their respective geographical origins. These Hausa Bakwai are the Daurawa, Kanawa, Gobirawa, Ranawa, Zazzawa, Katsinawa, Biramawa. (According to legend, a Persian prince whose original name was Abu Yazidu left Baghdad and wandered to what is today Hausaland. Arriving in the town of Daura, he slew the serpent/dragon [*dodo*] that had been preventing the townsfolk from using the well. Queen Daura married Abu Yazidu, whose name was later changed to Bayajidda, meaning "He didn't understand [Hausa] before [coming]." The two had a son, Bawo, who himself sired six sons. The seven and their descendants collectively constitute the "Hausa Seven." Seven other sons sired by Bawo outside of his marriage constitute the "Illegitimate Seven," or Banza Bakwai.) Thus, according to Hausa mythology, a person who can claim descent from one of the Seven Families is Hausa.[2] In the absence of any supra-Hausa tribe, affiliation with one of the seven is a traditional criterion for determining Hausaness.

Yet tacitly, and especially throughout the last two centuries, there has been a growing recognition in Hausaland itself that Hausaness need not be limited to affiliation with one of the Seven Families. Paden (1973) has described the process by which, for reasons of group status, mobility, and recognition of "Hausa power," "Northern Nigerian" has increasingly become synonymous with "Hausa." The well-known assimilation of the erstwhile conquering Torodbe Fulani into Hausa culture is added testimony

---

[2] True descent is not absolutely necessary. Abner Cohen (1969:49) describes how a person of even non-Hausa origin can become a Sabo Hausa if he "(1) speaks Hausa as a first language, (2) *can name a place of origin in one of the seven original Hausa states,* (3) is a Moslem, and (4) has no tribal mark on his face which indicates affiliation to another tribe" (emphasis added).

to the emerging (if unformalized) gratuitousness of the Hausa Bakwai criterion for Hausaness.[3] Barkow (1976:861) invokes the classic melting-pot analogy to describe the phenomenon of Hausa assimilation: "'Hausa' . . . are rather like Americans in that they have 'ethnic' identities—Fulani Hausa, Kanuri Hausa, Buzu Hausa, etc."

Guy Nicolas refers to the hyphenated Hausa as ethnic fractions (1975: 409). The sources of these ethnic fractions are "original groups" that first appeared on the periphery of local Hausa dynastic cores but have since, through pressures of war, slavery, and famine, migrated into the Hausa whole. Nicolas stresses the ease with which Hausa society assimilates, integrates, and incorporates members of other ethnic groups; the operative and encapsulating term for Hausa group dynamics is "hetereogeneity." Nevertheless, out-group Hausaization has proceeded by degrees: Beriberi Hausa are more integrated than Fulani Hausa, who are more integrated than Bouzou (Buzu) Hausa (410–22).

The contemporary political significance of Hausa cultural integration was driven home to me in a discussion with the village chief of Yardaji, immediately after the Nigerian coup d'état of New Year's 1984. When I learned that Sani Abacha, the army brigadier who announced the military takeover, was a Beriberi (Kanuri), I joked to the chief that, as in the olden times, Bornu would once again rule the territory. (Bornu and Sokoto were often at arms after the Fulani takeover in Hausaland.) The chief's response was unexpected but revealing: "Well, as long as he's Hausa, then it's all right."

Hausa ethnicity, then, is fluid, multilayered, and evolutionary. The Seven Families litmus test appears to be outmoded, yet no formal cultural myth has replaced it. Hausa identity *is* widening—but according to what standards?

Another factor complicating the determination of Hausa identity is the question of religion. Islam has certainly come to be included as a major element of the core Hausa identity (see Paden 1973:378, 380). Are non-Muslim Hausa then not truly Hausa? If they are not, what are they? Barkow has answered this question in the case of the Maguzawa, who consider themselves to be different from the neighboring Hausa Muslims and are so

[3] Between 1804 and 1812, the Toronkawa branch of the Fulani, led by Shehu Usman dan Fodio, waged a holy war to purify Islam throughout Hausaland and adjacent regions. Though at first they established themselves as foreign rulers in their newly created empire, these semi-sedentary Fulani (other Fulani clans are noted for a more nomadic lifestyle) came to adopt the Hausa language and culture. Some writers refer to the Shehu's descendants as "Hausa-Fulani" to signify their Fulani origins within an otherwise Hausa cultural ensemble. Hausa without such Fulani roots are known as Haɓe.

regarded in return. But what about those few Hausa who have converted to Christianity? Are they then no longer Hausa? They do not yet constitute a full-blown alternative community, as the Maguzawa do; what, for the purposes of group identification, are they?

The problem of Hausa ethnicity is further aggravated by the geographical bias of most studies of the Hausa. Despite the excellent work of Guy Nicolas in Niger, John Works in Chad, and Deborah Pellow in Ghana, most Hausa experts have concentrated on the Hausa of Nigeria. This focus has led to a virtual scholarly stereotype of the Hausa: a Muslim of Northern Nigerian origin whose mother tongue is Hausa. But millions of people who fall outside of these religious and geographic categories nevertheless, because of their linguistic situation, must (if only by default) be considered Hausa. These people include both Maguzawa (notwithstanding Barkow's findings) and Christians, as well as Nigériens, northern Cameroonians, Ghanaians, Chadians, and even Sudanese, who may never have set foot in Nigeria. Does the degree of their Hausaness depend on the degree of their deviation from the norms of religion (rejection of Islam), geography (residence outside of Hausaland), culture (meals of steak and potatoes instead of *tuwo* and *fura*),[4] and even language (English or French instead of Hausa)?

It is curious—though perhaps not surprising—that so many of the social scientists who have focused on the specifically ethnic dimension of the Hausa people have studied them outside of Hausaland. Cohen's study of Hausa migrants in Yorubaland (1969), Works's (1976) examination of Hausa pilgrims in Chad, Salamone's research in Yauri (1985b, 1987), Mark Duffield's (1983) work on Takari (Hausa Settlers) in Sudan, and Mahdi Adamu's (1978) study of the Hausa diaspora throughout West Africa are cases in point. Even Barkow's sample of "Hausa" outside of Zaria is not quite typically Hausa: over a quarter of the villagers described themselves as Fulani, and half of the household were recent immigrants to the region (Barkow 1976:862). When we deal in situations of migrants and migration, definitional problems of ethnic identity tend to recede behind the more prominent issues of intergroup dynamics. In short, it is easiest to tackle Hausa ethnicity when distinctly non-Hausa foils are at hand.

Far from lying on the thorny extremes of a fluid, variable, or relative Hausa status, our two villages have unimpeachable Hausa credentials:

---

[4] Tuwo and fura are the traditional staple dishes of the Hausa. Tuwo is a doughlike food consisting of pounded millet or sorghum that is cooked in boiling water and served with sauce (*miya*). Fura is gruel made of cooked millet balls mixed in sour milk (*nono*).

their locations, religion, language, economy, and history place them in the Hausa cultural mainstream. This is not to say that the Hausa communities of Yardaji and Yekuwa are ethnically pure or that they have not experienced their share of migration, integration, and assimilation—processes common to Hausa history and society. The ethnic status of urban Hausa society is commonly said to be "in constant motion" (Nicolas 1975:407)[5] and the same can be said of rural Hausa society as well: our two villages would be exceptional were they totally immune to group interpenetration. Some people of Fulani and Kanuri origin live in both Yardaji and Yekuwa; for all intents and purposes, however, they are wholly Hausa.[6] The contextual, relational, or situational significance of Hausa ethnicity and identity becomes most clear when we examine the juxtaposition of ethnic (qua Hausa) and national (qua Nigérien and Nigerian) identities.

Identifying and Measuring Components of Hausa Identity

In his study of communal identity in Kano, Paden (1970b:259–63) proffers eight bases of ethnic identification that define the population of this unofficial Hausa capital. Although Paden's study is limited to a particular (and urban) Hausa society, these components of identity may be adapted to analyze Hausa identity in toto. The eight components are *addini* (religion), *garin haihuwa* (birthplace), *asali* (ancestral home), *jama'a* (clan/community), *ƙasa* (country), *kabila* (tribe or language), *birni* (city), and *fata* (skin color). Paden insightfully demonstrates how these traditional bases of identity have evolved historically, particularly as a result of changes wrought during the colonial era. Thus two new identities—"a combined 'Hausa-Fulani' and/or 'Kano City'" (267) have emerged, and urban, linguistic, and religious bases of identity (birni, kabila, addini) have overcome clan/community and ancestral home (jama'a, *asali*) in salience (268).[7]

5 Here Nicolas acknowledges (although later he criticizes) John Paden's (1970b) work on Hausa urban ethnicity.

6 Inhabitants of outlying Fulani and Bouzu settlements, of course, do qualify as members of distinctive ethnic categories.

7 The absence of gender in this list of recognized categories of Hausa identity and its omission from my own survey (see below) must be acknowledged and corrected in future investigations of self-identity within Hausaland. "The long-standing acceptance of gender asymmetry and the subordination of Hausa women as 'facts' which define all aspects of their experiences should be set aside in favor of an approach that explores gender as an element in all social relations and processes" (Coles & Mack 1991:25). Until gender consciousness penetrates common Hausa language use, this task will remain operationally difficult. Even Roxana Ma Newman's (1990) English-Hausa dictionary employs only the linguistic meaning of gender

Paden does not prioritize his bases of ethnic identification in an operational way; neither does he include in this schema other possible bases of identity that have surfaced as a result of colonial and postcolonial political and administrative changes in Hausaland. In particular, the superimposition of citizenship (Nigerian and Nigérien) would seem to be a crucial addition to the Hausa concept of self. ("Kasa"—usually rendered as "land" or "country"—is an ambiguous term, and is more commonly used to mean local district or region than "nation-state.")

In an attempt to tackle this question of identity among the Hausa more rigorously, I devised and conducted a two-part survey among one hundred randomly selected heads of household in Yardaji and Yekuwa.[8] In addition to Paden's categories (except for skin color), respondents were asked to provide their citizenship, province, and county. (Subethnic group [e.g., Daura Hausa] was substituted for clan/community; village residence [gari] naturally replaced city [birni]). Respondents were then asked to list, in order of personal importance, each of the following attributes of identity: village residence (Yardaji or Yekuwa), birthplace (usually the same as village residence), religion (Islam), ethnic group (Hausa), subethnic group (e.g., Daura), and citizenship (Nigeria or Niger). Information on family guild, secondary occupation (since all villagers are farmers), age bracket/life station, education (religious and secular), travel and residential experience (urban and rural, domestic and international), and pilgrimage experience were also elicited to cross-test, along with ancestral home, the possible significance of these factors on the pattern of responses. Though no such relationships were found, it is interesting to note intervillage differences in these identity traits before we focus on the contrasts between national and ethnic consciousness.

Descriptions of Samples

The profiles of the two samples varied slightly. In Yardaji, 40 percent of the respondents were categorized as "middle-aged," 28 percent as "young

---

(*jinsi*) in her example of use. The *Modern Hausa-English Dictionary* of the Centre for the Study of Nigerian Languages, Bayero University (1985) has no entry for *jinsi*, limiting its selection "to those words likely to occur in everyday conversation and in modern books, newspapers, and other mass media" (p. v). Though gender consciousness is indeed rising in Hausaland (as the contributors to Coles & Mack, eds., 1991 demonstrate), it has not yet reached the point where *jinsi* joins *jama'a* (clan/community) as a vernacularly recognized term among ordinary Hausa women and men.

[8] A more detailed statistical analysis of this survey may be found in Miles & Rochefort 1991. A preliminary study, conducted in 1983, appears in Miles 1986c. This discussion is based on 1986 fieldwork and data.

heads of household," and 23 percent as "aging"; in Yekuwa, the propor-
tions were 37, 37, and 19 percent, respectively. All respondents were men.
Life station is a fairly subjective attribute, however, and it became apparent
during a parallel census taken of the entire population that the use of the
terms dealing with ageset differed somewhat from village to village: while
in Yardaji *samari* applied exclusively to an unmarried adolescent, in Yekuwa
a recently married young man might also be called samari.

A few more Yekuwa than Yardaji residents were born outside the village where they now live (18 percent and 13 percent); approximately the
same number of migrants in the two villages had come from across the
border (6 percent and 5 percent). Interestingly, virtually half of the respondents in each village claimed that their ancestral home (the area or
place from which their ancestors had sprung) was now situated across the
international border (47 percent for Yardaji and 50 percent for Yekuwa).
This finding indicates a significant degree of early colonial or precolonial
migration, which is consistent with the recorded history of the area.

Since virtually all men in both villages are farmers, only secondary occupation responses were elicited. In both samples, 17 percent gave their secondary occupation as Islamic study or practice; merchant came second,
15 percent in Yardaji and 9 percent in Yekuwa. The earth in and around
Yardaji is red, hard, and claylike, and 13 percent of the Yardaji workers are
potters. In Yekuwa, third place went to butchers, with 8 percent. In perhaps the most significant difference in occupational profile, twice as many
respondents in Yekuwa as in Yardaji—a full quarter of the sample—had no
secondary occupation at all.[9]

Yardaji respondents had received more education, especially religious
instruction: 85 percent had studied or were still studying the Koran, as opposed to 72 percent in Yekuwa. In both samples, 3 percent had received only
a secular education. Whereas only 5 percent had received no education,
religious or secular, in Yardaji, this proportion shoots up to 20 percent in
Yekuwa.

---

[9] The occupational profile of this random sample is at some variance with the results of
a more comprehensive census of the two villages reported in chap. 8. Most striking is the
large proportion of 'yan Yekuwa in the random sample who mentioned Koranic study as their
secondary occupation in comparison with those who did so at the general census. The proportion of 'yan Yekuwa with no secondary occupation rises even higher in the general census
than in the random sample. My surmise is that in the survey, where the focus was on self-
identity, respondents were more likely to mention Koranic scholarship as a (pre)occupation
even when it was unremunerated. In the general census the notion of occupation as livelihood
prevailed, and an activity was mentioned only when it was a source of significant income.

Yardaji villagers were slightly more traveled than those in Yekuwa: 84 percent of 'yan Yardaji had resided in another village or town for at least a month versus 77 percent of 'yan Yekuwa. Those 'yan Yekuwa who did such traveling, however, had more international exposure, 50 percent having resided outside Niger (mostly in Nigeria) as opposed to only 23 percent for Yardaji travelers, exclusive of those who had made the pilgrimage to Mecca. Surprisingly (given Yardaji's greater ostensible wealth and religious education), substantially more men in Yekuwa (49 percent) than in Yardaji (24 percent) had done so.

Men in Yekuwa were less familiar than those in Yardaji with their place in the local governmental structure: 22 percent were unable to identify their arrondissement or identified it incorrectly, versus 18 percent in Yardaji who could not correctly identify their county; and 38 percent—twice as many as in Yardaji—could not supply the name of their *département*. In no case did anyone have difficulty identifying his country or citizenship.

Analysis of Samples

Not surprisingly, the attribute "being Muslim" was of overwhelmingly greatest importance to villagers on both sides of the border; this was the first priority of 88 percent of all villagers. Village residence was the second most salient attribute; 47 percent of the total sample named it as their second or even first choice. (Thus the caveat raised in chapter 1 about acknowledging informants' own priorities is heeded.) It is noteworthy that order of self-identity does not follow distance from self: both the most universal and local levels of identity (religion and village, respectively) were at the top of the scale. At the bottom were provincial affiliation (proffered by only 5 percent as first or second in importance and by 62 percent as fifth or sixth) and birthplace (of the 31 respondents who had not been born in the village where they currently resided, 36 percent mentioned birthplace last or next to last; only 3 percent put it first or second).

Of particular theoretical interest is the relationship between ethnicity ("being Hausa") and national consciousness (identifying with Niger or Nigeria). The survey indicated a pattern of expressed preference for nation-state (presented in terms of country or citizenship) over ethnic affiliation. As a first or second choice, citizenship was chosen 28 percent of the time and ethnicity only 17 percent. This preference for the national over the ethnic component of identity assumes even greater significance when we compare the response patterns between the two villages. The relative weighting of nationalism and ethnicity alters as one crosses the boundary.

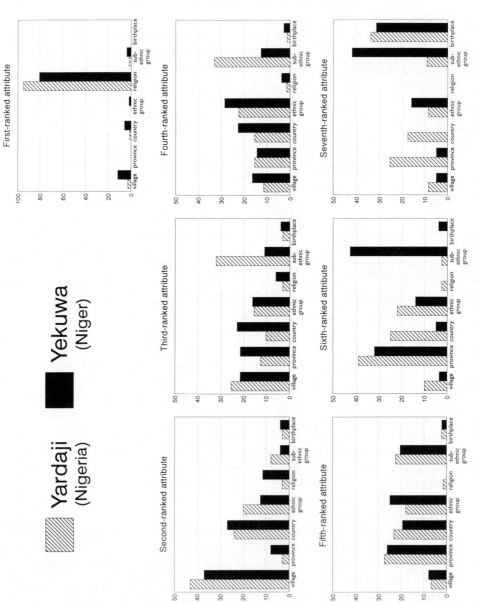

Figure 3. Rank-ordering of seven attributes of social identity by respondents in Yardaji and Yekuwa (percent)

Comparative Analysis

Although men in Yekuwa and Yardaji agreed that religion and village residence were the most important attributes, the weights they accorded these two variables differed significantly. In Yardaji, 96 percent of respondents gave top priority to religion; in Yekuwa, however, 81 percent placed Islam first and a full 12 percent gave their village the highest priority. (In Yardaji only 2 percent placed village over religion; see Figure 2).

Subethnic group (i.e., being of the Daura Hausa "family") clearly emerged as being more important for the residents of Yardaji. It first surfaced as a third-place priority for 32 percent of the Yardaji and only 11 percent of the Yekuwa samples; as a fourth priority, it was claimed by 33 percent in Yardaji and 13 percent in Yekuwa. Historical reasons, both precolonial and colonial, will be invoked to explain this variation. For the moment, suffice it to say that as a result of the 1906 Anglo-French boundary demarcation, Yardaji was restored to an emirate bearing the name of its ancient ancestry (Daura emirate) and today also forms part of a similar-sounding Nigerian government administrative unit (the Daura local government area). In contrast, the colonial partition reified Yekuwa's detachment from Daura suzereignty.

The differential strengths of national and ethnic consciousness become even starker when we compare Yardaji with Yekuwa. As a first or second priority, Niger was mentioned in Yekuwa only slightly more than Nigeria was in Yardaji (30 percent to 25 percent). Once the core attachments to religion and village were expressed, however, national affiliation (coded as "country" in Figure 2) emerged much more strongly (as the third preference) in Nigérien Yekuwa than in Nigerian Yardaji (22 percent to 10 percent).

The flip side to this question—the prioritization of ethnic consciousness—was less obtrusive. It is worth noting, however, that while "being Hausa" was chosen as a first or second priority by 20 percent of the Yardaji respondents, only 13 percent of those in Yekuwa accorded it that much importance. It was chosen equally as a third position (16 percent), but again, at this level the national factor was higher than the ethnic one in Nigérien Yekuwa (22 to 16 percent) while the obverse was true for Nigerian Yardaji (16 percent chose Hausa and 10 percent chose Nigeria).

Thus, while Hausa identity did not submerge nationality in either village, national consciousness was measurably greater among the Nigériens than among the Nigerians.

Table 5. Affinity choices for non-Hausa cocitizens vs. "foreign" Hausa (percent)

Non-Hausa cocitizens	Yardaji (Nigeria)	Yekuwa (Niger)
Fulani cocitizens	86.7%	79.8%
Foreign Hausa	13.3	20.2
Bouzou cocitizens	72.7	73.7
Foreign Hausa	27.3	26.3
Maguzawa cocitizens	69.0	58.6
Foreign Hausa	31.0	41.4
Kirista cocitizens	45.0	23.2
Foreign Hausa	55.0	76.8
Yoruba cocitizens	65.7	—
Foreign Hausa	34.3	—
Igbo cocitizens	61.0	—
Foreign Hausa	39.0	—
Tuareg cocitizens	—	59.6
Foreign Hausa	—	40.4
Zarma cocitizens	—	77.8
Foreign Hausa	—	22.2

Ethnic Affinity

The second part of the survey gauged villagers' relative affinity to specified non-Hausa and non-Muslim religious groups within their own country. The question ran like this (in the case of Nigeria's Yardaji): "In your heart, who do you feel is closer to you—the _____ of Nigeria or the Hausa of Niger?" Four groups—the Fulani, Bouzou, Maguzawa, and Kirista— were common to both sets of respondents. In addition, Yekuwa villagers were asked about Tuareg and Zarma (two important minorities in Niger) and Yardaji residents were queried about the Igbo and Yoruba (along with the Hausa, the most important Nigerian ethnic groups).

For all but one of the choices (the Kirista), 60 percent or more of the respondents in both villages expressed closer affinity to their non-Hausa cocitizens (see Table 5). Yet this preference varied according to perceived cultural distance from the Hausa. The Fulani, seminomadic pastoralists with strong economic and historical ties with the Hausa, were most uniformly perceived as closer to the respondents than Hausa over the border. (That the village chief of Yardaji is himself of Fulani background may explain an even greater preference in that village [87 percent] than in Yekuwa [80 percent]).

Bouzou (*bugaje*) are the descendants of black Africans enslaved by the light-skinned Tuareg (Berber-related nomads), and live in proximity to Yardaji and Yekuwa. They pursue a lifestyle similar to that of the rural Hausa. Physically, too, they differ little in color and physiognomy. With little variation between the two villages, compatriot Bouzou were solidly preferred to "foreign" Hausa.

Maguzawa present an interesting case of group differentiation from the Hausa. Although ethnically indistinguishable from the Hausa, Maguzawa are regarded as different by virtue of their "pagan" (i.e., non-Muslim and animistic) background. Even when Maguzawa have individually converted to Islam, as most have done, the Hausa continue to see them as different from "their kind" of Hausa. Though the Hausa admire the Maguzawa as ace agriculturalists, they also find them (and consequently any question concerning them) quite humorous. Though the majority of Hausa still prefer the Maguzawa to Hausa across the border, perceived distance from Islam does seem to attenuate affinity, 'yan Yekuwa being more orthodox on this score than 'yan Yardaji.

This religious factor becomes even more pronounced when one considers the case of the Kirista (Christians). These people were presented as ethnic Hausa who had converted to Christianity (from either Islam or animism). Only here did communal (*qua* religious) sentiment overcome national affinity, with a majority in both villages saying they felt closer to Hausa (Muslim) foreigners than to Christian (albeit Hausa) compatriots. The villagers of Yekuwa were even more likely than those of Yardaji to reject the nonbeliever. (It is perhaps relevant to note here that while Nigeria as a whole is about 50 percent Muslim, Niger's population is 98 percent so.)

Yet religion is by no means an unequivocal basis for group acceptance or rejection by Hausa villagers, as we see when we turn to the preferences among country-specific ethnic groups.

Many Yoruba in Nigeria are not Muslim; very few Igbo are. Still, 'yan Yardaji stated that they felt closer to them than to the Hausa of Niger. As between Igbo and Yoruba, though, the religion variable seems to predominate: Yoruba were preferred to Igbo, 84 percent to 16 percent.

In Yekuwa, even the nomadic Tuareg (a traditional raiding enemy of the sedentary agriculturalist Hausa) were given preference over non-Nigérien Hausa. The Zarma minority, whose members have dominated the government of the Republic of Niger since independence, were also preferred to foreign Hausa. Zarma were also much more popular than Tuareg.

When we consider the cumulation of all 600 responses in which foreign Hausa were a choice in a pair (100 respondents, 6 paired questions), the

Table 6. Cumulative summary of affinity choices

Preferred group	Yardaji		Yekuwa		Both villages	
	No.	%	No.	%	No.	%
Non-Hausa cocitizens	397	66.6%	369	62.1%	766	64.4%
"Foreign" Hausa	199	33.4	225	37.9	424	35.6
Total	596	100.0%	594	100.0%	1,190	100.0%

overall trend is clear: preference is expressed for cocitizens (even of different ethnicity) over coethnics (who are of neighboring but foreign nationality). Had the mitigating cases of the non-Muslim Kirista and Maguzawa not been included (as they deliberately were, to control for religious vis-à-vis ethnic affinities), the results would have been even more heavily weighted in the direction of national, as opposed to ethnic, consciousness. As it is, in almost two-thirds of all cases (64.4 percent) national preferences prevail over ethnic ones (see Table 6).

Affinity in Hausaland

It would be naïve to invoke the influence of national consciousness uncritically to explain expressed group preferences that fly in the face of historical animosity and common-sense expectations.[10] What else can explain the expressed affinity for ethnically alien cocitizens to foreign coethnics? (See Tables 5 and 6.)

In the case of Yardaji, it may well be general Nigerian condescension toward perceived Nigérien poverty that is operating. Nigerian Hausa may not be enamored of their Yoruba and Igbo cocitizens, yet both groups (and particularly the Igbo) are respected, if begrudgingly, for their economic success. If asked whom they would prefer (or allow!) their daughters to marry, Yardaji heads of household would almost certainly choose Nigérien Hausa rather than Nigerian Yoruba or Igbo. But when they are asked to identify with a group personally, the stated choice for these non-Hausa ethnic communities may reflect a desire to join economically prosperous cocitizens up the economic ladder (and thereby avoid poor Nigériens on the bottom rungs) as much as it does pure and simple nationalism.

---

[10] Elsewhere (Miles 1986c:440) I have addressed the methodological challenge posed by the possibility that villagers may have wished to provide me with "politically correct" answers to these potentially sensitive queries.

Such normative identification with the wealthy would be consistent with Hausa culture but would require the Hausa to extend their standards of social respect (such as the "good man" concept of A. H. M. Kirk-Greene 1974) to non-Hausa communities. In that case, this principle could explain Nigérien Hausa's expressed affinity for Zarma and, to a lesser extent, Tuareg groups.

The clientelistic nature of Hausa culture links political loyalty to material responsibility. Social affinity is a question less of affective attachment than of hierarchically stratified duty. (American citizens support a presidential candidate because they "like" him [or dislike his opponent]; Hausa subjects support an emir on account of clientelistically developed loyalty [*barantaka*].) Asked why they feel closer to the Zarma than to "foreign" Hausa, 'yan Yekuwa spoke of "wealth pass[ing] through their hands," of being "in their power," or of the Zarma's "authority over" them. Dependence and deference are inseparable from affinity; in Hausaland, to feel "close to" is also to respect, defer to, or be in awe of. In like measure, rural Hausa remain beholden to Tuareg because in the past they were at the raiding Tuareg's mercy.

Such hypotheses are necessary only if the more basic invocations of nationalism are deemed insufficient to explain the ethnic affinity responses. The fact that there *was* one paired choice in which foreign Hausa were consistently preferred to cocitizens (the Kirista) does strengthen the validity of the response patterns. While nationally defined preferences predominated over ethnic ones, the control for religion demonstrated that villagers *were* discerning in their responses and not merely trying to prove their nationalism.

Hausa Ethnicity and National Consciousness

Three major findings of the survey are: (1) 'yan Yekuwa express higher national consciousness (as Nigériens) than do 'yan Yardaji (as Nigerians); (2) in Yardaji, ethnic consciousness (i.e., being Hausa) is slightly more salient than it is in the (Nigérien) village of Yekuwa; and (3) in both communities greater affinity is stated for non-Hausa cocitizens (with the exception of those who have left Islam to embrace Christianity) than for "foreign" Hausa. In short, while national consciousness (being Nigérien, being Nigerian) is strong in relation to ethnic consciousness (being Hausa), it is somewhat stronger on the Niger side of the boundary than on the Nigeria side.

In and of themselves, the survey results should be seen as more indicative than definitive: indicative of processes and phenomena in various domains but not alone sufficient to prove the dominance of national over ethnic bases of social identity in rural Hausaland. They do help establish, nevertheless, that modern nationality constitutes an important element of contemporary Hausa identity, even—indeed, especially—among borderline communities.

Ethnic identity simultaneously assumes both lesser and greater prominence in a partitioned borderland. Since 'yan Yardaji and 'yan Yekuwa lie solidly within an ethnic Hausa universe and have relatively limited exposure to the other major ethnic groups in their respective countries (Yoruba and Igbo in Nigeria, Zarma and Tuareg in Niger), the fact that they are Hausa has relatively little salience in their daily lives. Nor do the villagers usually stop and ask themselves if they feel more Nigérien or Nigerian than Hausa. Being Hausa in middle Hausaland is quite different from being Hausa in Accra, in Yorubaland, or in Chad. It is thus common in Yardaji and Yekuwa for the word *hausa,* as a noun, to designate "human being" as well as "Hausa person." [11]

[A]n absolutely isolated hypothetical tribe's ethnic identity model is totally congruent with its human identity mode. It can cease to overlap with the latter only after the group enters into contact with another group and establishes its differences from the latter. (Devereux 1975:53–54)

In partitioned Hausaland, where the aggregate population is united by ethnicity but divided by nationality, citizenship assumes greater prominence than otherwise would be the case. National distinctions not only come to assume greater prominence but tend to supplant ethnic ones in the construction of "basic group identity" (see Isaacs 1974). It is not that national consciousness replaces ethnic identity. Rather, national identity (especially under conditions of partition) comes to serve functions similar to those of ethnicity in providing a meaningful basis for group differentiation and an instrumental means of group support. Fredrik Barth's model of ethnic groups and boundaries (ed., 1969) may thus be extended to international boundaries and adapted to national groups.

Though the relationship is not zero-sum, the superimposition of colonial and postcolonial bases of identity does seem to have occurred at the expense of ethnic identity. Certainly it has supplanted one well-established

[11] "Hausa" may also mean any language, not just the one we know as Hausa.

traditional basis of parochial Hausa loyalty and fealty, that of belonging to one of the Hausa Bakwai, the Seven Families. As Nicolas has put it, "Belonging to a modern State—Niger, Nigeria—plays a more important role than the vestiges of ancient States or of an ethnic group."[12] In more personalistic terms, one might say that the republican successors to Seyni Kountché in Niger and Ibrahim Babangida in Nigeria today command greater obeisance among the Hausa than do the royal descendants of Queen Daura and Prince Bayajidda. Political affiliations *have* followed boundary lines.

[12] Nicolas 1975:426. In this regard, Nicolas also observes:

In our days, the political cleavages in place at the beginning of the century have in part disappeared. . . . The Hausa principalities are no longer what they were when they served as military strongholds, when each prince was master in his own domain. . . . If the ethnic factor plays an important role in modern political and administrative life, it is subordinated to or mixed with other collective identities. (Ibid.)

4

Boundary Considerations

Garin dadi ba kusa ba ne.

The happy land is never near.

—Hausa proverb

Although fixed boundaries were the products of Western notions of space and demarcation, what came to be the Niger-Nigeria borderland region was divided in precolonial times by indigenous frontiers and zones of separation. Contrary to expectation, the Anglo-French demarcation did take these local political divisions into account. But because African and European practices of geopolitical division differed the colonial boundaries assumed new functions and reified previously dynamic spatial relations.

Borderline villagers have accepted the partition with equanimity. Precolonial warfare had created a climate of personal insecurity for inhabitants of the Sokoto-Damagaram borderland; this period is still described ruefully. Partition and pacification went hand in hand, and the imposed peace is recalled with gratitude.

Although outright warfare ended, the existence of an intercolonial boundary initially created new turbulence in the borderland. Smuggling, banditry, and cross-border migration are all recorded in the colonial archives. Once these disruptions were brought under control, colonial jealousy operated to minimize cross-border interference. Chiefs cooperated in this containment strategy.

African administrators internalized this pattern, and after independence they continued the colonial preoccupation with territorial integrity. A relative absence of official cross-border visitations, combined with periodic border closings, has reinforced the separating function of the boundary in the postcolonial era. Such policies reinforce the significance of the boundary for the villagers who live along it and heighten their consciousness of the state that lays claim to their side.

60

Boundary Creation and Maintenance

The colonial division of Hausaland was part of a larger, ongoing process that irrevocably changed the political shape of Africa. For purely Eurocentric reasons European diplomats, especially British and French, reorganized the peoples and territories of Africa into colonies, the embryonic units of statehood. By doing so they unwittingly set the pattern for those political allegiances and spatial identifications that characterize Africa today. However cruel or arbitrary, the turn-of-the-century partition of Africa is crucial to an understanding of the history, politics, and society of the continent today.

Students of Africa are particularly critical of the insensitivity with which the European continent carvers split indigenous ethnic and cultural groups into separate spheres of colonial influence: one expert graphically refers to the partition as a kind of "political surgery" that created "mutilated ethnic groups" (Asiwaju 1985a:2, 248. Jeffrey Herbst [1989:673], arguing that "the present boundary system represents a rational response . . . to the constraints imposed by the demographic and ethnographic structure of the continent," reflects rare dissent from this perspective.) While few observers seriously entertain the undoing or redrawing of the (originally colonial) international boundaries of Africa today, several proposals and suggestions have been advanced to mitigate the hardship and injustice that superimposed boundaries are believed to occasion. Such remedies include delegating authority to local governments to deal with cross-border affairs, targeting frontier communities (often dismissed as peripheral or marginal to national and urban interests) for special development, softening border restrictions, engaging in transfrontier developmental (especially agricultural) programs, and creating and reinforcing Pan-African political entities within which subnational and cultural groups may have greater freedom and autonomy (Asiwaju 1985a:11–13, 245–48; Samatar 1985:188; Southall 1985:101–2).

Most treatments of the African partition, whether they are general and theoretical or case studies, assume two problematic positions. The first is an apparent paradox concerning the long-term effects of the partition on the peoples actually divided. On the one hand it is contended that, since in Africa cultural linkages and influences are greater than state penetration, the international boundaries arising from partition do not act as effective barriers, and are indeed often ignored. Thus "partitioned Africans have . . . tended in their normal activities to ignore the boundaries as dividing lines

and to carry on social relations across them more or less as in the days before the Partition. . . . Judged . . . from the viewpoint of border society life
in many parts of Africa, the Partition can hardly be said to have taken place"
(Asiwaju 1985a:3–4). (The Hausaland example of "clandestine" groundnut
trade [Collins 1976] has been invoked in this connection.) On the other
hand, if the lives of partitioned groups were not significantly disrupted,
there would be little need for the kind of policy recommendations mentioned above.

A second problematic assumption is that partitioned groups are without exception distressed by their division into separate political entities
(cf. Asiwaju 1985a:14). Certainly Somali irredentism highlights the potential trouble that colonial partition has engendered. Yet the Somali case is
the exception. Most partitioned groups in Africa have accepted the reality
of political separation from their cross-border kinsmen, and it is not so
sure that they would wish now to have it otherwise. For the borderline
Hausa, at least, the yanken ƙasa is a fact of life, and few would dream of
challenging it. At least four factors explain why.

The first factor is time. Few inhabitants who knew Hausaland before it
was divided are still alive. During the more than eight decades that Kasar
Inglishi and Faransa, Nigeria and Niger, have existed, two distinct sets of
national identity have emerged. As surely as the colonial boundary was
superimposed upon Hausaland, so have two new identities, Nigerian and
Nigérien, been superimposed upon the Hausa people.

In addition, memories of prepartitioned Hausaland are not happy ones.
Before the country was split, war, slave raids, and famine were common
events. Hausa villagers who graphically recount the ravages of war between competing indigenous empires (specifically, Kano and Zinder) feel
no nostalgia for any precolonial Hausaland. Multigenerational irredentism,
such as Zionism, flourishes when the prepartition (or predispersal) memory is favorable or when the partitioned (or dispersed) people are not well
integrated into the host state. That is not the case here.

Third, it is important to realize that Hausaland before the partition falls
into the category of what Asiwaju calls "culture areas which were not necessarily organized into distinct sovereign states." It is thus an instance of
"culturally coherent territories where peoples of definite cultural identities have [been] split into two or more units, each fraction being placed
in the area of jurisdiction of a distinct state which functions to integrate
such a part of pre-existing culture area into a new socio-economic system
removed from the original cultural whole" (Asiwaju 1985a:5–6). Already

divided into indigenous imperial rival regimes, the Hausa had little unity to lose in the first place.[1]

Perhaps the most important reason for acquiescence in the boundary is the process that in the context of the Senegambian elite has been called "parallel socialisation," the overlaying of divergent languages, educations, and political loyalties onto a partitioned people (Renner 1985:75–78). It appears appropriate to extend this notion of parallel socialization, or parallel politicization, to the nonelite as well, even where they have not been exposed to colonial modes of inculcation as directly or intensely as the elite. This process has certainly occurred among the partitioned rural Hausa, who are forced to confront their Nigerian or Nigérien identity more directly than their Hausa identity.

Especially for the villagers who live along the boundary, the tangaraho is a vivid reminder of where one kind of life ends and another begins. The tangaraho may not act as an effective barrier to personal movement and commerce across the border, but it does serve as a powerful symbol and physical marker of two competing claims of sovereignty. Far from ignoring or dismissing it, the borderline Hausa, precisely because they are closest to it, are extremely conscious of the boundary's potential and real impact on their daily lives. Most conscious of it are those who cross it regularly, and thus most frequently witness the legacies of partition.

Precolonial Boundaries

To appreciate the significance of the colonial division of Hausaland, it is important to recognize the novelty of imposing Western-style territorial boundaries, fixed and firmly demarcated through invisible points in space, on indigenous African polities and kingdoms. This lack of precedent must be taken into account before we consider the argument that the division of Hausaland into British and French spheres of influence was not entirely arbitrary and did reflect preexisting ethnic and political divisions (Thom 1975, 1970).

Two key words used to describe the separation of chiefdoms, kingdoms, and empires in West Africa before the partition are "fluid" and "fluctuating" (Anene 1970:248, 256). Particularly in the Central Sudan, it was the actual exercise of power and control over a given territory that

---

[1] Omolade Adejuyigbe (1976) takes a similar position.

determined the outermost limits of any sovereign's territorial jurisdiction. This jurisdiction, moreover, was constantly being challenged by rival states. As one Yardaji villager expressed this principle of precolonial frontier indeterminacy, "The limit of one's strength, that was the boundary" (Bakin Ƙarfi, shi ne iyyaka). The Western concept of a geometric boundary, by which an invisible line drawn through two imaginary points in space is supposed to separate the intervening land and people into distinct entities under different political sovereignties, was quite alien to this part of the world. So was the expectation that "political loyalty" or "national consciousness" was supposed to follow these same geometric lines.

What mattered for mobile nonroyal Africans was not politics or patriotism but profit. "In the Central Sudan, merchants tended to be internationalists, indifferent to the political fortunes of states and apparently unaware of any special obligations to the states that happened to be their own. . . . [T]he peoples of the Central Sudan . . . completely . . . divorced trade from politics" (Anene 1970:263–64). Merchants from states technically at war with each other openly conducted normal trade (263). One might regard the trans-Sahelian caravan as the prototype of the modern-day multinational corporation, transcending mere political boundaries and allegiances to advance its paramount economic interests.

In addition to trade, the pervasiveness of slave raids rendered Central Sudanese frontiers porous to penetration and impervious to political consciousness. Slave raids occurred within empires as much as between them, providing little incentive for political loyalty among those populations who were the prey of slave hunters. "The inevitable result . . . was the perpetual fluctuation or fluidity (and often the non-existence) of 'indigenous' political frontiers in the boundary zone" (266).

The Boundaries of Hausaland

This picture of fluid and fluctuating boundaries subject to the vagaries of strategic and military power prevailed in Hausaland as throughout the Central Sudan. Despite the Bayajidda myth and the founding of the Seven Families, the various Hausa polities exhibited more rivalry than unity: "a state of chronic internecine war prevailed" (Anene 1970:236). The political fortune of this or that sarki did not engender much political allegiance among the inhabitants of the territories contested. Rather, the overwhelming majority of the Hausa were profoundly apolitical: "Throughout their history, most Hausa men were apparently indifferent to the ups and downs of politics which brought about the fluctuations of the fortune of the Hausa states. . . . The Hausa cared little who their masters were and were utterly indifferent to political frontiers as long as they were allowed peacefully to manufacture and peddle their trade goods" (236, 262).

Even the portentous Fulani jihad of Usman ɗan Fodio at the beginning of the nineteenth century did not substantively change this situation. As a result of ɗan Fodio's Islamic crusade, most Hausa kingdoms—including Kano—were conquered and their kings were replaced by Fulani overlords. Four Hausa kingdoms, however, reestablished themselves beyond Fulani control: the Katsinawa in Maradi, the Zazzawa in Abuja, the Gobirawa in Tibiri, and the Daurawa in Zango. (A fifth rebel kingdom, that of the Kebbawa, held out in Argungu until the Fulani definitively destroyed it.) These Hausa kingdoms in exile were hardly free and independent, however, but rather subject to another power; in the case of Maradi and Zango, to Damagaram (Zinder), which in turn was a vassal of Borno. Far from clearly delineating zones of control, the limits of these Sahelian superpowers were constantly being tested at the margins. The area around Daura, for instance, bore witness to the Damagaram and Kano armies that battled for control on the fringes of their respective kingdoms.

As a result of this conflict at the periphery, a "deserted frontier of separation" grew between the northern fringe of Kano province (under Sokoto) and the southern edge of Damagaram (vassal to Borno) (Prescott 1971:64; Thom 1975:16). To the Damagaram side of the frontier of separation lay the Haɓe (i.e., non-Fulani Hausa) resister states; those Hausa kingdoms that had succumbed to the Fulani were on the Sokoto side.

J. R. V. Prescott's and Derrick Thom's descriptions of a postjihadic "deserted frontier of separation" should not be construed as a clear and neat boundary division between Sokoto and Damagaram, however. For one thing, frontiers remained fluid and fluctuating: Sokoto was "loosely organized" and characterized by "considerable decentralization of government" (Anene 1970:248–49). It was also constantly challenged from without. In addition, it is not certain that the so-called frontier of separation was as deserted as it was claimed to be. Both Yardaji and Yekuwa fall squarely within the area under discussion, for example, yet continous settlement can be traced back before the jihad. Political geography in this precolonial Hausa borderland exhibited both ambiguity and flux. A fixed political border is a relatively new idea to the Hausa.

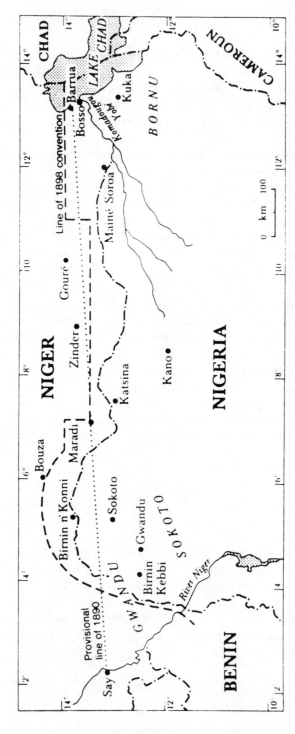

Map 7. Niger-Nigeria boundary demarcations. The final demarcation is shown by the line that combines dots and dashes. From Ian Brownlie, *African Boundaries.* Copyright © 1979 Royal Institute of International Affairs.

Dividing Hausaland

When the British and French first cast their eyes on Hausaland toward the end of the nineteenth century, they were only dimly aware of local conditions. Britain was preoccupied with expanding its influence northward from the coast and cherished suzerainty over the Sokoto empire. France desperately needed a water route to connect its eastern and western African holdings and in particular a viable corridor from Niamey to Zinder. It eventually appeared expedient to both sides to buttress their strategic claims by recourse to local cultural and historic conditions. The division between the Fulani and Zinder empires (the former encompassing the Hausa conquered during the jihad, the latter the Haɓe kingdoms in perpetual resistance) became a convenient way to agree to carve up Hausaland. It took considerable historical and geographic distortion and exaggeration and three separate treaties over the course of sixteen years before such a boundary was established and Yardaji and Yekuwa were collapsed into two distinct political entities.

The first European partition of Hausaland was effectuated by the Anglo-French Treaty of 1890. A straight, geometric line was drawn from the settlement of Say on the river Niger to Barruwa on the shores of Lake Chad. To the north of the line was the French sphere of influence, to the south the British. The Say-Barrua line cut substantially north of the present border and placed many of the inhabited zones of what is now part of Niger within British territory. This area included Magaria and much of greater Zango, including both Yardaji and Yekuwa.

The French soon came to realize that this first boundary demarcation deprived them of the *route praticable* that they were seeking. They also came to see that the basis of Britain's claim to much of this territory was an unfounded allegation that Sokoto had hegemony as far north as Asben. The French pressed for a boundary readjustment. The result was the Anglo-French Treaty of 1898.

The distinguishing feature of this second boundary agreement was the Sokoto Arc (see Map 7). A radius 100 miles north of Sokoto was traced, and then a border was drawn which dipped southward and eastward in three successive geometric lines toward Lake Chad. The British thereby renounced their claim to the northern reaches of the Sahel—but the French still were deprived of a convenient water route to Zinder, and were allocated little more than desert. Once again, almost all the populated areas of Hausaland came under British sovereignty, including Maradi, Birnin

Konni, Tibiri, and Magaria. Yekuwa too, along with Yardaji, was still part of Nigeria.

It was only at this point that the French proposed that the boundary be redefined to coincide with local political conditions. Observing that the Sokoto Arc cut through greater Damagaram, Adar, and Gobir, France asked for changes that would leave these indigenous polities intact. The British were willing to renegotiate their claims to Hausaland, for they were seeking concessions from the French in other parts of the colonial world.

In exchange for France's renunciation of fishing rights off the coast of Newfoundland, Britain agreed to give up a substantial portion of the Sokoto Arc and shift the final boundary southward. A new, wavy boundary was traced on paper that ceded many of the present-day settlements of Niger to the French; it also for the first time created an invisible line and irrevocable administrative split between Yekuwa and Yardaji. It is interesting to speculate what Niger, and especially Yekuwa, would be like today had Britain not preferred the fish of Newfoundland to the sands of the Sahel. Because it did, however, Yekuwa would belong to Niger whereas Yardaji would remain part of Nigeria. Such was the result of the final demarcation of Hausaland, the Anglo-French treaties of 1904 and 1906.

The Partition of Hausaland: Superimposed or Natural?

Because the French and British eventually had recourse to indigenous political and historical factors in partitioning Hausaland, it has been suggested that the final European partition of the Hausa did not conform to the classic colonial image of insensitive and arbitrary border superimposition. The British and French did not just draw a straight line through Hausaland and leave it at that; rather they devised "an anthropogeographic boundary whereby consideration was given to the indigenous political organization" (Thom 1975:6). However true this judgment may be at the macro level, it should be qualified on at least four grounds: politics, demography, ethnicity, and history.

The political qualification takes us back to the motivations of the Europeans for considering indigenous factors in partitioning Hausaland. As Thom notes, such factors were invoked not out of empathy for the Africans but rather out of expediency. Indigenous political circumstances were first advanced to buttress the colonial powers' claims to additional territories. The British invoked the argument to keep Sokoto "whole"; the French invoked it to leave Zinder "intact." Respect for indigenous boundaries was neither the first nor the most compelling concern.

> The European powers were less interested in maintaining the cohesiveness of the different ethnic groups within the borderlands than in acquiring the most territory with the minimum of friction between themselves. . . . Arguments were advanced for the maintenance of the political integrity of the traditional states; however, the Europeans discovered that it was also a convenient way to divide the territory." (Thom 1975:6, 30)

Settlement patterns also mitigate the anthropogeographic logic of partition. From a theoretical perspective, the idea of retaining the precolonial divisions between Sokoto and Borno, Kano and Zinder might have made sense, but it was often impossible to respect on the ground. For one thing, the indigenous boundaries were so fluid that no territory in the frontier zone was firmly established as part of this or that preexisting empire. The treaties provided for on-site boundary deflection to avoid splitting local communities, but it was not always put into practice; near the border station of Zango, for instance, the village of Gazabi is split into Nigérien and Nigerian quarters. On the macro level, despite the stated wish not to dismember indigenous political units, the larger states of Maouri, Konni, Gobir, and Damagaram were in fact truncated by the demarcation (ibid., 33). Inevitably, then, smaller, substate fiefdoms and vassals were also severed. Although the final partition was generally beneficial to the French, in some cases, such as Zango, it extended additional territorial control to local emirates now under British control.[2]

The ethnic reality of rural Hausaland also belies the possibility that the frontier partition truly reflected indigenous divisions. It is true that after the jihad of Hausaland the erstwhile Fulani conquerors quickly assimilated the customs and language of their supposed subjects. This is one of the hallmarks of Hausa culture, in fact—the ease with which it absorbs cultural, linguistic, and ethnic aliens. Yet this Hausa-Fulani mixing was more an urban than a rural phenomenon. In the cities and towns where the victorious Fulani established themselves, a significant interethnic mix-

---

[2] The British officer charged with administering the Zango and Daura areas, Captain H. C. Phillips, "found that, besides the villages which had previously been administered by Fulani Daura, Zango, or Baure, there were over six hundred settlements that lay between the previous boundaries of these chiefdoms and the international frontier" (M. G. Smith 1978:230).

ing occurred, certainly more there than in the Habe rump states beyond Sokoto's reach. But in the countryside, and therefore also in the frontier areas, the merging of the Torodbe Fulani into Hausa society was negligible, regardless of the side of the open Sokoto-Zinder fence on which the villages lay. No matter how valid the distinction between Fulanized and Habe states on the macro level, in the rural areas of Hausaland the border inevitably split ethnically homogeneous populations. Certainly in the case of Yekuwa and Yardaji, there was no preexisting cultural, historic, or ethnic basis on which to separate the two communities administratively.

The historical qualification relates back to the earlier discussion of national consciousness among the precolonial Hausa: there was none. In imputing a sense of political loyalty or belongingness among Hausa commoners to their overarching states or empires, one overstates the relationship with the *sarakuna* (rulers) as expressed by the *talakawa* (subjects). Commoners expressed fealty to their hierarchical superiors, but such avowals did not translate into patriotic attachment to an abstract political unit such as the "nation." It was the partition that sowed the seeds of a superimposed set of nationalities and political allegiances for the borderline Hausa. The partition did not split an already united Hausa people; it did, however, ensure not only that the Hausa would never achieve political unity but that their second-order differences would become intensified, accelerated, and bifurcated.

Daura, Yekuwa, and Yardaji

At the turn of the nineteenth century, the chiefdom of Daura encompassed between two and three thousand square miles and more than one hundred major settlements. Yardaji and Yekuwa were located in the geographical heart of the Daura chiefdom (see Map 8). "Even then its boundaries were probably uncertain, since the jurisdiction of its chief followed the movement of his subjects to new settlements" (M. G. Smith 1978:23, 59–61). Daura's chief in 1800 was the Hausa king Gwari Abdu.

Between 1805 and 1807, as part of the larger jihad then transforming Hausaland, Hausa Daura fell to the Fulani, led by Usman dan Fodio's flag-bearer, Mallam Ishi'aku. Sarkin Gwari Abdu fled Daura with his court and wandered throughout and beyond Hausaland for close to two decades. His goal was to keep the Hausa Daura dynasty intact, even in exile, in the hope of eventually recapturing Daura from the Fulani. Accordingly, most of his exile was spent in proximity to Daura town.

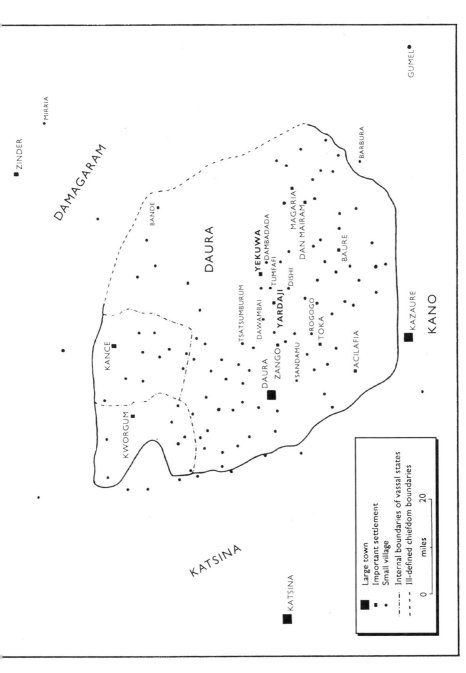

Map 8. The chiefdom of Daura, c. 1800. Adapted from Michael Smith, *The Affairs of Daura: History and Change in a Hausa State, 1800–1958*. Copyright © 1978 The Regents of the University of California.

ZINDER

MIRRIA

DAMAGARAM

BANDE

DAURA

YEKUWA
DAMBADADA
TSATSUMBURUM
DAWAMBAI
TUMFAFI
YARDAJI
DISHI
MAGARIA
DAN MAIRAM

KANCE

DAURA
ZANGO
SANDAMU
ROGOGO
TOKA
BAURE

KWORGUM

ACILAFIA

KAZAURE

KANO

BARBURA

GUMEL

KATSINA

KATSINA

Large town
Important settlement
Small village
Internal boundaries of vassal states
Ill-defined chiefdom boundaries

0   20
miles

Sarkin Gwari Abdu eventually settled in Yekuwa, approximately twenty-five miles east of Daura town. Yekuwa became his last capital and resting place. From Yekuwa he "reestablished his rule over most of his former territory except the southwestern portion close to Daura." M. G. Smith puts Abdu's death at around 1825 (1978:149, 152).

Sarkin Gwari Abdu's death was followed shortly by the splitting and fragmentation of the Hausa Daura. Lukudi, Abdu's brother and designated successor, continued to rule from Yekuwa. Rival pretenders to Sarkin Gwari's mantle, however, established competing chiefdoms to the south in Baure (under Tsoho) and to the southeast in Magaria (under Kitari).

To put greater distance between himself and Magaria, but also to move closer to Daura (which he always intended to retake), Lukudi moved his capital from Yekuwa eight miles to the west, to Yardaji. It was from Yardaji that he attempted, unsuccessfully, to take Magaria.

It was also in Yardaji that Lukudi succumbed to the greater power of Ibram of Damagaram. Ibram marched on and occupied Yardaji in 1845 or 1846. Lukudi was forced to abandon Yardaji and reestablish himself, under Ibram's tutelage, in Toka. (He was also forced to rule as cochief with his son Nuhu.) About five years later, pressure from Damagaram made Lukudi move again, this time to Zango, six miles to the northwest (eleven miles from Daura). During all this time, both Yardaji and Yekuwa remained under Zango and therefore were ultimately subject to Damagaram.

By the turn of the twentieth century, the Daura Hausa controlled more than sixty villages from their headquarters in Zango.[3] Hemmed in by Zinder, Fulani Daura, and Baure, however, the Daura Hausa in Zango enjoyed little independence or autonomy. By the time the Europeans came to take control of the area, prejihad metropolitan Daura was thus already fragmented into four sections: Fulani Daura sat in the western quadrant, Hausa Daura (from Zango) dominated the eastern quadrant. Zinder controlled part of the northwest quadrant, and the double renegade Baure chiefdom ruled the southeastern quadrant.[4] Despite this fragmentation of greater Daura, Yardaji and Yekuwa remained subject to the same superior powers (Zango and Zinder).

As a result of the first two Anglo-French treaties, all of Fulani Daura,

---

[3] This is the figure according to M. G. Smith's Map 4 (ibid., 193); but on p. 24 he writes that "in 1900 the chief of Zango, Tafida, controlled only about thirty-three settlements."

[4] A fifth chiefdom, Kazaure, may also be counted here, for it had appropriated part of the southwestern sector of Old Daura (ibid., 22–23). Magaria, which had fragmented from Lukudi's capital in exile along with Baure, had already been abolished as a chiefdom in the third or fourth decade of the nineteenth century.

Baure, and Zango were placed within British Nigeria. The final boundary agreement, however, ceded much of Zango—including Yekuwa—to the French in Niger. For the first time in their history, Yardaji and Yekuwa now found themselves in separate territorial jurisdications and subject to different alien powers.[5]

As compensation to Zango for the loss of its territory to the French, the British abolished the chiefdom of Baure and placed it under Zango. Shortly thereafter, in 1906, they also did away with the Fulani dynasty in Daura, and brought from Zango the original Hausa ruling family to govern a reconstituted Daura emirate under British sovereignty. At the same time the French abolished the sultanate of Damagaram, resurrected the chiefdom of Magaria, and ruled directly from Zinder. Yardaji thus found itself administered as part of a rejuvenated Daura emirate, itself a subunit of Kano (and later Katsina) Province, in the British colony of Northern Nigeria. Neighboring Yekuwa was now subject to Magaria, and the French *cercle* in Zinder, as part of Upper Senegal–Niger. As stipulated by Article 4 of the 1906 treaty, J. Tilho, captain of the French colonial infantry, and R. O'Shee, major of the British Royal Engineers, were dispatched to lead the joint Anglo-French Boundary Demarcation Commission. Their mission: to mark out on the ground, in Hausaland, what their respective diplomats had decided, on paper, in London.

Demarcating Daura

From 1906 until 1908, Captain Tilho and Major O'Shee surveyed the boundary, planting 148 beacons to mark the theoretical spots where Nigeria ended and Niger began. Sixty-three of these markers were class C beacons: "The upper length of an iron telegraph pole of Northern Nigeria pattern, 15 feet long, fixed in the ground at a depth of 4 feet to 5 feet, . . . and generally cemented at the base" (see Appendix D). Beacon 93

---

5 Colonial archives prove that, at least in Zango, the British were very much aware that the border with French territory was clearly dividing the local population:

> The Northern Frontier of this Province was delimited by the Boundary Commissioner in the latter half of the year. The French have acquired a very fertile tract of land immediately North of the Zongo-Machena line. *The boundary here cuts an important Habe population in two, the Daurawa.* . . . Zongo loses most of its territory and Dingas [sic] goes wholly to the French. . . . The final settlement of the boundary will at last[?] terminate the troublesome state of uncertainty on the frontier that has existed. . . . (National Archives, Kaduna [NAK]/SNP 7/9, 1538/1908, Kano Province Annual Report, 1907; emphasis added)

was of the class C variety, situated at 131° east longitude on the "North side of Herdaji–Tumfafi road, 1,700 meters from west gate of Herdaji" (Thom 1970:293). "Herdaji" is how alien European ears heard and rendered "Yardaji," as they went about determining the village's colonial affiliation. Beacon 93 is undoubtedly the tangaraho that juts out of the ground less than a mile northeast of Yardaji, along the dirt track that leads out from the village market.

Almost four miles to the east, beacon 94 was sunk on the "East side of Diehi–Yekua road, 900 meters from east gate of Diehi" (ibid.). "Diehi" corresponds to Diché, which is itself a distortion of the Hausa *rishin ruwa*, or "thirst." Diché's lack of water, though it causes serious difficulties for its inhabitants, is the butt of local jokes: one cannot return from a trip to this "dry" settlement without being asked, "Ka sha ruwa?" (Did you drink any water?").

Because of the town's proximity to the boundary demarcation, there are actually three Dichés now: Diché Mudi and Diché Nagaje on the Nigerian side of the border and Diché Faranshi on the Nigérien side. It is recounted that shortly after the border imposition, some of the cultivators of Diché learned that their farms were on French territory. They were told that they too would have to move to "France," or else their farms would be confiscated. The unlucky farmers of Diché therefore picked up and moved their habitations into Faranshi—just a few steps behind the tangaraho.

If the story is true, this event seems to have been a curious application of the 1906 treaty, which states: "It is understood that if the inhabitants living near the frontier thus determined should express the wish to cross the frontier in order to settle in the French possessions, or, inversely, in the British possessions, no obstacles will be placed in the way of their so doing, and they shall be granted the necessary time to allow them to gather in all standing crops, and generally to remove all the property of which they are the legitimate owners" (ibid., 282). Then again, the treaty was written by and for the European occupiers of Hausaland: there was precious little in the way of on-site verification of its terms. Even less likely was enforcement on behalf of individual Hausa.

A theoretical geometric line stretching between beacons 93 and 94 thus serves as the *iyyaka*, the local border separating Yardaji from Yekuwa and, ultimately, Nigeria from Niger. On one side of this unmarked boundary the land belongs to the village area of Yardaji, lying within the emirate and local government area of Daura, which are part of the state of Katsina within the Federal Republic of Nigeria. To the other side of this trigonometric calculation stretch the limits of Yekuwa, contained within the arrondissement of Magaria, itself under the département of Zinder and subject to the République du Niger. The line may be invisible, yet even small children can point virtually anywhere along it to the nondescript shrub, bush, or simple patch of sand where Nijeriya and Faranshi converge—and whence they diverge. At the tangaraho itself, other children climb for fun the metal pole that otherwise serves as the ultimate symbol of a Hausaland divided.

Local Perceptions of Partition

Postcolonial interpretations of West African history, many of them put forth by the elites who inherited the mantle of independence, foster the belief that Africans regarded the occupation and partition of their lands by Europeans as an unmitigated evil. Consequently, one might expect to find in Hausaland a degree of resentment, or at least regret, in the local perspective on the European partition. This, however, is not the case. Among the people most directly affected—the borderline Hausa—there is rather a continued appreciation that the partition heralded an end to the incessant warfare waged between surrounding and encroaching kingdoms. For this they are still grateful.

> When the Europeans came, they split the country, but pacified it. There was no more war, no more slavery. Just peace.
>
> —Yekuwa farmer

In the past, Yardaji and Yekuwa were witnesses to the armies of Zinder and Kano as they marched through the so-called zone of separation to do battle with each other. The ravages of precolonial war are not so easily forgotten by the descendants of those who suffered most directly from it. Even today Ibram of Zinder is still vividly recalled as having been a particularly fierce warrior, and few regret his passing.

> Damagaram made war, war. People were happy when the Europeans divided the country. From then on, there was no more war—until the one of Biafra, and Ojukuwu.
>
> —Yardaji farmer

Yardaji benefited doubly, for not only did it enjoy the Pax Britannica (a chauvinistic misnomer, for in Hausaland the French also imposed a peace) but it was also wrested from the heavy hand of Damagaram.

> Before the Europeans came, if your horse gave birth to a mare, it was
> yours. But if it was a steed, it would go to the Sarkin Damagaram.
>
> —Yardaji farmer

Conquest, vassalage, and suzerainty were nothing new to the peasantry. Now, however, the formerly fluctuating lines of demarcation were to become fixed and permanent. For modern Africanist historians and African politicians, the partition symbolizes an imposed European colonialism whose eradication came none too soon. For the nonwesternized inhabitants of rural Hausaland, though, the yanken ƙasa betokened a newfound political stability that, even eighty years later, is not blithely dismissed.

From a Yardaji-Yekuwa perspective, fairer-skinned invaders hailing from a great distance had but replaced a more familiar set of actual and would-be conquerors from whose *zalumci* (oppression) they had long suffered. The European occupation signaled an end to the tyranny of Damagaram, and it occasions few regrets. Even in those most acutely affected by it today, the original partition evokes little anger or sadness over any "arrested Hausa nationalism." People feel rather gratitude that, with Damagaram undone, Hausaland was finally to enjoy a modicum of *zaman lafiya*—peace.[6]

Border Life

The period immediately after the official partition of Hausaland but before the British and French actually established control there was marked by a degree of insecurity bordering on anarchy. Local brigands took advantage of the initial uncertainty surrounding the advent of European sovereignty to engage in criminal pursuits. One such method was

---

[6] Political violence was not the only kind whose suppression was welcomed by the common folk. Even after the formal colonization of Nigeria by Britain, talakawa were still subject to the slave trade:

Slave-dealing. The most serious case was the stealing of two children by a well-known slave-dealer . . . the dead body of one was subsequently found with a rope round its neck. . . . In one case two stolen slaves were found in chains in the home of a slave-dealer by the Bauchi frontier patrol. (Ibid.)

I should like to bring to your attention that a Fulani woman named Aminatou, from the village of Rinjim [in Nigeria], was arrested in French territory, near Mallawa, while seeking to sell two children who accompanied her.

Asked to explain, the woman declared that, out of necessity, she decided to sell the two children of a [female] prisoner, thinking that such things were tolerated on French territory. (Zinder Archives, letter addressed to resident of Kano, August 3, 1904)

Bush-Soldiering. . . . A man stole a horse and went into French territory, where he obtained a pass from the French authorities as a British deserter wishing to enlist in their forces, he then returned to British territory . . . when caught, he was wearing an M.I. [military insignia?] blouse with Sergeant's stripes, and a red fez. (National Archives, Kaduna [NAK]/SNP 7/9, 1538/1908)

An undesirable from French Country, whose apparent principal method of obtaining a livelihood was by means of false representation, has been sentenced. . . . After having hocussed several people he went to Kaura (one of the District Heads) and said that he had been sent by a European to prepare for his arrival . . . and asked to give him a horse in order to inform me of the fact. (NAK/KATPROF [Katsina Province] 3146/Quarterly Report, 1914)

The ease with which people—honest and dishonest alike—crossed from one colony to another made the frontier a high-crime zone.[7] Initially, at least around Daura, the British blamed the French for the state of lawlessness then prevailing:

There is . . . a considerable amount of thievery on the French border. The French authorities have of late insisted on the strict observance of . . . formalities and the delay involved certainly does not tend to the prompt repression of offences along the border. (NAK/KANOPROF [Kano Province], Annual Report, 1913)

A slightly earlier entry from the French side seems to corroborate the British position: "Survey the strip along the border. We have there thieves who operate in Nigeria and whose presence is tolerated by the canton chiefs" (Zinder Archives, report of 1909).

There was also at this time a chiefly competition for subjects, now that the old rules of suzerainty—takeover by force—had been supplanted by European norms of territorial sovereignty. The French at first tried to popularize that portion of greater Daura under their control by requesting that Musa, the restored Hausa sarki in Daura, send one of his sons to rule over the Daura Hausa of Niger from a newly created chiefdom in Dawambai. Musa refused, recommending a much more junior candidate instead (M. G. Smith 1978:312). Nevertheless, the French complained that it was the British—or the Hausa chiefs under them—who attempted to undermine French sovereignty in "their" portion of Daura:

[7] The same problem of lawlessness along a new frontier has been noted in the case of the Nigeria-Cameroon and Somali-Ethiopia boundaries (Barkindo 1985:43; Samatar 1985:178).

The Sarkin Daura is engaging in active propaganda to attract the natives of the canton of Dawombei into Nigeria. Threats, promises, gifts—all means are being used. He has started a rumor that the canton of Dawombei is soon going to be taken over again by the English authorities. Those who wish to come now to Nigeria, he says, will not be molested; the others, on the contrary, will be sorry later. (Zinder Archives, Rapport Politique, 1912)

In the competition between France and Britain (and between the Hausa chiefs in their respective colonies) for migrants, Nigeria won hands down. What Thom (1970, 1975) documents for Hausaland in general the colonial archives bear out in the Daura-Magaria region as well:

There is still a considerable amount of immigration from French Territory all along the Frontier. . . . In the Zongo-Baure district, settlers are coming over from that portion of Zongo territory, which has been ceded to the French. . . . Capt. Dyer . . . ascribes this to the higher rate of taxation in French territory. . . . (NAK/SNP 7/9, 1538/1908, Kano Province Annual Report, 1907)

Migration from French Territory continues, in fact it is on the increase. During June 300 came over and took up farms. The cause of this exodus is reported to be due to discontent with the system of taxation and the conduct of the French Native Troops. (NAK/SNP 17/9, report on Kano Province for first half of 1908)

It is interesting to see how the French characterized this same phenomenon of "Hausa flight," putting it in a light more favorable to themselves.

In this regard the English have not yet done anything from the administrative point of view: they don't collect taxes and they leave everything alone. . . . This situation will always be delicate because the malcontents who are on our side can take easy refuge on English soil without leaving their country of origin, Damagaram. (Magaria Archives, 1904)

It was at least a decade before the situation began to stabilize along the Daura-Magaria border. Renegades had to be caught, cross-border farming had to be resolved, and migration had to reach some initial equilibrium.[8] Relations between the "British" and "French" Hausa chiefs in Daura and

---

[8] Migration across the border never ceased entirely, however; in the 1930s, for instance, it was noted that "New farmland is being rapidly opened up in areas served by the [newly dug] wells and immigration from French territory is obviously considerable" (NAK, Northern Division Half-Year report, June 1934).

Magaria improved considerably, and relations between British district officer and French commandant were generally cordial.[9] Border incidents still
occurred, naturally, but they were handled with increasing alacrity:

> The best relations exist between the Emir [of Daura] and border chiefs in
> French territory and the smart capture of a stolen horse in Zongo market
> resulted in a most flattering letter from Sarkin Damagaram forwarded by
> the Commandant [of] Zinder. (NAK/KANOPROF 437/Northern Division
> quarterly report, September 1930)[10]

Still, the threat of cross-border flight loomed in colonial considerations
of justice and security in the borderlands:

> An unnecessarily large proportion of prisoners remain in chains, for the idea
> exists that the object of shackles is not primarily to prevent escape but rather
> that it is the right and proper hall-mark of the convict. *Proximity to the French
> border of course prohibits indiscriminate unchaining of prisoners.* (Ibid.; empha-
> sis added)

[9] This is not to imply that the observance of official protocol (another legacy of colonization in Africa) was not keenly observed where such contacts were concerned. The following
exchange between a British veterinary officer and his resident in Katsina illustrates how
seriously colonial bureaucratic sensitivities had to be taken:

Veterinary officer: I have received a letter from Veterinary Officer Maradi [Niger] welcoming my proposed visit. . . . As he has thus written to me officially I assume the visit
can be made without further ado?

Resident: If by "further ado" you refer to the letters of courtesy exchanged with the
Commandant le [sic] Cercle de Zinder on your behalf, I assume this was merely a
phrase, born of infelicity, in a moment of haste.

Veterinary officer: The words "further ado" were used in the sense of "trouble" or "difficulty" (Chamber's Dictionary) i.e. without further exchange of correspondence. . . . I
am sorry however that it should appear at all infelicitous. (NAK/KATPROF 2381, 1948)

[10] Even in the latter part of the colonial era, however, control of border regions remained
incomplete. The archives record a borderland conflict in the Daura-Magaria region as late
as 1952, when thieves from Nigeria entered a Nigérien village to steal. Three Hausa village
chiefs led a band of eleven archers to catch the thieves, and followed the culprits across the
border into "British territory." On the way back they were attacked by Nigerians. Casualties:
four wounded "chez les anglais [et] chez les français" (Magaria Archives, *Bulletin Mensuel*,
July 1952).
A year before, the Magaria French administrator recorded:

> Several murders of thieves have taken place and the gangs have moved into French
> territory. Nearly half of the incidents of theft that will be adjudicated this month con-
> cern persons from Nigeria. Usually these are cases of theft of millet and especially
> red-skinned goats, the price of which never ceases to rise in the English markets. (Ibid.,
> April 1951)

The outbreak of World War II did chill tensions along the border. The colony of Niger, initially under Vichy rule, officially closed the border in an attempt to prevent the flow of even local Hausa peasants between Magaria arrondissement and Daura emirate. Harshness on the French side, however, encouraged clandestine migration:

> About two hundred natives of French territory have entered Jibiya district of Katsina territory. It is alleged that they are dissatisfied because of demands made on them for labour, particularly the seizing of their women folk at Maradi. . . . They are regarded as temporary visitors who may return to their homes if and when conditions there seem to be easier. (NAK/KATPROF 2331, October 28, 1942)

Although it is usually difficult to assign precise dates to events drawn from oral history, the founding of Sabon Gari, the most recent unguwa (quarter) in Yardaji, can definitely be pinpointed to this period of time.[11] Residents of Tubé, less than three miles north of Yardaji (and therefore in Niger), were fed up with the forced roadwork and beatings they were subjected to under French rule. So a number of Tubé villagers packed up and walked over to Yardaji, in "free" Nigeria. As the Sabon Gari ward head recounts, "If you left Tubé to come to Yardaji, that was it, no one would come after you."

The normal pattern of colonial cooperation to maintain law and order in the borderlands was likewise disrupted by World War II. The archives recount the case of one Madi, a fugitive wanted by the French, who was at the time in British custody. The British were to hand him back to the authorities in Niger for detention by the French. However, "the French authorities decline official relations with our Government. Therefore, release the man. N.A. [Native Authority] Police better keep him in view lest he return to Prison!" (NAK/SNP 2934, November 1940).

The problem of cross-border migration is the most recurrent theme in the archives documenting the history of colonial Daura and Magaria. From the earliest entries until the latest ones, one encounters the familiar refrain of Hausa fleeing Niger for sanctuary in Nigeria: in this respect the late colonial era does not seem to differ much from the early colonial period. But what is perhaps even more striking is that the migratory phenomenon continues even after 1960, the year of formal decolonization and the acces-

---

11 A letter from the emir of Daura to the district officer in Daura, dated February 18, 1942, found in the old Native Authority offices in Daura town, speaks of eight heads of household residing there, along with seven women and ten children.

sion of Niger and Nigeria to independence. It appears that the pressures that impelled the Hausa to quit the district of Magaria ever since it was demarcated as French territory did not disappear when African (although not necessarily Hausa) administrators replaced the French rulers. In the last entries of the Magaria Archives, four years after independence, the African administrator in charge of Magaria subdivision still notes that "proximity to Nigeria [affords a refuge] for those who flee conscription [or] the census, [for] thieves, criminals, and subversives" (Rapport Annuel, 1964).[12]

For the colonial ruler on the spot, the boundary between Nigeria and Niger certainly did not remain an artificial division separating otherwise identical cultures and societies. As their respective colonies evolved, so did the local areas under their jurisdiction. Commandants and district officers alike keenly monitored developments on each other's side of the border and recorded the growing differences. The analysis made by the French administrator in Magaria is an apt illustration of what the border did in fact come to demarcate, even as he noted its interpenetrability:

> The subdivision of Magaria lives in symbiosis with Northern Nigeria. Most of the laborers [and] almost all of the shopkeepers are British subjects. We therefore know for the most part what is happening on the other side of the border. *It nevertheless seems that the very rapid evolution of this foreign colony has had little influence on us.* It is true that this evolution is attributable especially to the Ibos and Yorubas of the South and not to the Hausas. (Magaria Archives, Troisième Rapport Trimestriel, 1952; emphasis added)[13]

Twelve years later, when Niger was finally independent, the implications of Magaria's proximity to Nigeria was the subject of a comprehensive and perspicacious analysis by Magaria's (now African) commandant:

> Proximity to Nigeria is doing us considerable harm because of the difference in the administrative systems employed by our two countries.
>
> (a) Politics—It is the refuge for all our adversaries and all our wrongdoers who are aided and abetted by corruption. Also, our canton and Fulani chiefs consider their situation inferior to that of their counterparts in Nigeria.

[12] Naturally, no Nigérien administrator, French or African, willingly acknowledged that the major cause of migration out of Niger was the relative harshness of the administration there.

[13] The French administrator does seem to have been aware of the realistic limits of colonial control on "his" borderland Hausa: "Relations [are] still normal between French citizens and British subjects who pass from one side of the border to the other, royally mocking our decrees and orders, and knowing full well that they all are of the same race" (Magaria Archives, August 15–September 15, 1954).

(b) Administration—Because there is no systematic census taking, no military conscription, no vigorous control of foreigners, our people flee to Nigeria for the slightest thing. With such negligence we risk seeing all our peasants leave. Fortunately the oppression [of the commoners] by the traditional chieftaincy has served as a counterweight, with favorable consequences for us.

(c) Economy—The length of the border and the difference in merchandise prices result in a flight of capital and products into Nigeria.

(d) Social conditions—For lack of extensive medical treatment, Nigeria is contaminating us with many venereal diseases, smallpox, and several epidemics of measles and meningitis. (Magaria Archives, Rapport Annuel, 1964)

The transformation of the Niger-Nigeria border from a colonial to an international boundary has not diminished its role as the official line between different (though not necessarily hostile) sovereign powers. In some ways, in fact, the tendency of local people to regard the boundary as a legitimate, or potentially legitimate, separator of nation-states seems to be increasing. Situated as they are so close to the boundary, the people of Yardaji and Yekuwa are particularly knowledgeable about border crossings. Most border crossings are popularly accepted as proper; but when violations occur, the people are ready to step in. The following account of a borderline drama around 1980 was provided by a villager of Yardaji:

One Friday soldiers from Faranshi were following the hoofprints of a man on a donkey who was transporting beans to sell in Yardaji. A ward head of Yardaji was also on a donkey, searching for some of his sheep that had strayed. He was returning from the direction of Yekuwa. The soldiers came upon the ward head, thinking he was the bean man on a donkey they were looking for. They followed him all the way to the edge of Yardaji, to the spot on the outskirts of the village where women gather to pound millet. The women saw the soldiers were about to arrest the ward head.

So the women, still holding their wooden pestles, surrounded the soldiers. (There were two of them.) They beat the horses on which the soldiers were mounted. And they yelled loudly so that the village would come out.

Everyone came running, both men and women. They chased the soldiers, and threw *big* rocks at them. One of them, hit by a rock, actually fell off his horse. He was winded and faint—only with difficulty could he remount his horse. The soldiers fled to the east, until they regained Faranshi. Behind them were the cries and jeers of the villagers of Yardaji.

Disputes between settled agriculturalists and nomadic herdsmen have occurred from time immemorial in the Sahel. Nowadays, however, such tensions may be relatively concentrated along border areas, as offenders perceive that safe refuge is nearby, just across the border. In the following case, hot pursuit restored justice, despite awareness of territorial infractions. This story too is related by a Yardaji villager, and is said to have occurred in the early 1970s. It is known as the "story of the Udawa," who are a subgroup of Fulani herders.

> About ten years ago some Fulani from Faranshi had a large herd of big cattle. They went to the field of a Yardaji man. This was at harvesttime, and the cattle began eating the beans in the field. 'Dan Kagara [a Yardaji farmer] saw this, and came toward them with his hoe. He was about to strike one of them. But the Fulani had "medicine," so the hoe just fell out of 'Dan Kagara's hand. Issoufou, his son, came, and he too tried to strike—but for him, too, the hoe just fell out of his hand.
>
> Then one of the Fulani picked up a stick or a club and struck 'Dan Kagara on the head, so that he fell down. Then they struck his son Issoufou. He too fell, and started to bleed. Then Ladan, 'Dan Kagara's brother, was also clubbed, until he fell to the ground.
>
> Somebody saw what happened and came running to Yardaji to say that there had been a killing. "Kowa maza!" [Everyone, quickly!] he yelled. Men and women came running with clubs and sticks, bows and arrows. The Fulani took off on their camels, heading east [toward Niger] with their cattle and sheep. But the people followed them all the way to Yekuwa territory.
>
> They caught up with the sheep and drove them away. They drove the goats back to Yardaji. They caught one of the Fulani, beat him, and dragged him back to Yardaji. They even threatened to kill him. But the village chief stopped them.

Official Cross-Border Contacts

One of the most striking contrasts between colonial and postcolonial life along the border occurs on the official level. Interestingly, the Nigerian officials of Daura and the Nigérien officials of Magaria appear to have significantly less contact than their British and French predecessors had. Independence has resulted not in greater unity between neighboring African administrators and officials but less. At least in the Daura and Magaria districts of Nigeria and Niger, it seems, the attainment of national sovereignty has in actuality resulted in more inward withdrawal and preoccupation than the early Pan-Africanist visions promised.

At the local level the foreignness of Nigerian territory for Nigérien officials (and vice versa) inhibits official exchanges of the kind not uncommon in colonial times. In 1951, for example, the British provincial education officer in Katsina and his African but non-Hausa education officer visited schools in Niger; in 1955 an invitation was extended from the commandant in Magaria to the resident of Katsina (and the emir of Daura) to attend the opening of a dispensary and school in Sassambouroum, just north of Zango; and in the same year the chief of Baure paid an official visit to Magaria and Zinder (NAK/SNP 2934, November 1940; NAK/SNP 954, December 20, 1955; Magaria Archives, Rapport Annuel, 1955).

These visits were reciprocated by the French. In 1955, according to the annual report in Magaria, Daura received the *commandant de cercle* of Zinder (April 4) and the *chef de subdivision* of Magaria (May 29), who also visited Katsina (June 4–6); French officials visited a model farm in Daura, Administrator "Mac Couachie" in Hadeija (July 20), and the emir of Kazaure (July 28). In 1959, just one year before independence, the Magaria Archives still note visits to Magaria by District Officers Griffith (to see the state of the Kano-Magaria road) and Davidson (to discuss political parties and impending elections in Nigeria).

Today such transborder contacts by local officials and administrators are almost nonexistent. The subprefect of Magaria is not likely to pay a visit to the local administrator of Daura; neither is the chief medical officer of the Daura hospital likely to see his counterpart in charge of the Magaria *dispensaire*. The centralization of government and protocol are hallmarks of postcolonial African politics; when it comes to foreign relations and international contacts, local initiative is shunned all the more. The relative lack of official exchanges between administrators and functionaries of Daura and Magaria is representative of local-level relations not only between Niger and Nigeria but throughout much of the continent (cf. Asiwaju, ed., 1985).

In addition to centralization of policy making and execution, the relative dearth of local government exchange across the border may be attributed to the changed nature of rulership in the areas under consideration. During the colonial era, despite periodic second-order rivalry between them, British and French colonial officers of Nigeria and Niger shared a European commonality of purpose in Hausaland.[14] Both were alien overlords

---

[14] A precious insight into this ambivalent camaraderie of rivals is provided by the French officer who headed the Magaria district:

Peace reigns in the borderlands and in Kano, where there is still nevertheless a certain uneasiness between Peoples of the South and Peoples of the North. Little would be needed to fan the flames that are smoldering. If our own interests here were not tied to those of Great Britain, we could exploit the situation without much cost or trouble. (Ibid., July 15, 1953)

in a foreign land, charged with maintaining law and order and instituting a modest (especially on the French side) degree of infrastructural improvement to facilitate local production and commerce. Although they controlled their respective subjects and colonies, there were natural limits to the extent to which European rulers could identify with them.

Independence, with its bequeathing of power to African leaders, in fact diminished for the new rulers the commonality of purpose that European rulers had shared. National sovereignty, territorial integrity, and respect for inherited borders became more than lifeless legal concepts that the French and British periodically found it expedient to invoke in colonial settings: they were the very lifeblood of the newly independent African regimes. In these circumstances, a keener competition and a more zealous approach to national sovereignty emerged between bordering states. Niger was not to be confused with Nigeria; Nigerians were not Nigériens. Even if such distinctions were initially ambiguous—especially in border areas, and especially among the Hausa—the very least the governments of independent Niger and Nigeria could do was ensure that their own official representatives respect these differences. Official international (i.e., transborder) missions were not to be undertaken without high-level permission. Leaving one's own country to go to the next was not to be taken lightly; the foreignness of the neighboring state, not its similarities, was to be highlighted. This was not necessarily a conscious policy accompanied by formal directives and orders from the center, but it has nevertheless become the modus vivendi of African officialdom in its dealings with bordering states. Between Niger and Nigeria, as between most bordering countries throughout Africa, national sovereignty is a jealous preserve. Border permeability is least likely to be encouraged by government officials.[15]

Even among nongovernment officials who are nevertheless middle-level elites (for instance, schoolteachers), crossing the border is not something undertaken without reservation. Whereas peasants cross back and forth regularly without much ado, middle-level elites are more likely to find themselves subjected to the scrutiny of border and security agents. In gen-

---

[15] It is true that less official, quasi-governmental exchanges do go on across the border. For instance, when veterinary officials in Tumfafi, the small village just across from Yardaji in Niger, were inoculating cattle several years ago, Tumfafi's chief sent a message inviting Yardaji villagers to bring their cattle to be inoculated too. Alhaji Kosso, Mai Gari Yardaji's chief adviser, accompanied the Yardaji livestock herders for their two-day stay in Niger. And Sidi, the "needle man" (*mai allura*) in the Yardaji dispensary, would go to Kwabo to give shots to sick children there ("Because in Niger," he solemnly assured me, "there are no hospitals, there is no medicine").

eral, class bearings (dress, language, demeanor) easily serve to distinguish peasants from elites; Nigérien elites are even more easily identified. Their speech, if nothing else, sets them apart, for their Hausa is liberally larded with French loan words and in other ways differs from Nigerian Hausa.

Important chiefs (such as Nigerian emirs and Nigérien sultans) are more likely than government officials to represent their people across the border, but even they may do so only with the express permission of their national or state governments. A memorable meeting occurred in or around 1980, when chiefs from Daura and Magaria gathered in Yekuwa to pray at the grave of Sarkin Gwari Abdu, the Daura Hausa chief who first led his people in exile after the conquest of Daura by the Fulani.

Border Closings

The extreme permeability of borders in Africa (attributable more to logistical difficulties than to formal open-border policies) is a favorite theme of specialists on African borders (for an example, see Asiwaju 1985a: 3–4). The Niger-Nigeria borderland is reputed to be particularly porous, as John Collins's (1976) study of the groundnut trade demonstrates. In the past, the border between Niger and Nigeria was closed only under exceptional circumstances (as when the colonies of Vichy Niger and Allied Nigeria were technically adversaries). Yet in recent years a change in this pattern has begun to emerge, as governments—particularly those in Nigeria—assert their prerogative and power to control their populations and seal off their frontiers. While imperfect in execution, such attempts cannot help but have an impact on the consciousness, national and otherwise, of the villagers in Yardaji and Yekuwa.

Since 1983 Nigeria has had three mass expulsions of illegal aliens from its midsts. The first occurred in January 1983, when the civilian government of Shehu Shagari expelled over a million African foreigners from the country. In April of that year an army-police-immigration roundup resulted in the deportation of 6,000 more aliens. Then in May 1985 Major General Muhammadu Buhari, then head of state, ordered the third mass expulsion of aliens, 100,000 of whom (out of a total of 700,000) were forced back into Niger.[16]

Expelling foreign residents is one way of controlling the population; closing one's borders is another. Though it is commonplace to close the

[16] The expulsions were directed mainly at Ghanaian workers in Southern Nigeria.

borders for relatively short periods of time after coups and attempted coups, after the military takeover by Major General Buhari in January 1984 Nigeria's land border with Niger remained closed for the better part of two years, until March 1986. This is still a bitter memory for many Hausa peasants, especially those of Yekuwa.

When the closing of the borders was first announced, the ostensible reason was to prevent wanted politicians from fleeing the country. (Indeed, one such fugitive was caught in nearby Baure as he attempted to flee overland into Niger.) On January 23, 1984, the land borders of the country were duly reopened. On April 24, however, the government, as part of its plan to change the country's currency, again closed the border to stop naira outside of the country from being repatriated and converted into new notes. Even after the naira conversion was completed, though, Nigeria's military leaders decided that keeping the border closed would be an effective way of reducing the smuggling (particularly of petroleum products and imported foodstuffs) that was thought to be severely injuring the Nigerian economy. (Maintenance of "territorial security" was also invoked.) Closing the border did not just mean that people would be prevented from crossing at checkpoints, however; motorized border patrols were mounted by military, customs, and immigration services to police the open range. Not until March 1, 1986, was the border officially reopened.

Few residents of Yardaji ventured across the border when the patrolling was "hot." But villagers of Yekuwa, whose economic and logistical dependence on Nigeria is extreme, had little choice but to run the gauntlet of the Nigerian patrols. Although trading was the main reason for taking the risk, social obligations—attendance at relatives' naming ceremonies, weddings, funerals—also called them across the border. Usually they went at night by a circuitous route. Once they were inside Nigeria, roadblocks and mobile police units heightened the risk.

Hapless villagers who were caught faced beatings, confiscation of their money and possessions, and a kind of torture. A unique Hausa vocabulary is invoked to describe these humiliations: *rarrafe*, making people crawl on their knees on the pavement, sometimes with their elbows touching the ground, until they bleed; *gudun kare*, making people run and bark like dogs; *jan kunne*, making people hold their ears, sometimes with their arms under their legs, for hours at a time; *tafiyan agwagwa*, making people crawl like ducks; *ɓira*, making people jump on their hands like frogs; *jan gindi*, making people drag their buttocks on the pavement with stones under them; *asken kwalaba*, cutting people on the head with broken glass.

One Yardaji villager claimed that if one were caught while trying to leave the country, one's money would be either officially confiscated (if it amounted to 5,000 naira or less) or pocketed by the arresting official.

Another dan Yardaji differentiated between the "hotter" time for crossing the border, when Buhari was still in power, and the "cooling-down" period, after Babangida assumed power. Whereas one ran great risks when Buhari was head of state, under Babangida one could bribe the border patrol 50 kobo or one naira to get into Niger. (Thus, even with the border officially closed, 'yan Yardaji were able to walk across the border to Tumfafi for that village's annual wrestling tournament.)

Though the past few years have seen an intensification of border patrolling by Nigerian authorities,[17] people in both Yardaji and Yekuwa would point to Niger as the more forceful and effective patroller of their border area. Efforts by Nigeria to police the border are variable and politically motivated, waxing and waning according to politics, commitment, resources, and regime. Niger has demonstrated a more consistent policy, implemented mainly by the customs service, to prevent large-scale smuggling of livestock and agricultural products out of the country and manufactured goods into it.[18] One reason that the Nigériens are more effective in catching border smugglers is that they often patrol on horseback; the motorized Nigerians may be swifter, but the noise of their motors carries far in the empty bush, warning potential prey of their presence.

While both countries have increased surveillance of the border since independence, the greater concern expressed by Niger is a direct carryover from colonial days. It was the French in Niger who established, in 1913, the first customs barrier in the Hausa borderland region. Posts were established in small towns and villages next to the boundary, and traffic on cross-border trails was regulated. "In contrast, the British did little during this early period to control the flow of goods" (Thom 1970:159–60).

Only after World War II did the British in Nigeria establish customs stations at border checkpoints. (The closest ones to Yardaji are at Zango, six miles to the west, and Babban Mutum, thirty-one miles to the southeast.) The French, having abandoned their early customs infrastructure, instituted customs stations in the major towns closest to the border. Sassambouroum (Tsatsumburum), for example, is four miles north of the border at Zango, and Magaria is thirteen miles north of Babban Mutum (twelve miles north of the geometric boundary). There is also a Nigérien immigra-

---

[17] In announcing the establishment of border outposts in October 1984, Major General Buhari mentioned the need for timely information, intelligence gathering, and constant surveillance.

[18] This issue is treated more fully in chap. 8.

tion checkpoint at Tinkim, three miles from the boundary, nine miles from Magaria. From Thom one might infer that Nigeria's customs regulation was tighter than Niger's, for "the establishment of . . . control points at the boundary [entailed] a more efficient method of control" (163). But villagers living along the border today claim that Nigerian customs agents remain stationary at their border stations, whereas those of Niger (perhaps because they are posted farther away from the border) more aggressively roam the countryside. Naturally, it is with these Nigérien authorities that most Hausa villagers who live between the official border posts risk coming into contact. To adapt Thom's paradigm of dual boundary functionality (158), one may argue that whereas at the international level Nigeria may exercise greater control over the mass movement of goods to and from Niger (by regulating vehicular traffic), at the local level the authorities of Niger threaten greater disruption in short-range movement by individuals crossing the boundary for more immediate social and economic purposes. It is this latter activity that is in the fore of consciousness in both Yardaji and Yekuwa.

Implications

It is true that the boundary that divides Hausaland into Niger and Nigeria does not and cannot prevent local villagers from crossing back and forth with little governmental knowledge or control. Much of this traffic is innocuous—visits to friends and relatives in neighboring villages, shopping in nearby bush markets, and the like. Some of it is, at least in official eyes, illicit, such as the "clandestine" groundnut movement documented by Collins. And even when the border is officially closed, strategem and intimate knowledge of the open bush ensure that there is always some flow across the border, especially from Niger to Nigeria.

All the same, to imply that Hausa peasants are oblivious of the boundary, or haplessly ignore it, would be to oversimplify to the point of distortion. Those who carry goods across (either by donkey or on their heads) to engage in even small-scale trading in a neighboring village run risks of which they are acutely aware. The common fear is being caught by soldiers of Faranshi, whose reputation for fierceness goes back to the establishment of the earliest French military outposts in what was then the colony of Niger. Even without any official marker in sight, villagers know at precisely what point they have entered the other country, and are conscious of what then may confront them.

It is not only those who return to or enter Niger to engage in unauthorized (but vital) trade who feel the greater weight of authority in Faranshi. Villagers of Yekuwa returning from a dry season in Nigeria, as well as those of Yardaji who have only visited neighboring Niger, acknowledge the tougher exercise of power by authorities in Faranshi. The following story, recounted in Yardaji, was offered as a humorous illustration:

> A villager, while still a youngster, went to Niger for the dry season. He was in a village when Diori, then president of Niger, was coming to visit. They had all the youth line up along the road to clap and greet as the president passed. But this boy was a *dogo*—a very tall person—and stuck out in the otherwise uniform line. So they told him to bend down, so as not to stick out. But he was so tall, he still stuck out. So they told him to sit down on the ground! This he did, but not without dissatisfaction. And to this day, he swears he'll never go back to Niger, saying, "Faransa—shege mulki!" ("France—damn their system of government!").

Border Symbolism

Here, where Hausaland is most graphically divided, it is the border, the tangaraho, that clearly and definitively marks for local inhabitants and neighboring communities the transition from one kind of society and nation to another. It is a difference that for the villagers long predates the era of independence and is traced to partition. Yet the partition, as a subsidiary of colonial rule, contains a normative contradiction.

From the village perspective, European hegemony put to rest a longstanding intra-Sahelian conflict that killed and enslaved commoners caught in the middle. Putting an end to Kano-Damagaram warfare is an accomplishment for which the colonial rulers are lauded. But by instituting a colonial regime with fixed and immutable boundary divisions they introduced an arbitrary spatial inequity into the borderland. Whereas some villages enjoyed relative autonomy under the British, others suffered from a comparatively "hot" or "fiery rule" (*mulkin zahi*) as part of Faranshi. Mulkin zahi, moreover, did not disappear at independence. Its effective range has been a function not of time but of space. It is the boundary that delimits this disparity.

5

Colonizing the Hausa:
British and French

Watakila ya hana Bature karya.

"Perhaps" prevents the European from telling a lie.

Soja karfin Turawa.

The European gets his strength from the soldier.

—Hausa proverbs

The popular consensus is that French commandants practiced *mulkin zahi* (a harsh, severe regime), but that administration on the British side of the boundary was relatively light and unoppressive (*sauki*). Unlike Western analyses of colonial administration, which tend toward structural paradigms and bureaucratic formulations, the indigenous perspective is personalistic, reflecting Hausa norms in regard to the proper relationship between patron and client, ruler and ruled (barantaka).

Chieftaincy Policies

British Colonial Policy in Northern Nigeria

As a place to compare the effects of French and British colonial policy on the traditional chieftaincy, Hausaland is ideal. Not only was the British policy of so-called indirect rule developed by Sir Frederick Lugard in Nigeria, but nowhere in the British Empire was it implemented in such pristine form as in the Hausa-Fulani emirates of Northern Nigeria. To many observers "indirect rule" and "British colonial policy in Northern Nigeria" are virtually synonymous. Unlike East Africa—or indeed Southern Nigeria—where "warrant chiefs" were sometimes appointed to make colonial reality conform to colonial theory, that part of Hausaland in Nigeria presented the British with the optimal laboratory for their colonial experiment.

According to the policy conceived by Frederick Lugard, the traditional and therefore legitimate rulers of the Hausa people were to remain in place, albeit subject to British ratification. This policy was institutionalized by the "native authorities" system, under which five grades or classes of the chiefly hierarchy were established. British colonial administrators were there to advise their Hausa counterparts, to guide them toward a more rational, more efficient, more modern method of governance. The native authorities were the embryo of local government, out of which a postcolonial political system would eventually emerge. Change was to occur, but gradually; Hausa political systems and practices were to be modified, but without undue upset to Hausa society.

Structurally, the emirate system that the British inherited from the Fulani was to remain virtually intact, and in some instances even buttressed:

> The area over which each Paramount Chief has control will be marked on the map, and no alteration will be made in it except . . . with the Governor's approval. . . . [W]here immigrants from another jurisdiction, or remnants of a tribe, have been allowed to retain allegiance to the clan or tribe from which they emanated, this allegiance must gradually give way to the control of the territorial Chief in whose district they are. (Frederick Lugard, Political Memoranda, no. IX, Native Administration, pt. I, sec. 34, p. 312)

Maximum discretion and autonomy were given the emirs to oversee the collection of taxes and the dispensation of justice (through the Native Courts and Native Revenue ordinances). Limited British manpower and resources only partially accounted for this significant delegation of authority to "native institutions" in these two key areas: Lugard positively wanted

> the peasantry [to] see that the Government itself treats [the chiefs] as an integral part of the machinery of the administration . . . that there are not two sets of rulers—British and Native—working either separately or in co-operation, but a single Government in which the Native Chiefs have well-defined duties and an acknowledged status *equally* with the British officials. (Ibid., sec. 6, p. 298; emphasis added)

Elsewhere, he summarized: "[T]he policy is to support Native rule . . . and not to impose a form of British rule with the support of Native Chiefs— which is a very different thing" (ibid., sec. 46, p. 317).

The British and Daura

Perhaps nowhere else was British preoccupation with chiefly legitimacy so keen and yet so contradictory as in Daura emirate. In the first decade of the twentieth century, when the British began to consolidate their hold over it, Daura was still under Fulani control. This Fulani regime had been in place a mere century following the conquest of Daura by Usman dan Fodio's flagbearer, Malam Ishi'aku, in 1805–6 (M. G. Smith 1978:146). One hundred years later, the British still regarded the Fulani in Daura, the oldest of the seven Hausa states, as an alien set of rulers. The administration of Mai Gurdo, Mai Ishi'aku's descendant, was considered particularly corrupt and "degenerate." [1]

With Mai Gurdo's death in 1906, the British (and more particularly H. R. Palmer, the then resident in Katsina) saw an opportunity to restore the "legitimate" rulers of the emirate to their proper place in Daura. Since a rump Hausa Daura state had been in place in Zango, twenty miles away, ever since Sarkin Gwari's defeat in 1805–6, this was a particularly easy thing for the British to do.

Thus, one hundred years after the Fulani's rout of Daura, Malam Musa, the pretender to the Hausa throne, was returned to Daura. Of course, it was not purely out of a nostalgic sense of Hausa history and love for legitimacy that the British took this extraordinary step of restoring an exiled dynasty. From the installation of Musa in 1904 until the British left Nigeria in 1960, the success of this strategy has been unequivocal.

After Musa's death in 1911, Abdurrahaman became the Sarkin (Emir of) Daura. In place for half a century, he was thus not only the second Hausa emir of the restored Daura emirate but the one whose tenure most closely paralleled British rule in Northern Nigeria, Hausaland, and Daura Emirate. His reign was characterized by a high degree of autonomy, stability, influence, and relative power: a classic manifestation of British policy regarding the chieftaincy. By the time the British left in 1960, the prestige, status, and power of the emir, however modified by changes in the structure and operation of government, remained paramount.

Appointments to traditional offices, judgeships, and district headships were made not by the British but by the emir. These were not purely ceremonial or symbolic titles but fully functional administrative offices. Naturally, the emir based his selections on his own base of power:

---

[1] M. G. Smith (1978:306) cites as evidence the allegation that "the Fulani dynasty . . . no longer kept the Muslim fast."

> [T]he principal considerations that guided these chiefly appointments were the loyalty, lineage, status . . . and experience of the candidates and the entrenchment and gradual extension of dynastic and chiefly power. . . . Thus, by 1959, the dynasty enjoyed unchallenged supremacy in the political and administrative organizations of the state, and as head of both units, Abdurrahaman's preeminence was assured. (M. G. Smith 1978:334–35)

This is not to say that the British were oblivious of the administration within the emirate. Indeed, they were keen to ensure that tax collectors (usually district heads) did not engage in embezzlement. Violators were punished by both dismissal from office and imprisonment, and at one point the British threatened to remove taxation authority to Katsina. But never was it a question of directly taking on this responsibility themselves, or of abolishing traditional positions and offices. The British policy goal entailed a transformation of certain normative practices within Hausa administration but not its out-and-out repudiation:

> Under increasingly bureaucratic administrative procedures, district chiefs . . . were now required to conduct their administrations within the framework of impersonal rules and to live on their salaries or other legitimate incomes. Whereas they had formerly been lords, subject only to the orders of their superiors and the intrigues of their peers, they now had to conduct themselves like civil servants and officials; to divest themselves of arbitrary personal power; and, in administering the affairs of their districts, to act within their capacities and proscriptions, *solely as representatives of the emir and his Native Administration*. (Ibid., 334; emphasis added)

As early as the 1920s and 1930s, the chiefs' functions of law and order and taxation were being supplemented by development-oriented operations in agriculture, education, health, sanitation, forestry, livestock raising. Once again, these functions were initiated and implemented through the native authorities; in other words, the modernized traditional government. Most of the heads of these departments were members of the sarakuna family (see ibid., Chart E, 356).

Even greater autonomy seems to have prevailed among lower-level chiefs —village area heads (dagatai) and village chiefs (masu gari): "[C]hanges were more easily affected at higher levels of the officialdom than at its base in the rural areas" (338). Dagatai were salaried, as were their scribes (mallamai). Although the traditional rulers in Daura "did not recognize their offices as necessary parts of the regulative order," Smith does consider them "indispensable," and refers to the "remarkable improvements in their rewards and recognition" (356).

French Colonial Policy in Nigérien Hausaland

Unlike the British, who consciously attempted to adapt their method of governance to indigenous rule and custom (and used Northern Nigeria as a model), the French made no distinctions among the areas under their sovereignty so far as colonizing policy was concerned. Politically and administratively, the driving ethos behind French colonial policy in Africa was centralization: a single structure, a single hierarchy, a single set of rules. Structurally, this ethos was reflected in their policy of federation: unlike the British, who treated their various colonies throughout West Africa as discrete administrative entities, the French merged theirs into a single Afrique Occidentale Française. A direct line of command flowed from the president of the Republic to the minister of colonies to the governor general of Dakar for French West Africa to the governor of Niger. Within Niger, subordinate colonial administrators, wherever they were posted, received orders in the same bureaucratic fashion. In this sense, French administration in Niger was typical of French administration throughout West Africa.

In several respects, the differences between French and British colonial styles in West Africa are seen with particular clarity in Niger. Logistical problems—vastness of territory, difficulty of communication, the isolation of outposts from higher levels of authority—intensified the usual French effort to retain near absolute control: "[T]he administrators on the spot in Niger wielded . . . even more power than their colleagues in other parts of West Africa" (Fuglestad 1980:81–82). The farther from the capital in Niamey one went—in this case, hundreds of miles east, into Hausaland—the more powerful one could expect to find local administrators. If Northern Nigeria was as Lugardian as the British could get, eastern Niger was about as Jacobin as the French would go. Hausaland, then, experienced the logical outcomes of the French and British colonial styles.[2]

Unlike the British with their preoccupation with chiefly legitimacy, the French in Niger displayed relatively little compunction in dismissing chiefs whom they disliked and stripping the remaining ones of any semblance

[2] Senegal, with its longer experience with and exposure to French colonialism, is more commonly presented as the model case of French colonial rule in West Africa.

of autonomy. While the British were employing anthropologists to conduct painstaking research into the history and indigenous politics of their wards, the French were carrying out what Finn Fuglestad (1980:85) has characterized as a "crush and destroy" strategy in Hausaland. As elsewhere, the criterion for selection or retention of chiefs was demonstrated loyalty and ability to speak French. Being "legitimate" was less important than being "collaborative" (ibid). Indeed, until 1922 chiefs were subject to the arbitrary and harsh rule of the *indigénat,* by which even a low-level French administrator could unilaterally send an African to prison for up to fifteen days for such offenses as disrespect, carelessness, and reluctance to carry out orders (81).

It is true that the French later took a more conciliatory attitude toward the chieftaincy and that under Governor Jules Brévié a "neo-traditionalist policy aimed at . . . safeguarding the true nature of the chiefly institutions" was implemented in the 1920s (ibid., 122). As with the British in Northern Nigera, however, the initial actions, attitudes, and policies taken and expressed by the colonizers have made the deepest inroads into the subsequent and persisting role of Hausa chiefs in Niger, both in real power and influence and in the perception of their power and influence in the eyes of Hausa peasants.

British colonial administrators bent over backward to retain the broad external shapes of traditional Hausa-Fulani emirate boundaries. The French, in contrast, totally disregarded such considerations, preferring to split up traditional units of rule and replace them with administrative or artificial entities. The colony as a whole was divided into seven "circles": Zinder, Tahoua, Gouré, N'Guigmi, Agadez, Bilma, and Niamey. The first three lay within the traditional (if fluid) boundaries of Hausaland—more by administrative coincidence than by French design. Circles were subdivided into subdivisions, which in turn contained cantons and *groupements* (the latter for nomadic groups, such as the Fulani). Crucially, circles and subdivisions were administered by French commandants; only at the inferior level of canton and groupement would an indigenous chief (*chef de canton*) be in charge. With slight change (mainly in name) present-day Niger retains this administrative hierarchy.

In Nigeria the Hausa sarki was called "emir"; in Niger he was (and still is) called "sultan."[3] In no sense, however, was the sultan delegated the re-

---

[3] This title is given the top-ranking sarakuna of Niger. While the term "sarki" in Hausa is applied to royalty of various ranks, the French applied "sultan" only to those highest in the hierarchy; lesser sarakuna were called "chefs."

sponsibility or autonomy enjoyed by the emir. No native authorities, native court, or native treasury existed in Nigérien Hausaland, over which the sultan had authority: such tasks were the responsibility of the French commandant. Lower-level chiefs were responsible for the actual collection of taxes or arrest of wrongdoers—but only under orders from their French administrator. Fuglestad defines the commandant as "the local chief administrative officer, law-maker (in the sense that he could interpret local customary law as he wished), judge, police chief, military commander, prison superintendent, tax-collector, chief medical officer and much more" (1980:81).

The French and Zinder

Two years after the British—with appropriate pomp and pagentry— restored Musa to Daura in 1906 as the "legitimate" emir, "the French administration abolished the Sultanate of Zinder and placed French officials directly in charge of its dominions" (M. G. Smith 1978:309). Thus did the French show their concern for traditional political structures in Hausaland.

Part of the reason for this extreme administrative execution was the disgust of the French for the often brutal way the traditional rulers of Damagaram (the traditional name for Zinder) conducted business. Their reaction was almost as harsh. When it was determined that a tax collector of the sultan of Zinder (Ahmadu II) had in the course of his duties burned down villages and executed villagers, the French put him in front of a firing squad. However justified the punishment, it typified a severity of judgment and directness of action that the British were more hesitant to adopt vis-à-vis the most ruthless of "their" sarakuna.

The French abolished the Zinder sultanate by lopping it into three separate provinces, with unsurprisingly diminished powers and prerogatives. Even the selection and treatment of the succeeding *chefs de provinces* bespoke the colonizers' disdain for traditional norms of legitimacy. One of the provinces (Zinder proper) was given to a certain Bellama, "a former palace slave and a eunuch" (ibid., 74). (Three thousand people are said to have migrated in protest.) In 1921 the province chief of Zinder was even imprisoned (85)—a not uncommon practice that the French extended to even high-level sarakuna. Whereas the traditional prerogatives of chiefs were in many ways enhanced under British colonial rule, "the French severely circumscribed the power of the Hausa sarauta, including that of Damagaram, and in so doing reversed the dominant trend of the second half of the nineteenth century" (77).

Closer to Daura, but still on the French side of the border, the Sarkin Magaria was placed directly under the French hierarchy. Soon after taking control of Damagaram, the French removed Magaria from the jurisdiction of the sultan of Zinder and split it into six new cantons and one Fulani groupement, destroying the three indigenous entities that formerly composed it. A full-time French administrator was posted to Magaria, and there was no ambiguity as to who held the superior rank, he or the sarki. The Sarkin Magaria was even imprisoned in 1922.

In a decision that was to have long-lasting repercussions not only for Zinder but for Niger's Hausa population in general, the French decided to move their headquarters from Damagaram westward to Niamey, on the banks of the Niger River. (It is said that the decision was taken to please the colonial governor's wife.) Niger's new capital was thus in Zarma (Djerma) ethnic territory, and all attendant advantages—extended education, government recruitment, military dominance—flowed to that group. The French did not deliberately favor Zarma chiefs over Hausa ones, but the sheer advancement of the Zarma, in relative terms, has most probably helped that community's indigenous chieftaincy as well. Few Nigériens, for example, are ignorant of the fact that Niger's second head of state, Seyni Kountché, was not only a military commander but the son of a Zarma prince.

As I have argued elsewhere (Miles 1987), the differences between British and French policies toward their respective Hausa chieftaincies have continued beyond the colonial era. Whether the regime is military or civilian, one-party or multiparty, Hausa chiefs have in general occupied a more favorable position in Nigeria than in Niger; the emir of Daura and the sultan of Zinder but personify this situation.

Yet the imbalance between the chiefs of Zinder and Daura is not so striking as that between their respective subordinates. Inasmuch as Niger acknowledges that it needs the chieftaincy to implement developmental objectives, it now extends nominal prestige to the visible incarnations of the chiefly institutions. The lower on the hierarchical ladders of Zinder and Daura districts, the greater the relative weight of Nigerian Hausa chiefs. Viewed within a single precolonial and subethnic context—that of the Daura Hausa—the legacies of indirect and direct rule grow more striking the farther away from governmental headquarters one goes.

Mulkin Zahi, Mulkin Sauƙi (Harsh Rule vs. Light Rule)

Published reports clearly contrast French and British policies in Hausa-land.[4] But how do ordinary villagers along the border assess the colonial era? Do they also perceive important distinctions between British and French modes of goverance? How do they articulate those differences?

Indigenous Colonial Revisionism

For sympathetic observers of the African scene, one of the most difficult propositions to accept is the openly stated preference of many ordinary (that is, nonelite) Africans for the colonial era. It is a proposition, more-over, bound to nettle the African elite, those who struggled for independence as well as those who have since inherited the mantle of rulership. Yet however paradoxical or distasteful, it would be remiss, if not dishonest, to deny this familiar refrain of indigenous African revisionism.[5]

Usually such sentiments arise when postindependence infrastructural development, efficiency, and maintenance are compared, inevitably un-favorably, with those of the colonial era. Another comparison, however, is available—with precolonial society and government.

As we have seen, precolonial Hausaland, and particularly the "frontier of separation" in which Yardaji and Yekuwa lay, was ravaged by constant warfare between competing powers. In addition (or rather as an adjunct) to this interchiefdom and interdynastic warfare was the slavery into which hapless prisoners were impressed.[6] The *mulkin mallaka,* or colonial era, did put an end to this chronic state of political instability and violence, from which the rural peasantry suffered more than city dwellers and their elite successors. Old-timers in Yardaji and Yekuwa today still refer to the savagery of Tanimu and Ibrah, two of the more notorious warrior sul-tans of Damagaram (Zinder). As we have seen, frontier peasants were less upset by a newly imposed border than they were enamored of the newly imposed peace.

---

4 Obaro Ikime (1968) and Peter Tibenderana (1988, 1989) nevertheless dispute the "indirect-ness" of British rule in Nigeria.

5 The term "revisionism" is here used in its nonideological sense, to mean reexamination for correction or improvement.

6 One may certainly accept M. G. Smith's (1965b) thoughtful and thorough distinction between the systems of slavery as practiced in the New World and in Hausaland without denying that Hausa servitude too was morally tainted.

When the Europeans came, there was peace and general improvement [*gyaran dunya,* literally "repairing of the world"]. . . . There was more money available, and a real dignity of rulers [*mutumci sarauta*]. None of this useless talk [*zance*]. Today, if a chief says something, anyone can say it's a lie.

—Yardaji dispensary worker

When the Europeans came, if a man was arrested they at least made sure that he was given food, and something to lie on. Before that, a prisoner got nothing. . . . The British brought learning and justice. No longer could a man be evicted from his home just so the chief's son could live in it.

—Yardaji farmer

Two wells were dug in the village during the colonial era—and none since.

—Yardaji farmer

It was you *anasara* [whites] who put everything right. It's you who brought knowledge and learning [*ilmi*], it's you who opened our eyes. If things are any better today, even under the black rulers, it's thanks to you. Koranic learning has value. It teaches manners, it teaches correct behavior. But your ilmi is of another kind—knowledge of things, of how to do things. Now, if we're going to dig a well, we know to go and get cement, and plaster [the well].

—Yekuwa *griot*

Whites showed us marvelous engines, machines, and automobiles. When I read about the first explorers and how they suffered, I feel pity and shame for how they were treated.

—Yardaji resident, formally of Niger

Admittedly, these reflections are somewhat idealized.[7] After all, few villagers are still alive who can personally recall the precolonial period.[8] Still,

---

[7] Exaggeration of the power and abilities of whites is rife in rural Hausaland. On more than one occasion I was assured:

> You people live a long time. We, if we're fifty, we've grown old. You, if you're a hundred, you're still young. Yes, I know—you live to a hundred and fifty, some of you to two hundred. You have medicine against pain, against disease—that's why. And we—we plant, we harvest, all by hand. No wonder we age early and our bodies grow old. They just wear out.

[8] But Baba of Karo, whose published autobiography recounts the days of transition to colonial rule, is quoted as saying virtually the same thing: "When I was a maiden the Europeans first arrived. Ever since we were quite small the *malams* had been saying that the

this nostalgia for colonial days acquires an aura of credibility when one also hears criticism of the Europeans, particularly those of Faranshi.

Defining the Difference

> The whites did make things difficult. [But] those in Nigeria had it easier [*zaman da sauƙi*]. To this day, it's like this. For forty years there has been the "rule by the customs service" [*mulkin douane*]—patrolling the border, catching people, confiscating booty. Only the one that Allah helps will get through without getting caught. In Nigeria they've had customs for only ten years.[9]

This statement by a Yekuwa man may serve as a composite recapitulation of the perceived difference between Faranshi and Inglishi, Niger and Nigeria. From the earliest days the French took full control and held the reigns firmly. This was their mulkin zahi, or "hot" style of ruling. The British had a looser, less intimidating style of governing: sauƙi (ease, lightness). A Yardaji man says virtually the same thing as his Yekuwa neighbor:

> The English eased problems for the peasants: they abolished raiding, fighting. But the French squeezed [*matsa*] the Hausa: they confiscated millet, they made men carry *giginya* [a large, heavy palm tree used for construction] until they died.

When Europeans first arrived, Hausa peasants feared all of them. Soon enough, though, it appears that the initial fear engendered by any European dissipated in those on the British side of the border, while it was reinforced in those on the French side:

> In those days, people were afraid. If you yelled "*Salaud!*" a man would run away and crouch behind a tree. Fear!
>
> —Yekuwa griot

> The French are very prone to fighting. If you make them mad, they'll react very strongly. But Europeans of Ingliya are very patient and not easily

---

Europeans would . . . stop wars, they would repair the world, they would stop oppression and lawlessness, we should live at peace with them" (Mary Smith 1954/1981:66).

9 This is not literally the case: Thom notes the establishment of a Nigerian Federal Customs Service in 1961 (1970:165). But here as elsewhere in the oral narration, literal historical accuracy is less important than local belief. If it is perceived in the Yardaji-Yekuwa region that the Nigerians began a customs enforcement policy only in the 1970s, that is the relevant reality, as far as the villagers are concerned.

angered. When they left they didn't take everything with them—not like the French, who took everything that produced wealth.[10]

                                                          —Yardaji town crier

A subtle difference in the perception of the French and British is reflected in the names used to describe white people, a distinction that holds to this day. Early on in the colonial era, the British in Hausaland insisted on being called *bature* (pl. *turawa*), which literally means "European," rather than *nasara* (or anasara), Christian (see Paden 1973:53). The French either were oblivious of this ethnic-etymological distinction or did not care.

To the Muslim Hausa, naturally, colonization by turawa sounds marginally more palatable than domination by nasara. It is striking that this linguistic framework persists to this day, even in the Hausa hinterland. For whereas a white person is still referred to as bature in Yardaji, in Yekuwa he is labeled foremost as anasara.[11] On the linguistic level alone, it would appear that in Yardaji and Yekuwa, as throughout Hausaland, the language of the Muslim Hausa was more accommodating to the "European" colonial presence in Nigeria than to the "Christian" colonial presence in Niger.

Villagers on both sides of the border vividly recall the harsh conditions under which the Hausa in Faranshi had to labor. They recall the forced cultivation of groundnuts. ("People were forced to grow groundnuts, but were prohibited from eating them. Only surreptitiously, if no one was around, would one dare eat a groundnut, carefully burying the shell so no one would know.") They recall the obligation to work without pay on the laterite vehicular road (*debe*) built between Matameye and Magaria (and the punishment meted out to anyone who rode his donkey on it). They recall the men having to chop down enormous trees and carrying them on their heads all the way to Magaria.

No other white man inspired such fear and awe as the French commandant headquartered in Zinder. Bordeaux, nicknamed Sarkin Aiki (King of Work), has entered folklore for his toughness and ruthlessness.[12] It was under Bordeaux that people were prevented from eating their own crops; that lepers were forced to plant seeds; that blind men were made to weave

[10] Usually the image of the French departing a colony with all their capital and movable infrastructure is associated with the pullout from Sékou Touré's Guinea in 1958. It is interesting to hear a similar recollection in a Nigérien context.

[11] This practice invariably created some confusion as far as my own identity was concerned. Although white, I am neither European nor Christian, and thus I contradicted all local definitions of Caucasian racial/ethnic identity.

[12] Collins (1974) also chronicles the Bordeaux legacy.

ropes; that cripples had to shell peanuts; that both lepers and women were ordered to perform *guɗa* (a shrill joyful sound). Given the Hausa penchant for dramatic history, it is no wonder that a popular song has been recorded to immortalize the Bordeaux epoch:

> The whiteman said, "Even the Arab, the learned man,
>   the soldier,
> The soldiers' wives, married women (what an infidel!)
> Tell them that they are not exceptions."
> Young girls selling snacks, butchers, peddlars,
> Cripples and blind men and lepers,
> Even the old woman selling groundnuts,
> Baudot would not spare.
>
> CHORUS: Bordeaux, the Whiteman of Labor,
>   Not even an old woman selling groundnuts
>   Would he spare.
>
> The heathen would spare no one.
> Not even the old woman with her cornstalk stick,
> A cornstalk stick to keep away the animals,
> Animals coming to nibble at her groundnuts.
>
> From the city, from the hamlets, from the barracks,
> People taken for labor,
> Labor on the sultan of Damagaram's estates.
> One hundred men, seven days of labor,
> Impossible to complete.
> But when Baudot said "Finish it!"
> They made sure they finished,
> Finished so as not to suffer even more.
>
> Sidi the Holy Man,
> He told Sidi to farm.
> "I have never farmed in my life!" lamented Sidi,
> "But now I will."
> (Sung by Alhaji Mu'azu 'Dan Alalo of Zinder)

Bordeaux is not the only colonial ruler remembered in Yardaji and Yekuwa. The legendary Mai Tumbi ("Big Belly") came to the Daura region to make the first on-site boundary demarcation. Trees were cut down and burned to show the actual boundary. Goats were slaughtered for him and his soldiers, who ate and spent the night in Yekuwa before continuing onward.[13]

Whether they knew it or not, colonial administrators invariably received Hausa nicknames, by which they are remembered to this day. Nicknames and associated stories also distinguish Hausa perceptions of British and French rulers.[14]

By and large, British district officers and other colonial officials have humorous or descriptive (i.e., value-neutral) nicknames. Mai Izga, for instance, was never seen without a fly switch in hand. Mista (Mister) Kara promoted the cultivation of sugar cane. An apparently eccentric Captain Mai Jimina kept a pet ostrich. The strikingly white eyebrows gave Mai Fara Gera his name, and Gwamna (Governor) Mai Baza is associated with a fringed leather apron worn by dancers. (Just why is unclear.) District Officer Mai Hannu 'Daya had only one arm.

An interesting, if tragic, story is told of a certain district officer who committed suicide. It is said that he killed himself (by firing a rifle into his throat) because he disliked Daura and was unhappy about being posted to the bush. Some of his guards were arrested, but fortunately the unhappy Englishman had left a note absolving everyone else of guilt in his death.[15]

The meanest colonial officer in the Daura emirate seems to have been Baturen Shanu ("Cattle European"), but he was harder on the cows than on the people. Baturen Shanu distributed hoes and cattle. On tour, he would give a hearty kick to the side of a cow. If the animal didn't fall, then

[13] Mai Tumbi, or Captain H. C. Phillips, was dispatched in 1903 by the British resident in Kano to survey greater Daura and inform the inhabitants of Great Britain's newly established hegemony there. Phillips initially removed many villages—including Yekuwa—from French and Zinder rule to British and Zango administration. As we know, Yekuwa was returned to French jurisdiction a few years later (M. G. Smith 1978:230).

[14] Pierre Alexandre (1970a:11–12) whimsically draws on his own experience as a colonial administrator when he discusses this matter:

> The study of nicknames and drum-names is often instructive. . . . [A]ll those I know, my own included, are hostile. . . . But there is a world of difference between those which resemble certain customary royal names like 'Tornado', 'Male Gorilla', 'Panther-lying-in-wait' or 'Destroyer of Villages', and 'Little Bugger', 'Fat Arse' or 'Dirty Shirt'. To the eyes of the liberal European or even of an inspector of the administration, the behaviour of 'Little Bugger' would appear more acceptable, and strictly according to the book or even more democratic than that of 'Destroyer of Villages'. . . . The former was however, detested and despised by those he administered, the latter respected, accepted and finally popular even if not loved.

D. J. Muffett (1964: app. 1) also records the Hausa nicknames of the early British colonials in Northern Nigeria.

[15] Sarkin Daura identifies this unhappy officer as a Mr. Morgan, who took his life in 1956.

all was fine; but if the poor beast fell, the owner would be arrested and brought to the emir of Daura. The charge: failing to feed his livestock.[16]

In Yekuwa, French commandants leave a harsher legacy behind. Mai 'Dan Doro (the Hunchback) is, like Work King Bordeaux, associated with the forced cultivation of groundnuts in the Yekuwa-Magaria area. Specifically, he ordered people to remove the millet that was already planted in their fields and plant groundnuts in their place. Once he ordered four men to be stretcher bearers to carry his wife over long distances. It is said that this Frenchman was so unpopular that a mallam came to pray that the Hunchback would depart—and he did. Another story further explains the antipathy associated with this anasara:

> Once, when Mai 'Dan Doro was commandant, a census of the village was conducted. (It was for the purpose of collecting taxes.) A certain Fulani was spotted at the village edge. *Dogarai* [the chief's guards] were sent out to fetch him. When the Fulani saw them coming, he ran off. (At that time, one was always afraid to see or have to deal with the sarki.) The dogarai followed him on horseback and brought him back.
>
> When he was brought back to the village, he was beaten. Then they asked him, "Where were you going?" He answered, "To the market" (that is, Yardaji, for it was a Wednesday). They refused to believe him, so they beat him again.
>
> Chief Lalalu said, "I know him. I know his father. He was going to market. He wasn't fleeing. He's not from here, he isn't under my authority." The dogarai refused to believe this.
>
> Then a soldier (but a black man) stomped him so hard that he broke the man's ribs, and he collapsed on his other side. Mai 'Dan Doro said, "Tie him to a donkey and take him home." Lalalu said, "No, I won't have him taken home, because *you've* killed him. If I have him taken home, his father will say *I* had him killed. There's a donkey there—you take him home yourselves, since you are the rulers of the country. Nothing will happen to you."
>
> The soldiers and dogarai tied the man to a donkey and took him to his home. His father was afraid, so he kept silent. (Otherwise he was afraid he too might have been punished.) The Fulani had died on the way; his father buried him.

Then there was Barkono (Hot Pepper). "There was fighting in him, indeed!" If someone did anything wrong, Barkono would have his soldiers rip the shirt and pants off the hapless villager and flog him. ("The women would watch and cry.") It is said Barkono had people whipped less to punish them individually than to instill fear and discipline (*horo*) in all the

16 Several informants contributed to this account, but especially Alhaji Ali of Yardaji.

others. Barkono and his soldiers would confiscate goats and food, eat and drink, but never pay. They would then leave, Barkono alone mounted on horseback.[17]

The fear instilled by visiting commandants was so great as to lead to superficially irrational behavior. For example, a certain Satagumi, about to leave after overnighting in Yekuwa, shot a camel. When he saw that it was dead, he told the people to eat it. But the people were afraid to eat the animal, "in case [Satagumi] returned and demanded to know why they had eaten the camel. So they left the meat."[18]

The present chief of Magaria, Sarkin Harou, of course was familiar with a wide range of colonial administrators in Magaria, both before and during his accession to the chieftaincy. The earliest one he remembers is V. Prud-hon (1930–31) (nicknamed Mai 'Dan Wando for his wearing of shorts). It was a time, according to Sarkin Magaria, when "people suffered, men were beaten." If a commoner failed to work, Mai 'Dan Wando would hold the *sarki* responsible, even hitting him and suspending him for anywhere from two weeks to three months. As a lesson to others (horo), village heads would be forcibly brought to Magaria for between one week and one month.

La Hongrais (1934–35) was called Langa-Langa, which may be rendered loosely as Stringbean. (*Langa-langa* are the long strings used for tying loads or bales.) "He was tall, but didn't have much of a body." The lanky La Hongrais had so little strength than when he beat people, *he* would fall! Langa-Langa is also remembered for ordering people to work in the nighttime.

H. Boudy (1935–36) would get up *very* early in the morning to begin his tasks. The ever-observant and curious Hausa noted that he would not eat, defecate, or urinate until one o'clock in the afternoon. It was no flattering comparison to liken Boudy to Bordeaux: often silent, staring straight at you. . . . It was Boudy who deposed Sarkin Adamu for sending young men to Northern Nigeria to become soldiers (at the request of his "brethren" in English territory).[19]

---

[17] Hot Pepper seems to be G. Chabaud, who served as *administrateur-adjoint* in Magaria in 1933–34. Sarkin Magaria added this recollection: "He would address young people in French, who would be silent, and just stare. So he'd have them beaten. Then he'd tell them why—because they couldn't speak French! "Why don't you attend school?!" he'd demand. Chabaud would imprison fathers to get their sons to go to school, at a time of great opposition to mandatory colonial schooling. (Fights with knives and swords broke out over this issue.)

[18] The stories of the Hunchback, Barkono, and Satagumi were provided by Alhaji Moussa Makaho of Yekuwa, who gave his age as between ninety-three and ninety-five years.

[19] This incident occurred either later in Boudy's career or under one of his successors,

Sarkin Harou, chief of Magaria, and palace guard.

L. Braillard (1936–38) was called Azaga because he constantly cursed and insulted people (*zage*): "*'Salaud, bandit, cochon!'*"

Under Brouin ("Serkin Haousa," as rendered in the Magaria Archives) problems attendant on the French administrative mode of communication came to a head. According to the chief of Magaria, word was sent from Magaria to conduct a census. Lesser chiefs in the bush did so, but the sarki's rivals, resentful at having been passed over for royal appointment, made sure that the chief himself was kept ignorant of the matter. (They had befriended colonial government workers to sabotage the chief's work or spread malicious rumors about him.) Naturally, there was surprise in Zinder when the low census count arrived. The result was that henceforth any news communicated to the *bariki* (barracks) in Magaria would also be made directly known to the sarki.

J. Escher (1941–45) was Magaria's answer to Zinder's Bordeaux. Although remembered in Magaria as Koƙobiro (literally Woodpecker, but the word is used also to describe a thin person), he had a hump on his back and is probably the Mai 'Dan Doro referred to earlier.

Although it was Escher who had Harou named sarki, no love was lost between the two. He was a strange and wicked man (*mugun mutum, lalata*), according to the chief. He was sometimes friendly but at other times very hostile. Often he made as if to strike the chief—and sometimes did so. (Sarkin Harou claims that he returned the blows.) Unsatisfied with the small amount collected in taxes ("at a time when money was difficult"), the Frenchman would throw coins offered in payment to the ground. (The chief would patiently pick them up and insist that he take them.)

One night, according to Sarkin Harou, Bordeaux called Escher and told him he must bring tax money the next morning or face dismissal. Escher came running to the chief's palace in the middle of the night to ask if the chief had been spreading bad rumors about him. Tax money was immediately handed over, the clerks were called, and an accounting was made. Escher's problems with Bordeaux were over—at least temporarily.

Once Bordeaux sent word to the chief to meet him in the village of Kantché. Escher was not invited, and he was furious. He asked if the sarki was maligning him. Harou denied it, said he didn't want to hurt anyone, and prayed to Allah to protect the Frenchman. The sarki, however, was less

---

Escher. It was one of several cases in which chiefs in Niger during the Vichy era either encouraged or failed to prevent their subjects from joining the British forces in Nigeria. See Fuglestad 1983:141.

eager than Escher to meet with Bordeaux, and asked why Escher wished to depose *him*. Afterward the two ignored each other.

Many years later, however, Escher received Sarkin Harou in his home in Paris when a delegation of important chiefs was brought to France to attend Bastille Day celebrations. It was 1968—*lokacin de Gaulle*—and the sarki met the legendary general. By that time, Escher was an old man, living in an old house. . . .[20]

Serreau (1955) was nicknamed Saburo (Mosquito) and Sarkin Cizo (King Stinger) for his harassment of people. He was strict and stern, punishing people for little things: the Mosquito could not stand to see people playing checkers or just conversing—he would order them to get up and leave.

It would be unfair to leave the impression that all the French commandants are remembered as tyrants. Cunin (1947–49) earned the nickname Mai Lafiya (the One of Health); Voegtlin (1949–50) was called Mai Dariya (He Who Laughs); and Broussard (1952–53), who had white hair, was known as Tumkiya (the Sheep). Nevertheless, the overall impression left by the French in Magaria district and Yekuwa is negative. In this regard, given the contention that what counted most in European administration of Africa was not official colonial policy but rather the human relations between district offices and emir, commandant and chief,[21] these assessments of individual administrators by neighboring partitioned Hausa do contribute to an ultimate comparison between French and British colonialism in Hausaland.[22]

[20] Some of the details recorded here stretch credulity. But the comment made in n. 9 applies here as well: literal accuracy is sometimes less important than perception. Colonial oral history in Hausaland may be in a state of mythogenesis, and mythology, as is well known, derives its strength less from factual veracity than from the symbols, messages, and lessons imparted and received. See Alexandre 1970a:5 on the entry of the Great Bachelors ("the single men who invented colonial Africa") into local African lore and legend. See Mircea Eliade 1963 on the cultural importance of mythmaking.

[21] "On balance, no factor was more important in determining the nature of government than the personalities of British officers and African rulers and the way these blended in practice": Robert Heussler, "Indirect Rule in Northern Nigeria," *South Atlantic Quarterly* 67 (1968), quoted in John Smith 1970:17; "[T]he relationship between the *commandants* and the country was personal rather than administrative. . . . [T]he human qualities of the relationship of the chief . . . with the *commandant* depended essentially on the human qualities of the latter": Alexandre 1970a:6, 11.

[22] They also help explain the reaction to me, as a white person, in the two villages. While overall I was accorded as much hospitality and friendship in Yekuwa as in Yardaji, a greater reserve or reticence lingered among some 'yan Yekuwa (those whom I knew but slightly) than I encountered in Yardaji. Certainly, there was greater discretion in the overt expression of natural curiosity about me on the Niger side of the border than on the Nigeria side. It

Military Culture

The imposition of colonial rule throughout Hausaland, in Nigeria as well as Niger, was initially accomplished by brute military force. In order for Lord Lugard to apply his benevolent philosophy of indirect rule, he first had to conquer Northern Nigeria. Resistance was keen but ultimately futile, as bows and spears were pitted against maxim and gatling guns.

In his fascinating account of the British conquest of Hausaland, D. J. M. Muffet (1964) argues that C. L. Temple, directing the British forces, unnecessarily forced a military confrontation with the sultan of Sokoto, and even more unnecessarily had Major Marsh force a fatal showdown at the bloody battle of Burmi. Reading Muffet's book, one cannot help predict an incipient hatred of the British in Hausaland, as it recalls the useless and avoidable murder of their spiritual leader, the Sarkin Musulmi, Commander of the Faithful (literally King of the Muslims), Sultan Attahiru.

Yet this was not the case: Hausa and Hausa-Fulani accommodation to British rule was swift and profound, and thereafter relatively good relations prevailed between successive generations of traditional chiefs and colonial rulers. The spirit of the relationship desired by the British may be discerned from the conclusion of the speech delivered by Frederick Lugard in Sokoto on March 21, 1903:[23]

---

may have been due in part to the general caution in regard to foreigners inspired by tightly disciplined military governments. Yet I suspect that it was even more a carry-over from colonial-era memories of whites, especially among the elderly. An account that illustrates the point is adapted from my journal. The incident occurred when a Yekuwa youth brought me to interview Alhaji Moussa Makaho, a very old blind villager:

"Alhaji, you have a visitor."

"From where?" (that is, with whom is he staying?).

"From the chief's house—with Alhaji Aminu."

"What kind of a visitor? A Fulani?"

"No, an anasara."

"An anasara?! Put him on a mat, but away, away! What do I have to do with a white man? What possible business could I have with one?"

"He's come to greet you." (My wish to ask about village history was then explained.)

"I see. Let me get a mat for him from the mosque."

I said that I didn't need a special mat to sit on. But Alhaji Moussa insisted, and went to the mosque to get one. "Put it back there, back there." (He still didn't wish me to be too close to him.)

"But it's in the sun. The shade is next to you."

After the interview, the youth explained Alhaji Moussa's behavior as the result of fear: in the old days, people always feared white men here.

23 Lugard's famous speech at Sokoto actually was delivered four months before Attahiru's death, while the sultan was still in flight.

I hope that you will find our rule sympathetic and that the country will prosper and be contented. You need have no fear regarding British rule, it is our wish to learn your customs and fashions, just as you must learn ours. I have little fear but that we shall agree, for you have always heard that British rule is just and fair, and people under our King are satisfied. You must not fear to tell the Resident everything and he will help and advise you. (Kirk-Greene, ed., 1965:44)

The military method by which the British first established a political foothold in Hausaland soon gave way to a more bureaucratic framework. Colonial administrators may technically have been military officers, but governors, district officers, and assistant district officers dealt with their subjects (and chiefly advisees) more in a political and diplomatic manner than according to military norms of hierarchy and command.

In contrast to the general ease with which the British established their presence in the northern emirates and civilianized (or at least politicized) them, the French presence in Niger long retained a military stamp. Part of the reason may have been continued resistance to French rule (particularly in the Tuareg north). Part of it may have been a French penchant to colonize in a firmer, more direct, no-nonsense way. Whatever the ultimate reason, government in Niger remained permeated by a military culture whereas Nigeria has moved much further away from it.[24] Even in the villages, the image of *soji* (soldier) evokes reactions of varying intensity, from the serious to the humorous. Villagers in Yekuwa and elsewhere in Niger often greeted me with a flourishing mock salute; in Yardaji, this happened only once, the morning after the New Year's coup of 1984. But the impact

---

[24] This is the case despite a succession of military regimes in postcolonial Nigeria. Independent Niger came to be ruled by a military junta only in 1974, after fourteen years of civilian rule. In West Africa, such designations as "civilian" and "military" can be misleading. Niger under the civilian Hamani Diori and his one-party government experienced less freedom (because of its continuance of heavy-handed rule) than Nigeria under Major Generals Yakubu Gowon, Murtala Mohammad, and Ibrahim Babangida, to cite but three. In Nigeria, even the military has always accepted the inevitability and desirability of democratic government. (Some observers may cite the tenure of Major General Muhammadu Buhari in 1984–85 as an exception to this rule, but Buhari's overthrow by more liberal-minded officers only reconfirms it.) The vigorous Nigerian press has also been a guarantor of a continuing postcolonial civilian and democratic ethos in the country. In Niger, in contrast, Diori's Parti Progressiste Nigérien (PPN) can hardly be said to have fostered democracy either inside or outside of the party. Diori's successor, Lieutenant Colonel Seyni Kountché, was cautiously proceeding toward a centrally directed, no-party participatory democracy before his death. Multiparty elections in Niger were not held until February 1993.

of the military culture on the Hausa of Niger is not to be taken lightly. Repeated references to the uniformed border patrols and the punishment meted out to local customs violators are ample reminders. These figures are associated, moreover, with a long history of military power and coercion in the country.

> In the old days slaves, even the descendants of slaves, used to be looked down on. But then the French recruited them as soldiers. They would return wearing stripes and holding guns. Who would then dare insult them as slaves?
>
> —Alassane, Niger-born resident of Yardaji

> In the old days, if you saw a black man with a European, you knew he was a soldier. Wicked! If the European told him to shoot his own father, the soldier would do it. For sure he would!
>
> —Mimage, griot of Yekuwa

Unlike the British, the French conscripted Hausa villagers into their armies. The advent of independence to Nigeria and Niger has not altered this difference. It is one of the reasons given in Yekuwa for hiding the births of sons from census takers, for these census rolls are later used to determine the number of military-age youths in any given community.[25]

Also indicative of the extant military culture in Yekuwa is the way the town of Magaria, the district capital, is often referred to: bariki. It is invoked as a threat: wrongdoers are literally threatened with being taken to the "barracks" (i.e., the *gendarmarie, commissariat de police,* or *sous-préfecture* of Magaria). It is not, like Daura for the Hausa of Yardaji, a place of fun, gaiety, pomp, or profit; Magaria is a place best avoided.

Niger exercises considerable control over the populace by the use of national identity cards, modeled on France's own national identity card. The French penchant for control and centralization has been carried as far as the hinterlands of Niger. Nigeria's looser regulation of population and administration is all the more striking in comparison. In Yardaji terms, there is relative lack of *daraja* and *tsoro* (rank and standing, apprehension and discipline).

The recognition of a military culture in the national society encompassing Yekuwa, but not Yardaji, is also evident in attitudes toward authority, law and order, and corruption.

---

[25] Not all are inducted—in fact, only a handful are. But even the low odds of conscription are sufficient to create concern.

Faransa is not like here [Nigeria]. If a thief is caught [in Niger], he is severely punished. Here, there is only *surutu*—talk, talk, talk.
—Audu, migrant farmhand from Niger in Yardaji

In Niger, if someone commits a theft, they will make him suffer.
—Murtala, teacher in Yardaji's primary school

In the Hausa countryside, the penetration of Western cultural influence is nowhere more unexpected than in the use of *wewe* (marijuana) by a few youngsters.[26] Again, what one finds in Yardaji one does not necessarily find in Yekuwa. One reason is the threat of punishment: it is said that in Faranshi, one will be imprisoned for marijuana possession, no matter how large a bribe is offered. In Yardaji, users may be somewhat circumspect, but they are still relatively insouciant about their use of the drug.

Hausa villagers from Niger are struck by the lack of respect accorded to authority in Nigeria. People would never insult Kountché in Niger, claimed one; yet many Nigerians openly insult their head of state.

A Yekuwa man made an interesting comparison between the recognized agents of authority in the two countries:

In Nigeria, the *d'an sanda* [policeman] is not taken all that seriously. People may insult, strike, or even kill him. If a Nigerian policeman comes across a crime, they only need to pay him off, and the wrongdoer will not be taken to the police station. . . . Also, authority is divided in Nigeria: there is the police, there is the army, there is customs, there is immigration. . . .

But in Faranshi, a soldier is a soldier. There is no question of bribing, if a serious crime has been committed.[27] A rich man is treated the same as a poor person. . . . Just compare what goes on in the cities of Nigeria with the peace that we have here—there, there is constant fighting and killing.

Since it is not altogether fair to compare the cities of Nigeria with the rural areas of Niger, I asked whether the countryside of Nigeria (inference: Yardaji) also deserved such a negative characterization. The response was a mitigated affirmative: "They're on the way."

In the interest of balance, a Yardaji description of the *mulkin zahi* of Faranshi should be recorded here: "Niger is a bad, evil place. The common folk [talakawa] are mistreated. Their possessions are confiscated. They pay taxes but get nothing back for their taxes. There is no freedom."

[26] Traditional Hausa folk medicine does include local plants that may induce a hallucinatory experience, but wewe is not part of the indigenous medicine cabinet.
[27] The qualification presumably covers minor infractions, such as customs violations.

Relevant to any discussion of Hausa attitudes toward authority in Yardaji and Yekuwa is the evolution of Hausa political vocabulary in Nigeria and Niger. In both countries, the terms formally used to designate traditional chieftaincy and rule have been extended to encompass nontraditional rulers. In 1983 it was thus striking to hear villagers in Yardaji use the term "sarauta" (traditional title, position, office) to refer to the elected governor, while in Yekuwa *sarakai* (chiefs, emirs) was used to mean "soldiers."

One of the characteristics of centralized governance—indeed, one of the reasons invoked to justify it—is the ease of mass mobilization. Even at the village level, an order from the government can cause an entire community to gather together with little other prodding and with all due speed. Among the things that clearly distinguish our two villages are the mandatory village-wide meetings convoked by government directive in Yekuwa and the relative dispersion and communitarian political disunity in Yardaji. Field notes record the kind of village meeting in Yekuwa which had no equivalent in Yardaji. It took place on July 6, 1983.

> Kaiga, Limam Juma'a, Galadima, and Alhaji Ya'u were all called to Magaria. [These are the notables of Yekuwa. The chief was in Mecca at the time.] Sarkin Magaria was there, and so was Mai Kamfani [the chief's emissary to the district]. Assembled were chiefs of all the villages in the arrondissement—all 242 villages, each with its four representatives. They were told that an order from Zinder had come, that in every village the people were to be called together. The people were to be informed of the following matters:
>
> 1. If a stranger is seen, be it in town or field, he should be brought to the village chief. Because there are spies in the country.
>
> 2. There is an impending war between Faranshi [the speaker is interrupted and admonished to say "Nijer" instead] and Libya, Chad, and Russia. The people should pray to Allah that no war occur. But the country might need to recruit men into the army.
>
> There is no use of fleeing, even to Nigeria. Those who flee will be sent back to Niger. Everyone should know that his home is here, that this matter affects his home.[28]
>
> 3. There shall be a village farm. Young and old, even mallams, shall work on it to plant millet, sorghum, groundnuts, and beans. Money [raised from the sale of the these crops] will be used to fix the ward in the village dispensary.

[28] Relations with Libya, on Niger's northern border, have been periodically tense. Niger is considered a prime candidate for Libya's crescent empire, and has suspected Kaddafi of fomenting trouble, particularly among the Tuareg of Niger (see *Africa Confidential* 28:4). At the time of the village meeting, infiltration of Libyan troops into Chad (on Niger's eastern border) was intensifying.

4. Women are fighting too much among themselves, especially co-wives. Any woman who fights shall be taken, tied up, and brought to Magaria for judgment.

The instruction had nothing to say about fighting among men.

Colonial Continuity

> Now with the black rulers, there is deceit [*rikici*] again. We are the engines. We farm, we produce—and it's for them, the rulers. . . . Things are as bad now as before.
>
> —Yekuwa villager

Independence has undoubtedly brought change to Niger in general and Yekuwa in particular. Yet, from the point of view of the villagers on both sides of the border, it is not so obvious that it has been a qualitative change. Certainly in comparison with the evolution of Yardaji, that of Yekuwa reflects more than it contradicts colonial patterns of authority, governance, and military culture. In Hausa terms, it still deserves the attribute of mulkin zahi.

The Hausa language is rich in place-name epithets, both positive and negative. The epithet for Niger is said to date back to early colonial days, but it is still considered apropos today:

> It's full of trouble, this evil country:
>   Faranshi is like mouse broth.
> There is fat, and there is stench.
> The chisel never gets used
> To the carpenter's hand, and
> Will slash his hand.[29]

Another local saying assesses Yekuwa country more succinctly: "Faranshi is no good: there is difficulty/suffering/trouble, and no money."

Power and Authority in Rural Hausaland

For the talakawa (commoners) of rural Hausaland, government and politics have long been a matter of submission to the authority wielding the

---

[29] That is, in Niger even your friend will turn you in if you don't handle him right.

greatest *iko* (power). Only since the colonial era, however, has iko been exercised in such contrasting ways. Before the nineteenth century, the Hausa rulers of Daura controlled Yardaji and Yekuwa in what M. G. Smith characterizes as a "limited monarchy" (1978:83). The Fulani conquerors modified the Hausa governmental structure to suit their own ends (particularly concerning titled offices) but did not do away with it. It appears that the transfer of vassalage from Hausa to Fulani rulers did not change life in the countryside in any substantial way. Consequently, the rural Hausa in Fulani Daura did not evolve in a way that distinguished them from the rural Hausa in Zango territory.

With partition, however, the rural Hausa came to be split and ruled by two sets of overlords with sharply contrasting philosophies and policies. The talakawa had little inkling of the overall designs of colonial architects such as Lugard, and certainly no knowledge of such grand schemes as indirect rule and direct rule. They did, however, experience the results of French and British colonial rule, as they affected their local communities, in vividly recalled contrast. Regardless of the overall intention of European colonialism in West Africa, regardless of the constraints that mitigated official policy in the field, the people of Yardaji and Yekuwa are unambiguous in differentiating rule by France from that by Britain. We have seen why the former is dubbed a mulkin zahi and the latter is not.

With independence, European whites were replaced by black African rulers. Yet the ethnic identity of the new leaders did not, at least in the eyes of the talakawa, automatically negate the practices and orientations that for three generations distinguished rulership in Niger and Nigeria as zahi and sauƙi, respectively. (In this regard, it is significant that post-independence black rulers and elites are sometimes referred to in Niger's Hausaland as *baƙin anasara*—black white men.) Of course, the intention of the postcolonial leaders may have been precisely the opposite; that is, to decolonize in both polity and spirit. Yet the perception on the ground is that continuity outweighs disjuncture. For our purposes, the perception on the ground counts more than the intention at the top.

6

According to the Archives . . .

The saying is well known in Daura, "Bature yaro ne. Komi ka gaya masa, sai ya karba." [The European is a boy. Whatever you tell him, he'll swallow it.]

—Kaduna National Archives, 1916

I have argued that the French imposed a harsher, stricter, and less tolerable kind of regime (mulkin zahi) than the British, who are perceived as having been looser, freer, and more easygoing (mulkin sauƙi). Now that we have seen this issue from the indigenous perspective, it will be instructive to examine it from the colonial angle. Once again, I shall examine not the official and general policies of France and Britain in their African colonizations, or even the directives of their top-level administrators, but rather the day-to-day actions and perspectives of French and British field administrators in neighboring colonial districts of the same indigenous region. Although the colonial archives dealing with Daura and Magaria emanate from a completely different orientation from that of the colonized Hausa, they corroborate the indigenous oral legacies. They also provide the models on which local postcolonial African rulers have inevitably relied in their efforts at local administration.

Up until now, I have not questioned whether the asserted differences in colonial rule have been temporally biased and obscure more fundamental chronological distinctions. I have not distinguished the various periods of colonial rule, as more classic treatments of this subject do. This omission has been deliberate, for the villagers themselves do not make the temporal (and hairsplitting?) distinctions that historians do: they retain as comparative terms of reference the broad differences between French and British rule. The records written and received by French colonial administrators in Magaria and by their British counterparts in Daura do enable us to examine the differential administration of the Daura Hausa from a chronological and colonialist perspective.

Early Records, Early Stamps

From the outset the French commandants in Magaria ruled with unmitigated severity.[1] Punishments, especially imprisonment, were openly meted out for seemingly minor infractions, such as failure to follow administrative procedures, lying, and the unspecified "slightest mistake."[2]

Sometimes the methods used by the Magaria commandant raised questions even among higher-ups in the colonial administration. In response to an apparent challenge by his superior, the Magaria commandant wrote with unabashed authoritarianism: "My captain, the punishments I inflict are just and impartial. The problem is that the natives of the Territory are like those of Gabon—lying loafers. They resist with the force of inertia, and to this we must respond with severity, for only fear of the white man and of the fez makes them work hard" (Magaria Archives, September 21, 1916).[3]

We sense a personal commitment verging on the fanatical that is quite alien to the approach taken by any British officer in Daura: "As for the European and native staff who are under my orders, I look upon them as I must, and you can be certain that there is but one person who commands the subdivision of Magaria—it is I, for I know only the path of duty" (ibid., November 16, 1916).

Rather than impose their own personal authority, the British seem to have been more concerned with administrative restructuring to facilitate

---

[1] Although the records of the Magaria Archives list *chefs de subdivision* for Magaria (even at the low rank of sergeant) going back to 1908, the earliest reports extant there date back to 1914. Note in this context the 1912 archival entry for the British side of the Daura borderland:

> It is to be regretted that there are no French Officers nearer the boundary than Zinder. One official certainly visited Magaria, a post close to the border, during the latter half of this year but his stay did not last more than a day or two and the neighbourhood has the reputation of being lawless and devoid of authority. (NAK/North Division, Kano Province, Annual Report, 1912)

[2] "I have warned my subjects that the first one who goes directly to the circle [of Zinder] to make a complaint without going through the subdivision [of Magaria] will be punished upon his return by 15 days in prison. . . . I sentenced Kouchika to 15 days in prison for having lied to the captain commanding the circle in saying that the interpreter and scribe did not wish to receive him" (Magaria Archives, September 14, 1916).

[3] The initial warning apparently had no effect, for the next year another reprimand was sent to the Magaria commandant:

> I have been surprised to note extreme harshness in the exercise of your command. . . . While demanding firm discipline, you must strive to make it more bearable by natives whose mentality and customs are different from ours. . . . You have let yourself go because you lack experience in colonial matters and in certain abuses of authority and power. (Zinder Archives, no. 23, 1917)

governance by the traditional rulers whom they now endorsed. A 1912 entry conveys a spirit quite different from that of the Magaria commandant:

> One of the features which makes the Daura Native Administration . . . so much pleasanter to deal with . . . is the comparative absence of suspicion as to the motives of Government. In Daura the Emir and his Staff appear to believe . . . that the Government intends to deal straightforwardly with them, and so they themselves according to their lights, try to deal honestly and straightforwardly with Government. (NAK/North Division, Kano Province report, 1912)

Of course, the initial years of British rule in Daura were marked by the expulsion of the Fulani ruling house and the restoration of the exiled Hausa dynasty from Zango. These actions plus the abolition of the chiefdom in Baure (a rival Daura Hausa dynasty) provide M. G. Smith (1978:313) with grounds to assert that the British and French were equally callous in respect to indigenous government, and, by implication, administered the Daura region through a similar, undifferentiated European indifference toward indigenous Hausa government:

> These European political experiments were . . . profoundly unsettling . . . to the people involved. . . . [I]n 1906–7 the French and the British showed equal disrespect for the established dynasties of this area and removed or replaced them . . . at will. Simultaneously the new European rulers appeared completely indifferent to the rules of descent that regulated the traditional structures of official allocation. . . . Although the French and British did not intend to discredit traditional forms and principles of political structure, their actions in these chiefdoms had most disturbing effects. In Daura and adjacent chiefdoms, the European innovations of 1906–7 were widely understood to mean that traditional dynasties had no indissoluble or unconditional rights to rule and that traditional political units had no necessary or inviolable rights of existence. At this period, although the two European powers had shown that they wished to administer the local people through the chiefdoms familiar to them, they had also shown . . . that they regarded native chiefdoms as means rather than ends of political organization. . . . In effect, the French and British seemed to look upon chiefs and chiefdoms as subordinate administrative institutions whose future depended directly on their instrumental values for colonial government.

At the level and for the time period that Smith here addresses, he may be indeed correct; to agree that this initial phase colored subsequent colonial realities, and perceptions of those realities, is another matter. In the period that shortly followed the European partition of Daura Hausaland, the local archives reflect an ongoing preoccupation by the British with chiefly legitimacy (at least at the highest levels) in contrast to a determination by the French to assert their own authority directly.

This is not to say that the British believed in the equality of the Hausa under their ultimate sovereignty; in fact, those in charge of Daura displayed a classic variety of English paternalism:

> The visit [of the prince of Wales with the emir of Daura] generally seems to have been of the greatest interest and gratification to them. They have now actually seen in the flesh the Heir to the Throne and what was to them perhaps an intangible idea has now become a visible reality.
>
> Visits of this nature, I am confident, are of the greatest value and use in knitting together the Empire by showing to its more primitive peoples that there is a living and visible head to whom they [owe] obedience and allegiance. (NAK/KATPROF 3151, Daura Division report, July 7, 1925)

Of course, the line between paternalism and ethnocentric disdain was not always so clear:

> I hold the view that the time has passed when the Native Administration in this Province can be satisfied to carry out their responsibilities for dealing with counterfeiting, smuggling, motor traffic, produce adulteration and all the other offences brought about by modern conditions, with an inefficient and undisciplined corps that in multi-coloured dirty garments have not even the excuse of being picturesque. (NAK/29648, Annual Report, 1937)[4]

Corruption

The inevitable drawback to indirect rule, from the British point of view, was that a certain margin of indiscipline, if not corruption, followed from the administrative autonomy that traditional rulers (especially at the local level) were allowed. This is perhaps the most notorious colonial legacy in governmental practice that has carried over into independent Nigeria, and unfortunately it has continued to permeate much of the postcolonial bureaucracy. Early examples from Daura emirate may be gleaned from the archives:

---

[4] The writer is referring here to the *dogarai,* or *'yan doka,* palace guards and emirate constables, who were then exclusively responsible for maintaining law and order in the emirates. Only later on was a government police force established.

The Emir is always ready to deal severely with offences of this kind [impo-sition of exorbitant fees, unpunished theft, fines for trivial matters], but he complains that the people are afraid to come to him and that no one tells him what goes on in the Districts as they are afraid of the District Heads.

I have asked the Emir gradually to remove from the Districts all the depen-dents of District Heads who are not noted to assist the District Heads and to keep them in Daura town. If he finds that they still exercise influence in the Districts he can put them over the French border with the warning that they will be dealt with as rogues and vagabonds if they return. (NAK/KATPROF 3149, Report on Daura Emirate, November 1916)

Nearly a decade later, the indiscipline of district heads' dependents is attributed to the district heads themselves:

[S]ome of the District Heads are satisfied to remain in their District Head-quarters and such knowledge as they have of local current events is mostly second hand. The natural and logical consequence of this is that there is a lack of discipline and knowledge amongst certain of the Village Heads and an inclination to dispute or rather to carry out with hesitation the orders of the District Head. (Ibid., 3151, Daura Division Report, July 30, 1925)

The Magaria Archives do not provide parallel cases, of course, for the commandant was more inclined to bypass the Sarkin Magaria and deal with village chiefs directly. (There was no position of hakimi, or district head, within the French Hausa adminstrative structure.) Exercising greater direct control over the forces of law and order, indigenous agents of au-thority had much less leeway for abuse. Instances of such abuse over the border practically scandalized at least one Magaria commandant: "I have learned of a serious development about the police. Authorities bring to the station all individuals who strike them as foreigners. The gift is king and fines rain upon those who, not being in order, did not know enough to pay off the policeman" (Magaria Archives, May 1951).

Greater central control over both administration and its funding in French Hausaland has carried over into Niger Republic. Though it would be illusory to claim that governmental corruption does not exist in Niger today (Amuwo 1986 provides an insightful treatment of Nigérien corrup-tion), it does not come close to what occurs on the Nigerian side of the border. The difference cannot be attributed solely to the disparity in wealth (and therefore potential for self-enrichment) between the two countries. Rather, Nigeria's colonial administrative framework has provided an ethos and sheer opportunities that make *cin hanci*, *ha'inci* and *rikici* (bribery and corruption) more corrosive influences among the Hausa there than among those of Niger.

Heretofore, the most critical examination of political corruption among the Hausa has been M. G. Smith's (1964) study. Tracing the evolution of political norms and conduct from Habe to Fulani and then British regimes in Zaria, Smith documents the erosion of Islamic standards of conduct by Usman ɗan Fodio's successors, the relapse into prejihadic methods of oppression, and specific instances of political corruption in the early 1950s. Smith claims that as representative government, partisan politics, and independence are extended, abuse by officials diminishes. He concludes that "oppression and corruption tended to increase among Hausa with political centralisation and the increase of governmental tasks" (194). Given the perspective taken here, three observations should be made.

First, not all the Hausa became subject to Fulani rule (Smith's own classic studies of Abuja and Daura prove the importance of this distinction) and therefore the significance of the jihad for Hausa political morality must be tempered. Zango Daura never succumbed to Fulani sovereignty, and Daura itself reverted to Habe rule half a century before Smith's study of the phenomenon. However accurate the interpretation of the Zaria situation, caution must be exercised before it is applied throughout Hausaland.

Second, Smith shows how and why the British system of indirect rule created an administrative environment in which political corruption by Hausa rulers could flourish. But the administration of French Hausaland did not permit an equivalent degree of Hausa political corruption to take root. In other words, the kind of colonial system under which the Hausa were ruled serves as a crucial variable in the analysis of political corruption among the Hausa. It should therefore also be an important factor in an assessment of the differential experience with political corruption for Nigérien and Nigerian Hausa today.

Third is a point made by J. J. van Klaveren (1964:195) in his comment on Smith's piece: "The truth is that corruption is latent in any government . . . governments that are decentralized and oligarachic clearly tend to show a higher degree of corruption than those that are hierarchically centralized." Van Klaveren also notes that in Nigeria "corruption has increased since Independence. . . . Honest government depends above all on . . . civic consciousness and social ethics . . . not 'technical Western values'" (197–98). There is nothing uniform or inevitable about the degeneration of Hausa political morality, any more than there has been a uniform Hausa political experience. The experiences of the Hausa under French and British rule, as the Magaria and Daura records make clear, were as different in this domain as in any other.[5]

Administering vs. Administered Chieftaincies

The relationship between colonial administrator and Hausa chief depended largely on colonial policies toward the chieftaincy. In Daura the chief was regarded as an advisee; in Magaria he was a subordinate. From the outset there was no ambiguity as to who should be administering, judging, and ruling in Magaria: the commandant, not the chief. Instructions from on high make the situation clear: "I bring to your attention the necessity of resolving yourself the disputes that may arise between Fulani and Hausa, and not to submit them to the canton chiefs for adjudication" (Zinder Archives, October 10, 1904).[6]

In stark contrast, throughout neighboring Daura the chiefs were charged with doing their utmost to administer and monitor activities within their jurisdictions.

> The District Headmen in Daura are on the whole an intelligent body of men, and should develop into useful members of the administration. They have, I feel, done their best . . . to support the efforts that have been made to improve the general administration of the Emirate. (NAK/KATPROF 559, Daura Division Annual Report, 1926)

Even relatively delicate diplomatic matters could be entrusted to the traditional ruler in British territory: "[T]he Emir of Daura is largely instrumental in maintaining tranquillity and sympathy between the administrations [French and British] by his tact, good sense and long experience" (ibid., 14/1925, Daura Division Annual Report, 1924).

Such a position and status a Magaria chief would never attain. Political

---

[5] A local colonial perspective on the linkage between corruption and colonial policy is provided by this observation of those who habitually benefited from direct rule in a land of indirect rule:

> The French and Lebanese in Kano complain about the British authorities who totally withdraw from what is happening around them, leaving a large share of authority and administration in the hands of indigenous civil servants, whose venality is well known and is only worsening. In Kano and in the bush thefts are only on the upswing and very often go unpunished. (Magaria Archives, July 1952)

[6] The entry is handwritten and may be dated 1909 rather than 1904.

acumen dictated that a chief on the Niger side of the border demonstrate almost puerile fealty to France, and express gratitude for the grandeur of the French colonial mission:

> We asked in the Kaaba (where all prayers are granted) that God look over France and the French Union. We prayed that all the wishes of Great France be realized. We ended by praying that all Niger be blessed, especially the subdivision of Magaria where we hope to see abundance, happiness, health, and prosperity flourish for all. . . . I conclude by thanking for all time our mother France, thanks to whom we have been able to perform the pilgrimage to Mecca. (Magaria Archives, Laouan Moussa, canton chief of Mallawa, to commandant of Magaria, September 11, 1952)

If only to justify their own philosophy that native administration was upright and pragmatic, the British in Daura generally regarded the chiefs favorably. They were pleased to report that

> a definite atmosphere of well-being and contentment can be observed in all districts. . . . [S]teady progress has been maintained in the work of cooperation between the peasantry and the native authorities in managing local affairs. The Emirs of Katsina and Daura have continued to give evidence of their genuine interest in all things that concern the welfare of the people. (NAK/ 27811, Katsina Province Annual Report, 1936)

Chieftaincy appointments throughout Daura in the 1930s were looked upon through an unmistakably Lugardian prism:

> The death of several of the older District Heads during the year has provided an opportunity to introduce men of modern education and wider outlook into the machinery of local government, without in any way deviating from traditional practice in regard to the selection of the office holders. (NAK/ 29648, Annual Report, 1937)

Yet even as late as the 1950s, when the French were trying to turn back to the chiefs (Fuglestad 1983:159–60), the sarakuna of Magaria were still being denigrated:

> A definite strengthening in their authority and confidence can be detected. The chiefs have been confronted with their responsibilities, and the warnings they have received have made them understand that the command post will not catch wind of their laziness or shirking of duties without reacting. (Magaria Archives, Rapport Annuel, 1950)

The African chiefs were "without change. Much has to be demanded to get little out of them, and one has to refresh their memory continously for they have a remarkable facility to think about nothing" (ibid., Revue Trimestrielle, 1951).

The "ideal" posture of the Nigérien chief toward the French administration may be gleaned from this passage:

> The chiefs of the canton of Magaria are disciplined and respectful of superior authority. . . . Malka Harou, chief of the Magaria canton, a few years ago was surprised by the abrupt innovations in the political order, and has had difficulty finding the right path to follow. . . . He now understands what is expected of him. (Ibid., Vue d'Ensemble de la Subdivision de Magaria, 1952)

Whereas the French were now satisfied that the chief of Magaria "understood what was expected of him," across the border

> the 40th Anniversary of the reign of the Emir of Daura . . . was the major social event of the year. A very full programme was held, which was attended by distinguished visitors from Government, the neighbouring Emirates and from adjoining Niger Colony. (NAK/KATPROF 4183, Annual Report, Katsina Province, 1952)

Surveillance

One of the most striking differences between British district officers responsible for Daura and the French commandants in Magaria relates to internal surveillance: the French were constantly spying and reporting on their own people, whereas the British displayed a comparatively insouciant attitude toward internal security. Again, even if the degree of disparity in this respect has lessened somewhat since independence, the overall contrast still holds.

French local espionage in Magaria began early. Already in 1916 the Magaria commandant could boast: "I have some very diligent intelligence agents circulating from one end of the subdivision to the other. Their mission is the following: Watch closely all suspicious natives and prevent the export of millet."

Various categories of persons were under long-term surveillance, including chiefs, marabouts (Islamic priests), veterans, European and Lebanese residents (especially during Magaria's groundnut heyday), and eventually the *évolués* (European-educated Africans). A typical notation for 1937 notes budgetary allocations for *crédits politiques,* listing the names of persons to whom gifts had been given for information. (These people included migratory Fulani who had provided "interesting information" about what was happening in Nigeria.) Foreigners were especially suspect, no matter what the ostensible reason for their presence. An American pastor and his family were under surveillance in 1953. In the same year the presence of five ethnologists in Magaria's district elicited this assessment:

> The incomplete intelligence that I have obtained concerning some of these "ethnologists" and the excessive curiosity that all of them demonstrate about subjects quite alien to their discipline oblige me to take a wary attitude toward them. . . . May I ask you to keep a discrete but vigilant eye on the activities of these foreigners and to keep me apprised of anything that strikes you as suspicious about their behavior.[7]

Distrustful of all potential competitors for power and always less than magnanimous toward the indigenous chiefs, the French kept systematic tabs on their *chefs de canton.* A typical intelligence report in the Magaria Archives lists all the canton chiefs in Magaria with details concerning their age, income, religion, religious influence, political influence, authority, and "attachment to our cause." Rarely are the assessments very flattering: "Aboubakar Kode, chief of the Fulani community of Magaria, is loyal, considering his race" (undated). Ibra Yallo "is quite brilliant, a young man with panache, but vain, touchy, an operator. This chief must be watched closely and there is no question of trusting him completely" (Rapport Annuel, 1955). The chief of Ouacha "has the look of a musketeer and the soul of a skirt-chaser. All the same, loyal and devoted" (Rapport d'Ensemble, 1951). Even men who had already demonstrated the greatest loyalty to France— the African war veterans—could come in for disdainful criticism: "They are a bit too ready to listen to people who promise them the moon—fairly lazy, big spenders, most of them in debt" (Deuxième Rapport Trimestriel, 1954).[8]

---

[7] Issues of global importance and decolonization were not beyond the ken of even the local administrator. In a handwritten text the Magaria commandant reacted thus to a translation of Melville Herskovits's "Self-Government for the Natives": "The Americans, faithful in the last century to the Monroe Doctrine, took no interest in the partition of Africa. . . . They are [now] aiming for nothing less than to establishing themselves economically in Africa."

[8] A 1945 entry for Katsina Province, by contrast, notes that "vacancies in the police are being kept open for the most deserving [demobilized soldiers]. . . . A few men have been able to secure positions such as motor drivers, artisans, caretakers, etc. So far the conduct of demobilised soldiers has been good and no disturbances of any kind have occurred" (NAK/SNP 17/40123).

The greatest irony in official colonial policy concerned the surveillance of the "civilized" (évolué) class of Africans. The French strategy of assimilation was intended to create, through education and exposure to French language and culture, a Westernized elite class of colonial subjects, loyal to France and worthy to be clasped to the bosom of Mother Marianne.[9] In fact, however, the treatment of the évolués by the French colonials charged with executing this policy was marked more by distrust, disdain, and resentment than by liberty, equality, or fraternity: "Doctor Arou Kouka is incompetent, very badly thought of, stupid, pretentious, and the most spiteful of all. . . . Mahama Tchili is an outright scoundrel. Louché Djibo and Moussa Biga are two imbeciles" (Magaria Archives, August 1951).

The pettiness of the surveillance that the French conducted in Magaria is seen in a notation on one of the Chamchoums, a Lebanese family that had groundnut and other commercial interests in the Magaria of the 1950s: "Mr. Chaffie Chamchoum has really little influence. He's a decent sort who sponges off his brother, seemingly incapable of having any personal ideas in business matters—all the more reason that his influence in other respects is zero" (ibid., Vue d'Ensemble de la Subdivision de Magaria, 1952).[10]

The archives encompassing Daura under the British, in contrast, reveal virtually no scrutiny of specific individuals, no groups targeted for surveillance. Reports list the "African personnel" (clerks of first, second, and third class) who served in the province, but that is the extent of it. Only during World War II was there any concerted or coordinated attempt at espionage, and that was directed mostly toward what the British usually referred to as "French Territory."

"Civilized" Africans in Magaria

A fascinating and detailed analysis of the place of the "civilized" African in French colonial eyes is provided by an entry in the General Assessment of the Subdivision of Magaria for 1952. It appears under the heading "State of Mind of the Populations—Africans (a) Civil servants and civilized."

Before one attempts to study the state of mind of this category of the population, it would be fitting to define what one means by "civilized."

This is a difficult task, for depending on whether one uses this term in its

9 The official shift in policy from assimilation to association in the political arena does not invalidate this observation.

10 The archives even record a falling out between a Chamchoum and his mother-in-law!

larger or narrower sense, it will encompass many or few Africans. If one means by civilized every person who has attended school for awhile, can read and write, dresses like a European, then all the civil servants and employees of commercial firms are civilized.

In a narrower sense, one might call civilized only those who have truly assimilated the French European culture. In that case, in Magaria there would only be Mr. Chimère, the head of customs, whom we could call civilized.

It is thus fitting to use this term in its larger sense; all the civil servants and commercial employees certainly regard themselves as civilized.

This category of African has been much criticized, and they have been reproached for their arrogance, conceit, insolence, contrariness, and way of imitating the outward behavior of Europeans.

One can certainly reproach these people; but before criticizing, should we not examine our own conscience? For after all, it is certainly we, the French of Europe, who have made them what they are. Moreover, their habit of imitating us, far from being a reason to mock them, should rather be a source of satisfaction to us.

The civil servants and business employees of Magaria are similar to all the civilized natives of Africa.

They are very proud of their knowledge, many of them think it is quite wide; but the most intelligent ones realize that they still have much to learn.

They consider that their mode of life is highly superior to that of the other Africans, but some of them are beginning to realize that their home, their personal life hardly correspond with their outward behavior, and with what they really need. . . . They need women who can be true companions to them. . . .

They have left behind (or at least think they have left behind) the traditional African lifestyle. . . . Quite often transplanted outside of their country of origin, geographically as well as intellectually "detribalized," their pride generally prevents them from accepting a social order that they consider to have become outmoded.[11]

Perhaps this passage was inspired by a cynical analysis of what the commandant's predecessor referred to as the "semicivilized":

All influences are registered by our "semicivilized" elements, who all see themselves as big chiefs handling the money the day they are the masters of the country. They are pipe dreamers [*pêcheurs de lune*] whom we must neverthe-

---

[11] Contrast the detailed and extensive focus on the évolués by the French (which continues to the end of the colonial era) with the much blander (and relatively infrequent) distinction made by the British: "While the peasantry may be only vaguely conscious of the worldwide conflict in progress, *the educated members of the community* . . . are by no means oblivious of what is taking place, nor do they lack interest or insight" (NAK/SNP 34327, Katsina Province, Annual Report, 1941; emphasis added).

less watch and from time to time bring back to reality with some rather strong words. (Magaria Archives, Deuxième Rapport Trimestriel, 1950) [12]

Colonial Attitudes

Historical treatments of Africa customarily divide the colonial era into separate periods, emphasizing those tendencies most characteristic of the time frame under discussion. Thus, for example, Adu Boahen (1987:63–91) separates African colonial history in toto into (1) the 1890s to the end of World War I (characterized by differential resistance to colonialism according to education, elite status, and urban-rural locale), (2) the period 1919–1935 (when educated city dwellers and young rural workers and peasants replaced traditional rulers in wearing the anticolonial mantle) and (3) from 1935 to the 1960s (the overthrow of the colonial system and the "regaining" of political sovereignty and independence).

Closer to the case at hand, Finn Fuglestad (1980) dubs the period 1908–1922 in Niger "the decisive years," when the French first attempted to impose "direct rule." From 1922 through 1945 is the "great silence" or "classic period of colonial rule," during which an "indigenous chieftaincy-model" for French administrators flourished. The "new order" (1945–1960) prefaced decolonization, with the period from 1952 on characterized by "a new type of administrator, more interested in development planning and other such technical matters . . . more and more impersonal and bureaucratic" (192). Fuglestad adopts this approach to highlight "the changing nature of colonial rule" (18).

Even if the form and content of colonial reports for Magaria may be read to reflect these various periods, it is less evident that the colonial mentality of the administrator undergoes parallel changes. The early stamp of the all-knowing and all-powerful commandant, alternately suspicious and condescending, remains throughout, even into the 1950s. Likewise, British reports covering Daura maintain a consistent stance of personal detachment from local intrigue and a more businesslike approach to activities

---

[12] The colonial attitudes expressed in the Daura and Magaria archives are at variance with the generally accepted proposition that racism made British colonials intolerant and contemptuous of modern-educated African, whereas the French, because of their philosophy of assimilation, were more disposed to accept French-educated subjects as on a par with themselves. See Crowder 1968:397–98: "For the British the educated African was a gaudy, despised imitator of European ways. For them the 'real' African was the peasant or the traditional chief who, unlike the educated African, did not challenge their supremacy. . . . The French, however, were less closed in their aristocracy than the British."

under British jurisdiction. French and British colonialists alike certainly evinced prejudicial attitudes toward the Hausa under their jurisdiction. These prejudices were of different orders, but they changed relatively little throughout the colonial period. Even in the 1950s the Frenchman in charge of Magaria wrote:

> Carefree, liars like almost all blacks, the Hausa of Magaria . . . are obstinate and only with difficulty change the habits they have adopted. . . . We should not let this apparent apathy make us forget our role as guides and protectors of all these people. . . .
> The African masses, then, are becoming civilized laboriously. . . . We run up against the apathy of the masses, against an inertial force that is a fact of the Orient. The theme of our palavers in the bush has changed little over the past twenty years: "Be thrifty, look after yourselves, take care of your children, don't divorce so frequently, don't become drifters, keep your villages clean . . . buy soap and clothes before buying cognac or going to see girls, etc. etc." (Magaria Archives, Rapport Annuel, 1953)

The tone here differs considerably from that across the border, where a few years earlier it was noted that

> Daura Emirate, despite its position of comparative isolation on the Anglo French frontier, is now awake to the changing times and to the need for community development if the people are to remain happy and contented. But the greatest significance has been the progressive emergence of the spirit of self-help and desire for social advancement which will ensure that, whatever may have been the handicaps of their past history, the people can and will hold their place in the modern world. (NAK/KATPROF 45600, Annual Report, 1948)

Even after two generations had passed since the structures and spirit of Lord Lugard were introduced into Northern Nigeria, and at a time when "social development" was a major concern in colonial administration, the British were still acknowledging the importance of indigenous culture and tradition for the Hausa under them. One cannot conceive of a Magarian equivalent of the Katsina Historical Association, whose purpose was to

> stimulate interest in the history of Katsina and Daura Emirates. Amongst its activities the Association . . . records the tales of old men whose experience would otherwise have been lost for all time. Where so much is changing on all sides it is essential that educated and responsible citizens should not be ignorant of their own history so that a sense of the past should be present amongst those who will determine the future. (Ibid., 4410, Annual Report, 1956)

Just a few years earlier the French commandant expressed his disdain for the Hausa in a passage headed "Development of Material and Social Life":

> Very slow. The native receives money from his sales, goes to the shop to buy a few meters of white fabric, which he gives to the tailor, and a few minutes later throws over his dirty robe a stiff new one. He then buys a flask of pungent perfume and sometimes a dyed wrap for his wife. A piece of sugar cane, a leg of lamb or some goat chops, and he sets off satisfied. (Magaria Archives, Rapport Annuel, 1950)

Differential Development

Another contrast between the neighboring territories of colonial Daura and Magaria relates to the priorities of the two administrations. To be sure, a preindependence movement toward social and economic development is reflected in both sets of archives. Once again, however, a clear distinction emerges. Daura was approximately two decades ahead of Magaria in the establishment of a developmental infrastructure and ethos.

Only after 1946, according to Fuglestad, did the French turn an eye toward an economic renaissance of Niger; and only after 1954 did they allocate significant sums to investment (1980:170). That, of course, was a scant half dozen years before independence. M. G. Smith (1978:342) demarcates 1923–1933 as the initial period of significant activity for what may be regarded as developmental purposes (e.g., agriculture, sanitation, health, forestry). The Magaria and Daura archives bear him out. In the mid- to late 1950s Magaria undertook the kind of work that had already been done in Daura in the 1930s and 1940s.

After the initial amalgamation of the new Daura Emirate in the 1910s, the British soon turned to administrative and economic tasks, which in fact constitute the bulk of their reported activities. They made law and order only part of their agenda—unlike the French, who seemed most preoccupied with this aspect of colonial consolidation. Perhaps the most graphic way to highlight these differences in priorities is to compare the outlines of reports submitted by the British and French.

Daura Emirate was separated from Kano Province in 1934, and joined with Katsina Emirate to form Katsina Province. The Katsina Province Annual Report for 1934 was presented thus:

I. Provincial summary
II. Provincial affairs

        Administrative units
        Area and population
        European personnel
        African personnel
        Visits
III. Native administration and departmental affairs
        Judicial
        Revenue
        Expenditures
        Trade and economy
        Police
        Prisons
        Medical and sanitation
        Education
        Public works
        Well sinking/rural water supplies
        Agriculture
        Empire Cotton Growing Corporation
        Forestry
        Veterinary
        Missions
IV. General summary

In successive reports, other sections were added to part III of this model: mining, child welfare, road accidents, slavery, labor conditions, cruelty to animals, smuggling, counterfeit coins, water supply, posts and telegraph, housing and social welfare.

In Magaria at this time, the corresponding entries consisted mainly of political reporting of the type discussed above under the heading "Surveillance." Only by the 1950s do economic/developmental affairs assume any importance. Even then, however, as one may see from the following outline of the 1953 annual report, such affairs did not take on the same relative importance as they already did for the British in the 1930s:

    I. Political section
        A. State of mind of the populations
            1. Europeans
            2. Africans
                a. Civilized
                b. Chiefs and notables

        c. Natives (*Masse indigène*)
        3. Lebanese
    B. Political life
        1. Political activity
        2. Associations
        3. Press
    C. Social life
    D. Veterans
    E. Religious life
    F. Justice
    G. Foreign intelligence
    H. Arms and munitions
  II. Economic section
    A. Agriculture
    B. Livestock
    C. Waterworks and forestry
    D. Customs
    E. Communications and transport
    F. Commerce
    G. Public works
    H. Rural engineering
     I. Companies
 III. District tours

Some projects in Daura were never paralleled in colonial Magaria, such as the establishment of maternity and child welfare clinics, reading rooms, drainage schemes, and mosque and cemetery maintenance (NAK/KAT-PROF 47603, Annual Report, 1949). An "Information Service with its cinema van and tape recording machine, which record[ed] and broadcast speeches by the Emir and other influential people to the villages throughout the Province," would also have been quite alien across the border, as would an Adult Education Literacy Agency, which published news sheets, books, and booklets in Hausa (NAK/KATPROF 4309, 1954).

Democratization and Politics

Democratic representation, being a new and sudden element in a society that has hitherto been predominantly feudal in character, requires careful and patient fostering, but the fact that the needs of the peasant can now be expressed in representative assemblies possessed by powers infinitely wider than those of an Emir and Council will soon be much more easily understood by the people when the benefits of mass education become wider. (Ibid., 47603, Annual Report, 1949)

Deep down, the African masses believe that the white man has some funny schemes and that he perseveres in his oddness. . . . What an idea, to put some little pieces of paper in a box to send a representative—whom they don't even know—to the Chief in France! . . . The chiefs told them to vote "Blue," so they voted "Blue"; some of them, preferring to stay in their fields, sent their children in their place. For them, the blue paper is already forgotten. In their heads there remains nothing but the two words "millet" and "groundnuts." One can only admire their wisdom. (Magaria Archives, Deuxième Rapport Trimestriel, 1951)

After World War II, politics from on high dictated the extension of European democratic processes throughout the colonies.[13] Representative assemblies that had been instituted before the war were expanded in Northern Nigeria. Niger had virtually to begin from scratch to integrate indigenous elements into the governmental process. Although French and British district officers in Hausaland had equal influence in colonial policy making—that is, virtually none—the archival records make it clear that those in Daura willingly accepted and promoted the democratic ethos for "their" Hausa, while those in Magaria begrudgingly and cynically went through the motions of extending it to theirs. While the Hausa commoners of Magaria were being led and controlled by the French, those in Daura under the British were being encouraged to participate in the newly emerging democratic and constitutional systems of government.

Detailed accounts of preindependence politics in Niger and Northern Nigeria are provided elsewhere, and need not be repeated here.[14] Certainly the British did have preferences as to the outcomes of partisan battles, but there is little indication that they interfered as directly and intensely as the French in campaigns and elections. The British were satisfied that they had already created an institutional environment favorable to the Northern Peoples Congress (NPC); the French made sure that first the Union Nigérienne des Indépendants et Sympathisants (UNIS) and then the Parti Progressiste Nigérien (PPN) come out ahead. As a result of final-hour

[13] "From on high" signifies not merely metropolitan impetuses but pressures from colonized nationalist elites.

[14] For the story in Niger, see Charlick 1991 and Fuglestad 1980; for Northern Nigeria, see Dudley 1968, Post 1963, and Whitaker 1970. M. G. Smith 1978:350–55 discusses it for Daura.

colonial-era politics and administration, conservative Hausa elements retained control of Nigeria's Northern Region, and French antipathy for
the (Hausa-dominated) Mouvement Socialiste Africain (expanded into the
Parti du Regroupement Africain and also known as Sawaba, or Freedom
Party) ensured that "Niger [would fall] victim to the 'sub-imperialism'
of the Zerma/Songhay and the nascent political awakening of the Hausa
[would be] cut short" (Fuglestad 1980:187).

In the years from 1945 to 1952 the French saw their democratic partisan
nemesis in the Rassemblement Démocratique Africain (RDA). It was a
peculiar sense of democratization that prompted the commandant to suggest in 1947: "It is certain that if we know how to exploit the situation,
the PPN branch in Magaria will constitute an excellent intelligence agency
to report on the activity of this party [the RDA]." The rationale for such
partial democracy was explicit:

> Allying ever since its formation with the French Communist Party, which
> advocated the departure of the French from Africa, the activity of the RDA
> has become practically illegal because its goal has been the elimination of
> [French] national sovereignty. . . . By gathering in the malcontents, the em-
> bittered, and especially the riffraff who know no other way to live except as
> parasites, the RDA has discredited itself. . . . This party is short of money, and
> money is everything in Hausaland. (Ibid., Vue de l'Ensemble de la Subdivision
> de Magaria, 1952)

This approach easily translated into personal surveillance of évolués to fer-
ret out their political beliefs and activities.[15] Later, as the twilight of French
sovereignty in Niger loomed, the archives record several complaints lodged
by Issa Diop, a Sawaba organizer, including alleged instructions of the
chief of Magaria to kill Sawaba activists. (They were stoned instead.) The
action taken by the commandant in this case was rather lukewarm (ibid.,
handwritten correspondence, December 1959). Such attitudes and pressures may account for the rather low support for Sawaba in Yekuwa, where
the party received only 10 percent of the vote in the 1958 elections for the
Territorial Assembly.

As for Daura, there is no denying the heavy-handed tactics employed
by the NPC and emirate chiefs at this time to deny power to the North-

---

15 Example: "Politics still always interests them. Ousman Galadima, an employee of the
Agency, seems to have a baneful influence on the civil servants, who fear him terribly. He
is wicked, they say. Little, puny, often sick but with the tongue of a viper. . . . I would
have no objections to being deprived of his services" (Magaria Archives, Troisième Rapport
Trimestriel, 1950).

ern Elements Progressive Union (NEPU). Yet this was primarily an intra-Hausa matter, with conservative elements uniting to oppose the radical and populist ideology of the (also Hausa-led) NEPU. There is no comparable archival evidence to suggest that the British were as actively engaged in undermining the NEPU in Daura as the French were in sabotaging the RDA and Sawaba in Magaria. Later events were to prove that the British were misguided or naive in their colonial political faith, but they sincerely believed in democracy for Nigeria, for the North, for "their" portion of Hausaland. The French were less sanguine about the possibility that democracy could succeed in "their" *pays haoussa*. For at the same time that the British were routinely taking steps to ensure that "all districts [would be] toured by Administrative Officers and senior Native Officials and the purpose of the elections explained in all villages," the French commandant across the border was certain that "democracy, as we understand it, must have been an invention of Machiavelli" (NAK/KATPROF 4309, 1954; Magaria Archives, September 15–October 15, 1954).

Military Culture

If democracy had little opportunity to take root in Niger, the military culture did have much greater occasion to do so. Yet in French Hausaland, resistance to the military experience and its ethos has traditionally been the norm. This situation has certainly disadvantaged the Hausa of Niger, for in both colonial and postcolonial Niger military (and hence political) power has been concentrated in the hands of the Zarma. The result has been political subordination of the Nigérien Hausa, despite their numerical superiority in the country.

In Nigeria the Hausa have been in the political ascendancy because of their success in both democratic and military cultures. The two civilian heads of state, Tafawa Balewa and Shehu Shagari, have been Hausa or Hausa-Fulani; their integration within the military has provided several Hausa-speaking national leaders as well (e.g., Murtala Mohammad, Muhammadu Buhari [from Daura], Ibrahim Babangida).

Omens of the strength of the military factor in Hausa politics can be seen in the archives. Since the British accepted only voluntary enlistments in their colonial army, the role of the military was a nonissue in British-Hausa relations and was virtually absent from colonial reporting in Daura. Friction over military recruitment was, however, a hallmark of the French-Hausa relationship, going back as far as the recruitment drives of World War I.

The "basically egalitarian nature of the rural society of Nigerien Hausa-land" (Fuglestad 1980:72) rendered the Hausa less than amenable to military service; yet the discipline and obedience that French colonialism demanded made it imperative. The Hausa of Magaria and elsewhere, whose opposition to the French generally took the form of "passive resistance . . . were in a state of virtual rebellion" over this issue in 1918, and it occasioned periodic migratory flights to Nigeria (101). The records of Magaria show that military recruitment remained a touchy issue throughout the colonial era, and not (as one might infer from Fuglestad) only up until the 1920s. Three and four decades later, this issue was still not resolved.

In one of the rare entries in which the opinion of an indigenous chief is taken seriously, the chief of Kantché is quoted as stating, "Conscription is a scourge for the country and before the young people get used to it the country will be emptied of a portion of its youth to the benefit of Nigeria." A commandant himself was to comment on the "repugnance of the Hausa for the military profession. . . . All the conscripts fled their village, many of them to Nigeria." And only two years before the French were to grant independence and leave the colony, the familiar refrain was echoed: "The Hausa remain in general obstinately opposed to the draft and it will certainly take many more years before military service becomes part of their ethos" (Magaria Archives, Bulletin Mensuel, November 1950; Vue de l'Ensemble de la Subdivision de Magaria, 1952; Rapport Annuel, 1958). Inasmuch as the French had already tried for forty years or so to make military service "part of their ethos," one wonders how many more they thought were needed.

Religion

"In French West Africa Islam was seen as a problem in a way that it was never in British West Africa" (Crowder 1968:359). To a remarkable extent, this broad proposition, encompassing vast tracts of territories and numerous populations and cultures, is confirmed and even highlighted by our microanalysis of a single partitioned locality.

It is not that the British were oblivious of or indifferent to the possible threat of a West African Islamic uprising. Indeed, in 1906 the British were an early target of such a revolt at the town of Satiru, near Sokoto. Provincial headquarters reports on Islamic movements in Nigeria throughout the colonial era at the Kaduna National Archives make fascinating reading. Yet we may also accept Michael Crowder's observation that "once Lugard had secured the co-operation of the Emirs in Northern Nigeria, and the Sultan of Sokoto had shown loyalty after the 1906 Satiru rising, Islam was seen as the ally rather than the potential enemy" (ibid.)

The French were much more mistrustful of Islam, and they never did fully accommodate themselves to the Muslim presence in Magaria. Paradoxically, the Magaria Archives also indicate disdain for the version of Islam practiced there: on the one hand they do not take "Hausa Islam" seriously; on the other hand they are afraid of it. This ambivalence contrasts quite strongly with the policy and practice just across the border, where the British throughout Daura aimed to uphold, modernize, and use Islam in furtherance of their aims.

As early as 1915, Magaria commandants were reporting regularly on the marabouts (Islamic priests) in the district. Detailed lists included their names, ages, sects, villages, numbers of students, schools, texts used, and educational backgrounds. To read the reports, Magaria subdivision was a hotbed of Mahdist ferment and had to be closely guarded.[16] The village of Foudel was paid particular attention in these reports on Islamic schools.

In the 1920s, concern was overtly expressed about the potential danger of Islamic fundmentalist contamination from Nigeria, where the Mahdists were believed to be gaining strength. A report in the 1930s indicates the attitude of the French concerning Islamic education and the control exercised over Islamic priests: "The marabouts of the region are the targets of continuous but discrete surveillance. . . . Their comings and goings are controlled. . . . They do not move about without obediently informing the chief of the subdivision of their motives and itinerary." (Magaria Archives, Rapport sur les écoles coraniques, May 12, 1933). Another report on Koranic schools from this period refers to "a discrete but keen and costly surveillance" (ibid., circulaire 170, May 7, 1930). In the 1940s Governor Jean Toby was intensely interested in Islamic affairs, and the Magaria Archives contain copies of his many reports on this matter. This concern carried over into the 1950s, as proceedings from "Conference on Muslim Propaganda for Circle Commandants" attest: "Islam is in contradiction to modern development. There is therefore concern to neutralize its advancement in areas where it has not yet penetrated too deeply. . . . Christianity offers us an opportunity to give the natives a taste of living with us" (ibid.).

The Magaria commandant well understood the position of his superiors, and reflected it in his assessment: "The Muslim religion, as it is understood by the Hausa, is a hindrance to all social progress and to the improvement

---

[16] In the Islamic tradition, the Mahdi is an activist prophet who will unite the faithful in a rebellion agaist the infidels and foreign occupiers.

of the masses' standard of living" (ibid., Troisième Rapport Trimestriel, 1950). As late as 1957, French evaluation of Islam as practiced in Magaria was as pejorative and dismissive as always: "A very rudimentary knowledge of dogma that is practically limited to the most current ritual—a sort of syncretism that leaves little to Islam except its most superficial traits" (ibid., Rapport Annuel, 1957).

We look in vain for indications of comparable surveillance of Islamic schools and teachers in Daura, for a hint of anti-Islamic policy or administrative sentiment.

Education and Language

It is well known that the French practiced linguistic chauvinism, whereas the British tolerated (indeed, encouraged) instruction in indigenous languages.[17] These practices reflected the colonizers' respective educational policies, the French adopting a more elitist, numerically stringent, and generally assimilationist approach, whereas the British generally favored indigenization of the school system and practical training. In line with this thinking, as part of their colonial preparation British officers were themselves trained in indigenous languages, here Hausa. Information concerning Daura, usually written by chiefs schooled in the roman alphabet, dot the Kaduna Archives; for Magaria, the occasional Hausa (or *haoussa*) word in a commandant's report is as far as the indigenous language penetrates colonial officialdom. Such differences are intimations of enduring differential legacies of the role of both turanci (European) and Hausa languages on both sides of the border.

The educational philosophies imposed on the Hausa of Magaria and Daura are documented quite early. A December 1908 report records the establishment of a Daura branch of the School for Roman Characters (established to facilitate literacy in the "easier" European, as opposed to Arabic, script). Such efforts, later extended by the Adult Education Literacy Agency, culminated in the publishing of books and newspapers in the Hausa language.[18] The French never promoted a corresponding *vulgarisation* for the Hausa language in colonial Niger; in Magaria education and literacy were conceived in strictly francophone terms. Likewise, official

---

17 For an illustration of this contrast in Yorubaland, see Asiwaju 1976b: chap. 10.

18 *Gaskiya Ta Fi Kwabo* (Truth is worth more than a penny) is the oldest and most successful of the Hausa newspapers.

business could be conducted in Hausa on the British but not the French side of the border.[19] Early on the British adopted a pragmatic, generalist approach to education, unlike the more elitist French pedagogy. Thus Daura School was founded "to enable ex-scholars to return to their homes better fitted to carry on ordinary vocations of village life than those who had not been to school. Instruction in crafts and farming was introduced to teach the rudiments of these and to prevent boys despising manual labour or their father's occupations." And whereas a French Nigérien education *was* generally a ticket to future government service, the British explicitly wanted to correct the "general impression that a certain period spent at the school was 'ipso facto' a definite guarantee of employment under the Native Administration" (NAK/KANOPROF 14/1925, Daura Division Annual Report, 1924).[20]

A very significant contrast between the two educational policies concerns the relationship between government and religious schooling. British policy favored an integration of the two; French policy ill tolerated the Koranic schools. This factor added to the already important Hausa migration across the boundary, and sometimes dictated school establishment policy.[21] As a result, pedagogic philosophy clashed with administrative reality, and Magaria commandants occasionally opposed French educational policy on paper:

> The Koranic schools are still powerfully attractive, especially since Nigeria offers many sophisticated teachers. The way for us to attract more and especially higher-quality students would be to adopt our neighbors' solution: mixed [secular and religious] schooling. (Magaria Archives, Report from chief of Magaria subdivision to administrator-commandant of Zinder Circle, July 27, 1938)

> On the purely social level the role of the schools naturally appears very important. Certainly there has been improvement from the time when students

[19] "[T]he proceedings of the Native Courts of Daura . . . are now recorded in Hausa (in Roman script) which is the language of the Courts and the people" (NAK/KATPROF 29648, Annual Report, 1937).

[20] Such an observation contrasts neatly with the later problem concerning government employment: "The major problem which now faces the N.A. [Native Authority] . . . is that of recruiting N.A. Staff of the required ability and qualifications. Now those [students] who have passed out well prefer to take the immediately lucrative posts offered by the commercial firms" (ibid., 4183, Annual Report, Katsina Province, 1952). The private-sector option never did become a viable alternative for school graduates in Niger.

[21] The Magaria commandant recommended the establishment of a school in the border town of Sassoumbouroum, for example, "so that the children will not have to go to school in Zango-Daura in British territory" (Magaria Archives, Rapport Annuel, 1954).

parroted "our ancestors the Gauls," but it seems that little has been done but transpose what exists in France (the examinations are the same), whereas what was needed was a total rethinking about this country, whose civilization, social structure, and economic development are so different from those of continental France. (Ibid., Vue de l'Ensemble de la Subdivision de Magaria, 1952)

Such suggestions from the field were not implemented and the low standard of education in the district remained a sore point in subsequent reporting.[22] Perhaps more counterproductive was the friction that resulted as the French continued to impose an unpopular education program on an ever-resistant population—friction not unlike that engendered by military conscription.[23]

French education in Hausaland was perceived differently in Daura and throughout Northern Nigeria, where it appears to have been admired (probably for its rigorous academic standards). A handwritten report in the Daura local government office from Bashar Wambar Daura ("Educational Tour to French Territory," 1955) expresses this sentiment: "With regard to Education it is wonderful to us to see small children learning French right from the beginning, no other language's taught in the schools except French. This give the children good chance of learning very high standard of French."

Further insight into the contrast in colonial Hausaland schooling is provided by a report by C. Bell, the provincial education officer of Katsina, headed "Official Visit to Schools in Maradi Area, Niger Colony, French West Africa," and dated March 28, 1951:

2. The objects of the visit were (1) to . . . make contact with . . . colleagues, African and French, and (2) to provide . . . a view of the stimulating contrast between French and British methods of African education, based as they are on different political philosophies.

3. The first stop was made at Madarounfa. . . . The teacher, Monsieur Maida, who had been trained at Dakar, was a local Moslem, but was dressed in European clothes. We were much impressed by his cleanness, smartness and pleasant manner. We conversed with the teacher in Hausa and the children sang three songs for us in French before we left.

4. All the teaching is given in French and the pupils' writing reached a high

---

[22] "Magaria is quite backward in education. . . . Progress is slow and school attendance poor" (ibid., Rapport d'Ensemble, 1951); "There is much to do before the Hausa understand the benefits of education" (ibid., Rapport Annuel, 1954).

[23] "The young Hausa do not have the basic skills for learning. . . . There are many truants. . . . The parents have been summoned as well and all have received a warning" (ibid., Bulletin Mensuel, April 1952).

standard. The best of the children, after completing six years at Madarounfa, continue their education at the college in Niamey on the River Niger, and not at Maradi as one might expect. . . .

10. Education has recently been made compulsory and regular attendance by the children chosen for the school is enforced if necessary by Police action. (NAK/KATPROF 2387)

Perhaps in no other domain was colonial socialization so important as in the education and instruction of the young. This is a crucial colonial legacy of which the archives provide but a tantalizing hint. When the British and French did pack up and physically leave Hausaland, they left behind an ineffaceable and intangible presence that encapsulated fifty years' worth of starkly contrasting educational efforts. They may not have succeeded as they had hoped in inculcating their respective values and priorities; they did succeed, however, in shaping divergent mentalities among two sets of educated elites. These are the elites, it must be remembered, who took over when the colonials departed. While it is difficult to separate the layer of Western education from other factors in the makeup of otherwise similar young Muslim Hausa men or to measure its depth, there is no doubt that that layer does constitute part of these men's beings. This is perhaps the greatest source of the mental division of Hausaland.

Lessons from the Archives

Beyond the substantive differences in the colonial administration of Daura and Magaria, the archives reflect differences in form, tone, and style. Two different spirits emerge from the records of the administrators: the disengaged, tolerant, and paternalistic attitude of the British versus the judgmental, hypercritical, and frustrated sentiments of the French. We see dichotomies in security versus development, militarism versus civility, pragmatism versus moralism, delegation versus centralism, democratization versus authoritarianism, populism versus elitism. While such findings are not entirely new at the macro level, the graphic detail in which they are expressed at the micro level, and particularly in neighboring communities of similar ethnicity, religion, indigenous culture, and precolonial history, does add to the nascent colonial-era ethnography of Africa. It sets the stage for a current and general (if simplified and exaggerated) contrast between Nigérien and Nigerian Hausaland: enlightened despotism versus mitigated anarchism.

I had not expected to find any records from the postcolonial era available for inspection. A scholarly coup of sorts was made possible, however, by the inclusion of several years of postcolonial administrative reporting in the Magaria Archives. While a certain degree of balance is lost in that no independence-era reports for Daura can be offered, the general theme of colonial continuity after independence may be archivally documented for at least this one side of the border.

The first administrative report for Magaria immediately after independence is fascinating for its familiarity. That is, despite the fact that for the first time an African is in charge of the subdivision, neither the form, the spirit, nor the substance of governmental reporting changes significantly. From the text alone it would be difficult to guess that the author is Djibrilla Maiga and not Laurent Ravix. The accession to independence is acknowledged by the almost cursory notation under the listing of principal events of the report period: "The appointment of the first AFRICAN DISTRICT COMMANDANT FOR EASTERN NIGER."

In Magaria's postindependence reports some of the terminology changes, but little else: évolués are now referred to as *fonctionnaires,* and the term "masse africaine" is replaced by *populations rurales.* Yet these groups, plus all the others on whom the French reported (chiefs, marabouts, European cadres) are still discussed in terms of their loyalty, acquiescence in government, and political tendencies.

Traditional chiefs in particular retain a negative image in these reports. They are alternately characterized as anachronistic, superfluous, repressive, and incompatible with the aims of the independent Nigérien government:

> Remain obedient to the constituted authority but seem disoriented, because they enjoy neither our nor their population's confidence. Their role seems to have reached its final phase. . . .
>
> The traditional chieftaincy now evokes a theatrical decorum which should mark the continuing dismantling of an institution whose inefficiency is known by all. . . .
>
> There exists at present no possibility of making the traditional chieftaincy evolve in the direction of the masses. This institution shows such signs of senility that its maintenance poses serious problems. . . . The canton chiefs are feudal. . . .
>
> By loyalty and devotion to the French the majority have made themselves detestable to the population, by executing orders that they well knew to be unpopular. . . . The arbitrary and illegal conditions in which its members have been maintained for sixty years render this institution increasingly unpopular and undesirable. (Magaria Archives, Rapport Annuel, 1960)

Muslim priests and movements remain a concern for the administrators of independent Niger—one wonders whether out of habit or conviction. For the "progressive" new commandants, suspicion of a popular brand of Islam is joined with suspicion of Nigeria: "Please warn the Muslim circles against an enterprise which can quickly turn into a swindle, and is led by zealots of a sect foreign to our brotherhoods, and which until now has no root except in English-speaking countries" (ibid., November 28, 1960). The "*Mahdistes de Foudel*" also (still) merit an entry!

The difficulty of promoting, indeed creating, a sense of national consciousness comes through in the early independence records.[24] The problem is as rampant among the civil servants—accused of "a frightening lack of civic spirit"—as among the commoners: "The civil servants must get to the point where they understand that their duties are not confined to the accomplishing of daily routine tasks, but in the promotion of the masses who have not been educated" (ibid., Rapport Annuel, 1962). The "masses" are characterized as unenlightened, if obedient, sheep: "The submission of the peasant masses to the administrative and traditional authorities remains very great. . . . The majority of the population follows the party out of submission and not out of conviction" (ibid., Rapport Annuel, 1963).

The "new administration," moreover, has a heavy load to bear: "Its mission is to education, to direct, to lead, and to control these populations" (Rapport Annuel, 1964). One result is a certain long-standing migratory pattern: in 1964, the last year for which the Magaria reports were available for consultation, eight heads of family are recorded as leaving for Nigeria to avoid military conscription.

A Zinder police report conveys the spirit of the less than dramatic transition from colonial to independence-era politics: "Niger is the only country of the African states where it is permitted to criticize the work of the government. We shall put a stop to this very rapidly" (Zinder Archives, Commissariat de Police, October 1961).

[24] This sense of difficulty certainly helps confirm Fuglestad's conclusion that "no genuine nationalism, let alone any nationalist movement, existed in Niger before 1960 at the earliest. . . . [T]he very notion of political independence made [hardly] any sense to . . . the people of Niger" (1983:10).

7

Chieftaincy in Yardaji and Yekuwa

Magana ba iko maganar banza.

Talk without authority is useless.

—Hausa proverb

There is perhaps no better gauge of the difference between French and British colonialism in Africa than the policies of the two powers toward the chiefs. Granted that the ultimate wielders of power in each colony were the Europeans, the traditional chiefs still retained some measure of autonomy, and that measure varied considerably. At least in rural Hausaland, these variations persist today.

The British in Nigeria and the French in Niger consciously took opposing stances vis-à-vis the Hausa chiefs under them. If the Hausa chiefs in Nigeria were co-opted in the interests of British imperialism, we may say with Michael Crowder (1968:188) that those in Niger were "debased." The British ruled through their Hausa emirs; the French ruled over theirs.

But what about the "little chiefs"? Studies that examine the question of colonial chieftaincy policies have focused on high-ranking traditional rulers—the kings, emirs, and sultans. The village chief, the true linchpin with the majoritarian peasants, is usually excluded from intercolonial comparisons. In Hausa terminology, we know what colonial rule did to the sarki but not what it did to the mai gari.

Is there a substantial difference today between a Hausa village chief in independent Niger and a Hausa village chief in independent Nigeria? Are Hausa villagers sensitive to these differences? If we may judge by the Yardaji-Yekuwa data, the answer to both questions is an unequivocal yes. Villagers on both sides of the border concur that French rule was harsher in all respects, including the treatment of their traditional rulers. Moreover, they contend, there remain significant differences in the status, influence, and power of their respective chiefs, with those in Nigeria surpassing their counterparts in Niger. The difference is certainly visible in the villages themselves: both within his community and in his relationship with the external (i.e., national) society, the mai gari of Yardaji emanates more prestige, dignity, and authority (*girma, daraja, iko*) than his counterparts in Yekuwa. In short, the colonial relationship established between the rulers and the chiefs in the colonial era has continued, however unconsciously, after independence.

This is not to say that all variations in the role and status of the Yardaji and Yekuwa village chiefs may be attributed directly to the colonial legacy. Other factors, particularly economic ones, also contribute to the differences. Yet these other factors serve only to perpetuate and reinforce a pattern that was first established during colonial rule.

Nor do I argue that there have been no changes whatsoever in the government-chieftaincy dialectic from colonial days until now. Postcolonial policies have supposedly tried to counteract the British and French treatments of the chiefs: independent Nigeria has attempted to harness the chieftaincy, whereas independent Niger claims to "revitalize" it. A closer look at the chiefs in Yardaji and Yekuwa, however, shows that it is the colonial legacy that predominates. Even if the elites of the two nations are unaware of the link between the eras, the talakawa, the common folk, are quite conscious of the continuity. The general pattern of the (relative) autonomy of the Hausa chiefs in Nigeria versus the (relative) subordination of the Hausa chiefs in Niger remains unshaken.

Perhaps these continuing patterns are stronger in the bush, at the level of the mai gari, than in more urban areas, at the level of the sarki. After all, it is easier for the central government to influence nonstate actors and penetrate their institutions where its apparatus is more firmly entrenched. Even so, we should understand what has been happening in the countryside, where the vast majority of the Hausa live. Only in this way can we begin to assess the real degree of decolonization throughout Hausaland, or conversely, to evaluate the true extent of the liberation of the Hausa people.

The Mai Gari

In rural Hausa society the head of a village is known as mai gari. "Mai gari" literally means "owner of the town," although in actuality he (and it always is a "he" in Hausaland) has no proprietary hold over either the people or the land of the village (beyond his own personal plots of land). Although "mai gari" is usually rendered "chief" in English (and *chef* in French), it must be borne in mind that there are several levels of royalty in Hausa politics, and that the indiscriminate use of the word "chief" for such disparate positions as sarki and mai gari tends to gloss over crucial indigenous distinctions in status, authority, and power. The social distance between mai gari and sarki is enormous—arguably greater than that between mai gari and talakawa.

Because there is no governing chieftaincy or traditional rulership in the West, the very word "chief" (especially in an African context) often conjures up visions of grandiosity, reverence, and quasi-divinity. At the level of sarki such images may not too greatly exaggerate the esteem of commoners for their traditional rulers, but in respect to the mai gari such imagery idealizes reality: a village chief is a *village* chief. He is human, and no one—especially "his" villagers, who know him better than anyone— thinks otherwise.

In both Nigérien and Nigerian Hausaland, the mai gari is universally expected to perform certain established functions. The more generally acknowledged ones are dispute resolution and adjudication, tax collection, and accommodation of guests (Faulkingham 1970:181).[1] In addition to these functionalist activities the village chief performs some rather normative ones. Mai gari is perceived as the personification of the community, its symbolic head. In this capacity he acts as father, marriage counselor, and group therapist, as well as mayor and judge. All news relevant to the community, be it the passage of a stranger or the estrangement of a couple, normally passes directly to the chief, the heart, head, and hub of the Hausa micropolity.[2] The chief is the living symbol of the village, and his status, prominence, and respect may be regarded as a fair reflection of the spirit, or personality, of the village as a whole. The way the chief as an individual projects his character over his village is of less interest here, however, than

---

[1] Villagers in Yekuwa would add the following activities and duties to their chief's job description: He acts as a conduit for orders from Magaria and sends requests to Magaria as well (for example, requests for trees); he supervises work on the village farm and village-cleaning campaigns; he is brought any adulterer or thief and sends the transgressor to Magaria for judgment; he is informed of any perceived threat to the community (such as a plant disease); in times of drought, he arranges for the priests to pray for rain; to resident strangers he lends a field and even a house; he provides food for temporary visitors.

[2] Thus he attends or is represented at weddings, naming ceremonies, funerals, and even divorce proceedings.

the institutionalized differences that arise when chiefs perform these roles in divergent national contexts.

Mai Gari Yardaji

Sarkin Fulani Harou was turbaned chief of Yardaji in 1949, according to the records of a local history project. One of the first "sons of Yardaji" to have attended *makaranta boku* (Western-style school)—the primary school in Daura—he was also one of the first representatives to the Daura local government body under the old Native Authority system. As dagaci or *mai gunduma* of Yardaji Village Area, Mai Gari Yardaji oversees, in addition to the village of Yardaji itself, the outlying communities of Kanda, Rogogo, Diche, Kututuri, Bulungudu, and Rigage. In his own words, his job is "to look after the peace and welfare of the community". He acknowledges that he is there to arbitrate, to resolve disputes, to keep peace in the village. At one time he was also charged with collecting taxes, both *jangali* (cattle tax) and *haraji* (poll tax). The cattle tax, however, was abolished in 1975 and the poll tax in 1979. In his capacity as village area chief, Mai Gari receives a monthly salary of over 200 naira from the state government.[3]

Masu Gari Yekuwa

In Chapter 2 we saw why Yekuwa has two chiefs (masu gari). Both administratively and historically, Yekuwa is not one village but two: Kofai and Hamada. Each village therefore has its own mai gari. The villages have become physically joined to each other over the years, but in the minds of the villagers the two remain distinctly separated. Yekuwa is not one village whose chiefly power has been divided (and therefore diminished) between two masu gari; rather, it functions as two discrete villages, and each chief occupies in his gari the same role as the other does in his.

The current mai gari of Yekuwa-Kofai is Alhaji Adamu Danjuma. In 1983, when I first came to Yekuwa, Adamu had been chief for only three years, succeeding the late Sarkin Gabas Nalalu. (Sarkin Gabas is a princely honorific title meaning "King of the East.") Nalalu had been chief of Kofai for forty years before his death, and his loss still seemed to be a blow to the chiefly family, if not to the village as a whole. Although there is no

---

[3] When the military government reintroduced taxation, he also assumed the position of the village's chief revenue collector. Presumably he is entitled to a commission on the taxes he collects.

such thing as a village area in Niger ("gunduma" in Nigerian Hausa), Mai Gari Yekuwa-Kofai informally oversees the three outlying settlements of Kolfao Bugaje (which includes bush Fulani as well as Tuareg slave descendants), Madata (a Hausa village), and Diché Tsamiya (another small Hausa village.) When absent from the village (as during his pilgrimage to Mecca, when I first arrived in Yekuwa), Mai Gari Adamu is replaced in his chiefly post by his brother, Alhaji Aminu.

In Yekuwa-Hamada, Mai Gari Sule is chief. Sule's longer tenure as chief and his winning disposition lend him an aura of the consummate village chief. Like his counterpart in Kofai, Mai Gari Sule of Hamada is responsible for resolving disputes and collecting taxes. Since the cattle tax was abolished in Niger when the military took power in 1974, only the poll tax remains to be collected. In 1983 this tax stood at 1 naira and 40 kobo (or 350 CFA) for every adult man and woman—about $1. Very old people, lepers, the blind, and the mentally ill are exempt from haraji. Despite their responsibilities, however, neither village chief in Yekuwa receives a fixed salary directly from the Nigérien government.[4]

Mai Gari Sule and Mai Gari Adamu are on good terms; competition between the two Yekuwas has not led to conflict between their leaders. In any event, the contrast between Mai Gari Kofai and Mai Gari Hamada is of less interest to us than the contrast between Mai Gari Yardaji and Masu Gari Yekuwa.

Symbols of Status: Residence, Visibility, Mobility

The residence of Mai Gari Yardaji occupies a conspicuous spot in the center of the village. It is a stately structure, marked by an enclosed inner chamber in which private or highly significant business is conducted. Through this chamber lie passageways to the quarters of the chief's wives and children, including the family of one of his married sons, Ibrahim. A large inner courtyard takes up a good deal of space. The entire compound is surrounded by a wall, and it is unlikely that any but a few villagers have ever penetrated beyond the threshold of the discussion chamber, or have had a glimpse of the inner compound. Two of the most important village

---

[4] They do, however, receive a commission on the taxes they collect: 7.50 on every 1000 CFA. The CFA (for Communauté Financière Africaine [formerly Colonies Françaises d'Afrique] is the currency used in most states of former French West Africa and is pegged to the French franc.

Chief Alhaji Harou, Sarkin Fulani of Yardaji.

wells—one hand-pumped and the other crankcased—lie in the square in front of the chief's compound.[5]

The chiefly abodes in Yekuwa are much more modest. The chiefs' compounds are similar in layout to the pattern found throughout Kofai and Hamada: a straw fence delimits the space within which the chief has his hut. Space is much more limited than in Mai Gari Yardaji's compound, but the house is more accessible. The hut of the Mai Gari Yekuwa-Kofai is relatively modern by local standards—the outer walls are sheathed in cement and it has an aluminum "pan" roof.[6] It is quite small, however, no larger than 10 by 15 feet. In sum, both spatially and architecturally, the chief's residence in Yardaji connotes prestige considerably above that of either chief in Yekuwa. It also contributes to greater girma and daraja among the villagers—greater respect, but a greater social distance as well.

The way the chiefs perform their jobs is indicative of their objective status in their communities as well as of the perception of their status (as chiefs) among the residents of their communities. In all cases, the most important obligation of the chief is to be present, visible, and accessible to the

[5] By 1986, however, the latter had broken down.
[6] Later Mai Gari Hamada also acquired an aluminum pan roof.

villagers. Mai Gari Yardaji fulfills this duty in a most regal fashion, spending most of the daylight hours sitting in front of his compound in one of the few chairs in all Yardaji. Accompanied by one or more of his principal aides (who are seated on a straw mat to the chief's right), he watches over his village, receives people who come to greet him (*yin gaisuwa*), hears about local events from passers-by, listens to regional, national, and world news on his transistor radio, and extends counsel or advice to villagers who come to seek it. This is a full-time activity, and not one entirely devoid of headaches: irate villagers who come to the chief for arbitration (*sulhu*) may vociferously and unceremoniously pour out their wrath against their neighbor in front of all present, leaving the chief in the unenviable position of having to reconcile the irreconcilable. Village rumor has it, in fact, that the chief once decided that the trouble was not worth the reward, and almost renounced his position. (Propriety forbade me to ask the chief outright whether this rumor is true or not.)

It is rare for the chief of Yardaji to leave his spot in front of his residence. On Fridays, of course, he walks over to the mosque for prayers, but the mosque is only a few steps from his home. Occasionally he travels to Zango and Daura (if he is summoned by the district head or the emir, for instance), but it is extremely rare for him to walk around Yardaji. This is a sign of his elevated social position: people are expected to come to him, not the other way around. On those few occasions when he does promenade in the village (usually carrying his green-and-yellow parasol to shade him against the sun), villagers withdraw a few steps to create an appropriate distance between themselves and the chief, and bow their heads as a sign of respect. These occasions give rise to wild discomfort, for any interaction with the chief in the villagers' own social territory is uncommon enough to be unsettling.

In the rainy season the chief leaves his chair more freely to inspect his fields. They are tilled mostly by his sons, though he occasionally hires itinerant laborers to work on them as well. (Such laborers often come from villages across the border in Niger.) Once a year a *gayya* is organized on the chiefs' fields: a communal work effort on the part of male villagers, accompanied by festive drumming and a collective meal. The chief supervises or oversees this work, but does not himself engage in any manual labor. In Nigerian Yardaji, the line between chief and commoner remains high and uncrossable.

In Yekuwa, over in Niger, the story is rather different. Though the distinction between talakawa and sarakuna (that is, between commoners and chiefs) is no less clear to the people of Yekuwa than it is to the people of

Chief Alhaji Adamu Danjuma of Yekuwa-Kofai.

Yardaji, it is apparent to all that here the chiefs do not (or cannot) perform their chiefly functions in as impressive or regal a way as the mai gari in the neighboring Nigerian village. The masu gari in Yekuwa are available for consultation and arbitration, but they do not spend the greater part of their day royally waiting for people to approach them. Mai Gari Kofai, for instance, may spend a portion of his time and energy taking care of the shop owned by his brother Alhaji Aminu. Although a chief, he also helps his brother as a trader, and so sells the array of goods common to any Hausa *mai tebur* (petty merchant): oil, kerosene, flashlight bulbs and batteries, soap, tinned fish, candy, perfume, matches, pastes, and a long list of other things, though nowhere near so many as in any mai tebur in Yardaji.

Although no one questions that Alhaji Adamu is the chief of Yekuwa-Kofai, the actual process of executive decision making is unusually collective in Kofai. The chieftaincy is almost more a family affair than a matter of individual incumbency, perhaps because of the relative recency of Adamu's accession: as in any position of government or authority, some period of time is required for a newly appointed chief to grow into his new role. Until he does so, it is natural for him to turn for advice to his brothers and cousins. Given the persisting memory and legacy of the late chief Nalalu—

in whose shoes Adamu must have felt small indeed—this lack of individual initiative and dynamism is understandable.

The exceptional astuteness and ability of Adamu's brother Alhaji Aminu is also relevant here. Aminu not only is "replacement chief" in Adamu's absence but serves as his assistant. A man of extroverted and take-charge personality, he tends to overshadow the chief on occasion. The upshot is a significant diffusion of chiefly authority and responsibility.

In view of these idiosyncratic differences in chiefly stature, stemming principally from differences in length of incumbency and perhaps personality, how can we hope to make any significant comparison on the basis of national affiliation? Fortunately, we also have the example of Mai Gari Hamada to examine, whose tenure as chief is not an issue. Once again we find that the Nigérien mai gari is unable to incarnate the chieftaincy as impressively as his Nigerian counterpart in nearby Yardaji.

Though the Hamadu chief is not so visible as Mai Gari Yardaji, he does regularly "come out" (fito) and hold consultations with his aides and passers-by. He does not possess much in the way of a royal abode, as we have seen, and perhaps for this reason his preferred spot for holding court is not in front of his own compound but outside the nearby neighborhood mosque. More strikingly, especially in contrast with the Nigerian village chief, Mai Gari Yekuwa-Hamada sits on a simple mat. Neither chief of Yekuwa, in fact, ever uses a chair, even when performing official duties.

The seemingly innocuous difference between chair and mat actually has great significance for comparative chiefly status. As far back as Lugard's *Political Memoranda* of 1918, great attention has been paid to such distinctions, under the rubric of "native etiquette." Lugard wrote:

> Official etiquette and ceremonial are matters of great importance to African Chiefs, and are strictly enforced among themselves. . . . The assumption . . . of privileges by petty Chiefs . . . tends to lower the dignity of the rulers whose sole right such privileges used to be. . . .
>
>   Chiefs of the second grade should be given a small carpet or mat, and of lower grades a Native mat. In the Southern Provinces there has been a somewhat indiscriminate use of chairs without distinction of grade. This should not be suddenly altered so as to cause offence, but when possible a reed platform, raised a foot or so off the ground, should be substituted, so as to preserve the privilege of the chair to the Paramount Chief. Whenever a Resident visits a Native Chief, he should take a chair with him. . . . Office holders or *Sarakuna* in the Northern Provices should not be given mats. (Kirk-Greene, ed., 1965:81–82)

Whether Lugard's instructions accurately reflected native etiquette as it was then practiced or created new norms for chiefly protocol is beside the point. What is crucial is that the current-day prerogatives and trappings of Hausa chiefs remain quite significant, especially in the eyes of the talakawa. Such prerogatives and trappings have generally been overlooked, however, on the village level. When Hausa custom in the 1980s demands that the mai gari of a Nigerian village be spatially elevated through use of a chair but that a Nigérien mai gari remain at ground level with his villagers, a significant wedge between the status of Hausa village chiefs is indicated, on the basis of differential and inherited colonial and postcolonial patterns. Nowhere are these differences more apparent than in Hausa villages along the Nigérien-Nigerian border.

Like Mai Gari Kofai, Mai Gari Hamada is frequently to be seen moving about the village and engaging in relatively commonplace activities. In Yekuwa the chief attends naming ceremonies for newborn infants, as any member of the community would do. In Yardaji the chief often sends one of his sons in his place. Once again, though Mai Gari Hamada is indisputably chief, his status in his Nigérien community does not preclude his mixing with the people in a way that Mai Gari Yardaji is not expected to do.

Manual Labor

A more dramatic difference may be seen during the rainy season, when even the chief of Yardaji is likely to be somewhat mobile as he inspects his fields or supervises gayya (communal labor). For in Yekuwa the chiefs not only go out to their fields but themselves engage in agricultural labor. No gayya on the chief's farmland here: the Yekuwa chief physically works his land like any other Hausa villager. No elaboration is needed to convey the impact and lesson this practice has for everyone in Yardaji and Yekuwa alike.

Transportation

Indicative of the status of any chief in Hausaland is his mode of transportation. Nowadays important emirs and sultans own cars or limousines and hire chauffeurs. They keep horses for ceremonial occasions. The way a chief gets around is paid no less attention in the countryside.

On those occasions when Mai Gari Yardaji leaves the village to travel to Zango or Daura, he does so in his own Peugeot pickup truck; one of his

Chief Sule of Yekuwa-Hamada.

sons does the driving. Mai Gari is the only person in Yardaji to own a private vehicle, although several Japanese minibuses in the district do come to
Yardaji to pick up passengers for hire.[7] Mai Gari Yardaji also owns a white
horse, as befits his station. The chief mounts the horse when he visits his
fields during the agricultural season and when he participates in religious
and ceremonial events in Daura. (Someone else rides the horse to Daura
on the eve of the holiday, and one of the chief's sons drives him there the
next day in his Peugeot.) In sum, the chief of Yardaji relies on his car for
serious transportation, but retains his horse for prestige and ceremonial
purposes. In modern Nigeria, moreover, ownership of a vehicle is a sign of
great prestige in its own right, and confers more status than either a horse
or a camel.

In Yekuwa, a horse is not only a matter of prestige—it is the only means
of transportation available (unless one stoops to riding a donkey or walking). Mai Gari Hamada thus has a horse—a white horse—and is often seen
on it as he travels to outlying villages and settlements around Yekuwa. His

[7] By 1985 the chief's vehicular status had been upgraded by the acquisition of a Peugeot
504, nicknamed Saloon. It was given him by a cousin, the managing director of a large textile
and construction firm. Saloon is actually the chief's third automobile; he was given Lada in
1973 and Pickup in 1980.

counterpart in Kofai, however, has no horse at all: in this chief's family, only Alhaji Aminu owns a horse, which he acquired from me when I departed from the village. Once again, the Nigerian Hausa village chief is seen to overshadow his Nigérien counterparts in the trappings of chieftaincy, even in mode of transportation.

Border Crossing

Not only the mechanism of chiefly movement but its direction is of comparative significance. As we have seen, the prestige (girma) of the chief of Yardaji is such that he is relatively immobile: he leaves his village if he is summoned by the hakimi in Zango or the Sarkin Daura, or to participate in religious observances in Daura, but otherwise he rarely leaves Yardaji. Even within Yardaji he seldom strays far beyond his compound, and never lowers himself to attend the village market.[8] Any public commercial transaction is considered unbecoming for Hausa royalty, if not outright vulgar. (Hill 1977: 12 provides historical evidence of this phenomenon.) Since most Nigerians disdain Niger for its poverty and severity of rule, Mai Gari Yardaji has hardly ever set foot in Nigérien territory, though it is barely twenty minutes away by horseback. When his presence is desirable there, he is more likely to send in his place Alhaji Kosso, the mai unguwa (ward head) of Yardaji-Galadima and his chief counselor.[9]

The village chiefs along the border in Niger, in contrast, periodically travel not only out of their villages but into Nigeria. They are particularly in evidence in Yardaji on Wednesdays, when the village holds its weekly market. Mai Gari Kofai and Mai Gari Hamada are both quite familiar with the marketplace of Yardaji, as are most Yekuwa residents, whose own market is rather paltry in comparison. In fact, Yardaji exerts almost as strong an attraction for the Yekuwa chiefs as it does for the villagers of Kofai and Hamada.

Inasmuch as exceptions are often as instructive as general rules, it is worth mentioning the one time during my initial year of fieldwork when the village chief of Yardaji did set foot on Nigérien territory.

On May 19, 1983, occurred the appointment (nad_a, or "turbaning" of the new hardo (chief) of the Fulani camp of Kogai, just across the border in Niger, east of Yardaji. Kogai is a typical "bush camp," a fairly desolate area where seminomadic Fulani set up their tents about the open Sahelian

---

[8] Postcoup revenue-collection duties imposed an exception to this rule.
[9] Now deceased.

plain. Officiating the ceremony were the subprefect of Magaria, who was accompanied by armed gendarmes, and the Fulani district chief, the Sarkin Sassambouroum, who was driven in a new Range Rover.[10]

After the departure of the Nigérien government official and the Fulani chief of Sassambouroum, Mai Gari Yardaji arrived in his pickup truck in the company of his chief counselor, Alhaji Kosso. The mai gari acknowledged the importance of the occasion by wearing a ceremonial pink robe and white turban. He congratulated the new hardo (who ranked below him in chiefly status) and gave him 10 naira. Not only did the hardo receive nothing tangible from either the subprefect or the Fulani chief of Sassambouroum, but custom had obliged the community of Kogai to offer these visiting dignitaries much food, including coveted guinea fowl and *dambu,* a millet-and-milk specialty. The chief of Yardaji then offered the new Fulani hardo some chiefly advice: "Be patient with the people. If you are patient, then Allah will show you the way. If you feel yourself becoming angry with someone, just try to be patient—it is best that way. Let Allah alone know of your anger."

Reflecting on the installation of the hardo of Kogai the following day, Mai Gari Yardaji expressed his opinion that the naɗa had not been conducted properly by the Nigériens responsible for it. He wondered why the hardo had not been presented with a gown (*babban riga*), a turban (*rawani*), and a red cap (*ɗara*). In Nigeria, he assured me, these things would have been presented either by the hakimi or by the dagaci, acting in the hakimi's and sarki's names. Thus, on one of the few occasions when the chief of Nigerian Yardaji did have to travel to Niger, in his capacity as the local area's most influential traditional leader, he came away confirmed in his belief that the status of traditional chiefs in Faranshi continues to be diminished by that country's rulers.

Chiefly Views on the Chieftaincy

Mai Gari Yardaji's reflections on the role and treatment of traditional rulers in Niger prompted him to assess their role in his own country. In the northern states of Nigeria, he claimed, the traditional leaders (*sarauta na*

---

[10] Administration of Fulani communities in Niger and Nigeria also continues colonial administrative patterns. Whereas the British included Fulani settlements within the districts and village areas they set up throughout Hausaland, the French established a separate structure for the Fulani within their territory. To this day, therefore, "bush Fulani" within otherwise Hausa areas in Nigeria are subject to Hausa village area chiefs; those in Niger answer to a separate hierarchy of Fulani leaders.

gargajiya) commanded more respect and more loyalty among the people at large than did the politicians ('*yan siyasa*). The people obeyed the government, yes—but they obeyed their sarki even more (here he made reference to the 1981 riots in Kano, set off when the governor was thought to have insulted the emir) because the traditional leaders had been there since the beginning of time and would be there forever. Politicians (he really meant nontraditional rulers) were changed all the time: if any one in particular were not liked, he could just be thrown out (here the reference was to the 1980 impeachment of the Kaduna State governor). Continuity and longevity—these are what, in the eyes of Mai Gari Yardaji, lend legitimacy to power.

He repeated this refrain on several occasions: the longevity and legitimacy of the sarakuna na gargajiya (traditional rulers), as opposed to the uncertainty and impermanence of the "modern" kinds of leaders. Politicians, he noted, were continually fighting among themselves; but "when the sarki speaks, there's no dispute." Subsequent events in Nigerian politics can certainly be invoked to support the analysis of Mai Gari Yardaji. Not only was the elected president of the country (Shehu Shagari) to be overthrown shortly in a military coup, but even his successor (Major General Buhari) was to be ousted after only nineteen months in power (by General Babangida). In the eyes of the village chief, only traditional rulers could be relied upon to survive the instability and uncertainty associated with powerholding. Soldiers, no less than civilian politicians, are vulnerable to overthrow. But whatever else might happen in the political arena, the people could always look to their traditional leader, be he an emir or a village chief, as a symbol of stability, permanence, continuity, and legitimacy.

Even in a village as close to the Nigérien border as Yardaji, the point of reference in these discussions was not the situation in the nearby Republic of Niger but what was happening in Nigeria itself. For it was taken for granted that sarauta na gargajiya in Niger had little of the prestige, influence, and power of their counterparts in Nigeria: the chief's experience in Kogai was hardly an eye-opener, but rather confirmed long-standing belief concerning the denigration of the chieftaincy in Faranshi. The more problematic issue was how well the chiefs were holding up in Nigeria now that the Second Republic had reintroduced competitive party politics into the Nigerian polity. Even here, Mai Gari Yardaji was confident that in the final analysis, true leadership was provided by the chiefs, who invariably outlived other regimes and heads of state. He conceded that the chiefs were subordinate to the national government in actual iko (power) at any given time, but in a society where legitimacy is measured (at least in part) by longevity, he viewed the institutional authority of the chieftaincy as superior. For even if the chiefs had less power to allocate resources and impose sanctions to achieve their goals, their constant presence and intimate knowledge of the affairs of the people conferred upon them a permanent authority that so far has eluded the nonchiefly rulers of Nigeria.

Succession and Legitimacy

Paradoxically (at least by Western democratic norms) it is not the chief elected by the village who has the highest status but the chief who has been selected, according to the traditional norms of Hausa chieftaincy, by the emir or his agents. Ultimately, in both Niger and Nigeria the choice of the chief must be ratified by the state; but since ratification of village-level appointments is usually a formality, the mode by which a village chief is initially chosen is more important for his legitimacy. Once again, the structure and process on the Nigerian side of the border more strongly reinforce the position of the chief.

In Yekuwa a vacancy in the chieftaincy is filled by popular election. Viable candidates, generally the brothers or sons of the late chief, demonstrate their interest in the position. They then stand at the various corners of an open-air square as the entire village assembles. Then, in this open forum, in the presence of the sarki and subprefect, all male heads of household vote for one of the potential candidates by moving toward their choice and standing behind him. The candidate who has the greatest number of people behind him (in both the literal and figurative senses) is the village's next chief. The final appointment and ratification of the village chief is made by the state through its representative, the subprefect. Though this is ordinarily no more than a formality, the villagers are reminded, by the subprefect's physical presence, that the absolute authority of the chief is ultimately subject to his acceptance by the national government. In fact, however, the villagers themselves choose their chief.

In Yardaji, succession and legitimacy are established not by popular election but by a combination of local government and traditional chieftaincy criteria. In Kaduna State, in which Yardaji used to lie, when a chief of Mai Gari Yardaji's rank is to be replaced, the local government selects three candidates from among the chief's family and then rank-orders them. This list is then forwarded not to the government but to the emir (in the case of Yardaji, to the Sarkin Daura). It is the emir who makes the final choice (though his choice is subject, at least under the Second Republic, to confirmation by the governor). Investiture is primarily the affair not of the national government (as throughout Niger) but of the traditional chiefly hierarchy (hakimi, sarki, etc.). Although the local government chairman is present at the investiture in Daura, he takes a back seat to the sarki.

Although certainly less "democratic" than the method of election in Yekuwa, the choice of the chief in Yardaji, largely according to traditional Hausa norms of sarauta selection, confers a higher, not lower, degree of legitimacy. This is not to say that the chief in Nigérien Yekuwa has less legitimacy in the eyes of his villagers than the chief in Nigerian Yardaji has in his. Rather, to the extent that the selection of the mai gari in Yardaji is largely the affair of the traditional political hierarchy within Daura emirate, the chief's status and legitimacy are enhanced.

It is in his capacity as dagaci (that is, village area head) and not mai gari (village chief) that the appointment of the chief in Yardaji becomes a matter for the Daura local government area and emirate to decide. Recall that the position of dagaci does not exist within the Nigérien Hausa hierarchy; if it did, the demographic and economic importance of Yekuwa would inevitably make it a village area headquarters. The decision not to create such a position—whether by the French colonial or independent Nigérien regime—reflects a deliberate policy of extending to chiefs in the bush no greater autonomy, responsibility, or authority within the political hierarchy than is absolutely necessary. The failure to upgrade the position of the chief in villages such as Yekuwa (by title, salary, or autonomy) reinforces direct, centralized control over the population and chiefs throughout the Nigérien bush. The sarauta level of the indigenous Hausa political structure has been avoided. As a result, the chieftaincy at this level falls short of the status it retains in nearby Hausa villages in Nigeria.

This is not to say that there is no link in the indigenous Hausa political structure between, say, the canton chief of Magaria and the village chief of Yekuwa. There is such a link, but its form and operation are again indicative of the subordination of Niger's rural chiefs and talakawa to the rulers above them.

Hakimai and Jakadu Today

Before the European conquest, the administration of rural Hausaland was characterized by the direct subordination of all local communities and their local leaders (masu gari) to a fiefholder, or hakimi. The hakimi's title to the fief was granted by the sarki, or emir, in whose name the hakimi ulti-mately wielded authority. Significantly, however, the hakimi did not live in the district or territory over which he held power; he lived in the capital, near the emir. M. G. Smith (1978:24) thus characterizes these precolonial fiefholders as "absentee lords." One hakimi generally oversaw a number of fiefs, not necessarily in the same area. This was a deliberate stratagem by the emir to fragment any territorial power base of a hakimi. After the Fulani conquest of Daura, when the exiled Hausa state finally reestablished itself in Zango, the Sarkin Zango's fiefholder over Yardaji was the *kaura* (who eventually designated 'Dan Kwaba as his "acting administrator" over the village). The fiefholder of Yekuwa was the *yerima*.

Since the hakimai did not live in the areas under their jurisdiction (Hill 1977:9 refers to them as "city aristocrats"), an intermediate level of sarauta was established: the *jakada*. Variously characterized as "titled intermedi-aries," "administrative agents" (M. G. Smith 1978:24, 73), "executive or political officers," and "civil servants" (Hill 1977:9, 23), the jakadu (plural) were the ones who actually ventured into the villages to collect taxes and to gather information on behalf of their patrons (the hakimi and, by ex-tension, sarki). The jakada was also obliged to act as host, lodging villagers whenever they arrived in the capital from one of "his" fiefs (M. G. Smith 1978:112). In this way, fiefholders were remarkably well informed about fiefs that they rarely visited in person.

Inasmuch as the jakada's function was primarily extractive (he was, after all, a tax collector above all else), his visit to the village was hardly a cause for celebration. (Hill 1977:43 refers to the "stranglehold of the *jakadu* over ordinary farmers.") When the British consolidated their hold over Hausa-land, they regarded the extant setup as nothing short of inefficient, tyran-nical, and corrupt. One of their earliest priorities was to require the *hakimai* to establish permanent residence in the districts they were to supervise. Calling them now "district heads" (rather than "fiefholders"), the British put them on regular salaries. The effect was that "whereas they had for-merly been lords, subject only to the order of their superiors and the intrigues of their peers, they now had to conduct themselves like civil ser-vants and officials; to divest themselves of arbitrary personal power; and, in administering the affairs of their districts, to act within their capacities and proscriptions, solely as representatives of the emir and his Native Ad-ministration" (M. G. Smith 1978:334). The British also strengthened (and in some cases created) the position of dagaci (village area head) as a direct link between the central administration and the villages, giving him the major responsibility for collecting taxes there.

The upshot is that the position of jakada disappeared in British Hausa-land. In rationalizing and strengthening the chain of command from emir to district head to village area head to village chief (sarki to hakimi to dagaci to mai gari), the British left no place for the roving jakada, acting as occasional messenger or intermediary for an otherwise absent fiefholder and exercising an unmonitored and unaccountable discretion in his fief-dom. Thus today in Daura Emirate the emir communicates with the chief of Yardaji through the district head of Zango, and the district head of Zango knows that his dealings with the chief of Yardaji are subject to the orders and approval of the emir. As a result of this modification of the traditional hierarchy, the chief of Yardaji, while consciously subordi-nate to both the hakimi and the sarki, is secure in exercising his authority (and limited autonomy) in his capacity as village area head without the unpredictable intervention of a jakada. The British reorganization of the traditional Hausa political structure has so greatly enhanced chiefly status and prestige (girma, daraja) at the local level that "the present-day system of village administration . . . [still] basically resembles that created in the 1920s" (Hill 1977:49).

Paradoxically, it is in Niger that the anachronistic institution of jakada lives on. For although the French were ruthless in disrupting or eradicat-ing some aspects of the traditional chieftaincy, their very disregard for (and relative ignorance of) traditional Hausa modes of governing permitted some practices that posed no threat to them (even if they were repulsive to the talakawa) to linger on.

Thus, although the term "jakada" may have disappeared, the institution lives on in the guise of the *mai kamfani*. (This seems to be a Hausaiza-tion of the French *compagnie* in the sense of a military group.) Nine masu kamfani operate as the Sarkin Magaria's representatives throughout the Magaria district. The mai kamfani who is responsible for Yekuwa has the title of Yerima, as in precolonial days. (The other eight are Tarno, Yakou-dima, Maroussa, Turaki, Waziri, Mai Fulani, Murka, and Kaura.) The mai kamfani is not a government agent, but the villagers feel that he does wield considerable power (iko). In the past, up to forty years ago, he was feared for the beatings he might order when dissatisfied; a certain unease asso-ciated with such abusive authoritarianism lingers on. For this reason, when he does come to Yekuwa, the villagers give the yerima money—50 kobo, a naira—as a kind of protection money (*gaisuwa a gyara*) so that no evil will befall them. Although as far as the government is concerned he lacks the standing (*makami*) of the mai gari, in some respects he is more powerful in the eyes of the people than their own village chief.

For this reason, the presence of the mai kamfani is especially important around tax time. For although it is the mai gari who is officially charged with collecting taxes from the villagers, it is only the presence of the mai kamfani that really impels the people to come and pay. In the past, delinquent taxpayers would be shackled by the foot on the orders of the mai kamfani (who was executing the instructions of the commandant through the sarki). Even today some villagers believe (incorrectly) that he is the official tax collector. Without his "help," it is said, the mai gari would not succeed in getting people to pay; for after all, "he is always together with them" (that is, living among the villagers) and has to bear the brunt of their discontent after the tax season and throughout the year. On his own, the Yekuwa village chief could not command the compliance necessary to perform this rather unpopular function.

The mai kamfani has no fixed touring schedule, although he may send advance notice of his arrival when he is sent on a specific mission. He may come once a month, once every two months; sometimes he may spend weeks in his particular sector. There is no way of knowing in advance.

In this way the spirit and function of the precolonial jakada—that odious figure to the British, whose disappearance they championed—lives on in Nigérien Hausaland. Village chief and residents alike still live in anticipatory anxiety of the unpredictable but inevitable visit of the roving courtier of the sarki. There is no officially sanctioned and monitored link between the village and the Sarkin Magaria, such as the hakimi in neighboring Nigeria, who mediates between Yardaji's chief and the emir of Daura. The commands from above are not cushioned, as in Nigeria, by the existence of a local (and therefore more accessible) hakimi, passing on directives from his superior. Rather, the use of a jakada-like messenger from the sarki keeps villagers and their chiefs in the tight grip of their superiors, more faithfully reproducing the precolonial relationship between ruler and ruled, city and countryside, than their Nigerian cousins.

The Mai Gari in the National Context

So far, I have been concentrating on the relative role and status of our Nigérien and Nigerian chiefs within their respective communities and villages, according to traditional norms of behavior and conduct. But where do they stand in relation to their respective national societies? That is, in encounters with the state through its representatives on the local level, does the Nigérien chief still want in status in comparison with the Nigerian one?

Yardaji's primary school teachers.

Whereas a pretense of equality usually masks social stratification in Western societies, the interaction between social unequals in African society becomes an occasion for elaborate and public displays of hierarchical ranking. In Hausaland the expression of such interactions is encompassed by the institution of *gaisuwa,* loosely translated as "greeting" or "salutation." A person of lower rank will never stand in the presence of his superior, will not look the superior in the eye, and will not engage in conduct or speech more appropriate for use among one's peers; for example, a villager will use the third-person pronoun *ana* when addressing the chief. He will bend, bow, or prostrate himself before his superior, demonstrating his symbolic subordination by physically lowering himself. One need only observe the act of gaisuwa—or note its absence—to determine the hierarchical relationship between any two persons in Hausa society.

There is basically only one class of permanent representatives of the state in both Yekuwa and Yardaji: the schoolteachers. (One could also put the *likita,* or "doctor" in charge of each village's dispensary, in this category, but this role is much more marginal in village life than that of the teacher.) The relationship between chief and schoolteacher in the two villages may serve as a microcosm of the relationship between traditional ruler and state authority in the two societies.

In Yardaji, the chief is the undisputed leader of the community. To the

Teachers in Yekuwa's primary school.

extent that orders are to be given within the village as a whole, he is the one to give them. The schoolteachers have no particular role or function beyond that exercised within the school and over their pupils. If ever they need to meet with or talk to the mai gari, they perform the obligatory gesture of gaisuwa, and sit or stoop at the feet or side of the chief, on the ground, with or without a mat. Instructions from authorities outside the village that affect Yardaji go directly to the chief, transmitted either by the hakimi or *kantoma;* the schoolteachers (*mallamai makaranta*) are not implicated.

In Yekuwa, in contrast, the authority of the schoolteachers—not only within the village but over the chiefs—is remarkable.

The Nigérien government has conferred upon the *maître d'école,* especially in the bush, the unofficial role of administrative link between government and village. Directives from the subprefect may go directly to the state's representative in the local community—that is, the village schoolteacher—who passes them on to the chief for dissemination and implementation. In Yekuwa, then, the schoolteachers may convoke the chiefs to give instructions or orders from the government.[11]

---

[11] During the school enrollment season, for instance, a schoolteacher may call the chief and tell him, "The son of So-and-so will go."

The hierarchical relationship between chief and teacher found in Yardaji has been reversed in Yekuwa. There is no question of the schoolmaster's performing gaisuwa in the presence of the mai gari here; in fact, the teachers show utter lack of respect (at least according to Yardaji standards) toward the chiefs in Yekuwa. In one such interaction the twenty-five-year-old primary school principal called a "mandatory" meeting (*presence exigée*) with the chiefs of Hamada and Kofai. When Mai Gari Hamada and Mai Gari Kofai's brother (the chief himself was making a funeral call at the time) arrived, the teacher was playing cards. (Although perhaps not actually *haram*, or forbidden by Islamic law, card-playing is certainly a suspect activity according to the traditional Hausa code of conduct.) The teacher continued to play with his cards as he instructed the chief of Hamada and the chief of Kofai's representative to raise money among the villagers to replace the roof of the primary school. Such conduct before the mai gari would be unthinkable in Yardaji, even if the situation itself could be imagined.

The differing relationships between village chief and state authority in Niger and Nigeria are to be seen again in the occasional visit of soja (soldier) and ɗan sanda (policeman) in Yekuwa and Yardaji. Members of the Nigérien gendarmarie, as part of their patrol, alight in Yekuwa every few weeks or couple of months. Inasmuch as one of their major functions is to try to catch Nigériens engaged in illegal smuggling across the border, their presence sows apprehension in the village. Throughout their stay they are responsible for law and order, and any major disputes may be brought to them for resolution. Thus the mai gari becomes subordinate to even low-ranking state representatives. Although I never witnessed such a scene in Yekuwa, in other Nigérien villages I have been struck by the spectacle of village elders performing gaisuwa to minions of the Nigérien military.

Visits to Yardaji by uniformed members of the Nigerian police or immigration bureau are much rarer, and do not challenge or diminish the authority of the mai gari in the way they do in Yekuwa. During the national elections in the summer of 1983, for instance, armed policemen were dispatched to all polling centers throughout the country. The two assigned to Yardaji (one a southerner, the other a northerner) conducted themselves civilly, if not deferentially, in front of the chief and were treated as his guests. At mealtime, for example, they were served inside the chief's compound.

Before the coup of 1984, immigration officials from the nearby Zango border station paid sporadic visits to Yardaji, incognito, on market day, to look for traders or vendors from Niger. After the coup, when Nigeria's land borders were closed, the border police were more in evidence in Yardaji, searching at first for fugitive politicians, then for illegal frontier traffickers. In neither case, however, did their activities impinge on the authority or jurisdiction of the chief, whose position had never entailed regulation of cross-border movement. Thus, whereas interactions with agents of the Nigérien state in Yekuwa—whether schoolteachers or gendarmes—only tend to reinforce the diminished stature of the chief in the village, Yardaji's chief suffers no loss of status or prestige in interactions with agents of the Nigerian state.

Villagers' Views of the Chieftaincy

Eliciting from the villagers direct comparisons between the actual chiefs of Yardaji and Yekuwa (their relative status, prestige, authority, etc.) would have been awkward and might possibly constitute a breach of social etiquette. It is not merely a question of seeming to solicit negative comments about the local rulers: for the talakawa to speak about their leaders in any personalistic sense is just plain embarrassing. On such subjects, the Hausa sense of shame and discretion (kumya) limits affective expression.

Villagers can speak freely, however, about the general differences in the roles and treatments of the traditional rulers in the two countries. Although the perceptions they express are somewhat generalized, and their examples are drawn from a higher level of chieftaincy than that of their own village mai gari, one may implicitly translate their accounts of Hausa chiefs in Nijeriya and Faranshi in general into a more specific contrast of the chiefs in Yardaji and Yekuwa, as the villagers perceive them. These are the prevailing perceptions, as a villager in Yekuwa expressed them to me:

From the advent of European rule, the chiefs (sarakuna na gargajiya) in Nigeria remained strong, whereas those in Niger were subordinated to the new rulers. The new rulers included the *masu ilmi,* or modern-schooled black men, as well as the Europeans. In Nigeria, if the government wanted something done, it would have its desires communicated through the sarki, who would in effect oversee the execution of the task. In Niger, in contrast, the government would send a mai ilmi (in this context, a technician) to do the thing directly, bypassing the traditional ruler. And to this day, this is the way it is.

In Nigeria the sarki is still strong. If he wants to speak out, he will, and he will not be silenced by the governor. If the governor does not agree with the sarki's speech, he may speak to him privately, or tell him in writing, but he will not chide the *sarki* publicly, in front of the people. (If ever he tries, he will have a riot on his hands—as did the governor of Kano in 1980.) The sarakuna do not have as much girma (prestige) as in the old days, but they still have a considerable amount, especially in comparison with those in Niger.

In Niger, if the bariki (colonial commandant) did not like something the sarki was saying, the sarki was made to stop saying it. The chief is definitely beneath the government's representative (now the subprefect), who is a man of modern education (mai ilmi). The subprefect may refute or denounce the sarki in front of the people. The chief retains no daraja (respect, rank, standing) in the presence of the government agent, but rather suffers *ƙasƙasta*—a lowering of status, or humiliation. The sarki may go out on bush tour (*rangadi*) only at the behest of the government, and does so without any military bodyguards (*gardi*); he will go accompanied only by his dogarai (traditional palace guards), who are not even paid by the government.

In Nigeria the sarki tours in a motorized vehicle (probably a Mercedes Benz) and accompanied by policemen. (They even blare their sirens!) In Niger the government does not provide the sarki with a horse, much less a car. Why, even recently the Sarkin Magaria had to go on tour on horseback (and there are 244 villages under his jurisdiction!). He used to tour in his Land Rover, but no longer, not since it broke down. None of this is a surprise, though—his loss of maƙami and girma (standing and greatness) from the olden days is well known.

In his depiction of the differences in grandeur of the Hausa chiefs in the two countries, this villager may have overdrawn the reality of the situation. During his narration, for instance, another villager felt compelled to point out that today even a Nigerian sarki needs governmental permission before embarking on tour. Yet the broad thrust of his argument would go uncontested on both sides of the border: as measured by the trappings and accoutrements associated with prestige and status in modern Hausa society, the chief in Niger is a pale shadow of his former self. (The real significance of these outward symbols of status and prestige should not be underestimated. In Hausa society, it is impossible to separate physical and visible manifestations of greatness from the actual exercise of power and influence; a man of true importance who does not live, dress, or travel as do *manya-manya* ("big men") is a contradiction in terms. Cohen [1969:167–68] provides a wonderful illustration of this situation in his discussion of the "big malams" of Sabo.) In the light of yesteryear, but more particularly in contrast with his current-day counterpart in Nigerian territory, the position of the chief, in the eyes of Hausa border peasants, has substantially weakened in Niger.

Children of the Chiefs

As extensions of his own person, Mai Gari Yardaji's children give him cause for pride. Several of his daughters are married to wealthy and important personages outside the village, including the royalty in Daura. But it is by one's sons that the prestige of the Hausa family is judged. As of 1983 Mai Gari Yardaji had twenty-four living sons. The eldest, Alhaji Galadima, was kantoma, or the administrator for the Daura local government area. (When asked how the son could be above the father—for, in the institutional hierarchy, the kantoma has jurisdiction over the dagaci—one villager commented: "*Juyyin mulki*—it's the topsy-turvy government of today.") Three of Mai Gari's sons lived in Kano: one as a truck driver for a brick manufacturer, the second as a clerk for a garment company,[12] and the third as a driver of a Peugeot passenger car. One son was an office worker in a nearby town and another was employed in public works in far-off Lagos. Two sons were in Zaria, one attending a college, the other primary school. Seven other sons were attending secondary school in Mashi, Dutsin Ma, and Zango.

In Yardaji itself, the chief's two favorite sons, Ibrah and Hassane, farmed, tended cattle, and looked after Mai Gari's horse. Aminu drove his father's pickup truck and Kabiru taught in the village primary school. Magagi and Mansour were drivers of passenger minibuses, and Adamu and Issafou attended primary school. Kurma, the deaf one, just "wandered about."[13]

The large number of drivers among the chief's sons is not surprising: driving an automobile for hire is not only lucrative in highly mobile Nigeria but socially prestigous as well. It is a "modern" vocation fraught with excitement for young Hausa boys and one to which they can realistically aspire. In Hausaland, as elsewhere, knowledge is perceived as conferring power—hence the large number of chief's sons attending school—but so is being the man at the wheel. In a rural society reliant on motorized transport for long- and medium-distance travel, but in which there is a relative scarcity of vehicles and people who know how to drive, being a *direba*

---

12 He has since become a clerk in a local government education department in Kano State.

13 Kurma later enrolled in a school for the deaf in Kaduna. Aminu became a laboratory attendant in Katsina Polytechnic, and Adamu went on to the Day Secondary School in Zango.

(driver) does indeed confer a special status. Driving trucks, cars, or buses, far from reflecting negatively on the chief's family, in fact attests to the importance of Mai Gari's sons.

In Yekuwa, Mai Gari Hamada had eight living sons at the time I first met him. His eldest, Awali, was a tailor. Two other sons, Moutari and Salissou, were working for the government as agricultural extension agents, having completed secondary school. Si'udi was a farmer. Sons Abdusalaam, Bachiru, and Ado all attended school—a teachers' training college (*école normale*), a secondary school (*collège d'enseignement général*) in Niamey, and primary school, respectively. The youngest, Musaba, was still too young for school.[14]

Mai Gari Kofai had six living sons, only two of whom were adult. Alhaji Malam Ibrahim, the eldest, had become a lifelong student of the Koran. The second son, Abdurazaki, also claimed religious studies (*karatu*) as his profession. Oumarou was enrolled in the government school in the village—the only son of the chief to have received any Western-style education. Habibu, Aminu, and Idris were still young children.

Given the recency of Alhaji Adamu's tenure as mai gari in Kofai, it would perhaps be more instructive to look at the professions of his brothers—that is, the sons of the late chief Nalalu—for an indication of the success of the village's royal family. Issaka, the eldest son of Nalalu and already deceased, had been a farmer. So was Habou, Nalalu's second son. (Adamu was Nalalu's third son.) Muhamman attended primary school in Magaria for two years and then continued with Koranic study. Malam Rabiu, before his death, had also been renowned for his knowledge of the Koran. Nalalu's youngest sons, Aminu and Issoufou, were both farmers. Of Nalalu's thirty-one grandsons, eight became students of the Koran, eight farmers or herders, two merchants (of grain and kola nuts), one a worker at the local mill, one a washerman, and one a migrant laborer in Nigeria. Three grandsons were then attending primary school; the remaining seven were still preschoolers. Only five of these adult grandsons had attended any government school, and their maximum attendance was six years at the primary level.

Clearly, the sons of the chief of Hamada are, overall, farther along the road to success than the sons and grandsons of the late chief of Kofai. But how do they compare with the sons of the chief of Yardaji? We can see

---

[14] In 1986 Abdusalaam was a civil servant in Niamey, Bachiru had obtained his brevet diploma and would be continuing his education, and Moutari was preparing to be taken to Iran. Two more boys, both named Saratu, had also been born.

that the paths taken by the chiefs' sons in these two neighboring Hausa villages actually reflect the social and economic state of their respective nations. In Nigérien Yekuwa, upward (and outward) mobility occurs primarily through Western education and subsequent government service. Boys who eschew this path, as most of Nalalu's descendants have done, engage in traditional village activities and cannot realistically expect opportunities for significant prosperity. In Nigerian Yardaji, on the other hand, several of the chief's sons have prospered by entering the dynamic, free-wheeling free enterprise system so characteristic of the Nigerian economy as a whole. (Hearsay has even suggested that Mai Gari Yardaji has been paid as a consultant for one of his sons' contracting operations.) And though many of the Yardaji chief's sons have obtained or are in the process of obtaining some Western-style education (makaranta boko), it is by no means the prerequisite for economic success that it is in the more statist economy of Niger.

Colonialism or Materialism?

One could challenge my main argument here—that postcolonial manifestations of the chieftaincy essentially reflect continuities in the colonial patterns—thus: Cannot the differential levels in status of the chiefs in Yardaji and Yekuwa be attributed to sheer economics? If Niger is an uncontestably poorer country than Nigeria, then its villages and their chiefs will be poorer as well. Niger will suffer in any material comparison with Nigeria; why should the chieftaincy be any different? If Nigeria can afford to maintain its local chiefs by putting them on state salaries and Niger cannot, is this not more a reflection of economic exigency than an expression of Niger's hostility or indifference to its traditional rulers? If status and prestige in Hausaland are bound up with symbols and expressions of material wealth, then Mai Gari Yardaji's "luxury" compound, chair, Peugeot pickup truck (*and* white horse), successful sons, and so on, and hence his greater girma vis-à-vis his Yekuwa counterparts, are to be attributed to the trickling down of Nigeria's greater wealth to Yardaji, not to greater inherited solicitude for traditional institutions of government. It is not Lugard and indirect rule that have made Mai Gari Yardaji the envy of Mai Gari Yekuwa, but petrodollars and the allocation of state revenues.

There is truth to this argument, but only partial truth. For although the relative wealth of Nigeria has indeed tended to strengthen the status of Yardaji's chief, a more accurate view is that these economic factors have basically reinforced tendencies otherwise in operation. The challenge presumes that one can separate economic forces from political ones, and this presumption falls as far short of explaining West Africa today as it does of explaining the original scramble for Hausaland.

On the most basic level, the fact that Niger is a poor country (in comparison with Nigeria) and Yekuwa a poor village (in comparison with Yardaji) is itself a result of colonialism and, more specifically, the colonial partition. To a large extent, the material fates of today's independent Federal Republic of Nigeria and Republic of Niger were sealed at the turn of the century. When the British managed to claim for themselves a heavily populated, resource-rich, and topographically diverse territory and the French were left with a harsh, vast, underpopulated, largely Saharan expanse, the economic prospects of Nigeria and Niger were already set in place. Of course, the British in Lugard's day could not have imagined the incredible oil wealth that would later be discovered offshore in the Niger Delta, any more than Governor Jules Brévié and the French could have foreseen (much less understood) the discovery of uranium in the mountains of Arlit. Yet Nigeria's relative wealth and growth began not with oil but with agriculture; and no amount of nuclear fuel mined in northwestern Niger has overcome the natural stringencies of this landlocked Sahelian nation. Economics ex nihilo do not account for the respective positions of Nigeria and Niger, Yardaji and Yekuwa, and their chiefs; rather, their respective economic fortunes have emerged out of earlier colonial imperialisms, rivalries, and happenstance.

Moreover, the geopolitical changes that the European partition imposed in Hausaland helped shape the respective colonial policies of the British and French there (as elsewhere), and in turn their differential treatments of the Hausa chieftaincy. Although most explanations of the source of direct and indirect rule are Eurocentric—contrasting, for instance, the "Cartesian," "centralizing," and "universalistic" traits of French philosophy, government, and society with British "pragmatism," "empiricism," and "aloofness"—there were also situational reasons (geographic, demographic, economic) why these colonial policies were deemed suitable for the areas under French and British control. Despite the vastness of the area and the initial difficulties in communication, it was still easier for the French to exercise direct control over the relatively small number of Nigériens under them—and consequently to bypass or downgrade the indigenous rulers—than for the British to administer similarly the tens of millions of Nigerians under them. Topography also facilitated direct rule in French territory: the flat and open Sahel was more accessible to French touring and resident officers than the hill and mountain dens of many of the "pagan tribes" in southern pockets of Northern Nigeria. Furthermore, the economics of colonial administration threatened to place greater financial demands on the British in huge Nigeria than they did in demographically diminutive Niger—a burden the British were happy to pass on to indigenous rulers. Lugard himself justified the adoption of indirect rule this way in 1918:

> [T]he Political Staff available for the administration of so vast a country, inhabited by many millions, must always be inadequate for complete British administration in the proper sense of the word. . . . [It is] therefore imperative to utilize and improve the existing machinery . . . (Kirk-Greene, ed., 1965:70)

—that is, to rule through the chieftaincy already in place.

Differential patterns of rulership in French and British Hausaland can also be explained, then, by the spatial parameters that the colonial powers established: indirect rule fitted British Hausaland; French Hausaland was an inevitable candidate for direct rule. The key to the different fates of Hausa chiefs on both sides of the border lies in geographic and administrative variables whose origin is colonial, not economic; economically oriented explanations are pertinent, but only insofar as their basis in colonial political realities is acknowledged.

Finally, it should be stressed that within the (admittedly constrained) margin of maneuver open to the postcolonial governments operating over Hausaland, fundamental inroads into the inherited treatments of the chieftaincy at the village level have not been seriously made. Although I have suggested that the conditions established by colonial rule in Niger and Nigeria may affect (and somewhat limit) the parameters of change available within these two postcolonial states, the colonial legacy neither wholly precludes nor predetermines the policy options open to them. Nigeria could have tried to eliminate the perquisites of the chiefs' power (by reducing or eliminating their government salaries, for instance); rather, successive governments and rulers, civilian and military, have generally tried to use or exploit the chiefs' influence over the talakawa, indirectly confirming the chiefs' continued importance. Niger could have restructured the French-imposed chieftaincy hierarchy, or granted local chiefs more formal autonomy vis-à-vis the subprefect, or granted the masu gari some token stipend as a gesture of governmental support; but it has not done so. Despite the changes within their respective societies, the role and status of the Hausa chief have not fundamentally changed since the British legitimized the sarakuna na gargajiya (traditional rulers) in Nigeria and the French subjected them to ƙasƙasta (status loss) in Niger.

From Chieftaincy to Economics

No other institution demonstrates the continuity of indigenous African political life so well as the chieftaincy. Perhaps none other enjoys the same degree of legitimacy among African publics, or at least the rural African publics that constitute the vast majority within the nations of Africa. Yet perhaps no other institution was so deliberately manipulated or transformed during the colonial regime. The treatment accorded the chieftaincy by postcolonial states in Africa is therefore a good indicator of the extent to which independent African republics have either departed from or maintained colonial policies in local-level administration.

Hausa symbols of status regarding dwelling, accessibility, mobility, transport, and labor all favor the Nigerian village chief vis-à-vis his neighboring Nigérien counterparts. Chiefly succession, even at the village level, more strongly upholds traditional norms of power transfer in Nigeria than in Niger, where the state is more interventionist. A more bureaucratic and stratified approach to the chiefly hierarchy, introduced by the British in Nigerian Hausaland and retained after independence, also gives the Hausa village chief in Nigeria more autonomy than the mai gari enjoys in Niger.

Interviews with both chiefs and villagers underscore the local perception that the debasement of Nigérien chiefs by the French and the relative promotion of Nigerian chiefs by the British continue to this day. So do certain discrete events: the appointment of a Fulani hardo (chief), encounters between schoolteachers and village chiefs, visits by soldiers and police.

Material differences in life conditions and prospects are of great interest and concern to Hausa villagers along the Niger-Nigeria boundary. Perhaps in no other respect can the impact of the division of Hausaland be seen so clearly.

8

Arziki vs. *Talauci:*
The Economic Comparison

Da abinda mutum ka samu da abinda ka samu nai tun ran halita shi ke.

What a man gets and what happens to him is written from the day of his birth.

—Hausa proverb

The groundwork for an economic comparison between Yardaji and Yekuwa has been laid by several superb studies that have investigated the structure and dynamics of the economies of discrete Hausa villages in both Niger and Nigeria. M. G. Smith paved the way for modern Hausa economists with his description of the traditional economies operating throughout Hausaland, particularly in the countryside (1965a, 1978). Guy Nicolas (1960) has taken a case-study approach in Niger (Tassao, inter alia), assessing the impact that French colonial economic policies and changes have had at the village level. Polly Hill (1972, 1977) has broken ground in investigating economic variation in two Nigerian Hausa communities (Batagarawa and Dorayi), weaving into her analysis such diverse variables as British colonial indirect rule (which she characterizes as "rural non-rule") and population pressure and density. Numerous unpublished market and village studies have been conducted by and for aid/development agencies on both sides of the border in Hausaland, while the studies of Robert Charlick (in Matameye County, Niger) and Earl Scott (in Katsina Province, Nigeria) straddle the boundary between purely academic analysis and action-oriented development prescription (Charlick 1972, Scott 1978). Nevertheless, although Derrick Thom's (1970) dissertation ("a politico-geographical analysis") does brilliantly explore many of the economic implications of the Niger-Nigeria partition for the Hausa in the Katsina-Maradi-Zinder borderlands, no study to date has specifically contrasted the economy of a single Hausa village in Niger with one in Nigeria. Research in Yekuwa and Yardaji fortunately provides such an opportunity.

The thoroughness of the earlier studies liberates me from the necessity of comprehensively rehearsing all those aspects of the rural Hausa economy which are similar throughout Hausaland and therefore common to both villages (e.g., agricultural cycle, farming methods and crops, dietary regime, food preparation, secondary occupation, sexual division of labor, inheritance, etc.; see the appended Commentary in Hill 1972 for an extensive list of relevant topics). I may concentrate instead on the elements that have tended to differentiate Yardaji and Yekuwa economically. The extent to which both real-life possibilities and aspirations of material advancement have been conditioned by the colonial legacy cannot be overstated. For whereas Yardaji is perceived by the people of both villages as incarnating *dukiya* and *arziki* (wealth and good fortune), the consensus is as great that Yekuwa, at least in its outward appearance, is a place of *wahala* and *talauci* (suffering and poverty).

To assess the significance of these findings, it is necessary to place them within the wider context of colonial patterns of economic exploitation and development in and beyond rural Hausaland. We need to see how and why the most predominant elements of economic life in Yardaji and Yekuwa today—intervillage trade, cross-border smuggling, customs surveillance, currency usage, taxation, transportation, migration, and so on—issue from preindependence policies and processes. I find support not only for Thom's evaluation of the Niger-Nigeria borderlands in Hausaland—"with the emergence of Niger and Nigeria as independent States . . . the patterns established during the colonial period have intensified and become more firmly entrenched" (Thom 1970:240)—but for A. I. Asiwaju's findings in another African setting (Western Yorubaland) that even today the "widespread impression [remains] that the French was the harsher of the two systems" (Asiwaju 1976b:115).

Before we embark on this task, however, some mention must be made of the precolonial economy of the rural Hausa of Daura.

The Precolonial Economy

"Although based primarily on agriculture, the mixed economy of precolonial Daura was diversified by the raising of cattle and other stock; by the gathering of sylvan produce; by the exploitation of mineral resources, particularly iron; by craft production; and by long-distance caravan trade (*fatauci*)" (M. G. Smith 1978:35–36). Smith's account of Daura before and immediately after the Fulani jihad goes into great detail concerning the taxes that were levied on various classes of residents and producers throughout the emirate (113–20), but we have little additional information concerning the daily operation of the precolonial Daura rural economy. Hill (1977:1) makes a similar admission in discussing precolonial economic life in rural Kano before 1900: we have but a "smattering of knowledge" about "rural craftwork, trade and markets, the role of farm-slavery, land tenure, and so forth."

We do know, however, that for a time after the Fulani conquest of Daura city, Yekuwa and Yardaji were not mere villages but served as capitals for the Daura Hausa state in exile. It was to Yekuwa that Sarkin Gwari Abdu moved shortly before his death in 1825 and from there that his successor Lukudi initially ruled. (Smith relates that Yekuwa initially "lacked a[n] . . . earth wall, the essential sign of a chief's headquarters and a chiefdom's capital," but that under Lukudi it was built up into a "stockaded town" [1978:155–56].) Lukudi eventually moved to Yardaji, establishing it as his new capital, complete with town wall and gates. Smith estimates that at the time of its fall in 1845, Lukudi lost at least 1,300 subjects in Yardaji (165); for the time, it was a rather substantial settlement. But the fall of Yardaji to Ibram of Damagaram spelled the end of the Yekuwa-Yardaji period of Daura Hausa independence, and of whatever economic prominence the two towns had derived from it. Yardaji in particular had to start again from scratch, for, according to local informants, Sarkin Daura Musa forced the remaining inhabitants to abandon their settlement and build a new one outside the limits of the original town.

Thus, in the half-century between the conquest by Damagaram and the European occupation, Yardaji and Yekuwa became once again rural Hausa villages, without external political forces to disrupt their agricultural routine. Elderly informants recall those years before *zamanin turawa*—the "time of the Europeans"—as a time when life was harsh.

Slavery

Although M. G. Smith concentrates on the institution of slavery at the highest levels of the Daura Emirate (that is, the throne slaves), he does indicate that slaves lived and worked in the rural areas as well (1978:43–44). Up to perhaps 10 percent of the entire population of Daura Emirate in the nineteenth century were slaves. This proportion is not high in comparison with that elsewhere in Hausaland (especially in Kano and Zaria emirates) but high enough to indicate that slavery was a significant feature of precolonial rural Daura Hausaland.

Smith attributes the relatively low incidence of rural slavery in part to the distance that separated Daura from the areas that commonly supplied Zaria and Kano with slaves (1978:44). Informants in Yekuwa, however, consistently mentioned Damagaram (Zinder) as the central magnet and marketplace for slaves from their territory. These reports are consistent with Fuglestad's observation that "slavery was of prime importance in nineteenth-century Damagaram, as was slave-raiding . . . against neighbouring entities. . . . [B]ecause of the insatiable demand for slaves and funds, the gulf between the ruling elite and the masses seems to have grown ever wider" (1983:48, 46). Villagers recall that people who had been caught and enslaved were taken to Damagaram and given to the sarki, who sold or used them as he saw fit. Little boys, for instance, might be castrated to become palace eunuchs. By custom, however, the Sarkin Damagaram gave one-fifth (humushi) of the slaves to the people who had captured them. All booty was dealt with thus.

Informants also recall that women slaves were more expensive than men, for men were more likely to run away from their masters. This explanation is at variance with Hill's, that women slaves were more expensive "presumably mainly because they were a superior long-term investment, the children of a slave-couple usually belonging to the mother's owner" (1977:208). Hill does, however, present evidence that the price of slaves was somehow linked to the probability of flight when she quotes Lugard's memorandum 22: "young men . . . 'were not regarded as so safe an investment as boys, as being more liable to run away'" (221). My informants also said that in the days of slavery "one could go to market, buy a woman, and marry her." This is a new interpretation of the possible relationship between masters and slaves in Hausaland. Of course, it was not unusual for women slaves to bear the children of their masters (see ibid., 204).

Alhaji Aminu of Yekuwa proffered a rather sophisticated, if unconventional, economic analysis to explain the evolution from a noncurrency, slave-bound economy to the relative wealth of today. (In comparison with Yardaji, of course, Yekuwa is poor; but overall improvement in material life since the precolonial era is recognized.) Some of the terms I use in translation may be somewhat modernized, but the ideas are Alhaji Aminu's:

In the old days, there was no money at all. (Actually, there was relatively little trading or commerce outside of the cities—partly for lack of a market outlet, partly for lack of security throughout the land.) One of the few ways to get wealth was to trade in people. So slave raiding and slavery became a most popular means of rapidly acquiring a valuable free good. These slaves were taken by the sarakai (rulers) and sold to *attajirai* (big-time traders) in the markets. Today, though, there is more money in circulation, and therefore no need to resort to such methods to acquire wealth.

Of course, in reality it was the coming of the Europeans that both gradually ended slavery and established a coin and paper money economy throughout Hausaland, particularly through the introduction of such cash crops as cotton (farther south) and peanuts (in the north).[1] The Europeans outlawed the slave trade, thus inducing the owners and traders of slaves to seek other avenues of wealth, such as commercial trading.[2] This task accomplished, the economic necessity of slavery slowly diminished, and therefore its lethargic but inevitable disappearance was met with little resistance or subversion. Nevertheless, Alhaji Aminu's ingenious argument, coming as it does from a thoroughly indigenous and non-Western intellectual framework, does interestingly link the abolition of slavery in Hausaland with the broader processes of a widening and more diverse economy, one of whose most prominent features was monetization.

Hill's conclusion that slave ancestry has virtually no social and relatively little economic significance in Dorayi today (1977:219–20) appears to hold true for modern-day Yardaji and Yekuwa as well. However, M. G. Smith's observation (1978:32, 43–44) that "institutional traces" of slavery persist in the form of Bugaje ("Negroid serfs owned by Tuareg of Asben") settlements scattered around the emirate also is relevant to contemporary ethnic interaction: while relations are cordial between our Hausa villages and nearby Bugaje (or Bouzou) communities, the former continue to look down on the latter, usually expressing their derision in jokes.

Precolonial Poverty

Although it is natural to concentrate on slavery when one examines the harshness of the precolonial economy in rural Hausaland, modern-day villagers in Yardaji and Yekuwa (or at least the elderly ones) are still conscious of the burdens and obligations under which even "free" men labored under the pre-European regime. To hear the graphic descriptions of village life in the "old days" (*zamanin da*) is to appreciate why the advent of colonial

---

[1] Cowry shells were used as a medium of exchange before the introduction of colonial currency. In precolonial Hausaland grains served this purpose.

[2] Slavery itself, however, was not abolished outright. See Hill 1977:200–202, 209–11 for the British perspective and Suret-Canale 1964:81–89 for the French side.

rule is generally lauded by Yardaji and Yekuwa villagers even today, over a quarter of a century since their countries gained independence.

Far from living out any Rousseauan myth of "noble savagery," Hausa *talakawa* in the bush were engaged in a perpetual struggle with survival. However dramatic and lamentable the recent droughts and famines throughout Africa—the Sahelian drought of the late 1960s and early 1970s, the Ethiopian crisis of the mid-1980s, Somalia in the early 1990s—it should not be forgotten that these calamities have occurred in an era when national governments and international organizations have been able to respond, however slowly or inadequately, to massive starvation throughout the continent. Before the twentieth century, peasants faced with periodic hunger and starvation had little hope of assistance from any quarter. The talakawa were on their own, and famine was as uncontrollable as the fickle clouds on which their lives depended.

Even in normal times the standard of living was abysmal. Although Hill contends that "in former times most long-distance traders (*fatake*) were farmers who were rurally based" (1972:243), information gathered in Yardaji and Yekuwa indicates that few villagers in this bush profited from long-distance trade. Fear of slave raiders was one constraint on travel out of the villages, even for relatively short distances.[3] Local-level trade was accordingly moribund, and it appears that a weekly market was established in both Yekuwa and Yardaji (or reestablished, if we assume that some market was in place during Lukudi's day) only under the aegis of colonial pacification and rule.

The Hausa symbols of yesteryear's economic stagnation were the *walki* (a leather loincloth that covered the waist and thighs) and the *bante* (a strip of clothing that covered only the private parts). These were the garb of most male villagers. Elders in Yekuwa speak of the time when there were only two pairs of shirts and pants in the entire village; even in the early colonial days there might be only one *riga* (cloth gown) for twenty people to share. Today, of course, even the poorest villagers wear some kind of riga, or at least Western-style (and mostly Western-donated) trousers and shirts (*gwanjo*). Such donations—given as charity in the United States and Europe—are sold on the open market in the weekly *kasuwa*, just like any other good or merchandise.

---

[3] Fear of raiding and warfare is a recurrent theme in Baba of Karo's narration of precolonial life in Northern Nigeria as well: "In those days there was always fear; war, war, war—they caught a man and they made him a slave, or else they killed him" (Mary Smith 1954/1981:47; see also pp. 66–73).

Yet the precariousness of the distinction between "slave" and "free," in real economic terms, is highlighted best by the recollection of demands made on the villagers by the paramount chief of the area. In Yekuwa, for instance, "before the Europeans came, if a man's horse gave birth to a mare, it was his. But if it was a male, it would go to the Sarkin Damagaram." Such equestrian rapaciousness persisted into the early colonial era, and is confirmed (with slight variations in detail) by a 1914 report written by the commandant of Magaria:

> Tchikama [the province chief of Zinder] seems to have had a weakness for the animals of the region. Whenever a stallion or mare pleased him, he could not rest until he owned it. He had three ways of obtaining [the animal]: He would offer to buy it, take delivery of it, and then not pay. Or he might have it requisitioned on some pretext concerning the needs of the local administration. Finally, if the animal belonged to a chief, he would suggest that the chief make him a gift of it, promising him a thousand indulgences. And if that failed to work, he would wait until the chief committed an offense, furnishing him with an opportunity to step in, and to slap on a fine equal to the worth of the coveted animal. Considerable sums of millet have been expropriated by this greedy and venal chief. (Records of the subprefecture of Magaria)

In Yardaji it was said that even women from the village were taken away when they caught the fancy of some roving nobleman. Property—and "property" could be construed to encompass people—was not only vulnerable to confiscation by marauders but subject to expropriation by the "legitimate" rulers of the land.

Colonial Economics in Hausaland

Although histories of colonialism often attribute European intervention in Africa to unequivocal economic motives, in the case of Hausaland economic exploitation was more of an afterthought than a driving force. Only the most dogged Marxian historiographer could impute to the original European conquerers the imagination to view the harsh, dry, semi-desert Sahelian and Sudanese topographical zones of the rural Hausa as areas of great agricultural or extractive promise; that they constituted a vast reservoir of surplus labor could only have been an afterthought. Once Hausaland was assimilated into the greater colonial units of their European overlords, of course, the British and the French did have to construct some economic plan to justify and rationalize the acquisition of their Hausa territories, just as they did with all of their colonized lands. But it was more its connection to the larger Nigerian and Nigérien colonies than its presumed intrinsic value that caused rural Hausaland to be taken over and then exploited in the economic sense.

The notion that the Hausa lands of Nigeria and Niger were marginal contributions to the economies of these two colonial states (and did not represent tempting prizes in the eyes of would-be colonizers) is not entirely novel. (Rarely, though, has postpartition Hausaland been considered as a discrete economic unit in this way, rather than as an appendage to some more "fundamental" colonial unit.) Although Fuglestad disagrees with T. W. Roberts's thesis that, for the French, "the myth of an interior [in the central Sudan and Sahara] rich in resources and population was simply an explanation and justification for advances undertaken for quite other reasons" (Roberts 1972:378–79), he does accept the more plausible explanation that the larger area to which Hausaland belonged seemed to have considerable strategic and geopolitical importance, in view of France's desire to link the territories it had already acquired in northern, western, and equatorial Africa. And Fuglestad provides more than adequate substantiation for the contention that, overall, colonial Niger could barely pay for its own administration, much less turn a handsome franc for the *mère-patrie*. [4] Charlick (1991:109) makes the point most bluntly: "[S]ince France had little economic interest in Niger, it basically neglected the development of this colony."

Although Hausaland proved somewhat more lucrative to the British than to the French, only amalgamation with the more profitable southern

---

[4] Thus "the 'new' economic policy inaugurated by the French [after 1908] . . . was based on illusions about the economic future of Niger" (Fuglestad 1983:83). "By 1922 at the latest, it had been realized that Niger possessed few if any resources that could be tapped" (120). "[B]y the time the French began to 'catch up' with the moderate prosperity of the 1920s, signs of more difficult days ahead . . . were already evident" (128). "[T]he administration was not interested [in the inability of Hausa farmers to find buyers for their millet in the 1930s]. . . . Being left with a substantially reduced income, but forced to pay the same taxes as before . . . the Hausa had no choice but to break into their capital, in other words to sell their cattle" (135). "The drastic reduction of the Africans' contribution to the public purse [in the 1930s] compelled the French to limit their activities . . . [T]he administration had to cut back on the already small sums spent on education and social services" (137). During the Vichy regime of the early 1940s, French policy was to "supply . . . metropolitan France and North Africa inexpensively with whatever commodities the Africans could deliver. . . . In Niger, this policy . . . proved disastrous" (139). After World War II, the principle of budgetary self-sufficiency was finally abolished with the "development fund and associated programmes. . . . A cursory glance at the budget of Niger after 1954 [shows] that . . . Niger could not meet the maintenance costs. . . . [M]ost of the external funds . . . were simply used to meet the costs of maintenance and to support the already existing administrative and institutional framework" (170).

Protectorate of Nigeria made it a viable colonial territory: on its own, it is unlikely that British Hausaland could have thrived without considerable external subsidization. Michael Crowder makes this point most clearly:

> The immediate reason for the decision to amalgamate the two Nigerias was economic expediency. The Northern Protectorate [within which all of Hausa-land fell] was running at a severe deficit, which was being met by a subsidy from the Southern Protectorate, and an Imperial Grant-in-Aid from Britain of about £300,000 a year. This conflicted with the age-old colonial policy that each territory should be self-subsisting. Apart from the fact that it seemed logical to amalgamate the two territories, the one land-locked and the other with a long seaboard, it was felt that the prosperous Southern Protectorate could subsidize its northern neighbour until such time as it became self-supporting. (Crowder 1962:213)

By centralizing the Treasury, Lugard was able to divert revenue that earlier had been properly the South's to balance the North's deficit (ibid., 216).

The northern emirates in British Hausaland did eventually succeed in raising their own revenues for local administrative purposes, and even managed, as in Daura, to generate a surplus.[5] However, the extent to which such prosperity was facilitated by linkage to the greater Nigerian economy and market should not be overlooked. In particular, the development and extension of the Nigerian railway to Kano, from which agricultural products could be cheaply and efficiently transported to the coast at Lagos, and thence exported to overseas markets, was crucial to the economic viability of colonial Hausaland.

Cash Cropping and Colonialism

With slight deviation from the classic colonial pattern, one may say that the peasants of rural Daura and Magaria were compelled by the economic system introduced by the British and French to modify a mostly food-oriented (and largely subsistence) economy to one in which cash crops had to be grown.[6] This imperative stemmed primarily from the new requirement that taxes be paid in cash. To raise cash, peasants were obliged to grow and sell crops the European rulers promoted. In Western Yorubaland, where Asiwaju (1976b) investigated this phenomenon, cash cropping took

[5] See M. G. Smith 1978:338–53 for budgetary details.
[6] See Scott 1978 for a useful discussion of the "subsistence versus exchange economy dichotomy" as applied to rural Hausaland.

the form of the four *C*'s: corn, cotton, cocoa, and coffee. In the British and French territories of which Yardaji and Yekuwa were a part, the preferred cash crop was *gujiya* (groundnuts or peanuts), introduced to West Africa much earlier by the Portuguese but only now, with the demand in the European food industry for hydrogenated vegetable oils, given a substantial market boost (Thom 1970:152). The colloquial use of "peanuts" to mean "a trivial amount" is hardly felicitous when one considers the importance of this crop for colonial Hausaland: "the production of groundnuts . . . became the mainstay of the colonial economy of Northern Nigeria and the leading producer of foreign exchange for all of Niger" (ibid). Magaria in particular became the "peanut basket" for the entire country.

Groundnuts, Magaria, and Yekuwa

So far, our account reveals little difference in the operations of the colonial economies on both sides of the border. Hausa farmers in Nigerian Yardaji and Nigérien Yekuwa were similarly compelled to grow a cash crop to raise money for taxes. In both cases the choice of cash crop was determined in large part by European market demand. In both villages the cash crop settled upon was groundnuts. It thus appears that, without further elaboration, British and French colonial economic policies were alike.

Fortunately, further elaboration is possible. The recollections and perceptions of farmers in both villages are substantiated by John Collins's findings (1974, 1976, 1985). The way cash crop production was encouraged and generated varied substantially from one side of the border to the other, from one village to the next. Unequivocally, the French colonial mode of cash crop production is condemned by all villagers as having been much harsher than that of the British. Here again, the conclusions reached by Asiwaju in the case of Dahomeyan and Nigerian Yorubaland are replicated in Hausaland: whereas the British encouraged indigenous cultivation through free labor, the French implemented state control of production with compulsory cultivation.

Collins has argued that commercial groundnut production in Magaria did not originally stem from state intervention, but rather had its seeds in private, expatriate (often Lebanese and Syrian) merchants and trading companies. As early as the 1910s and certainly by the 1920s the groundnut trade was thriving in Kano. By the 1930s (the time lag is explained by the poor infrastructure in French Hausaland) the success of the Kano groundnut trade had induced merchants to establish buying centers in several villages near Magaria. Hausa farmers took up cash cropping in the first place, he demonstrates, less to raise money for taxes than out of "economic initiative and adaptability" (1974:24). Key to this new economic ethos were the goods (such as imported cloth and refined salt) that the trading companies offered for sale and that Hausa peasants were eager to buy.

Only with World War II did groundnut production become a financial and legal necessity on the French side of the border. Taxes were extracted more rigorously. More important, a program of compulsory groundnut production—enforced by physical punishment, heavy fines, and prison—was enacted in 1943, with quotas established even for individual families. The irony is that this obligatory groundnut production was imposed not by the Vichy government but by the "Free French" regime, and was continued for a year after the war ended.

None of the stories that elderly Yekuwa villagers recount concerning forced agricultural production in the colonial days are to be heard in Yardaji (except when they discuss how things were in Faranshi). For instance: "In the planting season, the French would force even the very old, the blind, and the lepers to work. The old men would have to plant and carry water. The blind were made to shell groundnuts. Lepers would have to carry felled trees away—the trees would be tied to their arms, and they would drag them off." Another: "They would force us to plant groundnuts, but prohibit us from even eating them. Once in a while, a man might eat a little while he was harvesting—but only secretly and furtively, on account of fear. One couldn't sell his groundnuts, either—not until they gave us permission to."

I must side with Fuglestad's unidentified informants, who apparently offered similar kinds of information, against Fuglestad himself, who inexplicably (given his own characterization of the French system as "despotic and arbitrary" [1983:82]) dismisses such reports, on the curious grounds that the measures they describe would be illogical or counterproductive:

> Some of my informants have argued that the French also made use of coercive measures in order to promote the cultivation of groundnuts, but there is no trace of such measures in the written record. This does not mean that such measures never existed, but if they did, they cannot have been very far-reaching, and were probably withdrawn very quickly. For groundnut cultivation was a field in which the interests of subjects and rulers converged. (1983:138)

Severity on the part of colonial administrators on Yekuwa's side of the border did not stem from any special difficulty associated with groundnut cultivation in the district under consideration. On the contrary, Magaria

District was the peanut basket of Niger, the most fertile and productive area for groundnut growing in all the country, ever since the export trade in the crop began in the 1930s. As Collins summarizes:

> [W]illingness to use force was not a result of war-time necessity. The pre-War history of forced labor in Magaria would belie any such claim. The need to use force to get farmers to grow groundnuts was however a direct result of the disappearance of normal economic incentives during the War. (1974:102)

Villagers of Yekuwa suffered what those of Yardaji were spared merely because they found themselves on the "wrong" side of the border.

The need to grow groundnuts for cash intensified after World War II, as both taxation and socioeconomic obligations (new consumption opportunities, Muslim largesse, greater demands by wives [Collins 1974:84, 7]) required the head of household to increase his kudi supply. (Just as the French word argent [for money] literally means "silver," "kudi" in Hausa literally means "cowrie shells.") Most significant for our purposes, the necessity to grow groundnuts to pay taxes predominated in Magaria after independence, as the Republic of Niger not only raised tax rates but moved rapidly to expand state control over the production and marketing of groundnuts. It did so not without "threats and veiled coercion" (302), and, "government rhetoric to the contrary, [by taking] a paternalistic . . . approach . . . [that] precluded any real local participation in the operation of the markets" (9). State control over groundnuts had more explicitly political ramifications as well: the groundnut cooperative agency set up by the government also served to "attack the traditional prerogative of the canton nobility" (303). One can hardly imagine a similar economic-cum-political policy operating against the royalty of Daura.

Daura and Nigerian Groundnut Boards

What is striking about groundnuts in M. G. Smith's (1978) comprehensive account of colonial Daura is their absence. Though purchasing of groundnuts through licensed buying agents did go on throughout the emirate (Alhaji Lassan, a venerable Yardaji resident originally from Kano, settled in the village as a result), the tuberous root does not seem to have marked society in the way it did in Magaria. For one thing, groundnut production was never compulsory in Daura Emirate.

Direct colonial government intervention in Nigerian groundnut production began during World War II, when the British set up the Ministry of Food. The ministry, offering relatively good wartime prices for groundnuts, purchased the entire crop. Full-fledged "national" marketing boards were first established in Nigeria in 1947 but were transformed into multi-crop and regional institutions in 1954. Nineteen-seventy-two was the last year in which the Northern States Marketing Board bought groundnuts in significant quantities; exports and production at the oil mills in Kano have been moribund since the mid-1970s.

In 1977 seven national agricultural commodity boards were established, including the Nigerian Groundnut Board. These boards did not function as intended, however. In 1986, acknowledging that agricultural market-ing had long been outside of effective government control and regulation, Nigeria disbanded all of its commodity marketing boards (Derrick 1986).

Long before the abolition of the marketing boards, and even during the colonial era, groundnut purchasing and marketing in Nigeria was con-ducted in a spirit more of free enterprise than of "participatory mobili-zation." Certainly the local colonial administration in Daura was not as directly identified with the crop's production and marketing as was the administration in Magaria. Groundnut farming for rural Daura peasants was a matter of opportunity, not necessity. Groundnuts are psychologically identified with colonialism in Yekuwa in a way they never were in Yardaji.

Legacies of Colonial Cash Cropping

Although Collins carefully differentiates Nigérien state intervention from antecedent private commercial trade in groundnuts, such a distinction was and is of little significance to the Hausa farmers directly concerned: they do not distinguish between private and state exploitation, any more than they do between the Vichy and de Gaulle regimes (see Collins 1974:67 and Fuglestad 1980:143) or between colonial and postcolonial oppression. They do, however, distinguish between conditions in Nijeriya and those in Faranshi, conditions that transcend the scholar's neat division into "colo-nial" and "postcolonial" eras. Thus when the Profeze brothers, some of the earliest private traders in groundnuts in Magaria district, offered submarket prices or even paid in matches and cloth (Collins 1974:38), this practice was taken more as the French way of doing business than as a capitalist one. (Magaria district farmers responded by hauling their groundnuts to Kano, and were harrassed by the sultan's guards for their pains.) When the French colonial administration in its turn imposed a heavy-handed ground-nut policy and periodically closed the border to groundnut traffic, this practice was perceived in the same light. And when the independent Nigé-rien government established its less than democratic system of groundnut cooperatives, this practice, too, was seen as but a variation on a familiar theme. Collins himself makes this point on at least two occasions:

> That [the] new head of the market was a cooperative agent and not a district officer or a representative of a private company was a fact which, even if realized, had little significance for the farmer selling his groundnuts.

> [T]he post-independence period . . . represents the most recent episode in a long history of State involvement in the market. This State involvement has seldom been motivated solely by the desire to benefit the producer. (Collins 1974:10, 370)

Today, as a result of the Sahelian drought of the 1970s and the catastrophic rosette groundnut virus that has devastated the local variety of seed, commercial groundnut cultivation around Yekuwa has plummeted. The county seat of Magaria, which in the 1950s and 1960s was producing between one-third and one-half of the country's groundnut crop and accounted for half of the country's self-generated revenues (Fuglestad 1983:168–69, 176), is now by comparison almost a ghost town. Those institutions that grew out of the booming groundnut trade have withered along with the peanut plants. The bank, the movie house, the peanut oil factory were all closed by the late 1970s, and remained so in the mid-1980s. Nabieh Chamchoum, the long-time resident Lebanese merchant, has long since left Magaria, and his boutique remains boarded up. The paving of the Nigérien section of the Zinder-Kano road has returned some commercial activity to the town, but it is based on transport of Nigerian products, not home-grown agricultural production. On the Nigerian side of the border, groundnuts have gone the way of most commercial agricultural products since Nigeria's mineral wealth began to pour in. In contemporary Hausaland, petroleum oil overshadows groundnut oil, just as Yardaji's market puts Yekuwa's in the shade. The dynamics of the economy operating throughout Hausaland may have changed, but the colonial patterns that were established there have not.

The Primacy of Food Crops

It should not be forgotten that, whatever the importance of cash crops for the colonial economy, for the Hausa peasants groundnuts have always taken a back seat to millet and sorghum. Though groundnut sales were necessary to pay taxes and for some other expenditures, "the local population was supported by locally grown foodstuffs . . . primary concern was with the production of food" (Thom 1970:153). Now that petroleum and uranium are providing most of Nigeria's and Niger's foreign exchange earnings, cash cropping has lost its former imperative for agricultural producers as well as for national planners. (Food self-sufficiency has also become an objective in the postcolonial state, though much more urgently in Niger than in Nigeria.) Today farmers in Yardaji and Yekuwa alike concentrate primarily on growing millet and sorghum, with groundnut cultivation increasingly marginalized. The peanuts that are grown are just as likely to be used for local consumption (cooking oil, *amaro* [roasted peanuts], *ƙuliƙuli* [small round fried cakes of peanut oil extract]) as for market sale. For those farmers who prefer *wake* (beans), groundnuts may be of only tertiary importance; and some farmers do not grow any at all. In this sense, the peanut in rural Hausaland may be returning to its precolonial place.

Taxation

A talaka (commoner) tends to judge the sarakai (rulers) by the taxes they impose. Taxation was by no means new to the Daura Hausa under the precolonial rulers, and its continuance by the Europeans, albeit in altered form, came as no surprise. Once again, however, we find an appreciable preference between the tax system and rates of the British and those of the French. Hausa peasants along the Niger-Nigeria border perceive a direct continuation of this pattern after independence as well: villagers in Yekuwa still bear the onus of a yearly tax, but those of Yardaji have been relieved of this bane.

Haɓe and Fulani Tax Assessments

Daura under the pre-Fulani Hausa regime seems to have engaged in the most onerous of taxation systems, at least as far as the talakawa were concerned. Although the initial impetus for the Fulani jihad was purification of Islam in Gobir of Hausaland, the Fulani warriors relied on the support of the disgruntled Hausa peasants—disgruntled by oppression of their Hausa overlords—for their victory. Taxation was certainly one of the most oppressive of the burdens the talakawa shouldered.

M. G. Smith (1978:113–20) describes a variety of taxes that were imposed by pre-Fulani Daura. They included *zakka* (a 10 percent grain tax ordained by Muslim law), humushi (the 20 percent levy on war booty), *mairam* (a tax on occupational specialists), *kuɗin garka* (a farm or garden plot tax), *al'ada* (customs or market sales taxes), *kuɗin baki* (a postharvest tax on strangers), *kud'in ciyawa* (a grazing tax on migrant pastoralists), *kud'in kabari* (a cemetery tax), caravan taxes, horse taxes, slave-sale taxes, and even a tax on the fathers of unmarried adolescent girls. In addition, pastoral Fulani had to pay a cattle tax, or jangali, and *karo* was a poll or head tax to which male commoners were liable. (Karo is also known as haraji.) A wide range of tax exemptions (*hurumi*) were permitted, particularly for Muslim priests, royalty, hunters, officials, slaves, women, children, footsoldiers, and the towncrier of the capital. Since currency (in the form of cowrie shells) was limited, taxes usually could be paid in kind. Scarcity of cash was also resolved by the use of *tukurda,* or *gaje,* a cloth currency.

Is it too farfetched to compare the Fulani fiscal reformers of Daura with Ronald Reagan in early 1980s America? Both set out to lower tax rates, simplify the tax system, and reduce the numbers and kinds of tax exemptions allowable. Although several of the older Hausa regime taxes were retained, "the economic organization of the Fulani emirate was simpler and perhaps more 'rational' than that of the Hausa state. . . . By comparison with arrangements in the Hausa successor states, [the] Fulani tax schedule [was] simpler, shorter, and less onerous" (M. G. Smith 1978:271–72). There was a price for such tax reform, however: the Fulani rulers relied more heavily on slave labor than their predecessors did, especially for the cultivation of their foodstuffs and grains.

Colonial Tax Reforms

When sovereignty over Hausaland passed to the Europeans, taxation remained a pillar of the state economy, but with some changes necessitated by colonial rule. For one thing, taxes eventually came to be paid in cash—colonial cash, as injected into the economy in the form of shillings and pounds (in British Hausaland) and francs (in French Hausaland). Cowrie shells gradually disappeared as a medium of exchange, as did lengths of cloth. Second, of all the myriad tax classifications in the Hausa and Fulani revenue systems, only two were ultimately retained: the community-assessed capitation tax (haraji) and the cattle tax (jangali, now applied to all livestock owners, whether Fulani or not). (In British Daura, zakka and some occupational taxes continued until the second decade of the century.) Despite these two taxes endured in common by peasants in both French and British territories, a significant difference has stood out in the recollections and continuing observations of Hausa villagers.

Although it is difficult to convert colonial shilling and franc tax rates into comparable numerical bases for strict quantitative comparision, there is no doubt that the tax burden was heavier on the French side of the border than on the British. (One archival comparison that we do possess suggests that the tax burden for Hausa in Magaria district was five to six times greater than for those in Daura Emirate; see Fuglestad 1983:174 and the corresponding note on 239.) In Yardaji *jangali* implied a tax on bulls and cows; in Yekuwa donkeys, horses, goats, and sheep were taxed as well. The most important difference is that while the British taxed only adult males, the French also taxed women and adolescent boys. (Of course, in Hausa society the male head of household, or *mai gida*, was responsible for the tax liabilities of his spouses and sons.) In the mid-1950s this differential burden was exacerbated when the French lowered the age of taxable boys from fourteen to about eight or nine (Collins 1974:95). The advent of independence brought no change in this pattern; the wives and sons of Hausa peasants were taxed if they lived in Niger, but not if they lived in Nigeria.

The British also used a more progressive method of tax assessment in their rural areas, estimating (by a somewhat complicated formula) the taxable capacity of individual areas and then calculating an "average incidence" for individual taxpayers within those areas. Thus within Daura Emirate (indeed, even within a single district) the tax rate could vary considerably from one village to another, depending on the estimated wealth of the community in question. The French, in classic centralized fashion, imposed a single, unitary tax rate throughout all the villages of Magaria district; no allowance for differential levels of wealth among individuals or communities was made.

In his comparative study of Western Yorubaland in the colonial era, Asiwaju (1976b) highlights the differing modes of tax collection implemented under the British and French. He notes that whereas the British collected taxes through local chiefs and used local treasuries, the French employed administrators and police for this task. A parallel may be drawn in Hausaland, where the British and French again had vastly different ideas about the way taxes should be raised as well as about the amount that should be raised.

Taxation as Colonial Symbolism

Although the system of *beit-al-mal*, or native treasury, was actually inaugurated by C. L. Temple, lieutenant governor of the Northern Region between 1914 and 1917, as early as Lugard's first term as high commissioner of Northern Nigeria (1900–1907; he served again from 1912 to 1914 and, as governor of all Nigeria, from 1914 until 1919) the importance of rationalizing and expanding the existing and indigenous system of taxation was paramount. In fact, the use of such "native treasuries" became one of the cornerstones of Lugardian indirect rule. The Fulani Muslim administrative and fiscal setup was to be retained (with modifications), at least as much to maintain the proper level of respect for "native authorities" as to facilitate the generation of governmental revenue per se. As a British colonial document states:

> If the Fulani were to be maintained in their position as rulers . . . it devolved upon the Government to assist them to levy the taxes they could no longer levy themselves [as a result of the advent of the British]. . . .
>
> [I]t is important to recollect that it was not undertaken merely—or even primarily—for the sake of creating revenue, but resulted inevitably as a part of the task involved by the assumption of administrative control in the country, and was the necessary result of supporting the system of native rulers in the Protectorate, without whom it would be impossible to administer the country effectively. (Quoted in Whitaker 1970:f42)

Tax collection was the direct responsibility of the emir and his administration, with substantial amounts of the revenues so collected (up to 50 percent) allocated to the emirate government. Salaries for traditional rulers and their retainers and counselors were thus fixed and legitimated by the British philosophy and mode of beit-al-mal, with the corresponding prestige and status of the collectors (subordinates of the emir, now resident in the rural communities they monitored) thus maintained.

Across the border there was no like concern for the symbolic value of "native" methods and institutions of tax collection. Taxation in French Hausaland was fundamentally a question of raising revenue for the colonial government, and little solicitude was shown for the reaction of the peasantry or possible loss of status for traditional rulers. These rulers were treated as little more than tax agents of the French. The French "system" of tax collection in fact replicated more closely the reality of precolonial methods of taxation than the British, since, from a village perspective, it still rested on direct extortion from the peasantry through the jakada, that intermediate tax-collecting agent of the emir whose position had been abolished by the British. None of the "rationalization" of the indigenous method of taxation which the British attempted to encourage, or a progressive policy of individual taxation, was considered by the French. Once the taxes had been collected, the French decided what to do with them; in French Magaria there was no "native treasury" supporting a "native administration" that would evolve into an embryonic local government, as there was in British Daura.

Daura and Magaria

M. G. Smith points to the years 1954 to 1958 as a time of particularly steep rises in the rate of taxation for the inhabitants of Daura Emirate. He associates this development with "equivalent increases in the emirate's taxable capacity, which was associated with upward movements in the world market for the prices of North Nigerian exports, cotton, groundnuts, hides, and skins" (1978:353). Collins, in contrast, focuses on the 1960s and 1970s—that is, the years after independence—as the period of particularly heavy tax burdens for the Hausa of Magaria. These increases were not, as in the case of Daura, commensurate with an "equivalent increase" in the general prosperity of the region, which would make such added taxes tolerable; tax increases could just as easily come in periods of lowered prices and yields of the cash crop. In fact, Collins claims that many farmers spent their entire earnings from groundnut sales just to acquit themselves of their tax obligations. It was in this period (particularly the 1960s), moreover, that the necessity to pay taxes became the key factor in groundnut production in the district.

The heavy obligation endured by the peasants in French territory is a consistent theme in Fuglestad's history of colonial Niger. "[T]he 'new' economic policy inaugurated by the French . . . consisted simply of imposing heavier taxes" (1983:83). The poll tax seems to have doubled in one year (1914–15) and tripled in the decade from 1906 to 1916. It doubled again in the second half of the 1920s, rose 60 percent during the Vichy regime (with further increases after the Gaullists assumed power), and skyrocketed sevenfold between 1946 and 1951. Not only was the postwar tax rate higher in Niger than elsewhere in French West Africa, but even within Niger tax rates were consistently and significantly higher in Hausaland than elsewhere in the colony. Hardship and migration were the results, particularly when heavy tax obligations coincided (as they frequently did) with famine. Although differential tax rates in British Hausaland did provoke some internal migration, it hardly generated the demographic shocks that it did in French Hausaland; the relative tax burden for the Hausa in Nigeria was minimal in terms of both rate and methods of extraction. Nowhere were these differences more acutely acknowledged than along the border, where neighboring villages would experience vastly different tax burdens, depending on whose colonial jurisdiction they fell under.

With the arrival of the military regime in Niger in 1974, Hausa villagers, in Yekuwa as elsewhere, were relieved to discover that the government was to reduce the taxes they had to pay considerably. Jangali (cattle tax) was eliminated outright, and haraji (head tax) was reduced by more than a third. Thus from a 1974 tax burden of 1,350 CFA (or the equivalent of 4 naira and 5 kobo at prevailing exchange rates), the villagers in Yekuwa a decade later had to pay only 350 CFA (the equivalent of 1 naira and 40 kobo). By 1986 this amount was up to 750 CFA. And, the villagers are quick to point out, very old people, lepers, the blind, and the mentally ill are still exempted. (Fulani in outlying settlements reported that their tax came to 400 CFA in 1984. Unfortunately, it was not possible to determine the reason for the 50-CFA discrepancy.)

With taxes drastically reduced in today's Niger, it would appear that the thesis I have been arguing—that the greater fiscal burden borne in French Hausaland, as represented by Yekuwa, has been continued into the postcolonial era—is disproved. When we return to Yardaji for comparison, however, we discover that the thesis does stand. For even though villagers in Yekuwa pay a fraction of the taxes they did in the past, they are even more conscious that their neighbors in Yardaji carry a lesser burden.

In federalist Nigeria, which has no national income tax, tax policies are enacted by the individual states. In 1979 the populist People's Redemption Party (PRP), controlling the Kaduna State Assembly, voted to do away with haraji. (Jangali had already been abolished by 1975, under the military government.) This popular move was a campaign issue even four years later, during the 1983 elections for state and national office. Yekuwa residents may have reservations about the restoration of civilian politics in their own country, but at the same time they certainly are jealous of people who live in a country capable of doing away with one of the most onerous "civic" duties imposed on the talakawa from time immemorial—the poll tax, whether in the form of grain, cowrie shells, or legal tender. The villagers view this important distinction less as a reflection of differential forms of authority—a Supreme Military Council in Niger, a state assembly in Nigeria—than as the logical legacy of differential colonial taxation policies in the two major portions of a divided Hausaland.[7]

---

[7] After the 1984 coup, Nigeria's military leaders attempted to make up for some of the civilian government's fiscal laxity. A Kaduna State development levy was imposed, for instance, obliging Yardaji heads of household to pay 20 (later reduced to 15) naira. These changes in tax structure still put Yardaji at an advantage vis-à-vis Yekuwa, for women and children were still taxed only on the other side of the border. At the same time, residents of Yekuwa were also obliged to pay an additional levy of about 8 naira and 50 kobo for the purchase of a

Currency

"Our five-franc bill is not in circulation except during the few months preceding the payment of taxes. . . . In four-fifths of the subdivision all transactions, miscellaneous payments, dowries, etc. . . . are conducted in English shillings." Substitute "naira" for "English shillings" and "CFA" for "francs" and this observation, made by the commandant of Magaria in 1926, could be repeated today.

Naira in Nigérien Borderlands

The Nigerian naira is the only significant medium of exchange in Yekuwa. Although for years it was technically illegal to carry more than 50 naira[8] into or out of Nigeria, naira and kobo traversed the boundary with as little control as the people themselves. (It is doubtful, moreover, if any villagers have ever heard of the law restricting the import or export of Nigeria's currency. Even at the nearby official border crossings of Babban-Mutum and Zango, only non-Africans are asked to fill out currency declaration forms.) CFA francs, in both bills and coins, are accepted in both Yekuwa and Yardaji, but are treated as a foreign currency in both villages.

Yekuwa is hardly exceptional in belonging to the naira currency zone. Thom (1970:198) has sketched a map in which he shows Nigérien villages within a 10-to-50-mile range from the Nigerian border as belonging to Nigeria's currency zone. Thom gives a twofold explanation for this deep penetration of Nigeria's currency into Nigérien territory: (1) Rural farmers need Nigerian naira to purchase items in Nigerian border markets (which are better stocked and more dynamic than Nigérien border markets) and (2) the exchange rate favors the holding of Nigerian currency. Payment in CFA in Nigerian border markets results in a dual loss, from both fluctuation of the exchange rate and reduced purchasing power. Inasmuch as the accepted rate of exchange is the same in Yekuwa and Yardaji, and the naira is infamously beset by instability and fluctuations in value (see Figure 3), this second explanation needs to be reexamined. It also needs to be pointed out that the CFA, unlike the naira, is a "hard" and internationally convertible currency; it is more likely to be sought, according to standard norms of economic analysis, than the more volatile and less valuable naira. Instead,

---

district ambulance that had not yet even serviced the village. (In 1986, 1,000 CFA were worth 12 naira, according to the local exchange rate.)

[8] Later reduced to 20 naira, before exchange controls were entirely revamped.

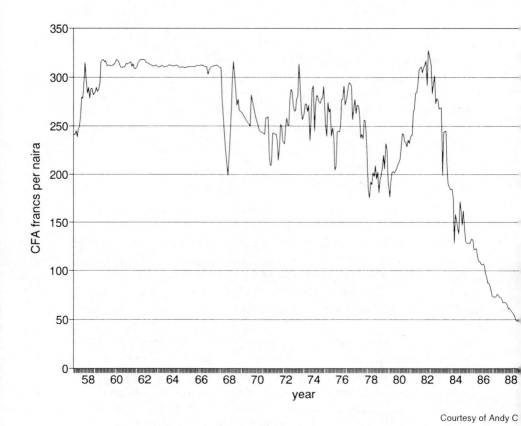

Courtesy of Andy C

Figure 3. Black-market currency exchange rate, naira vs. CFA franc, 1957–1989

at least at the village level, CFA have little utility (except in Yekuwa during the relatively short tax season). It would appear, then, that the Nigerian economy is so far superior in scope and accessibility in the border areas that it is more advantageous to hold Nigerian currency than "harder" CFA. Thus in Yekuwa the Nigerian economy overshadows both the Nigérien economy and international currency markets; as a result the naira "pushes out" the CFA and renders it superfluous (again, except for paying taxes). As the Magaria commandant put it in 1926, two currencies are operating in the district: "administrative money, which is French money, [and] commercial money, which is English money." Inasmuch as the marketplace is far more prominent than governmental administration (on either side of the border), the naira—that is, the "commercial money"—normally functions as legal tender in Yekuwa no less than in Yardaji.

CFA as a "Seasonal" Currency

In a relevant footnote, Collins (1974:71–72) observes that it was only with the introduction of the Vichy regime that the residents of Magaria district *had* to pay their taxes in French francs; he thereby implies that French authorities did accept payment in shillings before World War II. Fuglestad (1983:83, 102) notes, however, that between 1916 and 1920 the colonial administrators in Niger first refused to accept payment in anything but francs; Stephen Baier (1980:107) dates the requirement of tax payment in French currency to 1910. Regardless of the effective starting date, the requirement that the villagers in Yekuwa today acquit themselves of their fiscal duty not in the currency of their everyday transactions but in a de facto "foreign" currency is by no means a new problem, but rather an economic exigency inherited from the colonial past.

Village Views of Money

The physical, no less than the political, state of the currency is a problem shared by villagers in both Yekuwa and Yardaji. Paper banknotes—that is, naira notes—are generally in various stages of decomposition, and often remain in tenacious circulation by virtue of adhesive tape and the goodwill of the potential seller. Crisp, new notes may not carry any greater monetary value than ordinary drooping bills, but they do possess a certain prestige and confer on their bearer a measure of almost jocular respect.

In comparing the economic situations of the two countries, Yardaji's town crier explained Niger's relative poverty by the fact that the country has no "moneymaking engines." Whether he meant this in the literal or figurative sense is not clear. In any event, the perception that Nigérien poverty is linked, at least in part, to the lack of *kud'in Faranshi* (that is, "French money," or CFA currency) in Niger itself forms part of the local understanding of economic reality in this area of Hausaland.

In April 1984, Nigeria, in an effort to clamp down on illegal foreign holdings of naira, decided to undergo a currency conversion. Within a relatively short time, all Nigerians had to surrender their old banknotes and exchange them for new naira notes. This was some months after I had left Africa, but reports and letters indicate the confusion and hardship that the currency conversion entailed for villagers on both sides of the border. The following extracts are from a letter from a secondary school teacher, a native and resident of Yardaji. (Minor stylistic changes have been made for the sake of brevity and clarity):

Idi and Mallam Ja [two butchers in Yardaji] were coming back from Zango. They went there to deposit their old currencies [2,500 naira] but they found that the place was [too] congested. So they joined a motor [car] which was going to Yardaje; they were heading for Rogogo, which was another centre for the change. They stopped at Yardaje-Walewa junction, to wait for another vehicle to convey them to Rogogo.

All of a sudden, the patrol team [from the Zango border post] who were walking to Yardaje on foot saw them. The team came over to Idi and Mallam Ja, who were waiting to get a bus. They were questioned, and they answered—maybe [the patrol team] was not satisfied with their answers, or they mistook them for Nigériens. They beat them mercilessly and they gave them *gwale-gwale* [corporal punishment]. . . . [One of them] dipped his hands into their pockets and took away their money. . . . Up till now their money has not been refunded.

The letter then goes on to discuss the repercussions of the naira currency conversion for the surrounding communities across the border in Niger: "The horse races at Tumfafi stopped immediately after the Nigerian Govt. announced the change in her currency. You know that they are using the currency. The change has affected many Nigériens; they lost thousands of Naira."

Trade and Smuggling

The trade that is carried on between Yardaji and Yekuwa, despite the attempts by their respective governments to control or prevent it, is, in the eyes of the villagers, the single most significant fact arising from the existence of the border. It also colors their perceptions of their respective countries. The general theme is the one that has prevailed throughout the century: the rather severe policies and methods of the authorities in Faranshi to curb unregistered (and untaxed) cross-border trade, and the more lackadaisacal or laissez-faire approach taken by their counterparts in Nigeria. Once again, the harsher fate meted out to smugglers in "French territory"—beatings and seizure of goods—recalls what Asiwaju has recorded in the case of Western Yorubaland in the colonial era (1976:196). And once again, the distinction is as valid for our Hausa villagers after independence as it was before.

For Yekuwa residents, Yardaji represents a gateway to Nigeria and the Nigerian economy. It is also the source of many of the manufactured and processed goods that have become staples of village life today: canned fish, bread, flour for *taliya* (pasta), eating bowls and utensils, earthenware, cloth, flashlights, bulbs, batteries, plastic sandals and shoes, kerosene, bath soap, laundry soap, perfume, candies and bubble gum, matches, cigarettes, and so on. The only unprocessed raw good that is brought from Nigeria is *goro*—the kola nut—which is one of the few imports from outside Hausaland that remain from the colonial and precolonial days.[9]

Not all of these items are produced in Nigeria, and only two (bread and clay pots) are fabricated in Yardaji. The rest are imports, usually from East Asia. Virtually all these goods have to be procured in Kano, and are then transported, usually on market day, by either bus or truck to Daura, Zango, or Yardaji. Traditional fatauci, or long-distance trading by donkey or camel, is only a nostalgic memory in Yardaji and Yekuwa alike.[10] Some 'yan Yekuwa may go as far as Kano to purchase goods, but most procure them from small-scale retailers in Yardaji.

Intervillage Trade

It is the transport of these goods from Yardaji to Yekuwa that presents the greatest problems. There are only two ways to transport goods from Yardaji and Yekuwa: on the back of a donkey and on one's own head. This mode of transport not only is physically taxing and time-consuming but severely restricts the amount of merchandise that any individual trader can transport. It is for this reason that Alhaji Aminu of Yekuwa claims that the distance between Yardaji and Yekuwa (eight miles) is greater than the distance between Yardaji and Kano (ninety miles): whereas the former is a two-hour journey, the latter trip takes barely an hour and a half, and is much easier besides.

The real difficulty, however, is not walking the sixteen-mile round trip across the soft sand and under the hot sun, or in the middle of the night, often with a heavy load on one's head; the problem is to elude capture. *Sojoji* (Nigérien customs agents) may be lying in wait, perhaps in a jeep, perhaps on horseback, to seize the contraband that traders from Yekuwa are carrying. Villagers call this *kwatchewa*, which may be defined as either "taking by force" or "plundering property" (Abraham 1958:574). The goods are confiscated and the offender may be beaten. If the trader has been portering by donkey, the beast is usually seized as well. Both goods and pack animal are then hauled off to Magaria, where they are sold at public

9 See Cohen 1969 on the kola-livestock trade conducted by the Hausa in Ibadan.
10 See Hill 1972:195, 245–46 on the decline of classical fatauci in Hausaland.

auction. The goods are usually bought by wealthy Magarian merchants, who then resell them in the local market; the donkeys are generally bought back by their original owners, for whom training a new donkey is a task to be avoided. This cat-and-mouse game is played and replayed with tragicomic predictability: in Magaria on auction day, confiscating sojoji are said to greet their erstwhile quarry and to send the hapless villagers off with the traditional *sai anjima*—"Until next time." For such reasons the villagers say that "gwamnati Nijer, ba ta jin tausayin talakawa"—the government of Niger feels no pity for the peasants.

The risk of doing business this way is naturally reflected in the pricing of goods for sale in Yekuwa. A tin of Japanese sardines or mackerel, for example, cost 35 kobo in Kano in 1983. It would be sold in Yardaji for 40 kobo—a modest markup of 5 kobo, reflecting both transport costs and profit. In Yekuwa the tin of fish would be sold for 50 kobo. A Yekuwa trader justifies the price in this way:

> From Kano, goods are brought to Yardaji by truck. To bring merchandise to Yekuwa, it must be brought by foot [carried on the head] through the bush. For that you have to pay two or three kobo in transport costs. And then, if the soji catch the carriers, it is a total loss, since they confiscate it completely. And they may beat the people they catch! So seven kobo profit is not much, when you consider much of it may be just seized [*kwache*].

Economists refer to the added cost arising from the probability that some goods will be confiscated as "risk premium."[11] But when asked what portion of the final price is a reflection of the beatings that transporters might have to bear ("Mi ne ni kudin kashe?"), villagers just laughed. Intervillage traders fatalistically accept these borderland beatings as just another occupational hazard.

It is a risky enterprise, the trader went on, but there is no viable alternative to doing business in this way. He himself opened a small shop (*kanti*) in the village, but his merchandise is subject to confiscation should the soldiers or customs agents discover it. He could not afford the 50,000 CFA required for the permit to establish his business legally. Then there is a yearly tax, and all merchandise would have to be "weighed" (that is, assessed) and a duty paid.

The chase goes in the opposite direction as well, from Yekuwa to Yardaji.

---

[11] See Cook et al. 1988:21 for a calculation of the risk premium for steer smuggled across the Niger-Nigeria border.

Here the financial risk of being caught is even greater, for the merchandise transported, especially livestock, is more valuable.

Grain and Livestock Flows

Yekuwa is a kind of funnel through which surplus primary goods in Niger—particularly grains and livestock—are collected and sent on to Yardaji. Goats, sheep, and cattle are smuggled across the border, often at night, to escape detection by Nigérien patrols. The livestock may be sold in Yardaji's marketplace or transported farther for sale in a more lucrative, distant market. The price of a well-fed goat in Yekuwa in 1983, for example, ranged from 20 to 24 naira. In Yardaji it would be sold for around 30 naira, in Kano for 40 naira. Yet the risks of the trade are high. On June 28, 1983, forty-one goats, six of them from Yekuwa, were seized by mounted Nigérien customs officers as they were being brought to the Yardaji market. (The non-Yekuwa goats had been brought quite some distance, from towns and villages on the Zinder road.) Villagers report that even if the herds and their drivers enter Nigerian territory, Nigérien soldiers will follow them and chase them back onto Nigérien soil. Only if they are already in sight of Yardaji will they refrain from doing so: people are prepared to fly out of the Yardaji market to prevent such confiscations so close to their village.[12]

Cattle are particularly valuable. Large trucks arrive in Yardaji on market day to await the arrival of cattle from the other side of the border. The animals are then bought and transported to Danbatta or Kano or even directly to Lagos, where they are resold to butchers, who then slaughter them for the meat market. The markup at each transaction can be considerable—but the loss, if the animals are captured en route before reaching Yardaji, is total.

Grains, too—millet, sorghum, and beans—are part of the *simugal*. (The word, adapted from "smuggle," has entered the Hausa lexicon on both sides of the border.) Prices fetched for such foodstuffs are better in Yardaji than in Yekuwa, but two other considerations account for this transfer: In local markets in and around Yekuwa, no buyer can afford to purchase an entire *buhu*—that is, a large sack—of grain. Selling in volume in Yardaji is far preferable to selling in small quantities in Faranshi. Second, although the Nigérien government, through its cooperative agencies, does offer a good price for these products, agents buy only once or twice a season, and the burden of transporting the grains all the way to Magaria (about

---

[12] In 1980 Yardaji villagers reputedly beat up a Nigérien *douanier* and confiscated his rifle.

twenty miles away) has to be borne by the farmers. Convenience, no less than profit, accounts for these transborder grain sales.

Smuggling as a Vocation

The term "smuggling" has so many negative connotations that some caution must be exercised in applying it to the trade between Yardaji and Yekuwa. The illegality of the traffic is incidental, an alternative choice unavailable. Even if there were no price differentials, this "illegal" trade between the two villages would probably still go on, for Yardaji represents the only local market within walking distance of Yekuwa. From a village perspective, the efforts undertaken by the sarakai (rulers) to stop trade (and to punish the traders caught) not only demonstrates a lack of "pity" but runs counter to the normal, healthy, and ancient Hausa ethos of free trade.

This challenge to the Hausa ethos of free trade of course predates the establishment of Nigerian and Nigérien customs laws. Efforts to control transborder trade were an early and integral part of the colonial experience. The products involved may have changed as the economy evolved, but the struggle between trader and authority has become a virtual tradition. And as before, the trader usually prevails. As D. Hollis, reporting on Daura Division for the year 1911, wrote:

> Smuggling is common and with ordinary care and luck a smuggler can usually hope to avoid capture. . . . Smuggling is commonly practiced by men carrying small loads of salt or potash, who can easily cross the border by nights and, travelling through the bush, reach . . . some . . . market south of the Customs Stations in time to sell there [sic] goods there. . . . The smugglers of this kind who have been caught, have usually been caught by accident. (NAK/KATPROF 465)

Villagers know that it is "wrong" to engage in cross-border trade, in the sense that if they are caught, they will be punished. It is a question of submitting to iko (power and authority) but not really laifi (engaging in an activity that carries social opprobrium). People in Yekuwa are aware of the government's reasoning in these matters, even if it is "unreasonable" in its personal impact. The wealth of Niger, it is said, resides in that country's livestock. The government therefore tries to keep this wealth in the country; the flow of livestock to Nigeria is thought to impoverish Niger. It is not for want of patriotism that the people of Yekuwa nevertheless sell their surplus stock in Nigeria, but for lack of any viable alternative. Yardaji, as a window on Nigeria, does represent higher selling prices for primary goods, but more important, it is a nearby market where such goods *can* be sold, and where both "luxury" and other processed goods are available. Yardaji is thus a classic entrepôt, a center of exchange for primary goods from Niger and both imported and manufactured (consumer) items from the more industrially advanced economy of Nigeria.

Pattern Variations

Large-scale commoditization of cash crops, particularly groundnuts, constitutes an important exception to the local pattern whereby agricultural goods flow to Nigeria and customs patrolling is more intense and more effective on the Nigérien side of the boundary. Groundnuts have periodically brought higher prices in Niger than in Nigeria, and trade in them has shifted accordingly (Baier 1980:210; Collins 1976:264–70; Thom 1970:154). In the late 1960s surveillance by the Nigerian Federal Customs Service may have been marginally more effective than that of the Nigérien Service des Douanes.[13] From January 1984 to March 1986—the period after the collapse of Nigeria's Second Republic, when the country's land border with Niger were closed—patrolling on the Nigerian side was also exceptionally intense. The border was originally sealed to prevent political fugitives from fleeing, but was kept closed to crack down on cross-border smuggling.

Overall, however, the pattern of trade across a divided colonial Hausaland—once the trans-Saharan caravans had been superseded—continues between Yekuwa and Yardaji today: grains (especially millet) and livestock move clandestinely from Faranshi to Nijeriya, and the authorities in Niger move more aggressively to curb it.[14] Whereas Nigerian officials ply the major roads near and leading to the boundary, the Nigériens patrol the bush. Villagers still lament that the "French" are hurting local trade.

Markets

In view of the economic differences between the two villages, it is hardly surprising to discover that Yardaji's weekly market is substantially larger, more active, and more diverse than Yekuwa's. Perhaps nowhere else can the relative *arziki* (wealth) of the Nigerian Hausa village be seen so clearly.

[13] This switch is indirectly intimated by Thom (1970:160–61, 165–69). Thom's more basic point is the general weakness of both systems of border control.

[14] It has been contended that in the postcolonial era the aggregate net flow of grains has been from Nigeria to Niger. See Republic of Niger and USAID 1983.

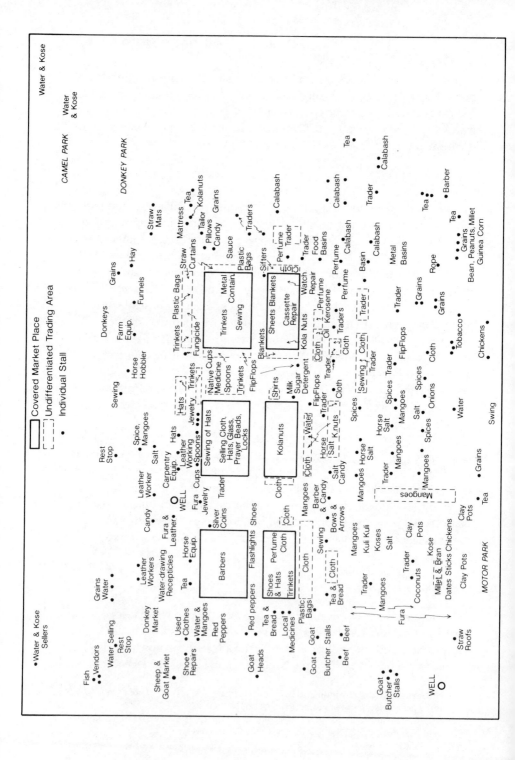

Wednesday—market day—is a bustling time in Yardaji. Trucks and passenger buses and wagons descend upon the village, bringing people and wares from Zango, Daura, and other outlying localities. Traders set themselves up at their habitual locations, either under straw-roofed open stands or at the market's concrete-and-aluminum display area (Map 9). A whole range of goods is for sale, many of them Nigerian manufactures, from enamel cooking pots to lengths of printed cloth. An interesting variety of food items is displayed, such as dates, coconuts, and granular salt. Naturally, large numbers of villagers make the trek from Yekuwa, almost all of them by foot.

The Monday market in Yekuwa, by contrast, is almost lugubrious. In terms of overall numbers of hawkers, Yekuwa's market is less than half as large as Yardaji's (see Table 7). In contrast to the diversity of consumer and household items sold in Yardaji's market (including sheets, blankets, and mattresses, jewelry and perfume, sewing and carpentry supplies), Yekuwa's offerings are more heavily weighted toward locally grown and prepared food products—fried bean and millet snacks, dried pepper, spices for locust-bean cakes. The most important item that can be traded in Hausaland, grain (millet and sorghum), finds a thriving commercial outlet in Yardaji but not in Yekuwa. Yekuwa's "comparative advantage" is reflected in those few sale items that are not so readily available in Yardaji: cattle, cassava, raw sugar cane, and fresh milk (brought and sold by pastoral Fulani women). Whereas the typical peddler in Yekuwa deals mostly in *koli* (small wares such as jewelry, incense, cosmetics, beads, charms, sewing materials, garlic), Yardaji's retailers deal in *tireda* (laundry soap, body oil, vaseline, razor blades, batteries, processed sauce, sugar, tea, candy, biscuits). Even Nigérien customs agents distinguish: tireda is confiscated, koli is not. The scale of commercial activity is significantly smaller in the Yekuwa market than in Yardaji.

Yekuwa's *kasuwa* (Map 10) is a "bush" market. It is attended by local villagers, outlying Fulani, and visitors from smaller settlements nearby, but not from as far away as people are willing to travel to get to Yardaji's market. No motorized vehicles bring either wares or clients; all travel to the Yekuwa market is by foot, horse, donkey, or camel.[15] Some hardy traders make the trek from Yardaji to do business, but nowhere near as many as go from Yekuwa to the Yardaji market.

The main impediment, which all frankly acknowledge, is fear of get-

[15] This was in 1983–84. By 1986 a Yekuwa vehicle had begun to take passengers—but not goods—between the village markets.

Table 7. Number of stalls offering goods and services at weekly markets of Yardaji and Yekuwa, 1986

Goods/service	Yardaji[a]	Yekuwa[b]
General trading	47	20
Trinkets	27	12
Grains	90	5
Chaff	15	—
Beans	10	—
Spices/sauces/pasta	74	66
Salt	12	9
Millet cake and balls, fried snacks and gruel	101	29
Boiled cassava	24	45
Roasted groundnuts	10	—
Kola nuts	4	3
Sugar cane and dates	—	3
Popcorn	—	1
Candy	—	1
Eggs	1	—
Rice	1	—
Oil	1	—
Chickens	18	1
Coconuts	2	—
Oranges	1	—
Guavas	1	—
Water	28	8
Tea and bread (includes 1 tailor)	11	4
Honey	—	1
Tobacco (2 also kola nuts)	9	6
Potash	1	7
Henna	—	7
Clay jugs	22	4
Calabashes	—	4
Metal bowls	6	—
Spoons	—	1
Rope	7	4
Fencing	3	—
Cover mats (*faifai*)	1	—
Donkeys	15	4
Goats	24	6
Cattle	—	6
Meat	30	8
Barbering	9	12
Tailoring	5	4
Fare collection (bus)	12	—
Motorcycle rental	4	—
Bicycle rental	4	—
Horse equipment	—	1
Cloth	16	4
Ready-made clothes	4	—
Secondhand clothes	1	4

Table 7 (Continued)

Goods/service	Yardaji[a]	Yekuwa[b]
Leather goods	12	—
Leatherwork	6	7
Shoe repair	9	3
Watch repair	5	3
Beds (metal spring)	4	—
Mats	4	7
Blankets and mats	3	—
Kerosene	11	5
Plastic bags	9	—
Flowers	4	—
Perfume	3	—
Medicine	2	—
Viewmaster	1	—
Swing (for children) and card gambling (for adults)	1	—
All goods and services	725	315

[a]September 10.
[b]August 11.

ting caught by Nigérien soji: only petty traders from Yardaji are willing to take the risk. Other residents of Yardaji will visit Yekuwa on market day, but more for amusement and distraction—to visit friends, see relatives, meet girls—than for their livelihood. Few of the household and processed goods for sale on Wednesday in Yardaji are available in the Yekuwa market. Just being in the Yekuwa market can be an exhausting experience: whereas shade trees cover much of the Yardaji market, that of Yekuwa enjoys no such protection from the sun.

These differences between the Yardaji and Yekuwa markets fit in neatly with Thom's four-class division of Hausa *kasuwoyi* (markets): city, border, route, and bush (Thom 1970:193–96). According to this classification, Yardaji is a border market: a market "located on the fringe of the two opposing political and economic systems [that] exert[s] an influence such that [it] attract[s] a considerable cross-boundary movement." As throughout Hausaland, a Nigerian border market is expected to "exert a greater attraction than [one] in Niger" (194).

Although geographically it is near the border, Yekuwa's kasuwa has little of the commercial significance of a true border market. Yekuwa thus has to be regarded as a bush market, "an outlet for locally produced products within a limited tributary area" (ibid., 196). The relative importance of the two markets particularly irks those Yekuwa traders who claim that "in the

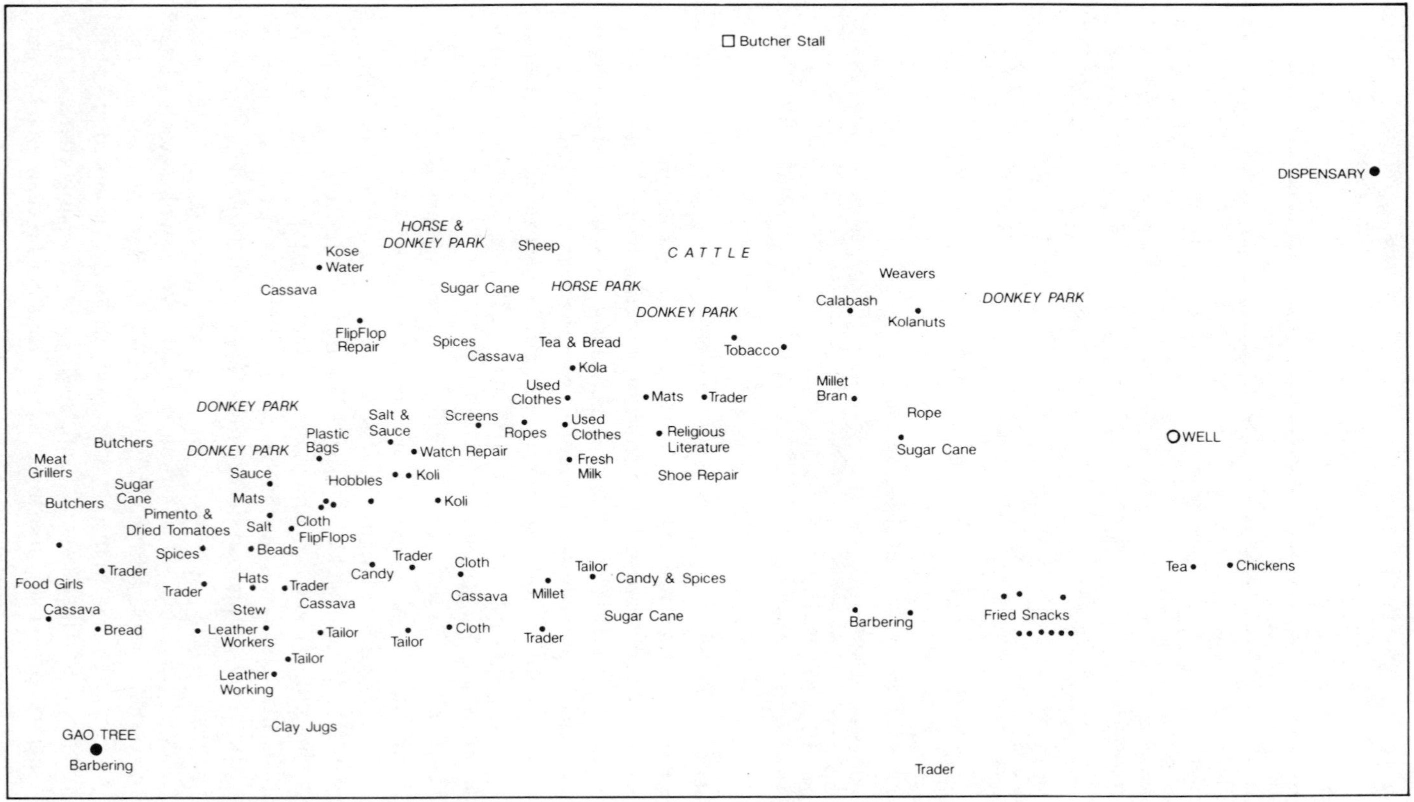

DISPENSARY ●

○ WELL

□ Butcher Stall

Tea ●   ● Chickens

DONKEY PARK

Weavers

Calabash ●   ● Kolanuts

Millet
Bran ●   ● Rope
         ● Sugar Cane

● ● ●
Fried Snacks ● ● ●
● ●

Barbering ●

Trader

C A T T L E

HORSE PARK

Sheep

DONKEY PARK

Tobacco ●

● Mats   ● Trader

● Religious
  Literature

Shoe Repair

Candy & Spices

Tailor ●
       Sugar Cane

● Millet

● Trader

HORSE &
DONKEY PARK

Sugar Cane

Kose
● Water

Cassava

Tea & Bread
● Kola

Spices ●
Cassava

Used
Clothes ●

Used
● Clothes
● Fresh
  Milk

Screens ●
● Ropes

● Watch Repair

● Koli

Cloth ●
Cassava ●
       ● Cloth

Tailor ●

FlipFlop
Repair ●

Plastic
Bags ●

Salt &
● Sauce

Hobbles ● ● Koli

● Cloth
● FlipFlops
Trader ●
Candy ●
      ● Trader
Cassava ●

Tailor ●

DONKEY PARK

DONKEY PARK

Sauce ●
Mats ●
Salt ●
● Beads

Hats ● ● Trader

Stew ●
Leather ●
Workers

Leather
Working

Clay Jugs

Pimento &
Dried Tomatoes ●

Spices ●
Trader ●

Butchers

Sugar
Cane ●

Butchers

Meat
Grillers

Food Girls ●
Cassava ●
         ● Bread

● Trader

GAO TREE
Barbering ●

Map 10. Yekuwa market

The marketplace in Yardaji on the weekly market day.

Yekuwa's weekly market.

old days" Yekuwa was by far the dominant market and settlement in the region, surpassing not only Yardaji but Magaria as well. With the choice of Magaria as the site of the French administrative headquarters in the 1930s and the establishment there of its "mandatory market," where farmers had to sell produce to pay taxes (Andy Cook, personal communication), Yekuwa lost its commercial profile. The subsequent road linkages to Zinder and Nigeria only put the final nail in the coffin of Yekuwa's economic paramountcy. Such an interpretation is consistent with other findings in the Hausa borderland region: Maradi's market, because of French political and economic decisions, came to replace that of nearby Tarné (which eventually disappeared); and Matameye, for similar reasons, eventually took over from Kantché (Thom 1970:146–48). Yardaji profited from both Yekuwa's eclipse by Magaria and its location along the boundary with Niger. As between Yekuwa and Yardaji, the market becomes a metaphor for the evolutionary paths taken by the rural Hausa economy under the British and the French, and under Nigeria and Niger.

Food and Agriculture

Though most village Hausa aspire to become traders, it should not be forgotten that the primary occupation of all is farming. For *noma,* in Yardaji no less than Yekuwa, is not only the basis of the village economy but the very key to individual prosperity, existence, and survival. Trading (or smuggling) may characterize the economic relationship between the two villages, but farming is the central activity and focus of everyone within each village.

Millet and sorghum are the basic foodstuffs.[16] The similarity of basic diet in the two villages reflects the similarity in food cropping. The seeds of the grain are pounded, by mortar and pestle, by women and girls. (The bulk of a woman's life in rural Hausaland seems to be spent on this incessant pounding, pounding, pounding. It is the sound to which one awakes in the morning and the last sound one hears before dusk. There is one gasoline-powered grinding machine in each village, but most grinding is still done by hand.)[17] The pounded millet, transformed into a doughlike texture, is

[16] Of the two, *hatsi* (millet) is the grain of choice in Yardaji and Yekuwa. Hill (1972:329) found *dawa* (sorghum) to be preferred in Batagarawa.

[17] In the summer of 1986 Yekuwa had a second grinding machine and Yardaji had a total of five. Two of them, however, had broken down.

prepared in one of two ways. Tuwo is an oval loaf of pounded millet that has been cooked in boiling water and then served with a sauce (*miya*) made of local condiments (e.g., okra, pimento, dried baobab leaves, salt, locust-bean seeds, goat meat). Fura is a dish of small balls of pounded millet, served in a bowl of sour milk (*nono*). This diet may be supplemented by dishes of beans or meat skewers, but by and large a Hausa diet is a constant rotation of tuwo and fura.

It is extremely difficult to quantify (and therefore to compare) the levels of agricultural production, and more particularly farmers' food reserves, in Hausa villages: "As no one save the owner, or sometimes his son, may look inside a granary, it [is] unfortunately impossible to estimate granary stocks, fundamental though this matter of storage is to any understanding of the working of this economy" (Hill 1972:20). Tool technology does not vary from one village to the next (small short- and long-handled hoes). Villagers identify only one variable that makes a crucial difference in agricultural production, a variable as important to agricultural economists as it is to peasants: the availability and application of fertilizer. Here an important distinction does prevail: *takin zamani* ("modern" or industrial fertilizer) is cheaper and more prevalent in Nigeria than in Niger. A sack of fertilizer can be bought in virtually any Nigerian town for 2 naira and 50 kobo. In Niger, only in certain designated centers (in the Yekuwa vicinity, Magaria, Satamawa) can this crucial factor of production be found—and the price is 2,250 CFA, or 12 naira.[18] In a graphic illustration of the difference in life on the two sides of the border, a villager from Yardaji pointed out the invisible line that cuts between the two countries and also serves to divide two farms. On the Yardaji side of the line the millet stalks were taller, more robust, and obviously healthier than those a few feet away on the Faranshi side. The reason, according to the villager, was simple: The "French" farmer could not afford (or obtain) the fertilizer that the Nigerian farmer was using.

The diet of the inhabitants of Yekuwa and Yardaji is not purely a function of village production, but reflects integration with broader regional and even national agricultural economies. This is more the case with Yardaji than with Yekuwa. In season, certain tropical fruits that are not grown in the region of Daura—guavas, mangoes, oranges, bananas, coconuts, pineapples—are hawked by young girls from baskets on their heads (*talla-talla*) or by petty merchants who have brought them from outside markets.

---

[18] By 1986 inflation had taken its toll on this commodity as well: the same bag of fertilizer cost 10 naira in Yardaji and 3,000 CFA (or 36 naira) in Satamawa.

Because of their perishability and the problems of transport, the residents of Yekuwa rarely see these delights.[19]

The availability of two other food products, bread and rice, reflects not only changes in the traditional Hausa diet of tuwo and fura but differential access to wider national and international food markets. The introduction of bleached-flour bread—an alien and not especially nutritious substance—is a phenomenon known throughout the developing world. In the Western Sahel, rice, too—some of it grown in Africa but most of it imported—has also revolutionized the diet of many people. Though *shinkafa* (rice) in no way has supplanted millet, it is quite popular in Yardaji, and is cooked and sold (with beans or meat) as a luncheon alternative. Bread is even more popular and more readily available, since it is produced in the village itself (from imported flour) in a bakery adjacent to the marketplace. (The Yardaji bakery began to function in the early 1980s. Bread had been brought to the village from Kano as early as the 1960s.) In Yekuwa, too, bread can be obtained—but it is Yardaji bread, and not only 5 kobo more expensive but invariably staler as well. Rice dishes are more infrequently found in Yekuwa.

Nigerian bread resembles American-style loaf bread. It has become so popular on both sides of the border that French-style bread is disappearing in parts of Niger. The chief baker of Magaria, for instance, has stopped making French-style baguettes entirely, so dramatically has demand for it dropped because of Nigerian *birodi* (bread).

In 1985, under the military regime, imports of both rice and flour were severely curtailed in Nigeria. Bread reportedly disappeared in Yardaji, and rice too was almost impossible to obtain. One would expect that Yekuwa's supplies of these foodstuffs suffered commensurately, although the Nigérien village's lesser dependence on them would have mitigated the effect of their sudden scarcity.[20]

Secondary Occupations

Although farming is the primary occupation of villagers in Yardaji and Yekuwa, most adults have secondary occupations as well. (Those that engage in *kiwo*, or livestock raising, rate that as a primary occupation along with noma.) The range of specialty in both villages is extraordinary, and

[19] In the summer of 1986 mangoes grown in Satamawa were available in Yekuwa.
[20] In Magaria, however, rice was available at 6,000 CFA per sack.

confirms classical descriptions of the vibrancy of the Hausa village economy (see M. G. Smith 1959:248–49; Hill 1972:175–88). Some occupations, however, are followed in Yardaji but not in Yekuwa.

Ibrahim Yahaya (1979:165–67) groups the secondary occupations of the Hausa talakawa (commoners) into four categories: commercial activities, crafts and skilled works, manual labor, and soliciting for gifts or alms. My own survey in 1986 identified 84 secondary occupations practiced by heads of household in Yardaji and Yekuwa (see Table 8), which correspond more or less to Yahaya's categories. The following "commercial activities" are engaged in in both Yardaji and Yekuwa: market retailing, food hawking, grain selling, poultry raising, kola-nut vending, tea brewing, selling of cloth or clothing, incense peddling. "Crafts and skilled works" in both villages include butchery, weaving (general or mat), construction, carpentry, tailoring, leatherworking, barbering, pottery making, smithing, (traditional) medical doctoring, and watch and radio repairing. Water carriers, launderers, head porters, cart haulers, guardians, firewood gatherers, and well diggers fall into the category of "manual laborers." Musicmakers (that is, drummers) and praise singers (*maroka*) may be categorized with alms seekers (*bara*).

Four noteworthy clusters of secondary occupations in Yardaji are not found in Yekuwa. The foremost is *direba,* driving passenger minibuses or other vehicles. Here are included drivers themselves, along with stationmasters, conductors, the petrol seller, and tire repairers, who also work on bicycles and motorcycles. The tire repairer in Yekuwa fixes punctures in oxcart tires. *Haya babur*—renting out (or "hiring") one's motorcycle for short-term transportation—may also be included here. Children with bicycles also engage in *haya* with other children, but this is more an "apprenticeship" for later business activity than a full occupation.

The harder but malleable soil in and around Yardaji gives rise to another cluster of activity: pottery, brickmaking, and bricklaying. (There are two potters in Yekuwa but they use earth carried from Yardaji.) Since bread is baked only in Yardaji, this is a third industry without parallel in Yekuwa. People in Yardaji can indulge in "modern sleeping arrangements," but beds and mattresses are not available in Yekuwa. (Fish frying, now discontinued, used to be a fifth unique activity practiced in Yardaji. The fish, obviously, were brought from farther south.)

Professions practiced more frequently in Yekuwa than in Yardaji (if at all) tend to reflect the traditional ethos and customs of Hausa society. There are fourteen drummers (*makaɗa*) in Yekuwa but only three in Yardaji; Yekuwa praise singers (maroƙa) outnumber their Yardaji counterparts nine to four.

Table 8. Occupations of heads of household, Yardaji and Yekuwa, 1986

	Yardaji		Yekuwa	
Occupation	No.	%	No.	%
Koranic scholar	100	14%	8	1%
Potter	83	12	2	
Herder	81	12	152	22
Grain merchant	42	6	10	1
Spice seller	27	4	11	2
Trader	25	4	21	3
Livestock/donkey agent	21	3	20	3
Butcher	20	3	28	4
Tailor	20	3	11	2
Vegetable seller	18	3	3	
Miller/thresher	15	2	1	
Driver	14	2	0	
Beggar	12	2	6	1
Teaman	12	2	3	
Water carrier	10	1	8	1
Peddler (*koli*)	10	1	2	
Oxcart driver	10	1	0	
Schoolteacher	10	1	a	
Traditional healer	9	1	5	
Porter/manual laborer	9	1	1	
Launderer	8	1	3	
Barber	7	1	7	1
Market revenue collector	7	1	0	
Candyman	6	1	6	1
Carpenter	6	1	3	
Snack/prepared food seller	6	1	1	
Stationmaster	6	1	0	
Kola-nut seller	5	1	10	1
Pot (jug) seller	5	1	1	
Kerosene seller	5	1	0	
Praise singer	4	1	9	1
Smith	4	1	9	1
Traditional ruler	4	1	5	1
Rope weaver	4	1	4	1
Tanner/leatherworker	4	1	2	
Musician/drummer	3		14	2
Poultry seller	3		3	
Repairer (general)	3		1	
Bus conductor	3		0	
Baker/bread seller	3		0	
Bed seller	3		0	
Brickmaker/bricklayer	3		0	
Mattress seller	3		0	
Motorcycle renter	3		0	
Calabash vendor/repairer	2		9	1
Wrestler/boxer	2		4	1

Table 8 (Continued)

Occupation	Yardaji No.	%	Yekuwa No.	%
Repairer (watches, radios)	2		2	
Cloth seller	2		1	
Incense seller	2		1	
Tire repairer	2		1	
Hay seller	2		0	
Mat seller	2		0	
Shoe/sandal repairer	2		0	
House constructor	1		3	
Travel agent (hajj)	1		2	
Magician	1		1	
Capmaker	1		0	
Date seller	1		0	
Dispensary worker	1		0	
Florist	1		0	
Forester	1		0	
Grain chaff seller	1		0	
Henna seller	1		0	
Horse trainer	1		0	
Manicurer	1		0	
Mat weaver	1		0	
Pesticide seller	1		0	
Petrol seller	1		0	
Prostitute	1		0	
Scribe	1		0	
Well digger/repairer	1		0	
Woodcutter	1		0	
Youth club chairman	1		0	
Hunter	0		5	1
Secondhand clothes vendor	0		3	
Tobacconist	0		3	
Weaver	0		3	
Sandal vendor	0		2	
Cap washer	0		1	
Donkey veterinarian	0		1	
Guard	0		1	
Lottery organizer	0		1	
Money changer	0		1	
Roofing material seller	0		1	
None	8	1	286	41
Total	702[b]		702[b]	

[a]Not present when census was conducted.
[b]Because some heads of household have more than one occupation, the totals exceed the number of heads of household reported in Table 1.

Table 9. Secondary occupations of heads of household in Yekuwa, 1986

Occupation	Kofai	Hamada
Herder	139	13
Trader	16	5
Butcher	14	14
Livestock/donkey agent	9	11
Spice seller	8	3
Tailor	8	3
Grain merchant	7	3
Koranic scholar	7	1
Beggar	6	0
Barber	5	2
Candyman/cane sugar seller	5	1
Kola-nut seller	5	5
Smith	5	4
Hunter	4	1
Musician/drummer	4	10
Praise singer	4	5
Water carrier	4	4
Traditional healer	3	2
Carpenter	3	0
House constructor	3	0
Teaman	3	0
Vegetable seller	3	0
Calabash vendor/repairer	2	7
Launderer	2	2
Wrestler/boxer	2	2
Potter	2	0
Poultry seller	2	1
Secondhand clothes vendor	2	1
Tanner/leatherworker	2	0
Travel agent (hajj)	2	0
Traditional ruler	1	2
Weaver	1	2
Peddler (*koli*)	1	1
Repairer of watches and radios	1	1
Cap washer	1	0
Incense seller	1	0
Lottery organizer	1	0
Magician	1	0
Miller/thresher	1	0
Money changer	1	0
Porter/manual laborer	1	0
Pot (jug) seller	1	0
Schoolteacher	1	0
Snack/prepared food seller	1	0
Tire repairer	1	0
Rope weaver	0	4
Tobacconist	0	3
Sandal vendor	0	2

Table 9 (Continued)

Occupation	Kofai	Hamada
Cloth seller	0	1
Donkey veterinarian	0	1
Guard	0	1
Repairer (general)	0	1
Roofing material seller	0	1
None	179	107
All occupations	475	227

Hunting, an extinct profession in Yardaji, has five practitioners in Yekuwa. Although the absolute numerical discrepancy is slight, it is consistent that twice as many 'yan Yekuwa as 'yan Yardaji are professional wrestlers or boxers. Novel occupations in the village include money changing, lottery ticket vending, and pilgrimage organizing. (The latter, listed in Table 8 as "travel agent (hajj)," does have an equivalent in Yardaji.)

Three general observations about the occupational structures that distinguish Yardaji from Yekuwa should be made. The first is the preponderance of men offering *mallamanci* (Koranic scholarship and teaching) as their "primary secondary" occupation in Yardaji (14 percent versus 1 percent). Yekuwa heads of household, in contrast, display a comparative advantage in livestock herding (22 percent to 12 percent). The most striking difference, however, is the third, null observation: whereas only 1 percent of Yardaji heads of household have no secondary occupation, over 40 percent of the equivalent Yekuwa population admit to being without a nonfarm occupation (see Table 9). This category ("none") is by far the dominant one, twice as large as the next largest group (herders).

It may also be worth mentioning that, although it is not listed in the table as a discrete occupation, simugal (smuggling) is an alternative definition for the activity carried out by many a Yekuwa (but not Yardaji) trader.

Women

Differences in the economies of Yekuwa and Yardaji have direct implications for the women in the two villages. Although scholars who have studied Hausa women have focused on their economic autonomy and parallelism (separation of their cash accounts from their husbands', retention of self-earned income, gender-specific financial activities; see Coles

1991, Frishman 1991, Hill 1972, Longhurst 1982, Schildkrout 1983), they concur on their economic dependence in one sense: the overall status and wealth of Hausa women is a function of the economic standing of their husbands.[21] The more dynamic, prosperous, and diversified economy of Yardaji provides greater opportunities for Yardaji women than for their Nigérien cousins in Yekuwa. This, of course, is a subsidiary effect of their belonging to the more vibrant economy of Nigeria.

The much greater incidence of *sana'a* (secondary occupation) in Yardaji is one indicator of the opportunities open to Yardaji women. Economic "space" is more limited for Yekuwa women because the meager amount of nonagricultural economic activity is dominated by the men. The division of labor by sex is quite rigid.

Women in rural Hausaland, unlike those elsewhere in Africa, are not encouraged to participate directly in farm operations (Callaway 1984:441). Seasonal participation in planting and harvesting may present a partial exception, but for the most part, farming is a man's occupation.

The most common economic activity conducted by rural Hausa women is the processing of food for sale. Whereas this is indeed a common activity in Yardaji, in Yekuwa precooked meals and snacks are sold mostly on market day.

Both the cultivation and processing of food by women are tied to the institution of *kulle* (wife seclusion, purdah). Women who are in seclusion are normally enjoined from leaving their compounds during daylight hours and hence cannot travel to the fields outside of the village to engage in physical labor. Within their compounds, however, cooking food and organizing its distribution (usually through their preadolescent daughters) are their major sources of independent income. Hill (1969) describes this as the "honeycomb market."

Although women in only a minority of households keep purdah in our two Hausa villages, its incidence is over three times greater in Yardaji than in Yekuwa. This finding may be attributed to the greater influence of organized Islamic orthodoxy in Northern Nigeria than in Niger, where the state has been much more interventionist in founding and using Islamic organizations to bring about social and economic change (Dunbar 1991). Because fewer wives are in seclusion in Yekuwa, women there are under less pressure to maintain their personal relations (a social aspect of "honeycomb life") from within the confines of their homes. Conversely, where purdah

---

21 Unmarried women obviously present a different case. See Pitten 1983, 1984 regarding Hausa "courtesans" (*karuwai*).

is less extensively practiced, Hausa women *are* more likely to spend time in the fields, but with less prospect of turning these activities into personal income.[22]

Wealth liberates. Because of the social prestige attendant upon a secluded wife, Muslim Hausa husbands prefer to hire workers rather than call on their wives when extra hands are needed in the fields. As we have seen, some Yardaji plots are tilled by paid migrant laborers (often from across the border in Niger). Some Yardaji women are thus "freed" from this physically arduous activity; many fewer Yekuwa women are. The same can be said for hauling water and collecting firewood, two traditionally female activities in Hausaland frowned upon by Islam, as newly interpreted.

When income in urban Hausa families declines, women are expected to make up the shortfall (Coles 1991). In rural Yekuwa, where income is low to begin with, economic independence is difficult to establish. But the increasing specialization and diversification of the rural Hausa economy does not necessarily bode well for Yardaji women, for they are even more vulnerable than men to "modern" goods and services. "[A]s tastes become oriented toward commercially prepared foodstuffs . . . [women's food processing] will diminish in importance," wrote Richard Longhurst in 1982 (114), and events in Yardaji bear him out: both the bread bakery and the fish-frying enterprises have been conducted exclusively by men.

Female living standards in Hausaland will continue to be dependent on the material conditions of the larger communities to which the women belong. Boundary-derived consequences, here heightened by different national economic experiences, seem to have privileged the women of Yardaji, at least for the time being, beyond those of Yekuwa. But within Yardaji gender inequities may increase as the village economy comes to resemble more and more the urban economy of the relevant three *K*'s: Katsina, Kano, and Kaduna. Comprehensive assessment of the implications of colonialism for gender relations in Hausaland will require further attention to the long-term implications of partition.

Transportation

The relative diversity and vibrancy of the Yardaji economy may be attributed in part to the village's infrastructural advantage: a level and network

---

[22] Barkow (1972) makes this point in the context of the Maguzawa village he contrasted with a Muslim one.

of transport without equivalent in neighboring Yekuwa. One might even claim that it is this variable more than any other—more even than colonial heritage or international boundary—that explains the economic differences we have seen. Again, however, the differential networks and opportunities for spatial mobility within and outside the villages are themselves reflections of a classical colonial pattern—little changed in the postcolonial era—in regard to transportation and communication between colonial jurisdictions and levels of infrastructural development within French and British colonies.

It is well known that railway and road links in colonial Africa generally followed a hinterland-coastal pattern that reflected colonial economic preoccupations and administrative boundaries. By and large, such patterns still predominate. One need only consult a map of West Africa in 1918 (see Afigbo 1973:426) to get a fairly accurate picture of the major ports, railways, and motor roads in West Africa today.

Despite some developmental changes in Hausaland, a Michelin map of the 1990s tells the same story as a colonial map of the 1920s. The Hausaland formerly under British jurisdiction enjoys a network of paved roads and functioning railways unrivaled in formerly French Hausaland. Though the Zinder-Kano road through Magaria, completed in 1979, facilitates trans-Saharan truck transport (Algiers to Lagos), it has not radically improved the general level of transportation for the majority of Hausa in Niger.

Yekuwa, for instance, is still spatially oriented more to Yardaji than to Magaria, its own district capital. The international boundary division obstructs the construction of a road to Yardaji, but there is no road to Magaria, either. The closest road to Magaria from Yekuwa is several miles away, and it is unpaved and unreliable in the rainy season. The trunk road from Yardaji to the Daura highway (a laterite road stretching about four miles) is also unpaved, but once the bumpy ride to Kwana junction is over, a smooth ride to Zango and Daura (and eventually to Kano) is assured. This access road to the Daura highway was built by village communal labor, and was completed in 1961.

Thus, whereas Yekuwa's transport is limited to donkeys (for merchants) and horses (for the "wealthy"), Yardaji bustles with bicycles, motorcycles, minibuses, and (on market day) trucks. There are no modern vehicles in Yekuwa at all: only on Magaria's market day (Saturday) may a Land Rover come to pick up passengers, but it will take them only as far as the closest road to Magaria, where they must wait for some other vehicle to take them the rest of the way. From time to time a gendarmerie jeep also arrives in the village, bringing soji to patrol the border. Yardaji, in contrast, has thirty-

Showing off in Yekuwa.

Showing off in Yardaji.

three motorcycles and nine motor vehicles, six of them for commercial use. Seventy adults and children have bicycles. It is true that Yekuwa's sandy soil is less well suited to bicycles than Yardaji's hard soil, yet bicycles *are* used throughout the Sahelian region, so this does not appear to be the decisive constraint. Yardaji's more extensive transportation facilities predate Nigeria's oil boom. The first bicycle in the village appeared around the late 1940s, the first motorcycle in the late 1960s. Modest innovations, yes—but not by Yekuwa standards.

Talauci—poverty—is one reason offered for Yekuwa's underdeveloped transportation; and yet it is the very lack of an infrastructural network that impedes trade, diversification, and growth. Even if Yekuwa is poor in relation to Yardaji, surely some individuals who have made money in either trade or livestock could invest it in passenger or commercial vehicles, as people in Yardaji have done. They *would* purchase such vehicles, it is claimed, if the duty on a motor vehicle did not approach the cost of the vehicle itself. (This may be an exaggeration in monetary terms, but the perception is just as inhibiting as if it were true. Cars, motorcycles, and bicycles do in fact cost appreciably more in Niger than in Nigeria.) For the same reasons, 'yan Yekuwa with means do not buy oxcarts (on which a yearly tax of 3,000 CFA is assessed),[23] nor do they invest in grinding machines (which are subject to a heavy annual tax). It is not the village's apparent poverty that inhibits Yekuwa's economy from reaching take-off but rather the harsh rule and rules under which Hausa in Faranshi (still) are laboring.

Another reason that Yekuwa villagers do not conduct their (already) illegal cross-border trade by motor vehicles is the fear that if they are caught, the vehicles will be confiscated by the soji. Yardaji traders are no less afraid of being caught in "French" territory with their unregistered (that is, unregistered in Niger) motorcycles or minibuses: even though they could easily ride or drive across the sandy savannah to nearby Nigérien villages, motorized 'yan Yardaji avoid the risk.[24] Hill (1972:193–95) points to a shortage of capital as a major constraint on Hausa farmers struggling to achieve some modest level of prosperity. Yet for Hausa villagers divided by a colonial-imposed boundary, the true obstacles to self-generated local-level investment (and possible prosperity) appear to be less economic than political. Were 'yan Yekuwa to perceive not risk but incentive in investing in what they already understand to be the means of arziki (roads, transport vehicles, machinery, agricultural equipment), they would undoubtedly do so. The perception persists, however, that whereas the government of their cousins across the border is benign (or at least unobtrusive), their own rulers take an adversarial view of their economic activities.

This is not, of course, the official policy of the central government of Niger, or the image that Niamey wishes its citizens to have of it. It is probably not the intention of the Nigerian government, either, to appear as distant from its citizens as Yekuwa and Yardaji villagers (happily) see it to be. This is, notwithstanding, the way the Hausa of both villages do perceive and interpret what goes on in their immediate communities. In stressing the perceptions of the villagers, I have deliberately downplayed the "big picture," or the policies of the governments and officials whose actions are more usually studied. My intention has been rather to note what actually goes on in a borderland setting, and to convey not the way Hausa villagers are "supposed" to see what their governments are doing for (or to) them but the way they actually do perceive their economic reality.

---

[23] By 1986 this tax had been increased to 7,500 CFA.
[24] In 1986 some 'yan Yardaji, confident that the risk of confiscation had lessened, were riding their motorcycles across the border.

Yekuwa and Yardaji from a Dependency Perspective

Studies of the international political economy usually describe the *dependencia* model in terms of the center and periphery nations, or the industrialized and nonindustrialized worlds. It might also be fruitful to consider economic relations between Yekuwa and Yardaji today as a microcosm of the dependency relationship that has developed within a Hausaland still divided according to colonial designs. This perspective could easily be expanded to encompass the contemporary relationship between a petroindustrializing and quasi-capitalistic Nigeria and its Fourth World and statist neighbor Niger. Though I prefer to argue according to my chosen units of analysis, the broader, national applicability of such a conceptual scheme should be borne in mind.

Yekuwa, we have seen, serves as the source of primary goods highly desired by Hausa traders in Yardaji and beyond. Yardaji is the supplier of processed or manufactured goods that Yekuwa needs. Yekuwa is the weaker player in this trade, and therefore the poorer one as well. Purchasing power is greater in Yardaji, as witness its more diversified economy and more dynamic weekly market. Economically, in fact, it regards Yekuwa as something of an economic backwater. This perception is reinforced by the people of other villages nearby, who look upon Yardaji as an urban center, in contrast to Yekuwa's more rural profile.

Yardaji men who seek work elsewhere during the dry season go to Kano; so do the enterprising young men of Yekuwa. Not only is the infrastructure more developed for transport in Yardaji, but Yekuwa is dependent on access to Yardaji to maintain its own (more modest) standard of living. And when access is curtailed—when the border is shut—it is Yekuwa, consistently the weaker and more vulnerable partner, that is hurt more.

Although it would be hyperbolic to speak of village-level "cultural imperialism," a certain resentment toward Yardaji's wealth, dominance, and sense of superiority does fester in Yekuwa.[25] I shall discuss these social dy-

---

[25] Some Yekuwa villagers vigorously asserted that there is only the *appearance* of greater arziki in Yardaji. In fact, they claimed, it is precisely because Yekuwa's greater wealth flows to Yardaji in the form of individual loans that the latter appears to be better off:

We have arziki, but it is hidden because our rulers confiscate it all the time. There is no profit to be made here. . . .

Our arziki is in Nigeria. For example, five sons of Yekuwa own six passenger cars that operate out of Zango and Yardaji. . . . There are many loans [*bashi*] given from Yekuwa to Yardaji, but none from Yardaji to Yekuwa. . . .

The way houses are built gives the impression of greater arziki in Yardaji. But if the

namics in Chapter 11. Suffice it to say here that they, like the economic contrasts between the two villages, have many of the hallmarks of the phenomena explained under the rubric of classical dependency theory.[26]

Colonial Arziki

On both sides of the border one hears that Yardaji had the arziki to be part of Nigeria and Yekuwa had the misfortune not to be. As Hill correctly points out, "arziki" means not only wealth or prosperity but also a philosophical or spiritual quality that brings good fortune. In considering why some people prosper more than others in a single community—in Batagarawa, in Dorayi—Hill naturally sees arziki as a quality that adheres to or rewards individuals ("a mysterious personal attribute necessary for success in this world" [1977:155; see also Hill 1972:185–86, 205–6]). On the Hausa border between Niger and Nigeria, however, arziki takes on a collective meaning—the luck or fate that has placed Yardaji within a land of prosperity but has placed Yekuwa in a land of hardship and suffering. Arziki, as good fortune or fate, is not so arbitrary or chancy as Hill represents it. Inasmuch as Muslim Hausa believe that nothing occurs that is not the will of God (*ikon Allah*), arziki is something that Allah, in His sometimes inscrutable wisdom, has distributed in the way He has seen fit.

Fuglestad (1983:113–14) broadens the notion of arziki (which he renders as "arzika") to explain how vastly outnumbered French Europeans could conquer Nigérien Hausaland and not have their power seriously challenged by the indigenes. He sees arziki primarily as "force" or "luck": in the eyes of the conquered Africans "the French possessed an extraordinary 'luck,' an unparalled 'force', which could only emanate from supranatural powers" (113). Arziki is equated with "the analagous Muslim notion" of *albarka* (blessing, grace) (151), but Fuglestad, like Hill, generally dissociates the principle of arziki from Allah—an approach with which few Hausa would agree.

In any event, arziki may be unpredictable, but its manifestastions are hardly hidden. In the context of Yardaji and Yekuwa, arziki primarily is a

---

earth allowed it [if the soil weren't so sandy here] there would be many more mud-brick homes. . . . After all, here in Yekuwa there is more money, millet, men, and livestock.

[26] Stephen Baier, writing about the integration of the Central Sudan into the world economy but sensitive to deviations from the classical "open economy" model which Central Niger represents, calls for "a more complex description of centre-periphery relations" (1980:222).

function of which side of the border one has been allotted. That a metal pole stuck in the earth by white men over eighty years ago should determine the life chances of a community and the individuals of that community is but one of the many vagaries of a world perennially subject to ikon Allah—the will of God.

9

Educating the Hausa

You were forced to release [your children] and they were taken to town,
To be educated and thus relieve you of your labours.
Your work is farming, but, you see, they know nothing of it,
They can only sit around on chairs.

—Alhajiya 'Yar Shehu

The phenomenon of parallel socialization, we have seen in Chapter 4, is generally invoked in discussions of the formation of distinctive sets of Westernized elites among partitioned peoples. Yet the nonelite may undergo a similar process, even in the countryside. A major vehicle for this process is the educational system. A simple trip across the Nigérien-Nigerian border highlights the process in fascinating detail.

Colonial patterns of education persist in astonishing continuity. Schooling is distinctly more efficacious in Yekuwa than in Yardaji, but also more oppressive. Curricula and textbooks reflect local culture, religion, and language much more in the Nigerian school than in the Nigérien. Teachers enjoy much greater remuneration and status in Niger than in Nigeria; at the same time, their integration within the local community may be more problematic. The written word evokes a combination of fear, awe, and inferiority among the borderline Hausa of Niger to a degree unknown among their counterparts across the border.

Colonial Schooling

Michael Crowder (1968:378–80) has succinctly summarized the general difference in colonial educational philosophy in West Africa:

> The French system was much more concerned with persuading children of the virtues of the colonial system and French culture. . . . [It] aimed at producing

227

"French" Africans, whose loyalty to France and indifference to local nationalism would be assured. . . . The British, less inclined to philosophise . . . were
concerned that the character of education given be adapted to the African
situation. . . . Britain sought to produce an "African" African. . . .

The difference can be seen in policies on language: "While the French insisted on children being instructed in French from the first day they entered
school, the British primary schools taught in the vernacular for the first
two years" (381). In West Africa, the French educational system, like the
French colonial system in general, had the reputation of being particularly
elitist and rigorous. Despite its authoritarian and culturally repressive aspects, it is recognized as having been more efficient and successful (in the
sense that it imposed higher academic standards) than the British policy of
mass and technical education. (Given the cultural and religious specifici-
ties of Hausaland, however, British colonial education never did become a
mass phenomenon in this portion of West Africa.)

Naturally, independence has changed the focus of loyalty in the former
colonies. No educational system in Africa today fosters loyalty to an assimilating France; and none promotes a strictly utilitarian and pragmatic non-
nationalistic vocationalism. Yet judging from what goes on in the schools
of Yardaji and Yekuwa, even if the direct objects of colonial veneration have
been displaced, the respective colonial stamps are still remarkably visible in
the schools' policies, methodologies, and pedagogy. These influences are
all the more striking when one realizes that neither village had a school
until after the British and French had left Hausaland.

Traditionally, education in Hausaland was conducted by the *makaranta
alkorani,* or Koranic school. Also known as the *makaranta allo,* for the
wooden slates (*allo*) on which children practice writing passages from the
Koran, these religious schools were run by both itinerant and resident
scholar-teacher-priests (mallamai), who imparted a strictly religious education to their students. These schools are very much alive throughout
Hausaland today.

The Europeans naturally introduced another educational system into
Hausaland, with the aim of exposing children to a more secular and "modern" education. The British in Hausaland, unlike those in other British
colonies, generally excluded all forms of Christian missionary activity.
Neither were Catholic missions encouraged by the colonial government in
French Hausaland. In neither French nor British Hausaland were government schools very widespread, but they did initially generate a considerable

amount of resistance among the Hausa on religious grounds. The foremost fear of the parents was that their children would be de-Islamicized.

The Hausa called these government schools "makaranta boko." The term *boko* has at least two meanings, both of which are relevant to their use in this context. "Boko" is considered a Hausa transformation of the English "book"; "makaranta boko" thus may be rendered as "any school or establishment where a secular (i.e., non-Arabic) education or training is given" (Hill 1972:212).[1] Yet the orthodox meaning of "boko" is "fraud," "false," or "mock" (Yahaya 1979:184, Abraham 1958:109). Western schooling thus acquires a pejorative connotation, which is carried over in the expression "'yan boko" to designate and stigmatize the Westernized Hausa (Yahaya 1979:198).[2]

"Ilmi" is another Hausa term that encompasses the differing types of education. In its original meaning, "ilmi" denotes pure learning and knowledge, particularly in the context of Koranic scholarship, or karatu (Kirk-Greene 1974:11). In the appropriate context, however, it may now be used to connote secular or Western-style education. Though "ilmi" is not so pejorative as "boko," when it is used in this way its referent is downgraded from moral or religious to technical or instrumental education.

The British attitude toward educating the Hausa was typified by Hans Vischer, one-time director of education in Northern Nigeria, who believed that "Western education 'denationalised its products' cutting them off from

---

[1] In French Hausaland the Hausafied term for school is *lekol* (from *l'école*).

[2] The indictment of *nasaranci*, or the creation of Westernized (literally "Christianized") Hausa (see Yahaya 1979), may be compared to that of assimilation in the French colonial experience (see Fanon 1967). One powerful medium in which both have been indicted is poetry. For a classic example in the French literature, see Césaire 1971. A Hausa example is provided in a poem by Ibrahim Yaro Muhammed, in Furniss 1986:8–9:

> Young people have taken up evil ways,
> They have abandoned all our respected traditions.
> All our customs have been abandoned.
> They have adopted European customs and they speak English
> To indicate their liberation and their worldly wisdom.
> Trousers they wear with a great big belt like a shield.
> They say their drawstring-trousers are broken.
> They no longer wear our traditional clothes,
> Preferring a jacket and trousers. . . .
>
> If you speak to them in Hausa they tell you to speak in English.
> Or else they move from Hausa to English and back again,
> They have forgotten the importance of the Hausa language.
> My advice if we are to look for liberation is to hold hard
> To our traditions and not let them die.

their society, customs and values." The schools that Vischer founded accordingly "related . . . curriculum . . . to the culture and aspirations of the people" (Clarke 1979:51–52). The Muslim Hausa establishment may have been slow to accept modern schooling, but local religion and culture meshed much more significantly with British Hausa education than with the French Hausa system.

It is true that the French established *médersas*, Franco-Arabic colleges, in which the French language and culture were taught alongside Arabic and Islamic sciences. But the establishment of the médersas reflected less a solicitude for the religion, language, and culture of the Hausa than a way of ensuring "a controlled, a malleable, a pliable Islam that they could twist and bend to serve their purposes" (Clarke 1982:190–91). The contention that this approach to Islamic education was continued even after independence is buttressed by the observation that the postcolonial Nigérien government established and controlled médersas not as part of the Ministry of Education but rather as part of the Ministry of the Interior: "The State is thus giving itself the means to intervene in the training of the dispensers of Koranic education—old dream of the colonial power" (Triaud 1981:19–20).

Postcolonial Education in Hausaland

At independence Niger inherited a skeletal school system, staffed largely by expatriates, whose aim was to teach a lot of academic subjects to a few chosen students. More than a decade into independence, outside of Niamey only about one in fifteen children managed to attend school (Donaint & Lancrenon 1976:67). By 1990, adult illiteracy nationally was down to 72 percent (compared with 49 percent in all Nigeria; see World Bank, *World Development Report 1992*), though as late as the mid-1980s UNESCO reported that 94.5 percent of Nigérien adults were illiterate. National statistics undoubtedly underreport the true extent of illiteracy among Nigérien Hausa adults, for they include the population of the capital, where enrollment rates have historically been highest and which lies outside of Hausaland.

Although the Ministry of National Education has attempted to "Nigérienize" the system, Niger's school system is still closely patterned on France's, both in curriculum and in administration. Thus we still find six years of primary schooling culminating in the *certificat d'études primaires* (CEP); six years in a *collège*, whose successful passage entitles one to the *brevet d'études du premier cycle* (BEPC); three years in a *lycée* (*baccalauréat*) or *école normale;* and, for the rare continuing students, university and postgraduate studies in Niger (there is a university in Niamey) or abroad (usually France). Virtually all education in Niger is government-run.

Nigerian education, like Nigerian administration in general, has deviated more from the British system than the Nigérien has from the French. The Nigerian system is relatively decentralized. Curricula, for instance, are established by the individual states. While the standard regional examination for secondary school students (organized by the West African Examination Council) is still based on a British model, it tests more for knowledge of local and national conditions (e.g., history, geography) than does the equivalent francophone *examen.* Twelve years of primary and secondary school are offered, followed by university or college studies. Private institutions, especially at the secondary level, abound. Each of the nineteen states had at least one university in 1983.

Since missionary schools provided much of the Western education in colonial days, and the British discouraged Christian emissaries and institutions in Muslim areas, Northern Nigeria has long lagged behind the South in educational achievement. The most recent innovation in Nigerian education, and the one to affect Hausaland most strongly, has been the Universal Primary Education (UPE) program. Peter Clarke (1979) has been monitoring popular reaction to UPE in Northern Nigeria.

Launched in 1976, UPE was Nigeria's attempt to institute a publicly financed Western-style educational system at the grade school level for all school-age Nigerians. Much of its rationale was developmental:

> The Nigerian government regards UPE as an essential element in its development strategy, and as vitally relevant to nation-building and national integration. . . . UPE will provide, it is hoped, an indigenous source of trained and skilled manpower for the administration, and the construction and maintenance, of development projects. (Clarke 1979:46)

In Northern Nigeria, however, Clarke found that UPE was met with resistance from the entrenched Koranic schools. This competing system opposed the introduction of secular education on several grounds, all of which directly or indirectly concerned perceived inroads into established Islamic belief and practice. Among these potentially disruptive effects are the breakdown of traditional marriage patterns (adolescent girls will become students instead of wives); a weakening of respect for elders and parents (by the introduction of an alien source of knowledge, custom, and belief); the introduction of a value-free (and hence valueless) epistemology; a growing alienation from village-based occupational roles (by the replacement of apprenticeship models and farming by civil service aspirations); and, most obviously, the loss to mallamai of their students (who also provide farm labor for their teachers) (ibid., 57–58).

Clarke notes that responses to UPE by the mallamai have been quite varied, ranging from "mini-jihads" to mere "protests of corrective censure" (ibid., 58, 61). He also acknowledges the "appeasement strategey" of UPE authorities in allowing curricular concessions to win over the local teacher-priests. Yet for all the importance of Clarke's emphasis on the criticism of and resistance to UPE in Nigerian Hausaland, its relational bias should not be overlooked.

In contrasting the attitudes toward UPE of northerners and southerners, Muslims and Christians within Nigeria (the latter of each pair being more favorably disposed than the former), one gets a different picture than one gets when comparing religiously inspired attitudes toward secular education among Hausa Muslims in Niger and Nigeria. Nigérien history and society have made any significant forms of resistance to secular education unlikely—even though in Niger incentive for such resistance is greater. The principal reason is the long-standing institutional divorce, in place since colonial times, between secular and traditional education in Nigérien Hausaland. The way the secular school is regarded by coreligionists and ethnic kin changes as the comparative frame of reference changes. In Hausaland, this comparative frame of reference follows directly from the European partition.

Village Schooling

In 1962 a primary school was finally built in Yekuwa. It was placed in an open space between Kofai and Hamada, and thus has become a physical link between the two Yekuwas. The archives record Mazongo Mijin Yawa and Garba Halilou (Hausa-sounding names) as the first schoolteachers in Yekuwa. However, Abdou Mallam (aka 'Dan Sanda), who attended Yekuwa's school in its early years, also recalls a Togolese schoolmaster.[3]

---

[3] In the colonial French educational system it was quite common to employ Africans from other French colonies, especially where local institutions and administration were rudimentary. A Togolese working in Yekuwa in the early 1960s would not be unusual; the secondary school in Magaria in the late 1970s employed several teachers from Benin. Neither the British

'Dan Sanda vividly recalls being repeatedly insulted by his Togolese maître d'école for his lack of academic aptitude: "I am an ass! I am lazy!" he
would joke, paraphrasing his former teacher.[4] 'Dan Sanda flunked out of
school; that is why he still resides in the village as a farmer, unlike the class-
mates who are now civil servants throughout Niger. Although he has had
virtually no opportunity to speak the language for decades, his fluency in
French is impressive. So is his ability to recite (and translate into equally
florid Hausa) extended passages from *Cyrano de Bergerac*. What a contrast
to graduating schoolchildren in Yardaji, who even today are incapable of
putting together a coherent sentence in English!

Yardaji's primary school, on the western edge of the village, officially
opened in 1965. (For five months before that, classes were conducted in
a small room in the village.) Mamman Umar Zango opened the school,
which began with a single class of forty pupils. In 1976, as part of Nigeria's
Universal Primary Education scheme, a second school was opened on the
eastern outskirts of Yardaji.

In 1983 389 children were attending school in Yardaji—244 in Yardaji
West and 145 in Yardaji East. Boys greatly outnumbered girls: Yardaji West
had 151 male pupils to 93 female ones. The schools have six grades (forms 1
through 6), form 1 accepting children of about six or seven years of age.

There is a fairly high teacher-student ratio in Yardaji, with eleven teachers assigned to the nine classes of Yardaji West alone.[5] They are generally
from the local area, such as Zango or Daura, and commute to school
by motorcycle. The teachers are specialists and rotate from class to class,
each teaching his specific subject: there is no single teacher for an individual class.

The schoolday in Yardaji runs from 7:00 A.M. to 12:45 P.M. for the two
youngest classes and until 1:15 for the other classes. This way, it is acknowledged, children may then go off to Koranic school in the afternoon. On
Fridays, the Muslim holy day, school ends at 11:35 so that all may prepare
for prayers at the mosque.

---

nor the postcolonial government would think of recruiting, for instance, cadres from Ghana
or Sierre Leone to teach in Nigerian schools. 'Dan Sanda's Togolese teacher may have joined
the Yekuwa school shortly after it opened.

4 Sékou Touré observed that many educated Africans came to accept their supposed inferiority to their European masters by internalizing *la mentalité coloniale* (see Crowder 1968:397).
'Dan Sanda's recollections show that a similar phenomenon has occurred even in the bush,
and even after independence.

5 All figures are as of 1983.

At the same time, neighboring Yekuwa had 164 pupils (118 boys and 46 girls) instructed by three teachers. According to one of the teachers, the low attendance rate is due to the "ignorance" of the parents. "They hide their kids—either by sending them to *makaranta haoussa* [i.e., Koranic school] in Nigeria or by sending them away to another village and saying they've died."[6]

Primary school in Yekuwa also consists of six grades, beginning with the *cours d'initiation,* proceeding with the *cours préparatoire,* and then continuing with two years each of *cours élémentaire* and *cours moyen.* First-graders in Yekuwa are also supposed to be six or seven years old, but they struck me as looking a bit older than those in Yardaji. This may be explained by the discretion that schoolmasters have in deciding which of the prospective pupils *appear* old enough to attend school.

The schoolday in Yekuwa still follows the French pattern: four hours of class in the morning until noon, a long break for lunch, and then two more hours of class in the afternoon. There is no special schedule for Friday. Although a detail, this decision not to adapt the government school schedule to Islamic practice is indicative of the long-standing divorce in Niger between secular schooling and religious reality—a divorce that colonial and postcolonial authorities in Nigerian Hausaland have been careful to avoid.[7]

Attending Classes

If one sits in on classes, one easily sees differences in the way children of the villages are brought up to view authority and government.

In Yekuwa, the schoolday began with pupils marching in paramilitary formation before one of them hoisted the Nigérien flag. They then filed

---

[6] Here is another example, extracted from my field notes:

It is school enrollment time. . . . The teachers came [to see the chief] today. When a paper was given to the grandfather of a girl, he said that the girl's mother had gone to Mecca, taking the daughter with her. But, lo and behold, the teacher saw the girl this morning! So he has come to mai gari to tell him—and to say that if the girl does not show up, the teachers will have to bring this to the attention of the sous-préfet of Magaria. Then the villagers will have to deal, not with the teacher, but with the sous-préfet.

[7] "[T]he British in Hausaland came to regard the traditional Islamic establishment as an ally; there was not . . . the distance between the British and their Muslim subjects in Northern Nigeria that continued to exist for many years over the border in French territory" (Hiskett 1984:277).

into class—the older grades into prefabricated classrooms, the younger ones into grass huts. (A storm had destroyed most of the school's permanent buildings, and the huts were erected as a temporary measure.) The teachers then went off to take their morning coffee.

After coffee, roll was called and the names of absent students were given to the principal. (He would later check up on the reason for their absence.) Since there were only three teachers for six classes, two levels were often in the same room (or hut) together. While the teacher was working orally with one level, the other would be doing written assignments.

Even in the huts the teachers had basic, if minimal, teaching aids: a free-standing blackboard, counting sticks, ruler. The first-year class, however, had no benches or chairs, and had to sit on the desks. The older, permanent classrooms were also equipped with maps of Niger, West Africa, and the African continent.

Lessons were administered in a tough, no-nonsense way. Errors, both oral and written, were met with both oral insult in Hausa ("*Shege! Shegiya! Uwarka!*"—Bastard! Your mother!) and physical punishment (being hit with a piece of rope or rapped on the head). One young girl, who had difficulty reading "Sani a la balle. Ali a une balle" was both rapped on the head and hit on the hand with a pen. In another class several pupils were whipped several times with a plastic rope when they failed to read a passage. Each wailed and whimpered while being punished, but when it was over just looked on silently when it was a classmate's turn to be beaten. All this administration of "discipline" seemed to be normal practice in Yekuwa's primary school classes. A more dramatic event is also instructive.

While one teacher was in the middle of a lesson, the principal arrived with a pupil who had not come to class. The principal, taking his rope, turned to the class and said in Hausa, "You see what happens to the one who doesn't come to school?" He then began thrashing the errant pupil while demanding, "Will you come tomorrow?" The hapless boy, through his wailing, answered, "If they bring me." The response merited more thrashing. "If they bring you? If they bring you?" Although the boy was now crying with all his strength, the beating continued until he gave the right response: "I'll come tomorrow! I'll come tomorrow!" Later, during the break, I learned that the boy had been absent because his father had sent him out into the bush to collect stalk.

After class, the teachers explained their methodology to me: "The kids must be thrashed to put fear in them. Without fear, they don't work. . . . The girls are especially bad. They make mistakes on purpose because their

The schoolday in Yekuwa begins with flag-raising.

mothers tell them that if they don't study, they'll be thrown out of school, and if they're out of school they can be married. And that's all they want anyway."

The schoolday in Yekuwa ended much as it had begun, with pupils marching round the flagpole. Then, in silence, they watched as one of them lowered their nation's flag.

Attending classes in Yardaji was considerably less traumatic (for me as well as the pupils) but equally revealing. In contrast to the marching and flag hoisting in Yekuwa, schoolchildren in Yardaji began the day by lining up outside their classrooms and, with cupped hands, quietly reciting Muslim prayers. Classes in Yardaji West proceeded with little drama, either pedagogic or disciplinary: none of the corporal punishment and verbal abuse I witnessed in Yekuwa was evident in Yardaji's schools. Although older students were supposed to be instructed in English, all lessons were actually conducted in Hausa. The learning process was more relaxed here than in Yekuwa. In Yardaji East, where there was a shortage of desks, the headmaster took his pupils outside and held class with the children sitting on the ground, as in a Koranic school. He taught them a song in Hausa, and even asked me to lead them in the chorus.

In Yardaji the schoolday begins with prayers.

Curricula

A comparison of the curricula in effect in the two villages graphically highlights the parallel socialization process, which is itself a reflection of colonial-era patterns. In Yardaji, of the forty-three class periods in a week, five are devoted to Hausa language instruction (reading and writing), two to Arabic language instruction, five to "Islamic and religious knowledge," and four to "cultural and creative arts." All classes—mathematics, science, social studies, English, home economics, physical and health education—are conducted in Hausa. The integration of local culture and language into the government school was part and parcel of educational policy under indirect rule, whose resonances may be found in the Kaduna State section of the 1971 *Report of the National Workshop on Primary Education:*

[T]here are certain subjects such as Hausa, Religious Studies, and Science, which because of their influence on the child's daily life, have to be given special emphasis. It is, in fact, the policy in this state that Hausa should be the medium of instruction for the first three years of Primary Education.

Certainly this policy has been adopted by those state authorities responsible for the curriculum and schooling in Yardaji.

Just a few miles away, other Hausa children are subject to the curriculum established by the Ministère de l'Education Nationale. This curriculum is designed to impart strictly Western (or secular) knowledge. A sixth-grader's week in Yekuwa, for instance, consists of six hours of French language and grammar, four hours of reading (in French), five hours of math, three hours of science, one hour of penmanship, and eight and a half hours divided among civics, history, geography, drawing, music, and physical education. Not only must all instruction be in French, but the Hausa language is banished from the curriculum.[8] I observed schoolteachers in Yekuwa addressing their pupils in Hausa very rarely—and then mostly to insult or punish them.

Religious instruction in Yekuwa's primary school is unthinkable. Unlike Yardaji's teachers, who accept Koranic schools as complements to the state's school, the Yekuwa teachers regard the mallamai and their religious schools as hostile to their mission. There is an ongoing struggle between government officials and village parents in and around Yekuwa over the enrollment of their children. One may just as easily substitute the term "conscription" for "enrollment," for many villagers still see the government's attempts to register their children for school as akin to military recruitment. Hence the reports of Yekuwa children being sent across the border for a "good" (i.e., Muslim) education in Nigerian Hausaland; and parents telling the teachers that their children are residing in some other village; and school-age children being reported as deceased. Reaction by Nigérien officials has been characteristically harsh. Here is one local story of an Islamic priest who more openly resisted compulsory government education:

> A mallam in Dunawa told the primary school teacher that he would not give his son to the school. The teacher then reported this to the subprefect in Magaria, who came with his "mustaches" [soldiers] and the Sarkin Magaria.
> The sarki asked the mallam if he would or would not send his son. The mallam supposedly answered, "May Allah protect you, but my son will not go to school." The sarki then turned to the subprefect: "You heard what he said."
> Then the subprefect himself asked the man, at first gently. Again the mallam

---

[8] A pilot project in Niger does now provide for instruction in the local language in the beginning years of primary school, and gradually incorporates French into the learning process. This is still an experimental program, however, and is restricted to a few schools in urban (by Nigérien standards) districts.

refused, this time swearing on the Koran, "My son will not go to school." But the subprefect himself put his hand on the Koran and declared, "I swear that the boy *will* go to school!"

At this point the mustaches grabbed the man and brought him to the subprefect's vehicle. Even before they put him in it, they began beating him. In the vehicle, they continued beating him, leaving his family behind to wail. They beat and kicked him all the way to Magaria.

In Magaria, the mallam was placed in the prison, and beaten even more. He was made to step in a bucket of feces which, punctured on the bottom, was then set above his head, dropping excrement on his head and body. He cried for the subprefect to come, for he had changed his mind.

When the subprefect arrived, the mallam said that he had repented, that his son would go to school, that all his sons would go to school, that the subprefect could even take his wife and put her in school! But the subprefect said no, he couldn't put any of the family into school, lest they die because of the mallam's oath on the Koran. But the mallam insisted and insisted.

Teachers as Role Models

Yekuwa teachers, like all Nigérien *fonctionnaires,* are periodically reassigned to posts throughout Niger, and may have little or no prior exposure to the local community where they teach. In Yekuwa the schoolteachers are given government housing and rarely leave the village. In Yardaji only the headmaster is provided with lodgings, and will, if he does not have another home nearby, live in the village.

If schoolteachers may be regarded as role models, then the models presented in Yardaji and Yekuwa in 1983 could not present a much starker contrast. Those of Yekuwa were relatively young—the principal was in his twenties—and virtually never socialized with the villagers. They wore Western clothes (shirts and tight trousers), always moved and acted as a trio, and, especially in public, spoke French to one another. Their demeanor, especially that of the headmaster, exuded authority and thinly veiled condescension toward the uneducated—that is, virtually everyone else in Yekuwa. As I mentioned in Chapter 7, they exhibited scarcely more respect for the traditional authorities of the community than for the populace at large. Even in the countryside they were consummate Nigérien fonctionnaires, a stereotype whose origin is colonial French.

Yardaji schoolteachers were a bit older and wore more traditional dress (flowing tunics, the pillbox fula). Their attitude, both in school and in the village, was certainly more easygoing and informal than that of their Yekuwa counterparts. They generally communicated in Hausa, not English.

They did not comport themselves as an elite apart, and did not challenge or demean traditional village authority. Unlike those of Yekuwa, the teachers of Yardaji demonstrably practiced their Islam.

The rupture between ilmi and addini, or between boku and karatu (that is, secular education and religion), is perceived in Yekuwa as giving rise to a generation that is disrespectful and arrogant (the sins of *rashin ladabi* and *jin kai*). Not only are the *'yan élèves* (pupils) ignorant of and disinterested in Islam, but some become outright disdainful of the religion, as well as of traditional authority. With their acquired ilmi they feel themselves superior to everyone else, including their teachers. Thus was an incident at the Yekuwa school explained to me: The teachers, acting harshly by thrashing their pupils, provoked a strike, legitimized by the claim that the teachers were no more educated or intelligent than the pupils.

According to 'yan Yekuwa, the Nigerian method of integrating Islamic studies with the makaranta boku is a preferable approach. Even if the parents have not themselves had formal instruction (in either boku or karatu), the children will not become alienated; on the contrary, they may bring their school-learned knowledge of religion back home and strengthen religious practice within the family. In Yekuwa, however, it is a foregone conclusion that once they start school, they will leave behind both religion and common courtesy.

UPE and Pupil Performance

In the Yardaji West principal's office hangs a framed, official portrait of the emir of Daura. Certainly no traditional ruler would receive comparable recognition in a Nigérien school, or in any other government establishment, for that matter. (A more central space on the principal's wall had obviously once been occupied by a picture of President Shagari; my visit, however, took place after the coup d'état.)

The headmaster expressed mixed views about Universal Primary Education, which was launched throughout Nigeria in 1976. On the one hand, he appreciated the value of mass education throughout the country. (The North has been particularly disadvantaged in respect to government schooling.) On the other hand, he questioned the sacrifice of quality that such a mass education scheme, unaccompanied by sufficient resources, entailed.

There is no way of knowing if UPE was in fact responsible for the disastrous results I obtained in Yardaji when I attempted to carry out a comparative pedagogic exercise in the two village schools. I suspect that the long-term neglect of educational training in rural Nigerian Hausa-land is probably at fault. Be that as it may, the findings were more than disappointing.

The plan was to have sixth-graders in Yekuwa and Yardaji write a short essay in response to the question "What do you want to be when you grow up?" The purpose was to see if the career interests or ambitions expressed by these rural Hausa youngsters varied in accordance with the side of the border they lived on. What I found instead was a shocking disparity in writing skills from one village to the next.

In the hour given them, Yekuwa students had little difficulty writing essays about one page in length. They wrote in French, and generally committed only minimal grammatical mistakes. Nevertheless, the ever-disdainful schoolmaster made predictably disparaging comments about the pupils' writing abilities.

In Yardaji, however, not one sixth-grader was capable of writing a single sentence in response to the assignment. When it became evident that they would not be able to do so in English, they were instructed to write their essays in Hausa. This change was of little help. Few got beyond scribbling a few letters—incorrectly—on the first line of the page. Certainly, a more comprehensive study of what goes on in Yardaji's schools would have to be conducted before a satisfactory analysis of these dismal results could be offered. Nonetheless, despite the outwardly pleasant features of education in Yardaji (lack of corporal punishment, culturally relevant instruction), the apparent illiteracy of the village's schoolchildren must be acknowledged as a sad reality, a reality that balances the negative picture of other Hausa schoolchildren being systematically beaten and insulted in Yekuwa.

A similar observation can be made concerning mastery of the official languages of the two countries and educational systems. In Yardaji, classes begin when the teacher enters the room and has the following ritualistic exchange with the pupils:

"Good morning, class!"

"Good morning, sir!"

"How are you?"

"We're very well, thank you, sir!"

Unfortunately, this is about the extent of Yardaji schoolchildren's oral mastery of the English language, the official language of Nigeria. In Yekuwa, pupils of the equivalent age and class (and even younger) demonstrate a markedly higher oral mastery of French, Niger's official language. It is true that Yekuwa children will grow up virtually illiterate in their native Hausa: they will be exposed to no books, newspapers, or magazines in the Hausa language. Yet, given the level of performance existing across the border, it is unsure that Yardaji children will attain much literacy in either English or Hausa.

Teacher Pay and Status

Inasmuch as pay may affect professional performance and educational results, this is perhaps the place to observe that the status and reward of the government primary school teacher in Hausaland appear to rise as one moves from Northern Nigeria to Niger. On paper, schoolteachers are paid substantially more in Nigeria than in Niger. In 1983 the monthly salary for a beginning primary school teacher in Kaduna State was 170 naira, or, according to the official exchange rate then prevailing, about U.S. $289. In Niger, the equivalent salary was 55,000 CFA, or about $130. In real terms, however (that is, at the black-market exchange rate prevailing along the border), 170 naira was worth only about 34,000 CFA, or somewhere between $78 and $82.[9] Moreover, because of rampant inflation plus the inordinate delays in Nigeria in paying salaries (schoolteachers went months without being paid), in real financial terms Nigérien schoolteachers were much better off than Nigerian ones (or at least those in Kaduna State). Whereas a teacher in Yekuwa is in a relatively comfortable financial position, in Yardaji his counterpart struggles to get by.

How this situation affects the relative self-esteem, motivation, and hence work performance of schoolteachers in Hausaland is difficult to measure. Yet it would not be farfetched to suggest that teaching in Yardaji does little for the morale or career expectations of ambitious Nigerian Hausa. Most would note that genuine possibilities for enrichment exist in business or politics. Neither the state nor the national government appears to expend the effort necessary to promote teachers' status and professional well-being. Being a *titsa* (teacher) in Yardaji carries less weight than being a *moshe lekol* (*monsieur de l'école*) in Yekuwa.

In Niger, government employment is virtually a sine qua non of financial security and moderate prosperity. While most primary school teachers

[9] In 1983 the official exchange rate for Nigeria's currency was 1.33 naira to the U.S. dollar, or 1.28 naira per SDR (standard drawing right) unit. Niger's shared West African currency was worth 417 CFA francs to the dollar, or 437 francs per SDR unit (1 SDR = U.S.$1.04695). Translated through a dollar standard, this converts to 542 CFA francs to the naira or, using an SDR conversion ratio, 558 CFA francs to the naira. In fact, in Yardaji and Yekuwa one naira was worth only about 200 CFA francs; conversely, 1,000 CFA bought 5 naira's worth of goods, not the (approximately) 1.8 naira that official tabulations would permit.

probably aspire to higher positions within the official Nigérien hierarchy and are not happy to be "banished" to a rural area, they would never look outside the civil service for a career. The Niger government accords education a high priority, and a *professeur* or *instituteur* has higher status than a teacher in the public school system just across the border.

Textbooks

An inspection of the school textbooks available in Yardaji and Yekuwa (especially those dealing with history, civics, and social studies) provides a valuable contrast in the way the children of these two neighboring villages are being educated and socialized by their respective states. In Yekuwa the emphasis is on patriotism, nationalism, and communitarianism. In Yardaji the textbooks stress tradition, local government institutions, and religion. All of the texts I inspected in Yardaji are of Nigerian (and usually Kaduna State) origin, but the Yekuwa school still has available a good number of books originally destined for schoolchildren in France.

One striking difference is seen in the treatments of contemporary traditional rulers. Yardaji's textbooks glorify the traditional rulers; Yekuwa's virtually ignore them.

> The Emir is the most important person in our area, town or village. . . . In this picture, the head of government greets the Emir. He is respecting him. The Emir is the father of all the people of our town. . . . When the whole community suffers from certain unpleasant happenings, everybody offers his solution through the Emir. [In the past as today] the King or Emir wanted people to live in peace. He did not want anybody to suffer. (*Living in Our State: Kaduna State* [Ibadan: Onibonje Press and Book Industries, 1977], 22, 27–28, 50)

Glorification of traditional leaders naturally has its roots in historical precedent:

> Our fore-fathers respected their leaders. These leaders were in villages. Leaders were also in many towns.
>
> Everybody cooperated with the leaders. There was peace in the villages. There was also peace in the towns.
>
> Everybody supported their leaders. The people gave their leaders anything they wished. They gave food to their leaders.
>
> The people also paid money. The money was used for the community. The gifts our fore-fathers gave their leaders are now called tax. (Ibid., 50)

The legitimacy of these traditional rulers followed from religious principle and practice. Islam is likewise legitimized in the school textbook: "The King or Emir was wise. He always prayed to Allah. He wanted Allah to help him. . . . Our fore-fathers always prayed. They prayed to Allah" (ibid.).

Concomitant with the glorification of traditional rulers and religion is a veneration amounting to idealization of ancestors:

> Our fore-fathers were peaceful. They loved people. They progressed. They had their own civilization. They did not concern themselves with the rise of the individual. . . . This is why every member of their families was important. . . . They did not envy anybody. They were happy at what God had given them. (Ibid., 54–55)

The preface to Boubou Hama's *Histoire du Niger* (coauthored by Monsieur M. Guilhem) lays out a different philosophy and raison d'être for exposing schoolchildren to their history:

> The teaching of history is full of interest. It is, moreover, one of the most efficient ways to develop the spirit and heart of the child *by helping the patriotic spirit to blossom in him.* A new and proud country cannot afford not to impart this to the youth of its schools. (*Histoire du Niger: L'Afrique—le monde,* 2d ed. [Paris: Ligel, 1975], 7; emphasis in original)

The same message is conveyed to the children themselves in the book's first lesson:

> [Learning] the History of Africa . . . *develops patriotism,* nationalism, and a civic spirit. . . . It alone is capable of nourishing in the heart of the little African a fervent attachment for his beloved Country in the dawn of its glorious destiny. (Ibid., 8; emphasis in original)

In Yardaji, we have seen, the textbook somewhat idealizes the African past, and thereby promotes a continuing linkage with it ("Our fore-fathers provided all the things needed in their own time"). Consonant with the "evolutionary" spirit of French/Nigérien education, we read:

> How privileged we are! How much more difficult was the existence of our fathers! They had neither our rapid means of transportation, nor our instruments for the battle against disease, nor our sources of information, such as the radio, which informs us daily about the events of the planet. They were far from enjoying our comfort! (Ibid., 11)

It is not surprising that *Histoire du Niger,* co-authored by a Frenchman and published in Paris, treats the colonial era much more lightly than the Onibonje book. The authorized Kaduna State text teaches:

> The European traders, especially from Great Britain . . . waged wars against many African Kingdoms. They also waged war against many Nigerian Kingdoms. They killed our chiefs. They also destroyed our towns and villages. They took our works of civilization into their own countries. They sold them at large amounts of money among themselves. This was because they admired them. They had not seen them before.
> The Europeans waged wars against our fore-fathers. They fought our fore-fathers at Bida. This was in 1897.
> They killed many of our fore-fathers. They also disgraced the leaders or our many villages and towns. They became masters of our fore-fathers.
> The European officials removed the leaders of our fore-fathers. They imprisoned many of them. They sent others to live outside their villages. Those who were not killed agreed to live with the Europeans. The Europeans banned and destroyed many of the ways of life of our fore-fathers. (*Living in Our State,* 54–55)

A more nuanced, almost apologetic treatment of the colonial period may be gleaned from the Hama and Guilhem text:

> We call "*colonization*" the sending of men to occupy and make the most of a far-off country, as a territory dependent on the "metropole" (the "colonizing" nation).
> We call "colonialism" an *abusive* and imperialistic doctrine that considers only the interest of the "metropole." Colonization, if it does not last, can be not always bad; it can assist, temporarily, the evolution of a country. Colonialism is an injustice: one must not thoughtlessly use one word for the other. (*Histoire du Niger,* 240–41)

The chapter then goes on to discuss, as "characteristics of the colonial regime," (1) the economic system, (2) Africa's entry into the circuit of world trade, (3) the construction of railways and roads, and (4) medical and cultural innovations. Even the most critical passage, dealing with the colonial economy (fixed prices, involuntary labor, cash and monocropism), is introduced by "All was not bad in the economic system instituted by the Whites in Black Africa."

The Francocentric treatment of history in the book subtitled *L'Afrique— le monde* is apparent when one considers what is treated as "Africa" and "the world." There is virtually no treatment of East or southern Africa—

"L'Afrique" here means West Africa—and the treatment of non-African society is in large part the history of France. We are given details on the French Revolution—with sections on Marat, Danton, and Robespierre— and four pages on Bonaparte alone.

The Cult of the *Takarda*

The respective practices and perceptions of education, even at the vil-lage level, buttress the contention that schooling in Niger perpetuates the French-initiated schism between (educated) elite and (illiterate) com-moners. Without modern education, one has no ilmi; deference must be paid to the educated (easily identified as the French speakers) who incar-nate both knowledge and power. While it would be inaccurate to leave the impression that educated Nigerians never condescend to the unschooled, the chasm is not so deep as on the other side of the border. Many modern-educated Nigerian Hausa who have risen in government, corporations, and enterprises "successfully reintegrate into their local community, con-forming to its norms and ways of life" (Yahaya 1979:195–96).

The existence and vitality of other avenues to success and power in Nige-rian Hausaland—religion, commerce, and even popular politics—offset somewhat the mystique of the almighty diploma. Another factor is the relative importance of the school-learned language: even without fluency in English, a Nigerian Hausa can prosper. In Niger, mastery of oral and written French is indispensable for societal advancement. Hence the cult of the *takarda*.

Receipt of a takarda (written paper) in Niger is a matter of serious-ness and concern. Takarda is associated with modern schooling, which is associated with government, which is associated with authority. It is gen-erally not a good thing to be confronted with (much less learn that one's name is on) a takarda, for usually only negative things—such as taxes, or school enrollment, or conscription, or police convocations—come of it. And of course, since official forms are written only in French, the takarda is unintelligible to most people.

In Nigeria the bureaucracy is so pervasive that everything—both good and bad—must pass by way of the proper (and endless) stream of takarda. The prevalence of paper neutralizes its impact (although not the takarda's aura of omnipotence). Since a takarda is indispensable for all sorts of ac-tivities, it does not necessarily entail negative results. In the same way that "going to Daura" for a ɗan Yardaji raises none of the apprehensions that "going to Magaria" does for a ɗan Yekuwa, the Hausa man of Nigeria does not fear the takarda as his Nigérien cousin does.

Education and Nationalism in Africa

Advocating national consciousness is one thing; inculcating it is quite another. Governments throughout the Third World have looked to the schools to create a new generation whose national consciousness will be unassailable. This strategy attains poignant expression when one compares two ethnically identical and neighboring villages separated by an international boundary. The adults of Yardaji and Yekuwa, unschooled though most of them are, already evince contrasting manifestations of what I shall call "village culture." This tendency should accelerate as greater numbers of young villagers are exposed to their respective governments' educational systems. The result should be an ever-widening differentiation between the inhabitants of the two villages in respect to character, personality, and worldview. It should also betoken greater social and psychological differentiation between the Hausa of Niger and the Hausa of Nigeria—a difference that reflects contrasting colonial mentalities and legacies.

The paradox is that independence and its attendant nation building were supposed to unify otherwise disparate ethnic groups within larger national wholes. This process, moreover, was supposed to be a first step toward Pan-African unity on a continental scale. The result, however, especially among partitioned Africans, has been quite the opposite: further differentiation on the basis of superimposed national (but antecedently colonial) identities. Government education will undoubtedly prove to be an increasingly important factor in forging and creating national identity, an identity that may take subtle forms of social behavior and psychological outlook as well as active expressions of patriotism. In socializing its youth, the village school imparts—intentionally or not—attitudes that are critical to the future identity of the nation's citizens. Even between these borderline communities, national inroads have obliterated whatever cultural homogeneity previously prevailed. Succeeding generations of Nigerian and Nigérien schooling are likely only to accentuate these differences.

10

Islam:
The Religious Difference

Sai an sha wuya akan tuna Allah.

When in trouble one remembers Allah.

—Hausa proverb

Despite the contrasts in education, economy, chieftaincy, and colonial history, life in villages throughout Hausaland has one common feature that might be expected to transcend all boundaries. For religion is the overarching feature of social life in rural Hausaland; it overshadows even language, history, culture, and economic base as a social cement. Yet even Islam—so fundamental to the belief system, outlook, norms, behavior, and daily life of Hausa villagers—has been evolving in different ways on the two sides of the border. The forms taken by Islam in Yardaji and in Yekuwa may be traceable to the different roles the religion plays in Nigeria and Niger today. These roles in turn are directly traceable to the Islamic policies of the British and French colonial regimes.

In Yardaji an "evolved" form of Islam is practiced, one that reflects wedding, marriage, and legal norms as articulated by autonomous religious leaders in Nigeria. In Yekuwa, religion, though legitimated by the state, is subordinated to it.

Islam in Hausaland

Islam made its earliest appearances in Hausaland—hitherto an animistic and polytheistic religious zone—in the fourteenth and fifteenth centuries. The Wangawara, itinerant Muslim traders from the east, combined mis-

248

sionary zeal with commercial prowess as they traveled among and traded with the Hausa. Trade at that time was an urban-based phenomenon that profited in the first instance from royal families and their clients. Hausa traders came to assume the religious roles of their Wangawara predecessors: the spread of Islam throughout Hausaland was a direct function of the expansion of economic networks among Hausa traders.

For hundreds of years Islam remained basically a religion of the urban elite. One element that restricted its expansion was its emphasis on literacy, ideally through mastery of the Arabic language but at least through *ajami*, the Hausa language written in Arabic script. From about the middle of the eighteenth century on, though, Islamic scholars and preachers made a concerted effort to include commoners and villagers—the least likely of literates—within the Muslim community.

At the same time, Islamic purists became increasingly intolerant of the "mixed Islam" (Hiskett 1984) practiced by the nominally Muslim Haɓe kings. Although the Hausa palaces had been the earliest havens for Islam, compromise with preexisting religious beliefs and practices made for a rather unorthodox brand of the faith. Unpopular authoritarian governance by the Hausa chiefs contributed to popular dissatisfaction. These two sources of tension acted as catalysts for the early nineteenth-century revolution in Hausaland.

Leading this revolution was the Fulani cleric Shehu Usman ɗan Fodio. Criticism of the Gobir aristocracy, leading to conflict with the chief of Gobir, was the spark that ignited the Fulani-led, religiously inspired jihad in 1804. Eight years later, when the fighting was over, the jihadists had control over most of the territory within Hausaland's traditional boundaries. Haɓe rulers were replaced by Fulani ones, and the area under control was consolidated within a single administrative caliphate. Sokoto became its capital. Although factionalization, dissension, and attack from outside challenged the backbone of the Sokoto caliphate, the successors of Usman ɗan Fodio ruled over most of Hausaland an entire century—until the next conquerors of the Hausa arrived.

Islam under Colonialism

In accord with the overall differences in colonial philosophy and instrumentation, the French and British approached the question of Islam in clearly contrasting ways. Where the British showed toleration, the French exhibited distrust; where the British allowed a measure of autonomy, the French strove to control and contain.

It is true that in the earliest stages of colonial rule in Hausaland—particularly the conquest phase—Muslim resistance to European invasion was as fierce against the British as against the French; early British attitudes and actions toward the Muslim establishment were accordingly just as ruthless. The British could not occupy Hausaland without first quashing the resistance led by the spiritual leader of the Muslims, the Sarkin Musulmi, sultan of Sokoto, Attahiru. It is a wonder that, after as brutal a battle as that of Burmi in 1903, the subjected Hausa and Fulani came to terms with British overrule as quickly as they did. It is all the more curious if we accept D. J. M. Muffett's (1964) thesis that not only was a military showdown between the British and Fulani-led forces avoidable but the killing of Attahiru was outright gratuitous.

Much of the credit for reconciling the surviving Muslim establishment to British rule must go to Lord Lugard. As early as 1903, in his famous speech in Sokoto, Lugard made clear that Her Majesty's crown was compatible with the sultan's crescent, and that Britain would not threaten Islam as the dominant creed of British Hausaland.

France's conquest of northern Hausaland was at least as violent as the British campaign. The infamous Voulet-Chanoine expedition (see Suret-Canale 1958 and Fuglestad 1980) is not only a lesson in militarism run riot but a case study in colonialist psychosis (comparable, in a sense, to Joseph Conrad's *Heart of Darkness*). Paul Voulet's and Charles Chanoine's actions not only terrified the Hausa (and others) who were unfortunately in the line of these French soldiers' march; they also alienated a segment of the domestic French population. Never was there any French equivalent to Lugard's speech at Sokoto, however, no overt attempt to reassure "their" Hausa that the violence against them was regrettable, no explicit guarantee of postconquest religious freedom. Whereas Lugard's words helped heal the wounds caused by Major Marsh in Burmi, the scars left by Captains Voulet and Chanoine were left to fester.

For France *was* hostile to the religious-cum-cultural competition that the Islamic establishment represented. True, the territory we know today as Niger never had a full-blown brotherhood or marabout structure comparable to what one finds in Senegal, for instance. Yet even in the influence exercised by local Muslim priests the French saw a potential threat to their "civilizing" objectives, in the political as well as the religious domain.

[The] French were emotionally involved with Islam, for . . . it [was] at odds with the French sense of mission. The British . . . felt more detached because [they] . . . presupposed from the start that the Muslim constituency . . . must eventually become responsible for its own political future. (Hiskett 1984:227–28)

Mervyn Hiskett's observation in regard to West Africa in general is perfectly applicable to the case of Hausaland—as Hiskett himself writes: "[The] British in Hausaland came to regard the traditional Islamic establishment as an ally; there was not . . . the distance between the British and their Muslim subjects in Northern Nigeria that continued to exist for many years over the border in French territory" (277).

Islam after Independence

The immediate postindependence government of Hamani Diori adopted an ambivalent posture toward Islam in Niger. Under the Francophile and internationally oriented Diori, Niger was officially run as a secular state, and its legal system underwent a formal laicization (Triaud 1981:16, 20). Though customary law was acknowledged in Niger's civil code, *shari'a* (Islamic law) was not directly mentioned as such. What is more, in this, the second most Muslim state of West Africa (after Mauretania [ibid., 10]), the Catholic church was given disproportionate respect and attention, as the colonizers demonstrated when they built the cathedral of Niamey two years before they permitted construction of the capital's main mosque.

Still, Diori was a Muslim, and he assured his countrymen of his faith. Along with his ministers, he publicly attended the services marking Id-el-Fitr and Id-el-Kabir (the end of Ramadan and Tabaski), and in 1962 he undertook the pilgrimage to Mecca. But the pilgrimage may have been motivated more by a desire to sustain his legitimacy in the eyes of his own and neighboring African states than by a desire to promote Islam as such, and certainly not to give it any institutional sense of autonomy. Rather, inheriting the French regime's Islamic concerns, "the postcolonial state will take the reality of Islam in hand and seek to structure it, out of a concern for control that perpetuates and prolongs that of the old colonial administration" (ibid., 13).

The concern for control is clearly seen in the continued cooptation of religious education (begun under the French) through the state-run médersa schools. Under Diori, administration of the médersas, we have seen, was placed not under the Ministry of Education, as might seem logical, but under the Ministry of the Interior, indicative of a greater concern for surveillance than for pedagogy: "The State thus gives itself the means to intervene in the training of the personnel involved in Koranic education—old dream of the colonial power" (ibid., 207).

The apparent rehabilitation of Islam under the Kountché regime was again inspired by a desire for religiously derived legitimacy, but also part of a broader foreign policy objective that brought Niger closer to other Muslim African and Arab countries. Notable in the latter category was Libya. Until Kaddafi's Pan-Saharan designs appeared to encompass northeastern Niger, Libya's promotion of Islamic and Arab religion and culture was quite marked. Now that a degree of caution colors foreign interest in Niger's Muslim population, the Nigérien government is striving to create and shape indigenous forms and structures of Nigérien Islam.

Under Seyni Kountché, an Association Islamique du Niger was established to "encourage the application of Islamic ideology at all levels of national life." It is clear to Niger's leaders that "Islamic ideology" means an official, recognizable, modern version of Muhammad's vision led by governmentally sanctioned and Arab-educated technocrats. Official Islam in Niger guards itself not against Christianity or other religions but against the Pan-African Muslim brotherhoods (especially the Nyassiste Tijaniyya) and entrenched class of marabouts (indigenous Muslim priests), which it regards as unorthodox and "reactionary." This is but an updated version of Niger's previous rulers' preoccupation: "The Chief of State echoes the tone of the French administration in his denunciations of maraboutic beggars and vagabonds" (Triaud 1982:38). Colonial continuity in the realm of religion, moreover, is a possible explanation for the Islamic Association's mitigated success, especially—as we shall see when we examine Islam in Yekuwa—when it comes to controlling and transforming religious life in the Hausa countryside.

The autonomy and vibrancy granted Islam in British Hausaland, in contrast, has naturally carried over into the postcolonial Nigerian state. Given Nigeria's religious pluralism, this freedom has given rise—especially in recent years—to conflicts as yet unexperienced in Nigérien Hausaland. Though religious outbursts have been confined primarily to urban centers, rural communities are not untouched by them.

The heyday of Islamic theocracy in independent Nigerian Hausaland was the First Republic (1960–1966), when the premier of the Northern Region was the *sardauna* of Sokoto, the national prime minister was a devoted member of the faith, and the sultan of Sokoto was still in his prime. A decade of military rule, followed by a more national system of democratic integration (the Second Republic), made secular inroads into the chiefly-cum-religious structure that had characterized the North. A comeback of sorts (favoring sarakuna and Islam) occurred under the regime of Muhammadu Buhari (Nicolas 1984:124), the Daura-born major general. But no matter what the official policy toward Islam (and the 1986 announcement of Nigeria's controversial membership in the Organization of Islamic Conference is here noteworthy), even more significant is the vitality of Islam in Nigerian Hausaland in its unofficial, nongovernmental capacity.

Nigeria's relative wealth, giving rise to greater links to the outside world (over 100,000 pilgrims to Mecca in 1981 alone; about 400,000 between 1979 and 1983), has been a boon to the propagation of Islam. The religion is taking on a more internationalist character than in Niger, and thus is evolving more quickly from the older mold of indigenous Sahelian Islam. The counterpoint to such Islamic evolution is the recent upsurge of violence spawned by populist and fundamentalist Islamic (or quasi-Islamic) movements in Northern Nigeria. These incidents are of two sorts: (a) riots inspired by the Maitatsine "prophet" and his followers and (b) clashes between Muslim and Christian groups (some at the university).

The spirit and power of revolutionary Islam in the African Sahel is not new, any more than is Muslim millenarianism. (Usman dan Fodio's jihad in the early nineteenth century is a phenomenon of the first sort; the Mahdi's populist revolt in the Sudan in the late nineteenth century represents the second.) In the 1980s, however, the rise in Nigeria of the self-proclaimed prophet Alhaji Mohammad Marwa Maitatsine and his followers, known as 'Yan Tatsine, cast quasi-Islamic confrontation within a characteristically contemporary context.

Maitatsine preached against "the widespread corruption of existing secular and religious elites and especially the orgy of Western consumption enjoyed by Kano's privileged classes" (Lubeck 1985:370). He denounced both the use and users of modern technology and luxury goods (cars, radios, televisions, watches, etc.), and modified orthodox Muslim practice and doctrine (e.g., the position and frequency of prayer, the rejection of accepted Koranic commentary, perhaps desacralizing the Prophet Muhammad himself). The 'Yan Tatsine (mostly youths, unemployed migrants, and Koranic students) began to control neighborhoods, harassed their residents, and, when eventually challenged by Nigerian security forces, broke out into armed insurrection. At least five such riots occurred in Northern Nigeria between 1980 and 1985.

Paul Lubeck attributes the rise and success of the Maitatsine phenomenon to the progressive marginalization of the *gardawa* (sing. *gardi*), the migratory, seasonal, and peasant class of Koranic students. Economic changes wrought by the colonial-mercantile capitalist period (1900–1966) and especially the petroleum boom of the 1970s and early 1980s transformed the gardawa from respected and useful conveyers of Muslim learning and magical power into an impoverished and distrusted lumpenproletariat. So marginalized, gardawa were prey to the charisma of a Maitatsine. By drawing on the power, passions, and convictions previously instilled by Muslim socialization, Maitatsine transformed this social dissatisfaction—the result of modern economic processes (and especially the socially disrupting impact of the post-OPEC oil-pricing bonanza)—into a fanatical and rebellious religious force.

Mervyn Hiskett (1987) discounts (without dismissing outright) the socioeconomic explanation for the Maitatsine explosion in favor of a "tribalistic" (i.e., ethnic-cum-linguistic-cum-cultural) one. For Hiskett, Maitatsine (of Cameroonian origin) appealed largely to dry-season "economic opportunists" (*'yan-ci-rani,* "eaters of the dry season"), largely of non-Hausa or non-Muslim background. He thus distinguishes them from the gardawa proper, whom he recasts as authentically Hausa and Muslim, and more urbanized, less peripatetic, and older than the people Lubeck describes.

If Hiskett is right, many of the followers of the Maitatsine not only spoke bad Hausa (*Gwaranci*) but were "culturally adrift" in urban and Islamic society. Staid city dwellers of Nigerian Hausaland disdain the 'yan-ci-rani; the latter, in turn, resent "Hausa linguistic and cultural pretensions" (Hiskett 1987:214–15). Maitatsine tapped into this wellspring of latent frustration and resentment and traumatized urban Hausaland. Such religious trauma, however, has been historically recurrent in the western Sudan and, though aggravated by contemporary material privations, does not require a predominantly economic (and particularly Marxist) framework of interpretation (210, 222).

Since the mid-1980s Islam in Northern Nigeria has been party to a different kind of violent challenge: communal tension between Christians and Muslims. In March 1987 an altercation between a female Muslim student and a Christian evangelist (the former accused the latter of publicly distorting the Koran, and slapped him) erupted into riots in at least six towns throughout Kaduna State (Kafanchan, Zaria, Funtua, Katsina, Ikara, and Kankia). Mosques and churches were burned, over six hundred arrests were made, and between thirteen and twenty-two deaths were recorded. Nigerian President Ibrahim Babangida claimed that the riots were "not just a religious crisis but rather, the civilian equivalent of an attempted coup d'état organized against the . . . government and the Nigerian nation" (*West Africa*, March 23, 1987, 552).

A real coup attempt in April 1990 also carried religious overtones. Although neither Christianity nor Islam was explicitly mentioned by the rebel military officers, their declared "expulsion" of the northern (Muslim) states from the Nigerian Federal Republic, combined with the discovery that they had been bankrolled by the multimillionaire benefactor of the Pentecostal Household of God Fellowship Church, demonstrated how vulnerable even the military is to religious divisiveness.

Several instances of Christian-Muslim unrest occurred in Northern Nigeria in 1991: riots in Bauchi State over the interdenominational use of an abattoir, rioting in Kano over the expected arrival of a German Christian fundamentalist preacher. Greater catastrophe erupted in May 1992 when a rural land dispute in northern Kaduna State (Zangon-Kataf) touched off riots between Muslims and Christians in the cities of Kaduna and Zaria. Upwards of two hundred persons were killed, hundreds of arrests were made, and several churches were burned to the ground.

Interestingly, much of the Christian-Muslim violence has occurred among the future intelligentsia of the country: during the 1987 troubles (which erupted at Kafanchan Teachers College), the chapel at the College of Advanced Studies at Ahmadu Bello University (ABU) in Zaria was burned, and twenty students were wounded in a clash at Bayero University in Kano (BUK). As a result, a ban was placed on religious associations and organizations in all institutions of higher learning. Such a measure could not, however, prevent student council elections at ABU from degenerating into pitched battles between Christian and Muslim students the next year.

Such overt conflict between Christian and Muslim is new in Nigeria, and perhaps presages another kind of change: the grafting of a newer (religious) form of polarization onto an historically more familiar (regional) one. It may be premature to offer a comprehensive sociohistorical explanation for this unexpected rise in Christian-Muslim tensions in Nigeria, although the widening scale of exposure to the greater Muslim and Arab world, thanks to modern transportation and communication networks, may be partly responsible. Whatever the root cause or causes, Nigerian Hausa society is experiencing heightened politicization of religious identity to an extent unknown in Niger. Colonial boundaries, which made Niger as religiously homogeneous as Nigeria is pluralistic, bear indirect responsibility.

Islam in Yardaji and Yekuwa

> In the past [here in the bush], there was no true Islam. Instead, there were pagan beliefs, medicines, and magic.
>
> Then one day a certain Mallam Hassan, a Beriberi, came to Damagaram from Bornu. He was really on his way to Sokoto, and was just passing through.
>
> But Tanimu, the Sarkin Damagaram, asked him to stay and live in Damagaram. Hassan said that he couldn't, because the people of Damagaram were not Muslim. "We aren't?" asked the Sarki.
>
> "How many wives do you have?" Mallam Hassan asked.
>
> "Fifty, sixty," replied the Sarki.
>
> "A true Muslim has no more than four," said Mallam Hassan. "Also, he prays [five times a day] and he fasts [during Ramadan]."
>
> Tanimu reformed and Damagaram was Islamized. And whatever was done in Damagaram was followed—it had to be followed—in the bush, by order of the sarki. And so Islam came here, too.
>
> —Yekuwa elder

The reminiscences of elderly villagers in Yardaji and Yekuwa are in the main compatible with the accepted historical account of the expansion of Islam into their areas. The veracity of the encounter between the mallam and the king is less important than the period in which it is said to have taken place. For by tracing the arrival of "true Islam" in the Daura bush to Tanimu's regime, the villagers themselves recognize the relative recency of their religion's entry (at least in its present form) on the local scene. In fact, if we take into account the religious backsliding documented elsewhere (Hiskett 1984:183–85) and the general expansion of Islam during the colonial era, it might be even more realistic to situate significant Islamization of the villages only within the twentieth century.

The everyday observances and manifestations of Islam are similar in both villages. Daily prayer (five times a day) is the norm, Friday afternoon prayers are communal, and daylight fasting during Ramadan is universal. Each village has a Friday mosque (Yardaji's is more elaborate), a village priest and "Friday mosque priest," and several Koranic schools. Yet while any person from one village would be comfortable with the daily rituals of the other, some institutions and phenomena linked to the exercise of Islam have been differentiating the villages since the colonial era and beyond. We have seen the relationship between Islam and secular education in Chapter 9. Three other spheres worth examining are pilgrimage, marriage, and law.

Table 10. Heads of Yardaji and Yekuwa households who have and have not made the pilgrimage to Mecca

	Yardaji		Yekuwa	
	No.	%	No.	%
Yes	142[a]	21%	287[b]	41%
No	545	79	407	59
Total	687	100%	694	100%

[a]Of whom 12 went twice, 3 went three times.
[b]Of whom 75 went twice, 13 went three times, 2 went four times, and four went five or more times.

The Hajj

The hajj (pilgrimage to Mecca) is one of the five pillars of Islam.[1] Before independence, colonial authorities in West Africa were able to control the departure of pilgrims for political reasons, granting permission in exchange for support by the clergy, withholding it as a means of coercion or punishment. Today, with jet travel and petrodollars fueling religious zeal, the airborne hajj has become a growth industry in Northern Nigeria (especially Kano), and one that Nigerian authorities are still trying hard to regulate. Curiously, though, the proportion of *alhaji* in Yekuwa (41 percent) is almost double that of Yardaji (see Table 10).

It is worth noting that Yekuwa has not only many more alhazai (plural of "alhaji") than Yardaji but considerably more repeaters: seventy-five alhazai from Yekuwa have been to Mecca twice, but only twelve from Yardaji have done so; thirteen went thrice (compared with three from Yardaji); and two went four times. Four have gone five times or more, and one of them has made the hajj nine times!

The goal of purchasing an airplane ticket to Mecca is one of the major incentives for livestock investment in Yekuwa. It is common to purchase young or skinny cattle and fatten them up for resale at a significant profit. Grazing is a "free" value-added stage, requiring no additional cash investment. Sheep, goats, and cattle are items of bulk wealth, indivisible in the sense that one cannot sell (or lose) part of one. The sale of one or a few can cover the price of a plane ticket.

[1] The others are affirming the unity of God and the prophetic rule of Muhammad, praying five times daily, giving charity, and fasting throughout Ramadan. The hajj becomes obligatory only when one has the means to perform it.

'Yan Yardaji tend rather toward petty trading, setting up stalls or tables to sell household goods. Profits from resale of the processed consumer goods (soap, flashlights, detergent, perfume, candy, etc.) come in small increments. Under such circumstances, savings are more difficult to accumulate; the desired hajj ticket appears more inaccessible.

A sociopsychological reason is also invoked by villagers to explain the greater number of Yekuwa alhazai: it is said that 'yan Yekuwa are more generous than 'yan Yardaji and therefore more prone to help their poorer relatives make the pilgrimage as well.

Whatever personal status may accrue to the alhaji, the savings and investments converted into pilgrimage tickets are not likely to contribute directly or substantially to the village's economy. Even the custom of returning from Mecca with luxury items (such as radios and watches) both as gifts and for resale provides little in the way of local investment.

One local effect of the hajj stems from the fact that flights to Mecca originate in Kano, Nigeria. Thus not only must tickets be purchased in Nigerian naira, but all would-be pilgrims need Nigerian passports. This is not a major obstacle to 'yan Yekuwa, for Nigérien citizens can readily obtain Nigerian passports through "dash." Virtually all Nigérien alhazai who live along the border and in relative proximity to Kano possess the green passports of Nigeria.[2]

For the purposes of conducting the pilgrimage, then, Muslim traders of Yekuwa are obliged both to conduct illegal business in naira and to pretend to be Nigerian. This is not to say that feigning foreign citizenship and dealing in foreign currency to fulfill religious obligations create a national identity crisis for Nigériens of Yekuwa. Nevertheless, both the necessity of conducting illegal business in naira and of pretending to be Nigerian do little to promote the Nigérien government's desire for economic autonomy and to instill a positive sense of national consciousness in its rural communities. Needless to say, parallel conflict between state interest and pilgrimage logistics does not arise on the Nigerian side of the border.

Marriage and Seclusion

"The Hausa have seven days festival. The first three take place at the bride's house. Then, after the contract ceremony, the bride is conducted to the groom's house where the ceremony is completed" (Trimingham 1980:72).

---

[2] They do not usually bother to obtain Nigérien passports, which are less useful and more difficult to obtain.

Bridal procession in Yekuwa. In Nigeria the mounted spectacle has been declared un-Islamic, so in Yardaji the bride is driven to her new home in a minivan, and cassette tapes replace drummers.

What is neglected in this account of the wedding ceremony (*ɗauren aure*) is a description of what makes the bride's trip to her groom's home so special in traditional Hausa society: she is wrapped in elaborate, colorful clothing that renders her completely unrecognizable (some brides also wear sunglasses) and placed on a horse, with a younger sister sitting behind her. Then, with a village crowd following, she is led, accompanied by loud singing, dancing, and drum beating, to her future husband's house.

There is nothing particularly Muslim about this custom, and its practice in Yekuwa seems to bear out J. Spencer Trimingham's assertion that "with marriage as a *rite de passage* . . . the indigenous element remain[s] dominant and the Islamic aspect negligible" (45). This ceremony has been abandoned in Yardaji, purportedly because such a traditional "pagan" custom is incompatible with (Nigerian) Muslim doctrine. Although some local inhabitants attribute the ritual's disappearance to the rising cost of renting horses (much scarcer in "developed" Yardaji, with its fleet of motorcycles and vans, than in Yekuwa), the real reason seems to be a judgment made by high-ranking mallamai in the country that subjecting a bride to such a spectacle is, according to Islamic principle, undignified, unseemly, and hence improper. It is worth noting, though, that even if the horse has been

Table 11. Married women kept in seclusion in Yardaji and Yekuwa

	Yardaji		Yekuwa	
	No.	%	No.	%
Yes	211	36%	76	11%
No	379	64	585	89
Total	590	100%	661	100%

done away with in bridal processions in Yardaji, the bride still is carried to her groom with music and song—now inside a Japanese-built minibus, and accompanied by the honking of a horn.

The extent of purdah or wife seclusion (kulle) also differentiates the villages along religious lines. Here again, the pattern indicates greater outward Islamic orthodoxy in Yardaji (influenced by Nigerian Islam) than in Yekuwa (within a Nigérien state more regulatory of Islam).

"Locking" or "tying" one's wife in kulle has traditionally been a prerogative of wealthy and urban husbands. M. G. Smith, noting "the spread of purdah-type marriage throughout the rural areas of Hausaland in recent years," links it with "the exclusion of Moslem Hausa women from active farming [according to] . . . the Hausa division of labour" (Introduction to Mary Smith 1954/1981:22). Yet Hausa women do engage in active farming; more important, the generalization about "Hausaland" does not seem to take the border differences into account.

My 1986 survey found that kulle was three times as prevalent in Yardaji as in Yekuwa (although it was a minoritarian practice in both). In Yardaji, 36 percent of husbands put their wives into seclusion; in Yekuwa, only 11 percent did so (see Table 11). In both villages, however, it was said that kulle had become more and more feasible, thanks to the increasing monetization of the economy: "Previously, there was no way to pay for water, for firewood, for clothing. Now because of money, women need not leave their homes to provide these things."

It would be rash to conclude on the basis of this evidence alone that 'yan Yardaji are more religious, or in a monetary sense more wealthy, than their Yekuwa counterparts. It is true that the demonstration effect of urban kulle in Kano and other Muslim Hausa centers in Nigeria probably has spilled over into Yardaji, adding social pressures to practice purdah. Yet 'yan Yekuwa point to another advantage of the 'yan Yardaji: The solid ground of Yardaji permits the digging of deep household latrines (a relatively recent innovation); the sandy soil of Yekuwa makes this practice much more difficult. With latrines, women may attend to their bodily functions within their own households, within purdah. Without latrines, they must be permitted to go into the fields, so kulle is impossible to enforce.

Shari'a

One of the thorniest issues bound up in the debate over the 1978 Constitution of Nigeria was that of shari'a, Islamic religious law. Should it—and how could it—be institutionalized in a modern, theoretically secular state? Under the British—generally supportive of traditional institutions—Nigeria had enjoyed a long history of coexisting parallel legal systems, religious and customary, along with British common law. In keeping with its pre-independence tradition, Nigeria did opt, in its 1979 and 1989 constitutions, for legally recognized, state-funded shari'a courts to handle issues that fell within the purview of Islamic law.[3]

For the people in and around Yardaji, shari'a, more than being a viable option, is the usual institutional channel for resolving disputes of a civil, commercial, or domestic nature that cannot be settled by the village chief. Permanent shari'a court offices exist in nearby Zango (seat of the local government area) and Daura (capital of the emirate). Both towns are easily reached by public transportation. The government police are a last resort. Few villagers would ever consider going to them on their own. Although theoretically Islamic law holds sway on the other side of the border as well, in practice the villagers of Yekuwa are normally cut off from shari'a avenues of dispute resolution. In the subprefecture of Magaria, cases brought to the palace of the chief may indeed be settled there, on the basis of Muslim law. But Magaria is twenty miles away, and no road connects it with Yekuwa. For logistical and economic reasons alone—lack of an adequate transportation infrastructure, prohibitive costs to travel—villagers in the Nigérien countryside are more likely than those in Northern Nigeria to eschew Islamic institutions of justice. Again, such constraints but reinforce the French colonial discouragement of traditional political and legal institutions.

At the same time, matters of a socially or economically disruptive nature in the community may more easily come to the attention of the government through its agents, patrolling gendarmes. Once these authorities catch wind of a problem, however justiciable by religious law, it is unlikely

---

[3] The proposal for the establishment of a Federal Court of Shari'a was not, however, ratified. See Laitin 1982 and Ibrahim 1991, esp. 131–32.

that the matter will be disentangled from the web of secular "justice." The following story, recounted by Alhaji Mallam H., a thirtyish grandson of the Yekuwa village chief, demonstrates how bizarre the results can become.

The Tale of Alhaji Mallam H.

First, you must know that memorizing the Koran is not the same thing as seeking wisdom. . . .

When my studies [elsewhere] were finished, I returned home. I had begun to acquire some knowledge, but I still had some way to go. I was here for about two years, preaching about the Muslim religion.

While I was preaching, there were some men [here in the village] who opposed me, for they hadn't learned the Muslim religion very well, and they feared that they might be caught in error. Although they didn't like me, they didn't express it—not openly, at least. For example, some of their wives would walk around town, draw water for them, collect firewood in the bush for them. But Allah doesn't like this—even in the Koran it's written that God doesn't like this. But these men wouldn't listen. . . .

In addition, there is something that they would read—*Sallatal Fatiya*. Myself, I didn't tell them that it wasn't a good thing. They also met up with someone who promised them Paradise next to God.

[One day] a certain itinerant preacher came to my place and said that he was going to preach. I said, "The government has prohibited preaching without authorization. I myself am a son of the town, which is why I myself don't have to procure it. But as for you, let's go to the village chief. If he forbids you, that's the end of it."

We went to the chief. I told him, "This stranger wants to preach. He desires permission to preach."

The chief said, "This is a matter for the mallamai." He told us to go to the Friday [i.e., head] *limam* [imam].

We went to the Friday limam. We greeted him in the mosque, in his ward. He said, "Mallam Alhaji H., is everything all right?"

I replied, "All is well. But there is something. I have come with a stranger, who seeks to preach. We went to the chief to seek permission, but he sent us to you."

He said, "What did the chief say to you?"

"He said that he himself was not going to forbid preaching, for this is a matter of the Muslim religion."

So the Friday limam said that since the chief didn't forbid preaching, he wasn't going to, either. He said, "Go and do it."

So this mallam began to study [the Koran], he began to preach. He said, "Taking water, wandering throughout town for no purpose, collecting firewood, going to the market—because of all these things that women are doing here, their husbands will not reach Paradise." Just as I had spoken, he too spoke. He also said that he who relies on the [man who promised salvation] will not reach Paradise either. He said, "How can it be that any man will receive seventy measures of greatness next to Allah, the Prophet, the Koran, and the angels? This is a lie." I listened to this mallam.

There were many people in town who sided with me. They asked, "Is it true, is it a lie?"

"Most certainly, it is a lie," I said. "I myself didn't tell you; [but] I wanted to draw your attention to it, for it is an important duty."

Now a certain old man—you know him, the stooped one—he went to the Friday limam. He said, "Limam, have you heard the news that Alhaji Malam H. has brought some stranger, and they are going to ruin the religion of our family and ancestors?"

He said, "Yes, they've come, they told me. They said that the chief let them be."

But the old man said, "No. Let's go to Mallam G."

They went to Mallam G. He told them he would see them in the morning, for it was night.

In the morning, the old man gathered many people together, and they came here [to the chief's hut]. They found me at the entrance to the compound. They asked, "Where is your stranger?" I said, "He's in my home." They told me to call him. "Is everything all right?" I asked. Mallam G. only said, "Just go and summon him."

I answered, "Mallam, if you've come with something to say, tell me, and I myself will tell the stranger."

"I've heard that he's claimed the *Sallatal Fatiya* is a lie."

I replied, "If this is what it's all about, I am not going to call him. I myself say it is a lie!"

"What is your proof?" they asked.

"The Koran says it's a lie. There is nothing that one may read or chant that will give him seventy measures of greatness next to the Prophet, seventy measures next to the Koran, and seventy measures next to the angels, and greatness equal to that of all men on earth."

Mallam G. said, "You are lying."

"Since you said it's a lie, let us swear by the Koran, you and I."

He said that he would not swear—only I myself should swear. So I swore by the Koran—but I invoked both of us, saying, "If I lied, may Allah punish me; but if he lied, may the punishment be his."

He said that I wasn't a Muslim. He got up and left, he and his people. He went to complain to the soldier in town.[4] The soldier came to me and said, "Where is your stranger?" And so I called [the stranger]. The soldier then

[4] This recourse to a member of the armed forces constitutes a critical turning point in the drama. The soldier in question was probably some low-ranking member of the border patrol who happened to be in the village at the time. There is no permanent military or police presence in the village.

asked, "Where is the chief?" "He's at home," I said. The soldier said, "Let's go to his place."

When he got there, the soldier told the chief, "I am arresting the stranger." "But why?" I asked.

"Because he has preached without authorization."

"If this is the way it is, then you have arrested us—since he is my guest."

So we left the chief's house and went to the guesthouse.[5] There we came upon Mallam G., who was sitting there. My guest told me to go and gather his things and his money—seven naira and fifty kobo—and bring them to him.

When he got there, the soldier pulled out a pair of handcuffs from his pocket and bound the guest's hands with them. Then, pointing to Mallam G., he asked the guest, "Do you know this man?"

The guest said, "No. I don't know him. I've never spoken with him, nor have I ever seen him before." The soldier asked Mallam G., "Is this true?"

"Yes. I don't know him either."

So the soldier asked Mallam G., "So with whom did you speak?"

"With Alhaji Mallam H.," he answered.

The soldier said, "Let's hold off speaking until he [Alhaji Mallam H.] gets here."

When I arrived, the soldier undid the handcuffs from the guest, and he put them on me. He said, "Aha, you're the wrongdoer, not the stranger. Stranger, get up, be off with you."

The guest said, "No. Where you bring this man, you'll bring me too."

"I'm going to take you to Magaria. Let's go."

Mallam G. said, "Don't take them—just make them promise not to repeat what they've done."

I refused. "We shall not agree to such a thing."

The soldier said, "I won't let them go. They will go to Magaria—and go to prison."

"We agree," I said.

Then the chief said, "You, Alhaji Mallam H., rather than be brought to Magaria, to prison, ask for pardon."

So I said to the soldier, "We are sorry. Forgive us."

He said, "Okay, it's over." The soldier undid the handcuffs. We got up and left.

But when Mallam G. returned home, he wrote a letter to the chief in Magaria. In it he said, "We have had a dispute with a certain youth, regarding religion—the grandson of the village chief, and his guest. [I write] so that you don't hear [it] from anyone else."

K. [a brother of Alhaji Mallam H.] was with the chief of Magaria when the letter arrived. The chief said, "K., a letter has been sent from your village. It is necessary to arrest this youth, your younger brother."

---

5 This is where visiting members of the border patrol put up at night.

K. said, "May you live long, whatever you say, are we not obliged to do it?" K. returned home, and he called me from the chief's compound. "The chief of Magaria said that they will come to arrest you. So flee!"

I said, "No. I shall not run from the truth. If I am in the wrong, I will run. But since I am in the right, I am not going to run."

"So that's it," said K.

Fourteen days later, a soldier came. He found me at the entrance to the chief's compound. He said, "Alhaji Mallam H.?"

"Yes?"

"Come! I have been sent here to arrest you—you and your grandfather [the chief], we shall all go to Magaria."

"All right," I said. "But I ask you to let me go and pray." It was two o'clock, time for the midafternoon prayers.

"Go ahead," he said.

When I finished praying, I said that I would go home and prepare my things. [The soldier said it was all right.] I went home. When I entered the house, and met my wife, and my mother, and my sister, I told them, "They have sent a soldier for me. We are going to Magaria. But nothing will happen. I'll go, but come back. After we're gone, do not cry. Just be patient, I'll return. They won't do anything to me."

They said, "All right then. It won't matter."

So we went off, myself, the chief, Alhaji A., Mallam G., his son, and the soldier. We went to 'Dan Kware by foot—the soldier was on horseback, and so were the chief and Mallam G., for they were old men.

We went to 'Dan Kware, and did our evening prayers. When we finished the prayers, a truck came. We got into the truck, and they asked us for our money. The soldier said, "The subprefect sent me, to bring these people to Magaria. Because of this, we aren't going to pay." The owner of the truck agreed. He had no choice.

We got to Magaria after dusk. The soldier said that the chief, Alhaji A., Mallam G. and his son should go into town. "But," he said, "you, Alhaji Mallam H., let's go home." The chief said, "Where is home?" The soldier replied, "Prison!"

The chief said, "No, leave him, he'll come along with us."

The soldier said, "No. If in the morning they look for him, and ask where Mallam H. is, what will I say? We have to go to the prison."

The chief said, "Did he kill anyone? Did he steal? For this you bring him to jail?"

"Yes, it's necessary."

I said, "Chief, don't worry. Nothing will happen." So the chief said, "That's it, then. All right, go."

We arrived at the entrance to the prison. It was closed, so he knocked at the entrance door. The guard asked who was there.

"It's me, M., from Yekuwa."

The guard opened the door and said, "It's you, M? Have you brought the Prophet of Yekuwa?"

I uttered, "Istingifari laha azimu."[6]

"Isn't it so?" asked the warder.

"You alone have said this. Not I."

Then the soldier said, "Here is my charge. Take him."

The guard said, "All right," and then "Where is the King of the Prison?"[7]

The King of the Prison appeared and said, "Here I am."

"You've got one [a visitor]," said the guard.

"From where?"

"From Yekuwa," I answered.

"Oh, are you the mallam from Yekuwa?"

"Yes."

"OK, come with me." He had already heard of me.

He led me to his mat and said, "Listen, everyone, I have a guest—a great guest." And so we went on chatting with him, the King of the Prison. I told him everything that had happened, from the very beginning up to that very moment. He said, "If this is what it's all about, tomorrow you'll be released." I replied [that that was fine news].

"Did you come with money?" he asked.

"I don't have any money—only one hundred francs."[8]

"OK, tomorrow morning you will chop some firewood, pound [millet], you'll clean up the latrine. Every guest that is brought here must do these things, because this is a house of hardship."

I said, "May God see us to tomorrow."

In the morning, at dawn, I got up and said my prayers. I picked up the Koran and began to read. I kept on reading, until the day had really begun. Before I finished my reading, the King of the Prison went out, and then came back. When he returned, I was still reading. We didn't exchange a word at the time.

He addressed an old man who was next to me, saying, "Don't let this man do anything. Don't let him give anybody any money. He isn't to move from this spot—I, King of the Prison, have spoken thus."

I was reading, but I heard when he said this. Nevertheless, I didn't stop reading. Only when I finished did I take out the one hundred francs I had and gave it to the old man, telling him to go and buy some bean cakes.

---

6 Words uttered when a man speaks profanely concerning Allah. If the hearer utters these words, he is relieved of responsibility for the profanity and protected from any consequences.

7 A senior member of the inmate community. Note how a kind of parachieftaincy is established among the prison population.

8 The equivalent of about 50 cents.

He bought the bean cakes for me. I took three of them, and I ate them. I said, "The rest of them, you divide up as charity."

After we divided these bean cakes as charity, five or six men came up to me, to get me to work. But whenever one came, the old man said, "The King of the Prison has forbidden him to work." A man asked, "Where is the money which he has given?" The old man replied, "Go and ask the King." So they took off.

I told the old man [that I was falling asleep]. He said, "Mallam, go lie down and sleep!" I started to sleep when the soldier [from the previous day] came to get me, to take me to town.

"Where is the mallam from Yekuwa?" he asked. I heard him from my sleep, but I ignored him. So the old man spoke. "Here he is, he's asleep." He came up to me and shook me, saying, "Mallam, wake up."

When I got up, we exchanged greetings. Then he said, "Get up, let's go."

I arose, and we went to the office [of the deputy subprefect]. We met up with the deputy, the chief of Magaria, the chief [of Yekuwa], and Mallam G., there at the office.

The soldier saluted the deputy subprefect and removed his cap. "Here he is," he said.

The deputy said, "Mallam G., do you know this man?"

"Yes, I know him."

The deputy pulled out the letter that Mallam G. had written from [Yekuwa], pointed to it, and said, "Do you know what this is?"

"Yes, I know," I replied.

"Read it, so that we all hear," said the deputy.

[Mallam G.] picked it up and started to read. His hands were trembling. The deputy said, "Mallam, calm down. Just read the paper properly."

Mallam G. [turned to me and said], "You, young man, not before you or Allah shall I be intimidated."

I said, "La' ilaha illa Allah."[9] Mallam G. said, "What? Did I do wrong?"

"Certainly you did wrong," I said. The chief [interjected], "Stop speaking." I fell silent. [Mallam G.] went on with reading the paper. He read:

"A letter from the Hand of Mallam G., to the Chief of Magaria,

"Greetings and prayers from grace, for the Chief.

"Lest you hear from another source, we have had deceit concerning religion, from the grandson of the chief of Yekuwa. Lest you hear by rumor. We have had the following deceit: The boy has said that *Sallatal Fatiya* is a lie. He has said, 'Do not have any intermediary for any man.' In addition, he said, 'Books are a lie.'"

The deputy said, "Is this so?"

---

9 Uttered when someone else speaks a falsehood, or wrongly.

I said, "No—it isn't so."

"So what [is the truth]?"

"Ask Mallam G. Did he hear this from my own mouth?"

Mallam G. said, "No, I didn't hear it from your mouth. But it has been said that the stranger in your home said this."

"So my guest spoke thus, [but] no one heard *me* say this."

"True," he said.

The deputy [stepped in]. "You there, we've heard you have been preaching."

"Yes, for certain," I said.

"So if you are preaching, you put your guest up to speaking this way."

"No," I said. "What I have been showing in my preaching is that they should put their women in kulle; that they [the women] shouldn't go to draw and carry water, or to collect firewood in the bush, or go to the market [idly]."

Mallam G. said, "It's a lie."

The deputy turned to me. "*Comment?* [10] You're going to speak lies in front of me too?" He called a gendarme on the telephone, telling him to come quickly. When the gendarme came, he took me away, to his—the gendarme's—office. When we got to the office, the gendarme asked me, "Why did they tell me to come and bring you to this office?"

"Well, the reason is that we've had a dispute concerning religion." I told him all that had happened. While I spoke, there was a man writing down everything I said. When I finished, the gendarme read it, and then read the notes that were taken when we were in the deputy's office. "That's it," he said. "The same thing—no mistakes."

He spoke to his "brother" in French. He said, "The deputy wants to do this boy wrong. He, the boy, is more in the right than that mallam. Because of this, here in Magaria, there is no one who will beat him or insult him." In French he spoke all this. I didn't know then what he was saying.

The gendarme got up and went out, and his colleague said, "Mallam, did you understand what the chief [i.e., gendarme] said?"

"I don't understand French," I said. So he told me what the chief had said. That was it for then. It was twelve o'clock, and everyone left work. The man said, "Come with me." We got up, went outside, to the foot of a tree. They brought food, and we ate together.

In the afternoon they went back to work. The chief returned.

"Mallam," he said, "you are going to become ignorant. Look at this," and he pointed to the wall. I saw three whips. He said, "If you don't tell me the truth, we'll take one of these whips and beat you with it."

In spite of this, he didn't frighten me. Thinking of what his colleague had told me, I repeated exactly what I had said earlier. He put the three papers together—from the morning talk with the deputy, with the gendarme chief,

[10] Note the occasional use of a French word to reinforce authority.

and now this third one—and brought them to the deputy. He came back and said, "I've been told to bring you back to the prison until the *sous-préfet* returns."

So that was it. They came with a vehicle and took me back to the prison.

When we got to the entrance to the prison, they opened the door. When I went outside and the King of the Prison saw me, he said, "Mallam, have you returned?" "Yes," I said, "I've come back."

"I didn't think you'd return."

"Well, you see what Allah has done."

"What happened?" I told him everything that happened [since I had last seen him].

"Let's see your hand. . . . Nothing has happened to it."

"Oh, no, they haven't done anything."

"All right, then, because if they had put it on, they would be taking you to Damagaram." He was referring to ink on thumb, in case of fingerprinting. If someone's case will not be settled in Magaria, he will be fingerprinted and taken to Zinder. "But if the *sous-préfet* arrives, we'll have to say goodbye."

So I resumed my life in the prison—for three days. But I didn't eat any prison food. The King of the Prison would bring food for me from the town. Good food, not the kind they have in prison. I have never yet eaten prison food. No fighting, no insults, no "black speech." The only work I did was reading [the Koran]—that and praying to Allah. I wanted to give charity as well, but I didn't have any money. So I borrowed money from the King of the Prison—two hundred francs. Every morning I could then buy bean cakes and give charity within the prison.

On the fourth day the subprefect arrived—it was a Sunday. He made a telephone call from his home [as a soldier told me later], and told a certain soldier (a different one) to come. He told the soldier to go to the prison and to come back with the "mallam from Yekuwa."

The soldier came. He went to the prison guard, and told him what the subprefect had told him. He entered and found me asleep. He told the King of the Prison that he was told to bring the "mallam from Yekuwa" to the subprefect.

The old man said, "Ah, Mallam, today you are released." The King of the Prison said the same thing: "Mallam, today you are being let out." All the prisoners gathered round and we exchanged farewells.

We went out [the soldier and I]. We chatted, since he knew I was no great wrongdoer—otherwise I wouldn't be taken out of prison on a Sunday. We went to the subprefecture, and found some people sitting at the foot of the tree—because on that day there was no work. When we got there, the soldier saluted the subprefect. I put out my hand to him and we greeted each other. I also shook hands with his companion. He asked me why I had been in prison for as long as four days. I told him.

"Is this the reason why you've been placed in prison?"

"Yes."

"But look how the chief [of Magaria] has done you wrong! For such a thing you bring a man to prison, and keep him there for four days? This kind of thing is not our affair. This is something that you mallamai are supposed to reconcile among yourselves. Where were you born?"

"In Yekuwa."

"And that's where you grew up?"

"Yes," I said.

"Where did you go to [Koranic] school?"

"In Nigeria."

"OK, fine. Look, I'm going to bail you out."

"Thank you," I said.

"Who do you know here in Magaria?" I gave him the names of two people I knew.

"OK, go to their homes. But come back tomorrow morning."

"All right," I said. I walked off, and left the soldier [who had brought me there] behind. He wasn't pleased—after all, a soldier is your escort, and then you go separate ways? A soldier doesn't feel happy when that happens.

After I had gone a little way, the subprefect called me back. "For God's sake, don't shame me and run away."

"May you live long, but how could you think such a thing? Two weeks before I was arrested I knew they would be coming for me, and I didn't flee. I certainly won't run off now."

The soldier walked off, and the subprefect said that he too was going to leave. "I too will go then," I said. "May you live long." The soldier went off one way and I another. The subprefect called me over again. He said:

"Tomorrow, when you come, whatever wrong I say you have committed, I want you to agree with me."

So I went "home," to where the chief [of Yekuwa] was staying. "Here is some food," he said when I arrived. So I ate some food. Y. came and found me sitting there.

"What?! How is it you've come here?" he exclaimed. He was afraid I had escaped from prison, and had come to his home.

"The subprefect told me to come."

"Impossible," Y. said. "The subprefect isn't around."

"He's returned," I said.

"OK," he replied. Then he went off to the chief [of Magaria, supposedly to tell him I had come to his home]. I did my afternoon prayers, and then went to the market to look around. When I finished wandering, I came back.

The next morning we all went to the subprefect's office. When we got there, before the subprefect said anything, the chief [of Magaria] spoke:

"This boy is a Jew. If we leave him here in Magaria, he'll corrupt the whole territory."

The subprefect nodded his head, but I knew he didn't agree, on account of our talk from the day before. At first he didn't say a word. Then he asked me the same thing from the previous day: "What have you done that they've put you in prison, for four days already?" I answered exactly as I had the first time. Then he said, "All right. I am not going to pass judgment on all this discussion that you have conducted. Chief, you must decide in this matter. Decide who is in the right, who is in the wrong, and treat them accordingly." [The chief turned to me.]

"What is your religion?"

"I'm a Muslim."

"Do you turn west to pray?" [11]

"No."

Then the council mallam [i.e., head of the Magaria Muslim Association] asked me: "What is your sect—Tijaniyya, or Qadiriyya, or Kabalu?"

"I'm not in any of those," I said. "I follow Malikiyya."

"But all of those are Malikiyya."

"So, I'm a part of it."

Then the council mallam asked me, "Do you have a permit to preach?"

"No."

"According to which commentary do you preach?"

"Upon the Koran I preach."

"You don't use any commentary?"

"That is correct."

"How is it that you preach—there is an official mallam association in the territory, and you didn't come to ask them permission?"

I was silent. I didn't say anything to them. He turned to the subprefect and said, "I asked him. He said he has no permit to preach. He said he doesn't use the *jalamaini* commentary. Without this, a person is not supposed to be preaching. Also, he knew there's a mallam association here in Magaria. Why didn't he come to ask them, and just went ahead on his own to preach? He knew, but he just didn't come!"

The subprefect said, "I'm arresting you for three wrongdoings. Do you know what the three offenses are that you have committed, for which I am holding you?" But in my heart, I knew he wasn't going to hold me, because of our talk from the day before. Nevertheless, I said [I was listening].

"The first offense: preaching in the country without authorization. The president told me that no man should preach without first receiving permission.

---

[11] A Muslim in Niger turns east, toward Mecca, to pray.

"The second offense: preaching without the accepted commentary upon the Koran.

"The third offense: you knew that there is a head of the Magaria Muslim Association, but you didn't go to ask him before preaching.

"Do you agree to this?"

[I said that I did.]

"All right, he has admitted his guilt. But we are going to forgive him for this."

Mallam G., the chief [of Yekuwa], the chief [of Magaria], and a certain mallam were all standing there. The subprefect wrote something down—I don't know what. I signed. He asked, "Are you going to go home now, or tomorrow?"

"We'll go now."

"Wait, I'll try to find a ride for you." He asked at the hospital, but there was no vehicle. He asked at the customs office—no vehicle. He asked at the agricultural office—no vehicle. He said, "I've asked all the services, but there aren't any vehicles around. Will you agree to go in a gendarme vehicle—a 'black car'?" He asked because when you see the "black car" of the gendarmerie, people are afraid and feel that something is wrong—nobody would wish to be seen inside of one.

"Yes, we'll enter it."

"Fine."

We took our leave of the subprefect and got into the vehicle—in the same vehicle as the chief [of Magaria]! We brought him to his palace. When we dropped him off, we went to get gas. Then we went to the home of the council mallam. He went into his house and called his servant to bring me water. After we finished drinking, we took off for home.

When we arrived [in Yekuwa], all the mallamai were assembled, along with the rest of the community. When everyone was there, the council mallam addressed them:

"People, good morning. How are you?"

"Fine."

"How is your worry for your brother?"

"No worry, as we see he has returned with you, in health."

"Fine. The reason that I have come to see you is to convey a message from the lips of the subprefect. Mallam H. was questioned about the three breaches [he committed]. They are: first, preaching without authorization; second, preaching without commentary; third, preaching without consulting the mallam association. This is what has brought us here. That is all. Peace be unto you."

Today there are many mallamai who have left off preaching, because of this requirement of authorization. But after the dry season, I continued to preach anyway.

Beyond illuminating the reason for the rather fearful reputation that the state and its agents have acquired among the villagers, Alhaji Mallam H.'s ordeal demonstrates the unfortunate consequences of state interference in religious and local controversies. The subprefect did seem to recognize a line between mosque and state; but should the matter have been brought to his attention in the first place? It is highly unlikely that a similar situation could occur in Yardaji. Such a matter would have been resolved entirely within the shari'a judicial system, bypassing the local police and local government administration entirely. In Niger, where no such institution is entrenched at the local level, the decision to turn to the secular authorities was natural. For Alhaji Mallam H., however, it was certainly not the most expeditious way of resolving the dispute.

A Partitioned Islam

Students of Islam have a multitude of dimensions by which to categorize and differentiate the various expressions of the faith: doctrinal (Sunni vs. Shi'a), ethnic (Arab vs. non-Arab), regional (e.g., Maghrebian vs. sub-Saharan), institutional (e.g., brotherhood vs. caliphate). Such dichotomies inevitably gloss over the particularistic national expressions of Islam which emerge even in historically and culturally similar contexts. Viewing Islam through the theoretical lens of partition sensitizes us to some of the more subtle differences that may arise.

In Chapter 3 we saw that Hausa villagers on both sides of the Niger-Nigeria boundary overwhelmingly specified that before they were Hausa, before they were Nigériens or Nigerians, they were Muslims. On the face of it, Islam would thus appear to transcend the second-order divisions occasioned by partition and resultant citizenship.

Yet Islam cannot be separated from the historical and national experiences of Hausaland. In the same way that partition has occasioned political and economic distinctions in Hausaland, it has affected the role and significance of religion. Although Islam certainly does unite people across the border, its formal expression, institutional autonomy, and political significance change as one shifts from Nigerian to Nigérien Hausaland. Contrasts in wedding customs and marriage arrangements between Yekuwa and Yardaji are mere epiphenomena of a much wider process. Colonialism and independence have given rise to a differential evolution of religion in the borderlands. In Hausaland, Islam too has been partitioned.

II

Village Cultures Compared

Yardaje, garin maza. Ta Ari, daɗin baƙo. Tuwonku naku. Matonku na baƙi. Garinsu ɗanwa kuke.

Yardaji of Chief Ari is a town of men. It is sweet for the stranger, but the porridge is not shared. Your wife goes with the stranger. They're always too inquisitive, asking, "Where do you come from, who is your father?"

Yékoua, Nalalu. Mai hayaƙin ƙato. Yaro, ko da mi ka zo, an fi ka.

Yekuwa of Chief Nalalu, a place of strapping lads. Whatever you can carry, boy, there is one who can best you.

—Local place epithets

The "national character" approach to comparative politics has lost much of its former attraction for most social and political scientists today.[1] National character studies fell prey to accusations of stereotyping and even ethnocentrism, accusations that were not entirely without foundation. When an entire society's mind-set is simplified so that members of other cultures and societies may easily grasp it, caution and skepticism are indeed warranted.

In this as in many other cases, however, social scientists did not throw out the baby with the bath water; instead they substituted another baby. National character was replaced by political culture, an admittedly more refined and circumscribed concept but one whose paternity national character cannot deny. Political culture theory focuses on those aspects of a nation's or a society's culture that help explain the activity, purpose, form, and function of that nation's or society's political processes. Whereas national character studies aimed to delve into the depths of a nation's

---

[1] For theoretical treatments of national character see Inkeles and Levinson 1954 and (for its critique) Almond 1956. Pye 1965, 1968, 1971 and Verba 1965 best represent the "political culture" offshoot of national character studies.

soul, those of political culture are content to give a plausible accounting of macropolitical behavior based on anthropological, sociological (including religious), and psychological factors. Though the methods differ, they come to similar conclusions.

Yet perhaps the true problem with the national character paradigm lay not in its disciplinary breadth but rather in demographic scale. That is, it is not that national character studies tried to do too much in delineating a community's sociopsychological profile but that they focused on communities too large and diverse. Whole societies encompass too many varying tendencies and tensions to justify comprehensive generalization. Yet by focusing on smaller communities one can with some confidence venture the kinds of generalizations that are risky in the aggregate. We may call this the "village culture" or "village character" approach.

"Village character" refers to the more intangible characteristics of a community. (In French, the nonspecialist term might be *ambiance;* the German equivalent might be *Geist*). It refers not to the commonalities existing among all villages or communities (which would probably be even more hazardous than national character) but rather to the specific profile of a given one. Of course, this profile or character will inevitably be affected and informed by the wider society around it, for few rural communities in the world are autonomous or isolated from a national or even international system. Rather than extrapolate from village character to national (or even subnational) character, here I attempt the opposite: to understand and explain the spirit, culture, and character of a specific community by virtue of its intrinsic and extrinsic influences. Admittedly, one cannot measure, test, or otherwise quantify the "spirit" of a community, and few political scientists today would dare employ such an "unoperational" concept.[2] Nevertheless, the most informative and meaningful of social observations may sometimes be the least demonstrable, at least by (social) scientific means.

Unexpected and strikingly different characteristics distinguish the cultures of Yardaji and Yekuwa. Such differences in village culture and character are not striking merely to the neutral observer but are freely acknowledged by the villagers themselves (albeit in somewhat chauvinistic terms). Moreover, the differences have arisen directly or indirectly as a result of the colonial partition of Hausaland, the local boundary demarcation, the respective colonial legacies, and the differential development of Nigerian and Nigérien politics and society. My argument is not that because Yardaji and Yekuwa are different, Nigerian and Nigérien Hausas must possess dif-

---

[2] But see Barkow 1973 for a most interesting experiment along just such lines.

ferent national characters, but rather that because the Hausa of Yardaji and Yekuwa belong to separate national communities with different colonial experiences, they have developed different village characters. Moreover, proximity to and acceptance of the border intensifies the distinctiveness that each village sees in the other. When we explore the various realms of village life—politics, development, group consciousness, law and order, morality, urbanization, psychology, language—we come to recognize a Nigérien rural Hausa culture and a Nigerian rural Hausa culture, but we find no "rural Hausa culture" apart from the state in which it is embedded.

Siyasa (Politics) vs. Iko (Power)

Elsewhere (Miles 1988) I have given an account of the Nigerian "democratic" and electoral process as experienced in Yardaji. As part of the Northern Region, North Central State, and then Kaduna (subsequently Katsina) State, Yardaji participated in the gradual if uneven extension of participatory politics which marked the late colonial (1946–1960), First Republic (1960–1966), and Second Republic (1979–1983) phases of Nigerian democracy. As C. S. Whitaker (1970) and M. G. Smith (1978) have shown for these first two phases, democracy in British Hausaland and Northern Nigeria was imperfect at best, and often subject to the will and interests of traditional authority (the *masu sarauta* or sarakuna class of traditional chiefs and titleholders). Imported European democratic norms of equality and constitutionalism still conflict with indigenous Hausa values and institutions such as clientage (barantaka) and social stratification (e.g., the distinction between sarakuna and talakawa.)

Still, over several decades the people of Yardaji have become acquainted with Western-style politics in the form of campaigns, elections, and voting.[3] They may take a jaundiced view of such "modern" innovations as *dimokiradiyya* (democracy) and at times express a preference for military over civilian rule; nevertheless, the democratic experiment (even if a failed one) has become part of the experience of being Nigerian and hence of being from Yardaji.

Yekuwa's "democratic experience" has been quite different. Only relatively late in the colonial era did the French accept even the principle of democracy for the subjects of French Hausaland. We have seen in Chapter 6 how weakly Magaria commandants assimilated and extended this

---

[3] At least the men have done so. Women gained the vote in Northern Nigeria in 1979.

principle. In any event, once the Parti Progressiste Nigérien (PPN) consolidated power and brought Niger into independence, it moved rapidly
to eliminate partisan opposition, particularly that of the (predominantly
Hausa) Sawaba movement. From shortly after independence until 1974
Niger was a one-party state: "[T]he Diori government pursued exactly the
same policy as the French after 1922, that of trying to sterilize all political
activity, to silence the voice of the average Nigerien" (Fuglestad 1983:187).
From 1974 until 1991 it was a no-party state, run, administered, and controlled by a military junta. Whereas Yardaji plunged rather raucously into
participation in national politics, submission to iko (power, authority) has
been the norm in Yekuwa. It is not necessary to reiterate how and why
these divergences reflect basic colonial legacies.

People in Yekuwa are quick to point out that the recent regime, even if
a military one, is preferable to the despotic rule of "Yardiar" (RDA, or
Rassemblement Démocratique Africaine, the Pan-African regional party
with which the PPN was affiliated). At that time, the sarakai (soldiers or
traditional rulers) came to the village at will and demanded whatever they
wanted—a house, food, anything. People were obliged to give them what
they wanted. If the Sarkin Magaria came, chickens, millet, meat had to be
offered—and he came frequently, perhaps twice a month. He might even
demand money from the village chief.

Now, it is said, the sarki needs permission from the subprefect to come
to Yekuwa. And the extortion and exploitation have stopped. No longer
can soldiers come and confiscate at will. Villagers may now feel free to ask
anyone, even a soldier, what business has brought him to Yekuwa.

During the time of RDA there was pseudo-democracy. The opposition Sawaba (Freedom) party did have the support of the talakawa, for it
alone was for the common people. RDA was supported by the big chiefs,
the French, the manya-manya (big shots). But if there were elections, the
people were forced to vote RDA. The sarki himself would come to tell the
people that they must vote RDA, saying, "Let not one person do otherwise. . . . Make no mistakes." And someone was always stationed at the
ballot box to ensure that no mistakes were made.

There was fear, real fear, during the RDA era. If an outsider visited,
people would not even pass by the place where he was staying for fear of
being thrashed, or having something taken away, or being forced to do
some very hard work. In fact, no political conversations could take place,
for fear that what was said would be heard by or repeated to an RDA
informant.

Despite the stated preference for life under the soldier Seyni Kountché to conditions under the civilian Hamani Diori, it would be an exaggeration to say that political freedom flourished in Yekuwa. The mitigation of repression is not the same as democratization. 'Yan Yekuwa are happier because they have in general been left alone by government and its agents, because they have not been confronted with siyasa (politics) as they have known it in the past. The notion of siyasa arouses a degree of wariness and suspicion, not only for what it has meant in Yekuwa's past but for what it is seen to represent across the border: chaos, lawlessness, and mass violence.

At the same time, even if some people in Yekuwa are attracted to the idea of democracy, they are less confident that they possess the requisite tools. In a classic instance of the internalization of colonial (and here postcolonial) prejudices by the colonized and ruled,[4] one young man from Yekuwa, an occasional laborer in Nigeria, said:

> Democracy can't work in Niger—people have neither the sense [hankali] nor the learning [ilmi] for it. Neither the soldiers (the older ones) nor the village chiefs have gone to school. How can you expect a democratic system to work here? And politics also means spending money, millions and millions.

Another ɗan Yekuwa put it more crudely: "Ordinary folk [talakawa] have no brains. If you don't hit them, they won't understand authority or governance."

By 1993 the Nigerian military was proceeding, albeit fitfully, to transfer power back to civilians from the local to national levels through a centrally managed two-party system that President Ibrahim Babangida had himself instituted. No matter how many times the military changes its timetable for national elections, there is little doubt that competitive partisan politics is returning to Nigeria, so deeply ingrained is the ideal of democracy among the country's elites, even the military. With the reestablishment of civilian governance, Yardaji is again obliged to participate in Nigerian elections and politics, with all the attendant challenges and risks. Factionalization, cynicism, and electoral corruption may emerge again, but there is no way of insulating the village from the influence of the nation's politics. This is all part of the Yardaji experience.

Intimations that a similar political process is unfolding in Niger must be treated much more cautiously. A transitional government has revised the nation's constitution, reduced the influence of the military, and seen the nation through its first multiparty elections since the 1960s. Undercut by

[4] On this point see Fanon 1967 and Mannoni 1964.

a Tuareg rebellion and severe economic austerity, however, Niger in the early 1990s has been experiencing an uncharacteristically high degree of political instability and indiscipline among the military rank and file.

Perhaps more instructive, and certainly more entrenched, has been the slowly evolving scheme of participatory, developmental democracy which Niger's military rulers instituted in the mid-1980s. Called the Société de Développement (in Hausa Kungiyar Hadin Kan Jama'a Na Kasa Ga Baki 'Daya, or the Association for Putting All the Heads of the Nation's Communities Together as One Voice), the system ostensibly allowed Niger's communities to choose their own leaders, organizing them in a hierarchical corporate structure from the bottom up. It explicitly circumvented (and in fact forbade) the establishment of political parties or any other political organizations not sponsored by the state, and thereby precluded the development of a competitive political system. At the same time, the government exhorted villagers to become involved in the scheme, accentuating the developmental over the political benefits. But viewed from Yekuwa, the government's attempts to motivate them missed the mark.

In the spring of 1986 a government meeting was held in Yekuwa, headed by the subprefect (still referred to as commandant) and the sarki of Magaria. They reportedly were accompanied by eight other important men, all but one of them government functionaries. The meeting lasted four long hours.

Each of the dignitaries made a speech "until he was tired"; then another would get up to make another speech. They spoke too long, it was said: "No one can remember what they said! If they had spoken for less time, we would have remembered. But such long talk, without anyone to write it down, must be forgotten." Eventually people got hungry and left. Children had also been gathered together for the meeting, but they of course could not understand. "It was all like a lecture on history [*zancen gargajiya*]. Whom did it concern? If it was about something useful, such as millet or groundnuts, we would care and remember. But all this long talk—what use is it to us? [*Ina amfani?*]"

Later on, perhaps not wishing to leave a wrong impression, the man did recall the substance of the talk: "They told us that all Nigériens are brothers: Hausa, Fulani, Bouzou, Beriberi, Adarawa, Zarma, Tuareg. All have the same father and mother. There is no discrimination." They also said that farmers and herders should be careful not to hurt each other.

In Yekuwa the input of villagers into the governmental process, both real and perceived, has been minimal and controlled. Few residents, if any, would challenge this state of affairs. In Yardaji, even if the input is in reality infinitesimal, people have been brought to believe that they *are* in principle supposed to participate in the formation of government. The alternating interregna of military rule in Nigeria may temporarily suspend politics, but they do not invalidate the expectation of future attempts at democratic structures of government. In neither Yekuwa nor Yardaji, however, do people believe that true democracy has ever flourished on either side of the border, and the very word "siyasa" has come to take on a pejorative tinge.

Differential Development

The contrast between a controlled and submissive populace in one village versus a politicized (if cynical) electorate in the other holds true not only for national political processes and institutions. Even at the level of local associations and activities, there are distinct differences in the way 'yan Yekuwa and 'yan Yardaji are organized (or organize themselves) for local development and in the spirit with which they approach local development activities.

Although both Hausa villages are part of developing countries, Yekuwa and Yardaji confront the dilemmas of development as differently as do Niger and Nigeria. Whereas the government in Niamey has actively promoted a collective "development consciousness" throughout the country, in Nigeria the spirit of private initiative and enterprise prevails. (Grand schemes for Nigerian national development—Operation Feed the People, Green Revolution, Universal Primary Education, War against Indiscipline —are periodically launched with great fanfare, but usually fizzle out or are replaced before they have achieved substantive success or institutional continuity.) Corresponding contrasts in local development efforts emerge in Yardaji and Yekuwa.

Compared to Yekuwa's, Yardaji's local associations and development groups appear somewhat disorganized and internally divisive. At the same time, they are self-motivated and self-directed in a way that those in Yekuwa are not. Such voluntarism and initiative are considerable advantages to all local development institutions.[5] In Yekuwa, development efforts appear more organized and cohesive—but that is largely because they are centrally directed, governmentally controlled and initiated, top-down endeavors.

---

5 See Uphoff 1986 on the importance of this factor in local institutional development.

'Yan Yardaji form local associations, however fitfully, because they want to; 'yan Yekuwa form them because they have to.

There are two parallel structures in Yekuwa for the Société de Développement, one for Kofai and one for Hamada. Each possesses a Traditional Rulers Association (Kungiyar Sarakuna Gargajiya), a Farmers and Herders Association (Kungiyar Manoma da Kiwu), a Youth Group (Kungiyar Samari da Yamata), an Association of Parents of Students (Kungiyar Iyay-yen Yara), a Student Association (Kungiyar 'Yan Makaranta), a Women's Association (Kungiyar Ta Mata), and an Islamic Priests' Association (Kungiyar Musulumci). It is said that a Soldiers Association (Kungiyar Sojoji) would also be part of the structure if any Yekuwa soldiers were residing in the village.[6]

The functions of each of these associations are straightforward and simple. It is said that the purpose of the Women's Association, for instance, is to arbitrate disputes among women (*jawon hankali*). The Association of Parents of Students and the Student Association are supposed to arbitrate between the teachers and parents of children beaten at school. The Islamic Priests' Association teaches prayers to both children and adults, and the Farmers' Association receives pesticides from Magaria if insects are destroying crops.[7]

The Youth Group is both the most complex in structure and function and the most active of Yekuwa's associations. The term "youth" can be confusing, for in the Hausa context it includes most able-bodied males. Numerical age is a very ambiguous yardstick in rural Hausaland. Eligibility for Youth Group membership is explained as follows:

> If you are between twenty and twenty-five years old, you are surely a youth and you must participate in the Kungiyar Samari. But if you get older and have a son who may himself participate fully—say, fifteen years old or so—then it is no longer compulsory that you yourself participate. But if you want to [*idon ra'ayi*], then you may.

[6] The official structure of the Société de Développement, as laid out by the government, also stipulates the formation of trade union, transport workers', and veterans' associations. For descriptions and analysis of the Société de Développement, see Dunbar 1991:77–78, Frélastre 1983:97–100, Guillemin 1982:102–3, Horowitz et al. 1983:15–23, Lanne 1983:41–43, Robinson 1991:11–14, and an anonymous article in *West Africa*, September 5, 1983, 2056–57.

[7] This discussion of the Société de Développement is based on conversations in Yekuwa in 1986. In 1983 more elaborate functions were ascribed to the society as well. The Islamic Association was to have the authority to approve or distribute religious literature (either from Niamey or from the Nigerian market) and to call for communal prayer (on instruction from Niamey) in case of national crisis (e.g., war or drought). There was also a Traders' Association (Kungiyar 'Yan Kasuwa).

In addition to the "youth king" (*sarkin samari*), the Youth Group has twenty-three officers. This number, established in Magaria, includes a "farm king" (*sarkin noma*), a "child king" (*sarkin yara*, to organize children to work and to discipline them), a "seed king" (*sarkin ɗi'a*), a secretary (*magatakarda*), a treasurer (*ma'aji*), and a village comptroller (*magajin gari*, who approves or vetoes proposed projects). The youth king was unable to recall the rest of his organization's officers, but he assured me that there was a list of all their names and functions. The paper was never located, however.

The Kungiyar Samari is in charge of the village farm (*gonar samariya*), on which all villagers, including the chief, work. (There are actually three separate plots: one for Hamada, one for Kofai, and one, by the school grounds, for both Hamada and Kofai.) Sorghum and beans are grown on the village farm. The sorghum is stored as food for visitors ("big people from Magaria," such as government officials or the district capital's own youth group officers). The beans are sold to raise money for village needs and benevolent activities: helping an old woman who needs to repair her home, cleaning and repairing the village wells, removing rubbish and rainy-season weeds from the streets, and so on.

A recurrent theme in discussions of the village youth association is *had an kai,* collective unity (literally, "joining heads"). Another word that crops up in this context is *dole,* obligation. Villagers *must* participate in these institutions, for the government has told them to do so. ("There should not be one person who says 'I don't agree' if the association has decided to do something.") Neither resentment of nor resistance to this compulsory participation is evident; it is unlikely to arise in any event. Still, among people habituated to following orders and conforming to programs established from above, a familiar Nigérien pattern seems to be repeating itself: the Société de Développement in Yekuwa appears to lack the requisite dynamism and initiative critical to the success of self-help movements. Despite its purported organization as a grassroots and bottom-up institution, there are far more instructions and orders coming down from Magaria to Yekuwa than requests for developmental assistance from villagers going up the hierarchical chain.

The head of the Women's Association explained that in reconciling fights between women (especially co-wives) in the village, she needed only to threaten offenders with being sent to Magaria (for "they fear being tied up"). When requested to do so by her association's superiors in Magaria, she collects money from the village women. Through her the women of Yekuwa were "asked to contribute" money for the construction of a building in Zinder. What building? She didn't know. Were the men's associations also supposed to contribute? "How do I know what goes on with them?" The radical, participatory change in village thinking which the Société de Développement is supposed to promote is not in evidence when the head of Yekuwa's Women's Association, in discussing the relationship between her branch and that in Magaria, explains, "What they tell us to do, we do."

Neither do the niceties of electoral procedure appear to have high priority in the Société de Développement. To choose the leaders of the Yekuwa local associations, "elections" were conducted thus: "It was asked, 'Who wants to be this, who wants to be that?' Someone would say, 'I do!' Then the town crier would call out, 'People, do you approve?' and everyone would say, 'Yes, we approve.'"

Another informant claimed that the mai gari chose all the heads of the local associations. The two accounts are actually compatible: at least formally, the village chief must ratify community decisions, so the "people's choice" would also have to be the chief's choice.

In Yardaji, dissatisfaction with the activity (or inactivity) of the Kungiyar Danwakeke (the village's long-time Youth Club) prompted others to establish an alternative association, the Kungiyar Kwantangwam. As the head of the (defunct) Danwakeke group explained, the major purpose of the club was to collect money from members to assist poorer villagers in need. In this sense, it functioned basically as a community chest, or even a social club. If a villager lacked the money to purchase a ram for the naming ceremony of his newborn child, say, the Youth Club's treasury could be tapped for a loan.

Some villagers felt that the Danwakeke club collected membership fees only "to have parties." When Alhaji Sali returned after seven years in Gongola State, where he was secretary of a club in Yola, he spread the idea of a more dynamic village association in Yardaji. Visits were undertaken to other towns and cities (such as Danbatta and Kano) to see how other youth clubs were operating. In the rainy season of 1984, the Kwatangwam Youth Club (named after the oldest well in Yardaji) was officially founded with a modest membership of twelve. It rapidly grew to one hundred dues-paying members (20 kobo for ordinary members, 50 kobo for officeholders) and an elaborate organizational structure. Titleholders include chairman (*shugaba* or *cayaman*), vice chairman (*mai taimakon cayaman*), secretary and assistant secretary (*sakatare, mai taimakon sakatare*), press secretary and assistant press secretary (*sakatare watsan labaru, mai taimakon sakatare watsan labaru*), treasurer and assistant treasurer (*ma'aji, mai taimakon ma'aji*), visitors' secretary and assistant visitors' secretary (*sakatare baki, mai taimakon baƙi*), head planner (*cif organiza*), auditor and assistant auditor (*audita, mai taimakon audita*), assistant counselor (*mai taimakon mai bada shawara*), sergeant at arms (*polis*), policeman (ɗan sanda), messenger (*mesanja*), public works secretary (*sakatare ayyuka*), and referee (*alƙalin wasa*). The club established a charter (*manufofin kungiya*) with the following principal aims and goals: (1) village maintenance, (2) assistance to the elderly, (3) community health, and (4) sports and the preservation of traditional games. The charter formally forbids the club to engage in politics.

Muhammadu Aliyu was elected first chairman of the Kwantangwam. He explains the club's activities:

Our first job was to repair the street running in front of Ilu's tea shop. [In the rainy season it collects mud and prevents vehicles from passing.] Then, with brooms, we swept *all* the streets of Yardaji. Then came the planting season, and we weeded the village cemetery.

After that we cleaned up the marketplace. Then we took care of repairing the Kwana road [the laterite artery running to the Zango-Daura tarmac]. We realized that we could not complete this work all on our own, carrying buckets of earth on our heads the entire distance. So we went to the local government for assistance. The local government gave us a vehicle—for twenty-one days we used it, working to repair the road.

When we finished we brought the local government chairman to come and inspect our work. He came and saw *all* the work we had done—the road, the market, the cemetery. He expressed great pleasure and thanks for the work we had accomplished.

We said that the work we had done was the equivalent of six thousand naira. He said it was worth ten thousand naira. When he returned to his office and made calculations, he said it was worth even more than ten thousand naira. Then we recalculated, and found it was worth twenty thousand naira.

Then we looked for other ways to help the community. We decided to acquire a motorized pump for our well. For this we collected two naira from every householder. We then got skilled workers from the government, so that we should have good drinking water. So we stopped collecting the two naira.

They came and inspected the area. One week later, the well diggers arrived. We gave them some of the money we had already collected, as thanks.

They completed the digging and erected the water pump. Then came the coup d'état [that brought Major General Ibrahim Babangida to power]. After that, the government forgot about the whole project.

So we said, "We ourselves will collect the money to purchase the engine for the water pump." But then the local government announced that we shouldn't proceed, because it hadn't been properly notified of the work undertaken up until then—that is, the erection of the water tank.

So we discussed the matter among ourselves. There were some very old men who informed us about an old abandoned well site—going back thirty-seven years—that had water. So we went to the site to clear it, and to dig. We discovered lots of water in it.

So we calculated how much money it would cost to build a proper well. We figured we would need thirty sacks of cement. We collected the stones ourselves and did the work. We repaired it, and got lots of water from it. So now the whole village, including Bulungudu [an outlying settlement], uses it.

We have also been repairing the wells within the village. It's a big job, too! Everyone recognizes the work we have done. Now, though, in this planting season, the club isn't working so much. Except for sports! We are organizing soccer games with youth clubs from other villages, and even wrestling matches with paying spectators (fifty kobo). But the walls to the wrestling area have fallen down. After the harvest, we'll fix it. . . . We now have about two hundred fifty members.

Aliyu's narration offers a glimpse into both the benefits and the pitfalls of an autonomously initiated and operating local developmental association. The spirit of voluntarism and initiative is evident, as is the importance of grassroots leadership and incentive. Yet the possibility of foul-ups due to misunderstanding with and by the Nigerian bureaucracy when a village group does act on its own is a potential hindrance. In Yekuwa the Société de Développement could have arisen in the first place only under the national government's direction. In Yardaji, the Kwatangwam Youth Club operated for some time before it received notice from the Daura Government Social Welfare Office that the club had to register with state officials in Kaduna and submit its charter, its membership list, and a registration fee of 50 naira.

Both types of institution have a common cultural heritage in the Hausa system of gayya, or communal labor, and the *samariya,* an age-group (youth movement) association. "Gayya" is often used to signify collective farmwork; other group activities may be so designated as well. "Although all recent investigators have regarded gayya . . . as of declining importance, it is possibly still common in some localities" (Hill 1972:251). Certainly the relative strength of gayya varies even between neighboring villages. What is of especial interest here is the different ways in which both the spirit and form of gayya have evolved in Yardaji and Yekuwa, a result, undoubtedly at least in part, of their national affiliations.

There is local agreement that classical gayya has virtually disappeared in Yardaji, although it is still alive in Yekuwa. The "love of money" (*son kuɗi*) in Yardaji is given as the chief reason. As one ɗan Yardaji explains:

Thirty, thirty-five years ago, there was no paid labor for the construction of houses, just gayya. You would call people together, and they would work together. You would cook for them a big pot of beans, or lots of porridge. You would distribute kola nuts and a little money—fifty kobo for the master bricklayer, and then ten or twenty kobo all around.

But then people started to move around, to travel. Some went to Kano, and would be paid forty kobo for a day's labor, straight out. They came back with the thought, "Why should I do this work free, as gayya, when I can be paid for the same labor in Kano?" And slowly, people had to be paid for their services, so that today there is no longer any gayya for home construction.

There certainly is much more consciousness of money in Yardaji than in Yekuwa, and much less shame (kumya) in asking for it. In Yekuwa I was often faced with the problem of not knowing how much to pay someone for his or her work or product. Men and women were reluctant to ask directly for payment, and often refused to specify the amount they expected. ("Give whatever you want.") In Yardaji the problem was that adults and children alike asked exorbitant amounts of money for small tasks or purchases. Whereas in Yekuwa I had on occasion to press people to accept my money, in Yardaji the challenge was to hold on to it.[8]

It is in Niger that the traditional and village-level institution of the youth group association—the Hausa samariya—has been most strongly promoted by the national government as an organizational instrument for development. It is also perceived as a link that enables the national government to reach down to (or "penetrate") the country's 8,000 rural communities. But this

> new role places an enormous burden on an institution that never had any formal organization beyond the village, and that drew whatever dynamic it ever had from purely parochial social and economic concerns. . . . In theory *samaria* are supposed to mobilize local self-help resources, and to initiate projects themselves. . . . In fact almost all *samaria* activities are undertaken in response to programs called opérations, decided upon at the national level. (Horowitz et al. 1983:13–14)

Pearl Robinson, who also investigated the Société de Développement from the perspective of a rural Hausa village (Tibiri), offers a similarly negative assessment:

[8] The way people in the two villages responded when I interviewed them is also revealing. People in Yardaji eventually came to ask for their kola nut (my token of appreciation) as soon as the interview was over. Some even wanted payment in advance. In Yekuwa, people often thanked me and gave *me* a present—kola nuts, eggs, macaroni, even money.

[T]he notion that all the social strata crucial to rural development were substantively incorporated into the *société de développement* does not hold up to scrutiny. Small-scale farmers and herders, women as well as men, were represented by councilors whose class, status, and personal circumstances differ markedly from their own. . . . As one woman in Tibiri put it, the councilors were "the people with money." (Robinson 1991:14)

Mobilizing the Masses

The samariya is not the only instance of the Niger government's adroit use of popular or traditional institutions to achieve both developmental and political aims. Hausa-language drama (*teyatur*) is a more entertaining tool by which the government emphasizes "the need for all citizens of Niger to work together for development [and] . . . national awareness and Nigerien unity" (Beik 1984:16, 19). Teyatur, however, usually touches only an urban audience. Potentially unpopular mass mobilization campaigns (which function in part to bolster legitimacy) are astutely cushioned when they are delivered or executed through traditional channels.

Not long after the aborted coup d'état against Lieutenant Colonel Kountché in 1983, the head of state set out on a nationwide tour. In anticipation of his arrival in Zinder, word came down to Magaria that the arrondissement was expected to contribute its share of the pageantry in the provincial capital. The Sarkin Magaria was charged with scouting through the countryside to select suitable horses that would be ridden by their owners all the way to Zinder, to be part of the welcoming procession at the entrance to the town. Although villagers were hardly disloyal to their head of state, horse owners did see this imposition as quite a burden: the distance was great, the possibility of getting fodder along the way meager, and the prospect of competing with all the other riders for horse feed in Zinder daunting. Many horse owners therefore hid, or found reasons not to be able to go. All the same, a sizable contingent of horses from throughout the district was dispatched, including at least three from Yekuwa.

The significance here is not merely the authority the rulers have to impose corvées and engineer obligatory demonstrations of mass support, but the mechanism by which they do so. To the populace, it appears as if the traditional rulers are extending their support to the secular head of state. In fact, only by order from the government can such instructions be delivered and the canton chief sent on such a mission. The governmental rulers, taking advantage of the distance between themselves and the populace, use the traditional leaders to ensure a display of popular support for themselves. They thereby avoid the impression that they are pressuring the peasantry to demonstrate openly in the government's favor—although that is precisely what they are doing. Be it for logistical, historical, or psychological reasons, it is hard to imagine the Nigerian government mobilizing the masses of Daura in an equivalent way.

The Nigérien government employs an even more eye-catching means to mobilize and raise national consciousness in Yekuwa: right in the middle of the village, obtrusively signaled by its erect antenna towering on high, is a solar-powered television screen. In the early 1980s the government installed these community television sets in cities, towns, and larger villages throughout the country. The one government channel broadcasts news, information, cultural events, and films for several hours in the evening. Naturally, the domestic news is consistently upbeat, and invariably portrays cabinet ministers, government officials, and, of course, the head of state in a positive light. There are rotating local-language broadcasts (especially for the news), but the major medium of communication remains French. As a result, relatively little of the population at large—virtually none in Yekuwa—can actually understand the broadcasts.

Television, of course, is a visual medium, and recurrently projected images and symbols of Nigérien sovereignty, even without substantive commentary, would serve the mobilizing aims of the broadcasters well enough. Thus, for example, coverage of the 1983 Franco-African summit in Vittel, France (which I viewed from Magaria), centered largely on Lieutenant Colonel Kountché's reception by French dignitaries (including President François Mitterrand) and other acknowledgments of Niger's place in this international forum. Reportage on the substantive aspects of the summit's tasks and political agenda was virtually nil.

Unfortunately, Yekuwa is often deprived of even the visual images from these nightly broadcasts. During most of my stay there (both in 1983 and 1986), the video receiving capabilities of the village TV had broken down— not an unusual problem in developing countries, where maintenance of infrastructure is more problematic than initial technological implantation. Villagers still gathered in front of the blank screen to meet and chat, as they often did even when the TV was in working order.

The TV sets Yekuwa apart from Yardaji, and bespeaks a more concerted effort by the government there to mobilize this remote rural community. Yardaji has two television sets, which may pick up the more commercially oriented (though state-run) station from Kano as well as the station in Niger. These two sets are privately owned, however, and not accessible to the village at large. (They are powered by rather noisy petrol generators, whose pumping sounds virtually drown out the audio.) Whereas television in Yardaji is a symbol of status, in Yekuwa it is a means for mobilization.

Law, Order, and the Economics of Justice

Although rural Hausaland is generally a safe place to live, one does find variation in the incidence and expectation of lawlessness. Neither Yardaji nor Yekuwa experiences violent crime (barring occasional disputes between Fulani herders and Hausa farmers over crop and grazing land), and neither is altogether free of petty theft. Between the two, nevertheless, there is consensus that Yardaji is *wurin sata* (a place of stealing), whereas in Yekuwa "one need not lock one's hut."

The sheer physical outlay of the two villages is indicative of different perspectives on the security of property. Yekuwa's outskirts are rimmed with granaries—large round structures with removeable stalk roofs—which contain individual families' stockpiles of millet and sorghum. Survival itself is bound up in these granaries, for it is in them that food is stored from one harvest to the next, as are seeds for the next season's planting. The greatest threat to these granaries on Yekuwa's rim comes from field rats and other rodents, which, along with the monkeys in the fields during the growing season, are Yekuwa's greatest thieves.

No family in Yardaji would dream of situating its granary outside the village proper. Indeed, each family keeps its granary within its own individual compound, where access to it is strictly controlled. Fear of theft is offered as the reason—not necessarily fear of neighbors, but fear of "outsiders." Professional thieves are unlikely to be looking for millet stockpiles, but one unfortunate shopkeeper did awake one morning to find that his shop had been pilfered of almost all its canned goods.

"Faransa is not like here," summarized one Nigérien who was living in Yardaji as a day laborer. "There, if a thief is caught he is severely punished. Here, there is only *surutu*—talk, talk, talk."

The tradition of a strong and comprehensive Muslim judicial system was maintained in British Hausaland from early colonial times. As far as possible, Lugard mandated that *alƙali* (Muslim) courts be retained and even strengthened, with the British intervening only to ratify or veto decisions in serious cases. In French Hausaland, colonial administrators assumed much of the onus of meting out justice themselves, with the corresponding denigration of the indigenous judicial system. The Napoleonic code prevailed over Koranic shari'a.

When instances of petty thievery are discovered today, they are treated in very different ways in the two villages. In Yardaji, given the rather unsavory reputation of the country's official security agencies (perceived as lacking in honesty, empathy, and efficiency), the police are generally avoided as much as possible. Mai Gari will try to resolve, arbitrate, or judge as appropriate, keeping any indiscretion within the confines of the village. When a situation exceeds his capacity, he will pass it on to the alƙali court in Zango, from which appeals may be brought to the alƙali in Daura. This procedure presents no problem logistically, for both the district and emirate capitals are easily accessible by a nearby paved road.

In Yekuwa, colonial and postcolonial factors relating to state authority, secular justice, subordination of chiefs, infrastructure, and poverty all combine to create a different attitude toward intravillage crime and a different process for dealing with it. An incident that took place in Yekuwa on September 27, 1983, tells the story:

Bala had gone to his farm and discovered that half a sheaf of millet had disappeared. He followed tracks that led from his field straight to Tsahiru's house, at the edge of the village. There Bala found his millet.

Bala told Alhaji Aminu, the acting chief, who summoned Tsahiru. Tsahiru had a long history of this kind of theft. What to do with him? According to Alhaji Aminu, the three of them should go to Magaria and turn Tsahiru over to the gendarmerie. He had even secured a rope to tie the thief up. But who would pay the fare, which was a naira each way? Custom dictated that the plaintiff pay. Bala's cost would be at least 5 naira for the fare (assuming the thief would not be returning) plus other expenses (such as in-transit meals) plus the next morning's lost labor. The monetary value of the stolen millet could not have exceeded 1 naira.

Having figured the cost, Bala decided to drop the matter and "forgive" the thief. But now that it had been brought to his attention, the acting chief did not feel that the affair could just be dropped. A thief had been caught. It would be dereliction of duty not to take him to the proper authorities in Magaria. Besides, what would happen to him if the gendarmes in Magaria caught wind of the fact that he had let a thief go free, in direct violation of the law?

So the argument was now between Bala and Alhaji Aminu. As the shouting grew in intensity, the thief seemed to grow bored. When he tried to join the discussion, he was ignored.

Alhaji Aminu finally said, "OK, but if the gendarmes hear, they will be told that I tied the thief up, but you untied him and let him go. And *you* will be responsible for catching him if they come to get him."

The farmer agreed. He had, in fact, prevented the thief from being bound, repeating the traditional formula of forgiveness: "Na yafeka, na yafeka."

Bala's misfortune is not unlike that of many would-be litigants even in the United States, who are deterred from pursuing justice when the cost of litigation is estimated to exceed the probable award. In Yekuwa the physical and attitudinal distance between villagers and adjudicating authorities may subvert the interests of justice in some cases. In Yardaji, where the judicial system is formally more effective, other influences make even graver inroads into law and order. Tsahiru was lucky, for in Faranshi a wrongdoer is usually punished, swiftly and severely; but in Nigeria, it is said in both Yekuwa and Yardaji, with the proper funds one can literally get away with murder.

Village Hospitality

Hospitality to strangers is part and parcel of Hausa (indeed, Muslim) culture. In Niger it has even become a source of national pride, with both humble farmers and powerful subprefects vigorously lauding and demonstrating Nigérien hospitality.[9] As is often the case, the claim is reinforced by reference to a supposedly opposite situation in Nigeria.[10]

Nigerians and Nigériens harbor some suspicion of each other, even when both stranger and resident are Hausa. Periodic expulsions of aliens from Nigeria have certainly not enhanced Nigeria's reputation as a haven for visiting African foreigners.

> In this country, a stranger will not be put up, even in a Fulani camp. He has to go into town. But even in town, unless he already knows someone, he won't be put up. In Yardaji, only the mai gari will give a stranger a place to sleep.
>
> In Niger, anywhere, people will automatically give a stranger accommodations for the night, and feed him in the morning. Then the traveler may continue on his way.
>
> Why is it like this in Nigeria? Maybe because of headhunters.[11]
>
> —Nigérien Fulani in Yardaji

[9] At least toward "authorized" strangers. Especially in border areas, at least as great a premium is placed on vigilance. See Lanne 1983:42.

[10] In Nigérien contexts other than Hausaland, there is distrust of Libyans and, by extension, even of Nigérien Tuareg. Nigerians accuse Ghana of exporting criminals. Border clashes with Cameroon and the Cameroonian origins of the violent fundamentalist Maitatsine movement have made that country also a candidate for Nigerian opprobrium.

[11] Headhunting is one of those sensational rumors that even the African media today pick up on from time to time. In the case of Nigeria, it is recognized as a "southern" phenome-

> When I first arrived, people said I couldn't stay, that word had come from Daura not to put strangers up. People in the village—especially the high school students home on vacation—said they'd be afraid to sleep in the same compound as me.
>
> —Visitor from Magaria

But if there is mutual suspicion between Nigériens and Nigerians, it is also generally acknowledged that Nigerians are less than trusting of their fellow countrymen.

In Hausa, the word *baƙo* is used to designate both "guest" and "stranger." It is in the former, positive sense that it is ordinarily used and understood. With the superimposition of a differentiating national identity over the ethnic one, however, Georg Simmel's already Africanized notion of *der Fremde*—the stranger who does not fit in, who remains apart—is being recreated even in the Hausa borderlands. This is a new phenomenon that transcends the one that Elliott Skinner (1963) contemplated for African "strangers" in the colonial era and, with William Shack (1979), documented in postcolonial times. In these studies, even if the role of the stranger was at times ambiguous, at least his identity was fairly clear-cut: he came from another colony, another state, and ultimately another ethnic group.[12] The suspicion and hostility that the stranger generated may have been regrettable, but it was comprehensible, issuing out of his obvious otherness. But here in Hausaland we are witnessing the creation of a stranger—a Hausa stranger—out of an a priori cultural similitude. It is one of the ironies of independence that while the struggle for decolonization may have created a temporary anti-European unity among the elite, it has given way to a longer-term and socially more pervasive alienation among neighboring kin.

Morality

In any Islamic society governed by shari'a, the distinction between individual morality and criminal behavior is not so great as it is in the West. All conduct, no matter how ostensibly personal, has ramifications for the

---

non; not even the source of this quotation believed that headhunting occurred in Northern Nigeria.

[12] In the case of Niger, the traditional "stranger" of disrepute was the Dahomeyan (see Challenor 1979:80–82). From my experience as a secondary school teacher in Niger, I would say that among at least part of the Nigérien elite, latent anti-Dahomeyanism persists as resentment toward the continuing role of Beninois in Niger's educational system.

entire community, and thus is governed by the Islamic code of behavior. These social considerations are of course in addition to the expectations that Allah has set forth for the relationship between the believer and Himself. In Hausaland, nevertheless, a subtle distinction is made between activity and behavior that is forbidden by the Koran—haram—and behavior that may in addition violate the law of the state—laifi.

If Yardaji looks down upon Yekuwa as backward and unsophisticated, Yekuwa in turn righteously condemns Yardaji as a den of iniquity. Three reasons may be invoked: *caca* (gambling), *karuwanci* (prostitution), and *wewe* (marijuana).

Caca in Yardaji takes the form of a card game in which petty amounts of cash are at stake—a kind of Hausa blackjack. Participants are invariably young men, who cluster on a mat or on the ground in groups of three or more, several games of caca going on simultaneously. Two locations in the village are recognized for this purpose: *mahaukacin gida* (the crazy house) and, after dark, *faskarawa* (the place of unruliness). After dark the games are conducted by flashlight, kerosene lamp, or moonlight. Even the participants acknowledge that gambling is wrong, and would probably agree it is confined to the lower stratum of village society. Still, at least to other Hausa, this village subculture inescapably imparts a less than savory reputation to Yardaji as a whole.

It would be misleading to suggest that there is no caca in Yekuwa at all, although it is hardly the common practice it is in Yardaji. I witnessed one night game in August 1986, as part of the unofficial festivities accompanying a naming ceremony. However, many of the participants were in fact from Yardaji, and it is probable that they brought the game to Yekuwa in the first place.

One kind of haram in Yardaji that has absolutely no counterpart in Yekuwa is karuwanci.[13] Prostitution is a fairly recent innovation in Yardaji, dating back only to 1984. It was introduced gradually, when a few *karuwai* (prostitutes) began to follow the local market circuit, arriving in Yardaji on Wednesday and leaving for Kanda on Friday, the latter village's market day. A man could be entertained for 5 naira. Eventually as many as ten karuwai settled in Yardaji permanently, until the local government area administrator, acting through the district head, ordered them either to get married or to leave. All did leave except for one, who, as of September 1986, was kept company by an older woman friend. (The friend made money by

---

[13] Karuwanci in Hausaland has many characteristics that distinguish it from prostitution in the West, and indeed from elsewhere in Nigeria. For a good treatment of this subject, see Pittin 1984:1301–13.

selling foods and snacks.) The remaining karuwa has had a child, and has succeeded in forcing the responsible client to recognize it as his own.

The smoking of wewe is less open than either caca or karuwanci,[14] but from a "moral" perspective its incidence still sets Yardaji apart from Yekuwa. As with caca, only young men indulge in the practice, and it is not inconceivable that Yardaji's influence may eventually spread across the border in this respect as well.[15]

It would be unjust to leave the impression of Yardaji as a rural Sodom, whose vices are contaminating both its own and neighboring populations. Most Yardaji denizens are upright Muslims and eschew even the thought of committing haram. Yet although Yardaji is only a village, on the social level it is becoming somewhat urbanized—or better, Kanoized. Not all of the social innovations imported from the city, of course, are tainted. The recent fad of "Nigerian haircuts"—a man sits in a chair, as in a Western barbershop, and is given a "fashionable" hairdo—falls into this category. (Traditionally, a Hausa *wanzami* sits on the ground or on a mat, faces his similarly seated client, and with a long blade shaves the head entirely.) For 'yan Yardaji, Kanoization is equated with sophistication; 'yan Yekuwa are less sanguine about such developments, especially in view of Kano's reputation as a veritable den of iniquity: "It's a big town, where the Dalla and Gwaburo hills are found. A place of women, a place of vehicles. A place of sheep, a place of donkeys. A red-light district, a town of infidels. A town where no one is conceived in wedlock. Only bastards."[16]

---

[14] Although not necessarily. In the middle of an interview about an unrelated subject, one Yardaji man lit up a stick of wewe. He acknowledged that such things were bad, but that that was the way of Nigeria—bad things go unpunished.

[15] Frank Salamone (1973) has noted the existence of a drug problem (the abuse of amphetamines, barbiturates, and hallucinogens) among fishermen, carriers, longshoremen, farmers, secondary school students, members of the elite, and cattle Fulani in Yauri Emirate, far to the west of Daura. In this case and at this point in time, illicit pills were smuggled in from Niger. As a secondary school teacher in Magaria in the late 1970s I know that a few secondary school students in Niger also took drugs, including marijuana; these drugs, however, came from Nigeria. Natural hallucinogens were also extracted from plants in rural Hausaland.

[16] These are standard epithets for Kano. Here is another description (offered in Yekuwa) of the mentality of Kano natives:

> Their guests are their food [Baƙonsu, su ne abincinsu]: when showing company around town, people in Kano will ask their guests for money to buy food, meat, etc. Then they will ask them for money to buy kola nuts. If a Kano man acts as a middleman, selling on his guest's behalf, he will sell high but say he received little, pocketing the difference. A Kano man only feigns joy at receiving guests [Kirki daga baki].

Other Hausa groups receive their individual stereotypes. The Katsinawa "are discreet [Suna da rifi] and display a proper sense of shame [kumya]. If someone commits a wrong, everyone will talk about it—but only behind his back. He himself will never hear about it." On

Complexes: Superiority and Morality

For the people of Yekuwa, Yardaji, although modest in size, wealth, and significance by Nigerian standards, is unmistakably part of greater Nigeria; likewise, Yekuwa for Yardaji represents Faransa. As a result, each village serves as a kind of stereotype for the other, a microcosmic reflection of the image that Nigeria holds for Niger and vice versa. The fact that the perpetrators of these nationally based value judgments are themselves spatially, culturally, and ethnically quite similar does little to mitigate this state of affairs.

However modestly, Yardaji shares in the more dynamic economy and greater wealth enjoyed by Nigeria. Yekuwa, like Niger in general, is accordingly regarded as a place of poverty (talauci). As we saw in Chapter 8, Yekuwa is quite dependent on Yardaji, not only for its market but also in its role as logistical gateway to other Nigerian markets (Zango, Daura, Danbatta, and Kano) and the greater Nigerian economy. 'Yan Yardaji are hardly discreet in vaunting their economic superiority over their poorer neighbors. In commercially conscious Hausaland, economic superiority (at least when balanced by karamci, or generosity[17] is often equated with superiority. This tendency has become more pronounced in recent times, when the generally favorable Islamic position on economic growth and development (Cummings et al. 1980, Ragab 1980, Sutcliffe 1975) has been strengthened by the transition to a merchant-capital and then semi-industrial (or petroleum-boom) economy in Northern Nigeria (Lubeck 1981, 1985). At the village level this general tendency has been translated into a collec-

---

the other hand, those of Sokoto "exercise no patience concerning wrongdoers. They'll come right out and accuse them, warning them not to repeat their behavior. They don't lie, speak only the truth—even if it is potentially divisive." Not surprisingly, the Daura Hausa (in the larger, prepartition and maybe prejihadic sense of the term) "are kind people. Whatever you want, they will give it to you. If you don't fulfill a promise to them, they will remind you of it. They like to receive visitors. They are not stern, strict or fastidious, but rather easygoing." Tuareg are known for their miserliness (rowa); Zarma for their maliciousness and lying (k̃eta da k̃arya). At the risk of self-exposure, here is the recently formed profile of Americans:

> They won't lend their horses. They cook only enough for themselves—if someone else drops in, he's out of luck. They always have questions: "Why this? Why that?" They have money, but say they are poor. They attend naming ceremonies, they go where charity is distributed, they go give condolences when someone dies. They know how to fast.

On a less idiosyncratic level, the United States is more generally noted for its impressive military power and arsenal of weapons. "Amirka, akwai faɗa!" (America sure knows how to wage battle!).

[17] See Kirk-Greene 1974:6 on the role of karamci in Hausa culture.

tive superiority complex in Yardaji and a corresponding inferiority and dependency complex in Yekuwa. Dependence on the international community (through the mystique of *l'aide internationale*) is also more prominent throughout Niger. I recall a discussion with a Nigérien extension agent posted to Yekuwa for whom it was self-evident that every secondary school in his country must have been built by some other country.[18]

Yekuwa villagers respond in two ways to their apparent economic inferiority. First, they claim that it is they who are making Yardaji prosper, and bitterly resent assertions by 'yan Yardaji that theirs is a *matsiyacir kasa* (an impoverished land). Because of the threat of confiscation (kwatchewa) by the customs agents of their own country, people in Yekuwa both hide their wealth (*boye arziki*) and send it where it will be safe—over the border. Thus 'yan Yekuwa, who have more livestock, millet, money, and people— all manifestations of true wealth—make many loans (*bashi*) to 'yan Yardaji. Moreover, the owners of six-passenger cars based in Yardaji are said to be residents of Yekuwa. There *appears* to be greater wealth in Yardaji than in Yekuwa, but the reality, they say, is the reverse.

The second reaction to Yardaji's superiority complex is Yekuwa villagers' assertion that theirs is a life imbued with peace and honesty—not the crime and immorality that pervade Yardaji. While 'yan Yardaji evince a superiority complex based on material advantage, 'yan Yekuwa respond with one based on their relative virtue: a Nigérien Hausa morality complex.

Villagers in Yekuwa clearly exaggerate the sins of Yardaji. Yardaji's major problem is guilt by association—association with Nigeria, which Nigériens are convinced is a land of violence, crime, and corruption. Although one cannot compare Yardaji to, say, Kano as a place of crime and personal danger, as one dan Yekuwa said, "it is on the same path." I suspect that Yekuwa's morality complex is proportional to the prosperity differential between Nigérien and Nigerian Hausaland.

Niger's self-congratulatory attitude toward its domestic integrity and international stature is captured in these prize-winning lyrics from the 1983 national song festival, memorized and recited to me in Yekuwa in the summer of 1986. Its theme may be summarized thus: "Niger may not be a land of material wealth [arziki], but our wealth is peace [zaman lafiya]."

> Peace is what advances our country, Niger.
> You come, you go, wherever your heart desires,
> You sleep in peace.

[18] Despite the many differences between Niger and Martinique (also a former colony of France), one may note a commonality arising from a shared *mentalité d'assisté* (Miles 1986a:213, 215).

Niger has become a beautiful virgin here in this world,
Niger has become a fragrant perfume among the nations
    of this world,
Peace is why we have come to Diffa.

We won't allow ourselves
To become entangled,
Like our neighbors.

We converse, everyone notices,
We play, we are admired.
Here in this world, everyone admires us.

Town and Country

Linked to the socioeconomic rivalry between Yardaji and Yekuwa is the more long-standing dynamic in Hausa society between *gari* and *daji,* or town and country.[19] Thanks to the European partition, virtually all the major urban Hausa centers (Kano, Zaria, Katsina, Sokoto) fell within British Hausaland. Also, as I argued earlier, as an indirect result of the partition the economy of British Hausaland took off—and is continuing to rise—while that of French Hausaland stagnated. Prosperity has accentuated the already existing urban bias of Nigerian Hausaland. This urban-rural bias also defines the Yardaji-Yekuwa relationship.

Within its immediate orbit, Yekuwa considers itself a full-blown gari. Several smaller settlements and villages around Yekuwa depend on it for economic and administrative transactions. One such hamlet is Sabuwa, which in 1983 hosted the local boxing, wrestling, and *sharo* (Fulani whipping-cum-initiation) spectacles. I was told that a man of Sabuwa expressed astonishment to see a friend of his from Yekuwa walking alongside an anasara (white man), sitting with him, and even taking him by the hand. This reaction generated much amusement among other Yekuwa men, who laughed at the lack of sophistication of people of the *ƙauye* (bush). When I asked why the games (which are rotated annually) were held only in small villages such as Sabuwa, not in Yekuwa, I was told, "People would be afraid to come. Yekuwa has gotten so big, people would be fearful. They're afraid something might happen to them." I am sure 'yan Yekuwa would be quite astonished to hear other people refer to them as 'yan ƙauye, as people in Yardaji are wont to do.

[19] See Dalby 1964; Hill 1975; Miner 1965; Olofson 1975, 1976; and Yusuf 1974 on the city-countryside dynamic in Hausaland.

For Yardaji, with roughly the same population as Yekuwa,[20] seems to bustle in comparison. Bicycles, motorcycles, and vans afford noise and mobility—both characteristics of city life. (At the same time, there are fewer horses and donkeys—unmistakable symbols of rural life.) Yardaji also has more commercial entrepreneurs (even if modest peddlers), greater specialization in secondary occupations, greater consumption of processed foods (including bread), a handful of residents with electric generators (two with their own television sets), some with employment (gainful or otherwise) in Kano, and more nighttime social activity (e.g., caca). Homes are generally made of "modern mud" (unlike the grass huts of Yekuwa), and more and more are plastered with cement. There are even some pit latrines in compounds. And, as the discussion of religion reaffirms, the more extensive practice of kulle (seclusion of women) makes Yardaji not only more orthodox Muslim but more urban as well. In short, though Yardaji is not a full-fledged city, its residents view it not as a mere village but as a relatively urbanized town. Of course, the residents of Zango, Daura, and Kano would hardly regard Yardaji in the same way.[21]

Language

A. H. M. Kirk-Greene (1963), conducting a preliminary analysis of Anglo-French influence on Hausa, has noted that "there has grown up a colonial vocabulary, and as long as these residual cultural institutions last so long will their terminology, albeit assimilated into Hausa, continue their separate existence." He has also "invite[d further] attention to the hitherto

---

[20] Residents of both Yardaji and Yekuwa assured me that their village was larger than the other.

[21] Ahmed Beitallah Yusuf (1974) observes that the town-country distinction in Hausaland should be viewed as a continuum rather than as a categorical division. David Dalby (1964:300) and Harold Olofson (1975:152–53) accentuate rather the relational and relative status of gari and ƙauye (or daji): Nobody admits being from ƙauye—even the most isolated Hausa's home is gari—but a Hausa can always point to others as being "from the bush." Both approaches allow me to propose that Yardaji is more urbanized than Yekuwa without accepting its self-designated status as an actual gari ("A town proper, which may be walled. Population . . . is large, dense, and heterogeneous. Markets [are held] about three times a week. . . . The community also contains an Islamic court headed by an alƙali (judge)" [Yusuf 1974:212–13]). Yardaji lacks all these things as well as some other phenomena associated with Hausa urbanity: drinking (shan giya), transvestism (daudu), and institutionalized courtesanship (karuwanci) (Yusuf 1974:209; Kleis & Abdullahi 1983). As Dalby and Olofson stress and as the Yardaji-Yekuwa example indicates, where one stands determines how urbane or bush a Hausa community is.

neglected field of a comparative vocabulary of Hausa colonial neologisms in Northern Nigeria and (say) Niger" (41).

Such a comparative study cannot be undertaken here. It is worth documenting, however, that more than two decades after Kirk-Greene's initial inquiry, the differential colonial impact on the Hausa language is still evident, even between two neighboring villages that have extensive and daily contact with each other. One generalization coming out of the Yardaji/Yekuwa experience is that while both villages have incorporated neologisms from their respective colonial languages, the Nigérien Hausa speakers have gone further in Frenchifying their speech than Nigerian Hausaphones have in Anglicizing theirs, the latter retaining a "purer Hausa" for their neologistic purposes.[22]

Administrative, legal, and political terminology most easily differentiates the languages and cultures of Yardaji and Yekuwa. Yardaji lies in the *karamin hukuma* ("small authority"), or district, of Daura. Yekuwa villagers are unfamiliar with this term, as well as the official Nigérien Hausa term for *département—lardu*. Instead, to designate Magaria, their district, they still use "bariki" (from the French *baraques*, barracks). Similarly, before Yardaji was transferred to Katsina its residents identified their *jiha* as Kaduna Sitay (Kaduna State), but 'yan Yekuwa refer to Zinder as *difatiman* (*département*), or just *babban birni* (big city).

People refer to sojoji (soldiers) in both villages, although there are also 'yan sanda (policemen; literally "men with sticks") in Nigeria. In Yekuwa one might alternatively refer to the *jandam* (gendarme). Whereas I often heard President Shehu Shagari referred to as *shugaban kasa* (head of the country) in Yardaji, I never heard this apt, modern Hausa title employed for the Nigérien head of state. Civilian politics in Nigeria gave Kaduna State a *gwamna* (governor), but perhaps most tellingly, the administrator in Magaria is usually referred to not as *sous-préfet* but rather as *komandan* (commandant).

Differences in Nigérien and Nigerian Hausa speech can prove serious on occasion. One way in which border patrollers and other officials test travelers' nationality is to ask them to identify certain objects. Woe to the hapless Hausa who says *montir* (from *montre*) instead of *agogo* (watch) in response to a challenge by a Nigerian immigration officer!

The town-country and center-periphery relationships discussed earlier

---

[22] Quotation marks are necessary for obviously there is no such thing as a "pure Hausa." Much modern Hausa vocabulary—political, technological, commercial—is actually Arabic in origin. See Kirk-Greene 1963:28, 33 on this point.

apply to language as well. Nigerian Hausaland—particularly its cities—is considered the throne of Hausa speech, from classical to slang. Accordingly, both radio broadcasting and newspaper publication are vibrant industries. The radios of both Yardaji and Yekuwa are tuned to stations in Kano and Kaduna. Although La Voix du Sahel, Niger's sole radio station, does do some broadcasting in Hausa, these broadcasts are limited to a few hours in the middle of the day, a not very convenient time for villagers to listen. Even for news and entertainment in their own language, then, villagers of Yekuwa rely more on services provided south of their border than on those available in their own country.[23]

In administering questionnaires in both villages, I was struck by the unfamiliarity with certain Hausa words and expressions, or lack of consensus on their meaning. The term *kabila* (ethnic group or tribe) often had to be rendered *yare* (language). The arguably highbrow Hausa *muhimmanci* (importance, significance) also was unfamiliar. A minor categorizing discrepancy arose when it became apparent that whereas any married man in Yardaji is automatically regarded as a mai gida (head of household), in Yekuwa, until the groom moves out of his father's compound (perhaps months or years after the wedding), he is still considered a saurayi (young man, youth). More revealing, perhaps, were two expressions that posed little difficulty in one village but often did in the other: *gadon gida* and *asali*.

"Gadon gida" may be translated as "inheritance" or "family guild," connoting the original occupation practiced by one's forebears. "Asali" is "pedigree" or "ancestral home" (as family regional origin). Respondents in Yekuwa generally had little difficulty providing this background information. In Yardaji, however, it was not uncommon for younger persons not to know the answer, or to confuse the two terms, or not fully to understand their meanings. It is tempting to extrapolate from this admittedly ambiguous observation the notion that some (urbanized?) Yardaji young people are less in touch with the referents and characteristics of traditional Hausa personal identity than are their rural counterparts in Yekuwa. Pending further investigation, it is sufficient to point out that these two nearby Hausa-speaking villages evince linguistic differences not only in colonially derived

---

[23] Because illiteracy is high in both villages, newspapers are rarely found there. It is worth noting, however, that no Hausa-language newspapers are published in Niger, but there are three in Nigeria (*Gaskiya Ta Fi Kwabo, Albishir, 'Yancin Dan Adam*). Niger's government publishes one newspaper in French (*Le Sahel*), which I never saw outside of Niamey. An independent newspaper appeared in Niger in 1991, bearing the Hausa name *Haske* (Light); its articles, however, are still written in French. At the newsstand in Daura, in contrast, Hausa-language papers sell briskly.

neologisms but also in comprehension of wholly indigenous concepts and idioms.

During school breaks, when secondary school students return to their villages, more French is to be heard in Yekuwa than usual. English is rarer in Yardaji, even when the students are home. As for villagers who do not really speak any European language, the non-Hausa visitor is more likely to be assaulted by fractured French in Yekuwa (*Ça va? Merci*) than by an equivalent English cacophony in Yardaji.

Halin Gari (Village Character)

The greatest difference in Yardaji and Yekuwa village cultures transcends the contrasts in politics, development, justice, hospitality, morality, psychology, urbanity, and language. The greatest difference is the most intangible of all, and the one that most defies substantiation through the recording of discrete events and processes. It is the difference that emerges when one actually lives in both villages and has innumerable mundane contacts and interactions with both sets of villagers. It is enhanced by observations of each set of villagers interacting with the other. This is the essence of what I have called village character; in Hausa, *halin gari*.

In Yardaji a brashness, an assertiveness, contrasts sharply with the humility, deference, and reserve that characterize Yekuwa. Yardaji men are aggressive where Yekuwa men are submissive; they are animated where 'yan Yekuwa are passive. The contrast in village character is even more striking among women. 'Yar Yardaji are more direct, more extroverted, more jocose than 'yar Yekuwa. Rarely did women and girls in Yekuwa treat me to the good-natured teasing and half-serious marriage propositions that made living in Yardaji such a harrowing delight!

One finds self-confidence bordering on conceit in Yardaji; in Yekuwa one finds self-effacement. The image of Yardaji is presented by its *samari*, its youth; in Yekuwa the *tsoffofi*, the elders, set the pace and tone. 'Yan Yardaji are ready to challenge where 'yan Yekuwa pride themselves on their respect. Humor is valued in both villages; but the male visitor to Yardaji will receive sexual jokes and inquiries, whereas in Yekuwa discretion prevails.

As a community, Yardaji is relatively diverse and individuated. These villagers tend to go their own ways. Putting aside the split between Hamada and Kofai (which, after all, are considered separate villages), the residents of Yekuwa present themselves as a tightly knit, organized, unified, and internally cooperative community. In Yardaji one finds tolerance for government and affinity with traditional authority. In Yekuwa one finds fear of everyone who has anything to do with authority outside the village.[24]

The most evocative contrast in village culture and spirit comes from the images employed by two villagers as they commented on each other's community. In Yardaji, according to one d'an Yekuwa, there is *jin kai* (an expression that literally means "feeling one's own head"; in other words, arrogance). Appropriate to the intangible nature of village character is the wordless way by which one Yardaji herder described the people of Yekuwa: placing an outstretched index finger to each of his temples, he stooped and began to sway, imitating mute, docile, and obedient cattle.

Village Culture on the Borderline

Although the framework provided by "village culture" and "village character" may well function independently of boundary considerations, it is doubly useful when placed within a borderline context. Many of the national differences embedded within local communities may very well distinguish other communities far from the borderlands. But consciousness of such differences is heightened when one need merely venture across a nearby invisible line to perceive them. The ease with which borderline communities can apprehend their national distinctiveness solidifies group identity. The otherwise invisible line is invested with special powers.

Crossing a boundary in a partitioned area is almost like viewing oneself in a carnival trick mirror: one recognizes one's basic self but is struck most by the mutation of the essence. The boundary functions as the trick mirror: it mysteriously strips partitioned peoples of their underlying sameness and distorts them with "national" differences.

Admittedly, when we leave the carnival and its mirror, the distortion disappears. Tricks of history are not so easily escaped, however. Division of people by boundary is one of colonial history's most cunning tricks. For not only does the boundary tend to outlast the colonizers, its magical powers remain obscure. How can boundaries *do* any of the things I have

---

[24] Thus, when in each village I announced my intention to ask people questions, in Yekuwa the town crier, having assured his listeners that "there is nothing to worry about, it has nothing to do with taxes," spontaneously added, "Ba abin sarauta ba ne"—"It has nothing to do with the government." It is also interesting that whereas in Yardaji a proclamation is made only with the prior knowledge and consent of the mai gari, no such custom prevails in Yekuwa.

attributed to them? "Iron curtains" and other hyperbolic aberrations aside, boundaries are invisible lines, imaginary constructs, artificial creations. Yet in Hausaland, as throughout the world, they take on politico-magical significance. The mirrors and tricks of humankind's historical carnival are indeed universal.

12

Transcending the Tangaraho

Ido ba mai gani ba, sai hankali ke gani.

It is not the eye that understands, but the mind.

—Hausa proverb

Below the surface of my description of the borderline Hausa tug some nagging theoretical questions: Why are colonial patterns being continued in the postcolonial era? What is the mechanism that keeps Hausaland divided? Why is there no grassroots resistance to indigenous neo-colonialism, of the sort currently heralded in new histories of the classical colonial era?[1] And why do colonial boundaries persist with such great force, even after the hegemons that originally drew them have disappeared from the scene? The explanation commonly offered in the African context—the fear of contagious destabilization, which underlies the principle of boundary inviolability enshrined in the charter of the Organization of African Unity—seems to have little force at the local level. Six mutually compatible hypotheses provide possible answers.

The first explanation might be dubbed the "internal hegemony hypothesis." It proposes that the new Hausa elite, having risen to positions of political and economic power in their respective states (and often in areas outside of Hausaland proper), have a personal, material stake in perpetuating the boundaries as well as ideologies of Nigerian and Nigérien nationalism. These "most favored lords" (as David Laitin [1991] calls the elite who became entrenched in the peripheral Soviet republics) depend on their respective states for their prestige and sustenance. Leadership within a nebulous, reconstructed "Hausaland" would, in contrast, be fraught with uncertainty. Village elites (state-paid teachers, health workers, and salaried

---

[1] I am referring in particular to the various chapters on "African initiatives and resistance" in the UNESCO *General History of Africa*, vol. 7, ed. Adu Boahen.

or tax-commissioned chiefs) also have an immediate interest in the maintenance of the quasi-colonial postindependence status quo.

The internal hegemony argument is buttressed by a second hypothesis, a modified version of Marxian false consciousness. Perhaps the Hausa
talakawa as well as sarakuna, commoners as well as rulers, just do not
sufficiently appreciate the linkages between postcolonial politics and colonial oppression; it would be too dangerous to do so. From this perspective, the boundary—the ultimate expression of property alienation—is
but one component of the ideological superstructure (along with legal,
educational, and accommodationist religious institutions) that reifies the
otherwise inauthentic partition of the Hausa people into inherently colonial units. The nationalism that legitimizes the continuing partition is a
classic component of the ideologically blinding superstructure.

Because the false-consciousness argument and, to a lesser extent, the
internal-hegemony hypothesis require the existence of a privileged and
transcendent observer, standing outside a Neoplatonic cave of colonialism,
I regard them as hermeneutically incomplete and conceptually suspect.
A more plausible explanation may be found in organizational theory: institutional inertia. Colonial legacies persist because the institutions and
demarcations established during the colonial era have acquired legitimacy
by virtue of their longevity. Educational systems, chieftaincy hierarchies,
customs regimes have all reinforced the originally illogical colonial borderline. In the absence of a competing institutional framework, the colonial
machinery just lumbers on. Dividing lines are reified. Alien divisions are
assimilated.

Paradoxically, much of the boundary's legitimacy is grounded in its functional irrelevance. Though the boundary does symbolize the division of
the borderline Hausa into separate nationalities, it does little to impede
cultural contact and exchange between them: in daily life, the border rarely
functions as a line of separation. Markets and marriages are two forces that
constantly nullify the boundary as a physical divider. If the boundary is so
porous, why actively oppose it?

A fourth explanation for colonial continuity in the postcolonial era lies in
nationalist ideology. It is important to retain the colonially inspired differences in identity because this is what imparts reality to Nigérienhood and
Nigerianhood. And why are such constructs as "Nigeria" and "Niger" important to borderline villagers eking out survival on the edge of the Sahel?
Because belonging to such internationally recognized entities elevates these
otherwise invisible agriculturalists to the status of members of the global
community. Independence, goes the theory of nationalism, promises to

the decolonized dignity and self-respect in the eyes of the rest of the world. Such Hausa terms as *mutumci* (manhood), *mulkin kai* (ruling oneself, independence), and *kishin kasa* (jealousy of/for the country; nationalism) convey the normative tone within this Africanized discourse of decolonization and nationalism. Boundaries, within this nationalist paradigm, are geographic symbols of the nation-state.

A fifth hypothesis for the perpetuation of boundaries and colonial-based identities comes from sociology: ethnogenesis. Indigenous communities in regular contact with other groups strive for distinctiveness. They tend to highlight their idiosyncratic differences rather than level them for the sake of benign (or banal) homogeneity. Partition, according to this view, has imparted to otherwise undifferentiated ethnic groups the ability to erect differentiating supraethnic identities. The process is not easily undone, even when the rulers who divided them have been ousted and the physical borders are dismantled. This uncomfortable fact was discovered in Germany when, after forty-odd years of separate rule, East and West Germans were taken aback by the profound cultural gap that separated them. Mental boundaries are more encrusted than physical ones; when European communism collapsed, the persistence of Croat-Serb differences in the interstices of the old Ottoman and Austrian empires not only annihilated Yugoslavian state-building efforts but murderously demonstrated the primacy of imperially cast differences over both economically grounded ideologies and "rationally" redrawn boundaries of the twentieth century. Even as economic logic tends to the formation of larger interstate pacts (such as the European Community and the North American Free Trade Agreement), ethnic assertiveness ensures that subgroups within such larger units retain, and indeed accentuate, their identificational differences. In the Hausa borderlands, where the people are ethnically and religiously homogeneous, national identity substitutes for ethnic particularity.

Yet though two group identities have been imposed on the Hausa, they remain linked by significant cultural elements. Some of these elements, ironically, serve to strengthen their separation.

Within Hausa society, especially rural Hausa society, the norms of *biyayya* (loyalty, obedience) and *zaman lafiya* (stability, peace) still prevail. With regard to political authority, Islamic-inspired rebellion of the type beginning to emerge in urban Hausa centers of Nigeria (see Ibrahim 1991) is still tempered by Muslim and Hausa principles of *ta'a* and *sulhu:* accommodation and reconciliation. Despite the assimilation of Fulani jihadists and their descendants into the community of the conquered, the Hausa, particularly those residing in the borderlands, retain an aversion to confrontation, outright resistance, and armed rebellion.[2] In this respect they differ from the nearby Zarma and Tuareg, not to mention other African peoples reputed to perpetuate the "warrior tradition" (see Mazrui, ed., 1977).[3]

I am not postulating the immutability of Hausa quiescence or forecasting the inevitable triumph of politically conservative Muslim groups over activist ones (see Paden 1992). Religious tension and interethnic conflict in Northern Nigerian cities, coupled with a dynamic rural-urban linkage throughout Hausaland, challenge any pretense of permanent peaceableness, even among the borderline Hausa. But as an explanation as to why colonial patterns have persisted in the postcolonial era, cultural normativism (as an unnumbered middle-level hypothesis) provides the glue that holds the more elusive hypotheses of internal hegemony, false consciousness, bureaucratic inertia, nationalist ideology, and group identity formation together. It also represents a more fully developed expression of the final hypothesis addressing the conundrums of colonial and boundary continuity, the one provided by political socialization.

Might we not extend to an aggregate level the usually individuated finding in political socialization that "there is a sequence in the acquisition of [political] orientations [e.g., sense of national identity, awareness of major political institutions], with the affective and evaluative orientations preceding the cognitive" (Kavanagh 1983:37)? In young states, critical systemic analysis may not build up until sufficient information on institutional shortcomings has been absorbed and processed by the new citizenry. Only after the postindependence honeymoon wears off can an honest appraisal of postcolonial vis-à-vis colonial transformation be made. Until then prevailing institutions are beyond criticism.

On the individual level, political socialization could account for an increasing degree of legitimacy conferred upon the boundary. Some borderland Hausa may have harbored a sense of the injustice or incongruity of

[2] Migration, particularly from Niger to Nigeria, may indeed constitute a form of resistance, as Asiwaju (1976a) argues for Upper Volta and the Ivory Coast before 1945. It is not, however, equivalent to more overt expressions of resistance and rebellion.

[3] This is not to say that the rural Hausa are by nature either passive or pacifistic. Indeed, as Kirk-Greene (1980) demonstrates in his (partial) debunking of the "martial races imperative," in the early colonial era the rural Hausa were regarded as excellent military material: witness their widespread recruitment in Glover's Hausa Constabulary and the West African Frontier Force. But Kirk-Greene also shows that the Hausa were subsequently superseded (at least in British martial race thinking) by recruits from Nigeria's Middle Belt. The point is not whether the Hausa are intrinsically a "martial race" or not (the very question is ludicrous) but the extent to which their present political culture eschews direct, physical opposition to duly constituted state authority.

colonial partition before independence, but not among the generation that came to political consciousness after independence. The Hausa born in the early 1950s and after have been politically socialized under nationalist regimes for which borders were not mere diplomatic conveniences but the very stuff of national sovereignty.

The lack of Hausa irredentism (to the extent that irredentism necessitates a preexisting state prepared to "redeem" its people and territory [Neuberger 1991:97]) represents the African norm. "Realpolitik and utilitarian calculations by the potentially redeeming states are the major reasons for the relatively small number of African irredenta and their failure to change the postcolonial map dramatically" (106). Neither Nigeria nor Niger, despite the political or demographic dominance of the Hausa, has sufficient interest in advocating the redemption of any portion of Hausaland beyond its current borders. To the contrary, such a prospect would be extremely destabilizing, in respect not only to international relations but to the delicate domestic ethnic balance prevailing within the two states.

One may indeed find a handful of urban-based Hausa cultural nationalists who seek to spread the doctrine of Hausa unity. Yet the notion that ordinary talakawa are aggrieved on account of the continuing partition of Hausaland, or that there is popular sentiment for Hausa ethnonationalism, is phantasmagorical. The mass media's focus on Third World ethnic foment notwithstanding, this accommodation to partition and its boundaries *is* the norm, at the grassroots as well as at the national level.

Policy Implications

For policy makers no less than for scholars, it is important to recognize, as Friedrich Kratochwil (1986) does, the changing functionality of boundaries. Though the molecular consistency of the iron pole jutting out of the sand changed not a whit when Nigérien and Nigerian flags were hoisted in 1960,[4] its functional significance changed dramatically. No longer symbolizing the separation of two empires' colonies, the tangaraho now represented the distinction between two successor states within a greatly expanded international system. It is not clear, however, that the rulers of the new states have regarded their boundaries in new ways. A fresh look at these inherited colonial demarcations is needed, not with the aim of dismantling them but rather with a view toward transcending them.

[4] Niger achieved independence first, on August 8; Nigeria's came two months later, on October 1.

Outside of Africa, the most important shift in boundary functionality has been "a tendency toward erosion of the exclusivity associated with the traditional notion of territoriality . . . because of the growth of transnational relations and interdependencies" (ibid., 27). While global microdiplomacy (the establishment by subnational governments of cooperative linkages with territorially noncontiguous foreign governments and private enterprises) is still beyond most African localities and borderlands, transborder regionalism is not. Transborder regionalism accepts and legitimates the idea—so uncomfortable to those who hold traditional notions of national sovereignty, particularly while sitting in the middle of "soft states"—that borderland peripheries may have more in common with the locality across the boundary than with the centers of their own states. Transborder regionalism is tolerant of the emergence of an "integrative transborder political culture"; it facilitates a "transborder regime," understanding that it refers to "geographically delineated regions that cooperate across an intersovereign boundary but do not aim at such integration as would give birth to a new 'transfrontier nation,' emotionally and structurally separate from the two respective political heartlands" (Duchacek 1986:18). Such transborder regionalism is to be found in the areas abutting the borders between Germany and Holland, Switzerland and France, and Canada and the United States.

An objection to applying West European and North American norms of transborder relations to the decolonizing world is based on the life-cycle argument of new state formation: Whereas nationhood preceded statehood in the West and North, in the South statehood has typically preceded nationhood. The temporal advantage that European nations and their offshoots enjoyed—hundreds of years of national identity formation before modern statehood was attained—finds few parallels in decolonized polities. In these states, national identity is as problematic as the transition to independence was abrupt. Nor do developing (and particularly African) nations enjoy a level of economic and technological development that makes transborder diplomacy as feasible, desirable, and indeed indispensable as it is between industrialized nations. The liberal notion of transborder regionalism and other relaxed views of national sovereignty are a luxury that young states and developing nations just cannot afford, either politically or economically.[5]

Such arguments, while encompassing kernels of historical and economic

[5] Contrast the northern Mexican states and contiguous American states, where "the practice of transborder regionalism is primarily telephonic" (Duchacek 1986:21), with the Hausa borderlands, where telephones are virtually nonexistent.

truth, also imply that developing nations must follow the same path as the industrial nations did, and perhaps a similar (though one would hope condensed) time frame. Such a notion is generally rejected by the leaders of developing nations. Yet however impatient political leaders are for economic development, they are correspondingly cautious when it comes to political development. Transborder regionalism is one area in which enlightened international diplomacy can leapfrog over outdated conceptions of national sovereignty.

Since my witnessing of frontier life in rural Hausaland, Seyni Kountché of Niger has died of a brain tumor in a French hospital and Nigeria has performed administrative surgery on Kaduna State: Daura Emirate is now grafted to the new state of Katsina. Even more significant, Niger has embarked on the road of recivilianization and political party pluralism[6] while Nigeria prepares, once again, for a sequential handover of power by the military. How these events will trickle down and affect Yekuwa and Yardaji remains to be seen. Whatever their ultimate effect, it is safe to assume that they will contribute to the continuing differentiation of Yardaji from Yekuwa, just as the two Hausalands will continue their disparate evolution.

The overarching continuity of pre-independence institutional norms in Hausaland today does not mean that Northern Nigeria and middle Niger reflect their colonial pasts in equal measure. Structures and processes of independent Niger more closely resemble colonial Niger than the Federal Republic of Nigeria resembles British Nigeria. Change has been more rapid, dramatic, and pervasive in postcolonial Nigeria than in postcolonial Niger. The dismantling of the native authorities, the creation of states, a succession of military coups and a civil war in the 1960s, the creation of popularly elected local government councils, the explosion of a petronaira economy, and the overnight extension of universal primary education in the 1970s certainly transformed Northern Nigeria in ways that the British who knew and ruled it could hardly have imagined. The 1980s witnessed civilian versus military and intramilitary political turbulence, the collapse of oil-greased development plans, and a rise in religious conflict both within the Islamic community and between Muslims and Christians. Change in Niger, despite the replacement of civilian authoritarianism by a development-oriented military regime and a fleeting (relative) prosperity from uranium revenues, pales in comparison. Even should the trend toward

---

[6] In 1993 Nigériens elected a Hausa, Mahamane Ousmane of the Convention Démocratique et Sociale (CDS-Rahama), as president.

democratization and political pluralism take root, as part of the wave of francophone African societies galvanized by pro-democracy, antimilitary national conferences, Niger will still have a long way to go to catch up with Nigeria.

Yet at another level, the greater divergence from colonial-era politics in Nigeria reinforces the overall argument for colonial continuity. For indirect rule, despite its overtly conservative bent, mandated greater indigenous political autonomy than the French afforded their colonials. Institutional dissimilarity between colonial and modern Nigeria is a token of the separation between state and society which the British tolerated but the French abhorred. The successors to British rule have been unable to restrict or mold change as they may have wanted; the societies and system they inherited have not made it possible. From this perspective, the apparent evolution away from colonial institutions in Nigeria is itself a legacy of a colonial system whose will to impose absolute norms and structures was relatively weak, and whose approach to governing at the local level was relatively loose.

Paradoxically, despite the legacy of indirect rule in Nigeria, I would further hazard the guess that, at least at the grassroots level, Nigérien Hausaland is more like precolonial (and especially prejihadic) Hausaland than is Nigerian Hausaland. For despite the preferential status of chiefs in Nigeria, control from on high is heavier, tighter, and more rigid in Niger. In its approach to ruling and governance, the military establishment of Niger has been more akin to the traditional, precolonial sarakuna than either civilian- or military-cum-chieftaincy rule has been in Nigeria. Authoritarian military rule may not sound attractive, but in the context of Hausa history, where clan-ridden Kano and despotic Damagaram were hardly paragons of democracy, it is the more familiar mode of governance. France's designs for change in Hausaland were more revolutionary than Britain's; but in the end, it is the mode by which change was imposed rather than the purpose for which it was attempted that has prevailed. Revolutionary change under the whip has yielded more mulkin zahi ("hot rule"); gradual change under the scepter has been more comprehensive.

Although African leaders and advocates frequently lambaste the legacies of colonialism and presumed ongoing neocolonialism, it is not recognized to what extent these same states and governments have themselves been perpetuating erstwhile colonial policies and attitudes in such critical areas as education, language, chieftaincy, and religion. It is perhaps more convenient (and less embarrassing) to draw attention to external relations (mostly of an economic nature) that may legitimately be used to buttress the neocolonial argument. Nevertheless, internal tendencies that prolong colonial patterns are arguably more prevalent than external economic relations that do the same, in part because fewer African elites and Africanist scholars are conscious of the paracolonial nature of national policies. If awareness is a prerequisite to action, then an honest recognition of the internalization and perpetuation of colonial mentalities (and I stress their plurality) is a necessary precursor to true decolonization.

Two examples will perhaps illustrate my point. One relates to levels and expressions of national consciousness. The other relates to the nature and discourse of political activism, particularly as manifested in student radicalism.

Patriotism (overt expressions of support to the government in power) is different from nationalism (a more general affective sentiment extended to one's people or nation-state.) Both phenomena are more prominent in Niger, where they are consciously engineered by state and school, than in Nigeria. To be sure, ethnic pluralism has presented greater challenges to national unity in Nigeria than in Niger, where the Tuareg challenge represents more a deviation from the general trend than a counterthesis. But more than manageable pluralism, the legacy of a fiercely nationalistic colonial France, imposing the idea of loyalty to state and nation, explains the postcolonial emergence of a Nigérien political identity. Born in revolution, steeped in the doctrine of assimilation, France's strong sense of nationalism became an exportable commodity, transplantable from the Champs Elysées to the Sahel. Although the direction of this loyalty has of course shifted from Paris to Niamey since independence, its content remains an important holdover. For all its imperial greatness, overseas Britain never succeeded in transferring a like degree of nationalist sentiment to either London or Lagos. (Is it because of the more tenuous nature of British identity, which Linda Colley [1992] has probingly exposed?) Britain's emphasis on local autonomy and governance overseas, a logical extension of indirect rule, is relevant here. Nigérien nationalism, a muted phenomenon in 1960, has been promoted by those Nigériens most familiar with the French experience.

For those of a rebellious nature, particularly student activists, the contrast between Nigérien and Nigerian forms of protest is also indicative. In Northern Nigeria the radical Hausa university student, gravitating to Islamic fundamentalism as a source of revolt, is likely to join the Muslim Student Society. But the Nigérien Hausa *lycéen* who wishes to show his fierce opposition to the establishment is more likely to flirt with atheism. Here again, even in countercultural terms, the French influence is manifest. Students of French culture and history will readily recognize this fiercely individualistic, anticlerical strain in French society. Forms of protest are no less inheritances of colonialism than forms of government. It is indeed significant that, whereas the mobilization of Nigerian Hausa students against authority is increasingly carried out in the name of Islam, the rebellion of their Nigérien counterparts is markedly secular in tone.

Hausaland in Comparative Perspective

Is the colonial legacy so ingrained as to shape the evolution of the Hausa in Niger and Nigeria indefinitely? At what point does contemporary social reality depart from historical antecedent and provide a nation with an independent basis of identity? When can we say that a nation has been totally, irremediably decolonized, having established a nexus of decision making and action that is authentically home-grown?

These questions are taking on new currency now that new states are reemerging out of old nations and borders are both crumbling and rising throughout Eastern Europe and the Commonwealth of Independent States. The Soviet Union may be defunct as a sovereign entity, yet surely its influence lives on, however differentially, even in those new republics that have most vociferously distanced themselves from "Soviet imperialism." Is the decolonization of the former Soviet socialist republics qualitatively different from that of the former colonies of Africa? To be sure, the racial component and the related history of slavery give European-African colonial history a special dimension that cannot be underestimated. Yet race was always a factor in Soviet society, too, and still accounts for much of the post-Soviet animosity ripping at corners of the embryonic CIS. Different strategies of accommodation to and assimilation within the former Soviet Union will also shape the pace and direction of decolonization within the new Commonwealth.

What needs to be more closely investigated is how individual cultures react to similar colonial strategies and the forms that such reactions take. This is a task no less pertinent to the former Ottoman and Soviet empires than it is to Africa. This perspective is necessary if we are to understand the dynamics of imperialism even in medieval Europe:

> The feudal state structures that emerged in northeastern Europe may have borne a strong resemblance to one another, but they did not interact in a uniform way with the regions that were subject to them. *The social structures of the areas that came under the control of kings and their servants played a significant role in determining the nature of the interactions between rulers and subjects.* (Given 1990:251; emphasis mine)

Alhaji Muhammadu Bashar (left), the emir of Daura, with S. M. Sanda Oumarou Haboubakar, the sultan of Zinder, at the Nigeria-Niger Transborder Cooperation Workshop, Kano, July 2–8, 1989.

This much emerges as a constant: comparative analyses of imperialism must focus at least as much on the cultures of the colonized as on the culture of the colonizers.

How ironic that Berlin, the city where the partition of Africa was conceived, has now become a symbol of the fragility of irrational boundaries! German reunification represents a strong argument against the retention of intraethnic partitions imposed by outside powers. Yet even as all traces of the Berlin Wall disappear, Hausaland remains divided. Nor is it likely that the reunification of Germany, any more than the breakup of Yugoslavia and Czechoslovakia, portends any change in the borders separating Niger from Nigeria.

The division of Hausaland is not so tragic as the more notorious partitions of Germany, Vietnam, and Korea. One reason is that African neighbors have generally come not only to accept but to rationalize the historically irrational. Although I have argued that, particularly in the Magaria-Daura gateway region, boundary-based national identities have become reified since independence, the last few years have witnessed an increasing number of transborder cooperative initiatives that have func-

Colonel Ahmad Muhammad Daku (left), military governor of Sokoto State, with his Nigérien counterpart, the prefect of Zinder, at the Nigeria-Niger Transborder Cooperation Workshop.

tioned to strengthen relations between Niger and Nigeria (Asiwaju 1990: 11). Significantly, such initiatives have been built largely upon the commonalities of borderland regions, exploiting the "boundary as bridge" paradigm (see Asiwaju 1984). The creation of the Nigeria-Niger Joint Commission on Cooperation, based in Niamey, is emblematic of the kind of institutional development that fosters cross-border relations in a nonthreatening manner. By creating a National Boundary Commission and institutionally housing it in the Presidency, Nigeria is also taking the lead in promoting a "transborder cooperation culture" (Asiwaju 1990:11) among African states. One of the most significant achievements of this commission has been the convening of transborder cooperation workshops with neighboring states, which commenced with the Nigeria-Benin Transborder Cooperation Workshop in Badagry in 1988.

The second transborder workshop, held at Bagauda Lake in Kano State in 1989, joined government officials, traditional rulers, and university scholars from Nigeria and Niger. Binational working committees proposed measures to strengthen cultural, judicial, economic, administrative, and security ties between the two countries, particularly in their border regions. Specific proposals included the use of traditional rulers in cross-border peacekeeping roles; sporting and cultural exchanges; implementing ECOWAS (Economic Community of West African States) codes for economic integration; collaboration in vaccination campaigns and sharing of veterinary information; and joint examination of the original boundary demarcations (Magari 1989).

By coincidence, a 1991 follow-up to the Bagauda Transborder Workshop was held in Magaria. The Nigérien and Nigerian ministers of the interior acknowledged ongoing border "problems"—smuggling and drugs, the need for rehabilitation and safeguarding of boundary posts, collaboration of security forces—but also emphasized peaceful coexistence and "scrupulous respect for goods and persons," as stipulated by the ECOWAS protocol on the movement of people and property movement (*Africa Research Bulletin,* March 1–31, 1991, 10039).

It is just possible that the Nigeria-Niger Transborder Cooperation Workshop constitutes a watershed in the evolution of postcolonial Hausaland. That local communities engage in cross-border activities is not new; that their respective central governments acknowledge this borderland dynamic and construe it in a positive way does represent an important development. It is a step, in at least this one region, toward demarginalizing the status of borderline communities (see Miles & Rochefort 1991:401–2).

Looking Forward

Throughout these pages I have tried to convey a sense of how a formerly colonized people, now divided into independent states, perceive their reality and interpret their past. For them colonial patterns of rule have accounted for significant differences in the way they and their parents and grandparents have lived; these colonial patterns still account for significant differences in life expectations.

Yet these people who most directly live out partition's legacy are not the ones who expend the most energy condemning colonialism. The struggle for survival is sufficiently exhausting. Life can be precarious in the border communities of Hausaland, and tilling the soil takes precedence over plowing through the past. Herein lies the element of pathos for the rural Hausa living on both the existential and geopolitical margins, an element I have only inadequately conveyed in relating their story.

After four generations, the tangaraho—the iron pole in the sand—still divides Hausaland into Niger and Nigeria. It still demarcates one kind of society, one type of regime, and one set of hopes from another. In another four generations will the tangaraho—and the myriad equivalents that dot the African landscape—become a quaint reminder of the continent's bygone partition, by then healed? Or will it be a nightmarish link in a chain of barbed-wire fences erected by future xenophobic politicians in the name of nationalism?

Europe planted the tangaraho; its weeding is up to Africa.

Fieldwork Strategy:
The Choice of a Site

With the theoretical task to be accomplished established—to compare Hausa villages on the two sides of the Niger-Nigeria border—the first
practical challenge was to select two appropriate villages. How to proceed?

Fortunately, logistical constraints helped to narrow the field. As research
associate with Bayero University, I needed to maintain reasonable access
to Kano, the site of the university. I also wished to be reasonably close
to Magaria, the capital of the arrondissement of the same name in Niger,
where I had already taught for two years at the Collège d'Enseignement
Général (College of General Studies, or CEG). Using an extraordinarily
detailed map originally prepared by the U.S. Army Corps of Engineers, I
settled on a manageable radius within which to seek my villages.

The next step was to choose among the half-dozen or so pairs of villages
that appeared fairly close to each other on the map. No two were linked by
any road, so this was not a consideration. (The "modernizing" influence
of a motorized vehicular link would probably have caused the rejection of
any such pair anyway; the object, after all, was to find as rural a setting as
possible.) Five remaining variables had to be taken into account.

Most important was the question of administrative and hierarchical comparability. Although the scope of the research project was to widen, my
original intention was to do a comparative study of the contemporary role
of the traditional chief in Hausa villages in Niger and Nigeria. Thus it was
crucial that the chiefs in both villages occupy parallel rungs in their respective chieftaincy hierarchies. This requirement, by extension, also meant
that the villages would occupy comparable places in the administrative
structures of the two countries.

Second, it was important that the two villages have populations of
roughly equal size. This imperative was to prove slightly more problematic,
as Chapter 2 explains, on both theoretical and empirical grounds. Never-

theless, it was important that neither village overshadow the other in size, lest a bias in demographic importance skew the comparability.

Third, it was necessary to satisfy the test of institutional equivalence. That is, state penetration—the existence, for example, of government education and health facilities—had to be roughly the same in both villages. Logically, this criterion would be met if both villages did occupy similar places in their countries' administrative structures.

Fourth, comparable economic importance in the respective local economies would also tend to control mediating variables of possible distortion. Here the question was whether each location had a daily market, a weekly market, or no market at all.

Fifth, the proximity of the two villages would affect the level of interaction between them and speak to the relative strength of the transborder linkage. The ideal situation would be greater interaction between the two villages than with any other community. Next best would be greater interaction between them than between either of the pair and any other village across the border. Finally, the two would have to be close enough so that I could travel from one to the other on my own. Inasmuch as commercial motorized transport between the two did not exist, and it would have been both physically risky and legally foolish to ride my motorcycle (useful on even dirt roads) through the empty, sandy bush, I would have to be able to negotiate the distance either on foot or on horseback. (Villagers, of course, had much greater stamina than I; what was reasonably close for them might have exceeded the limits of my endurance.)

At the earliest stages of fieldwork strategy, the two overriding criteria in village pairing were chieftaincy comparability and proximity. Conversations in Kano with individuals familiar with the border area under consideration helped narrow the choice. At this point Yardaji and Yekuwa emerged as possible candidates. Later reconnaissance revealed that the demographic, institutional, and economic factors converged positively. The choice was clinched when I discovered that the mother of Malam Souleymane ɗan Tata, a close friend and marabout in Magaria, originally hailed from Yardaji and still had relatives there. As it turned out, several of my former students at the CEG came from Yekuwa. Thus perhaps the most valuable asset in any fieldwork—entrée—was coincidentally assured in both villages.

Another felicitous element reinforced the aptness of the site selection and indirectly enhanced my entrée in the villages and surrounding territory. This was M. G. Smith's monumental historical analysis of the emirate of Daura, The Affairs of Daura: History and Change in a Hausa State, 1800–1958 (1978). Smith's work not only provided a solid historical perspective within which I could situate the modern-day villages of Yardaji and Yekuwa but, in the eyes of both commoners and emirs, rationalized and legitimized my interest in their communities and countries. The days when Europeans mounted their horses and went on bush tours throughout West Africa are long gone; in the 1980s, a white man commuting across an international boundary between backcountry Hausa villages naturally generates more than mild curiosity. The precedent of scholarly interest in greater Daura made the explanation of what I was actually doing in Yekuwa and Yardaji perfectly plausible. Smith's book was very well known to the sitting emir of Daura, Alhaji Muhammadu Bashar. Many of my conversations with the emir centered on or progressed from discussions of *The Affairs of Daura*.

Administration of Self-Identity Surveys

To obtain a random sample in the absence of local rolls or census counts, I drew a map indicating all discrete households in each of the villages. I mapped and listed approximately four hundred households in Yardaji, approximately five hundred in Yekuwa. I selected every fourth household in Yardaji for the survey and every fifth household in Yekuwa, for a total sample of one hundred in each village. Since Hausa custom demands that information relating to the household be provided only by its senior member, I asked the head of household (usually the eldest male) to respond. (In a handful of cases a widow or "prostitute" [karuwa] headed the household.) If the head of household was absent at the time of my visit, I returned as often as I had to until I found him in. Only if the head of household were away for an extended period of time—in Mecca, for instance—would I ask the next senior member of the household to serve as respondent.

After eliciting the individual profile of each respondent, I restated seven elements of identity for prioritization: birthplace, village residence (Yardaji or Yekuwa), citizenship (Nigeria or Niger), state (Kaduna or Zinder), religion (Islam), ethnicity (Hausa), and subethnic identity (Daura Hausa). Since village residence and birthplace were the same for three-quarters of the respondents, most had only six identity variables to choose from. I wrote the six (or seven) identity variables on separate index cards and laid them out on the ground or mat in front of the respondent. I then asked the respondent: "Of these six [or seven] items—that you are a 'son of Yardaji,' a 'son of Nigeria,' a person of Kaduna State, a Daura man, a Muslim, a Hausa—of these items, which is most important to you?" After the respondent indicated one item verbally, I removed the corresponding card and asked, "Which of the remaining five items [I repeated them] is of greatest importance to you?" I repeated this procedure until only one card was left.

I then said, "And finally, being _____ is important to you, right?" to avoid the impression that even the sixth chosen item lacked importance to the respondent, which might have been a breach of etiquette. I then repeated the items in the order in which the respondent had chosen them, giving him an opportunity to "correct any mistakes I might have made." The six (or seven) items were then duly recorded on an individual survey sheet.

Selected Characteristics, Daura Local Government and Magaria Arrondissement, 1978–1985

	Daura local government	Magaria arrondissement
Population	424,357 (1983)	297,902 (1982)
	(Zango District = 89,945)	(Magaria Canton = 64,800)
Area	2,600 sq. kms.	8,000 sq. kms.
Population density	163 per sq. km.	37 per sq. km.
Primary schools	152 (1979–80)	69 (1983–84)
Primary school teachers	1,018 (1979–80)	240 (1983–84)
Primary school enrollment	39,751 (1979–80)	8,931 (1983–84)
Male	65%	67%
Female	35%	33%
Teacher-student ratio	1:39	1:37
Adult literacy enrollment	2,128 (1980–81)	353 (1983–84)
Male	66% (1979–80)	88%
Female	34% (1979–80)	22%
Medical institutions	42 (1978)	13 (1983)
Medical staff	75 (1978)	28[a] (1985)
Youth clubs	288 (1982)	866

Sources: Kaduna State of Nigeria, Ministry of Economic Planning, Statistics Division, *Statistical Yearbook, 1983* (Zango, 1984); République du Niger, *Monographie* (Niamey: UNICEF, November 1984); Ministère du Plan, *Préparation du plan quinquennal 1987–1991, appui au SDP* (Paris: Société d'Etudes pour le Développement Economique et Social, December 1986).

[a]Does not include 663 trained health volunteers.

Extracts from Anglo-French Treaties Delimiting the Nigeria-Niger Boundary, 1906–1910

The Government of His Majesty the King of the United Kingdom of Great Britain and Ireland and of the British Dominions beyond the Seas, Emperor of India, and the Government of the French Republic, having agreed, in a spirit of mutual good-will, to confirm the Protocol with its two Annexes, prepared . . . by their respective Delegates for the delimitation of the frontier between the British and French possessions to the east of the Niger . . . have agreed to the following Arrangement. . . .

[Annex] . . . It is understood that if the inhabitants living near the frontier thus determined should express the wish to cross the frontier in order to settle in the French possessions, or inversely, in the British possessions, no obstacles will be placed in the way of their so doing, and they shall be granted the necessary time to allow them to gather in all standing crops, and generally to remove all the property of which they are the legitimate owners.

—Convention between Great Britain and France, respecting the Delimitation of the Frontier between the British and French Possessions to the East of the Niger. Signed at London, 29th May, 1906.

Protocol with Regard to Definition of Frontier
Article I. Description of the Frontier
The frontier follows a straight line from beacon to beacon . . . described according to the following system of classification—
Class A. A group of four palm-tree posts disposed round a fifth central post which carries a tri-colour enamelled iron plaque. . . .
Class B. A conical pillar built of dry stone, cemented on top, to which is fixed the numbered plaque above mentioned.

Class C. The upper length of an iron telegraph pole of Northern Nigeria pattern, 15 feet long, fixed in the ground at a depth of 4 feet to 5 feet, carrying at the top the numbered plaque above mentioned, and generally cemented at the base.

Class D. The cast-iron base socket, 5 feet long, of an iron telegraph pole, fixed point uppermost in the ground, at a depth of 3 feet. . . .

Class E. A tree, stripped of all except the upper branches, to which the numbered plaque is fastened at a height of 10 feet to 15 feet above the ground. A clearing has been formed around the tree. . . .

Article III. Maintenance of Beacons

The Commissioners are of the opinion that it will be to the interest of the two Colonies to maintain the frontier beacons which they have erected, and which are exposed from many causes to deterioration, and even destruction, if neglected.

They agree in recommending that the following precautions should be taken every year by both English and French authorities:—

1. Towards the close of the rainy season, before the natives have fired the bush, clear around each beacon a space of 10 meters radius in order to prevent the splintering by fire of the enamelled face of the numbered plaque.

2. Keep pruned every year the trees on which are fixed the plaques indicating the frontier in the same way as has been done by the Commission of Delimitation.

3. Should it happen that a numbered plaque fall from any cause whatever (such as oxidation of wire or nails, lightning, shock, &c.), it will be necessary that the Chief of the nearest village should immediately acquaint his Resident of the fact in order that the latter may take the necessary steps to insure that the plaque in question be immediately restored to the exact position in which it was fixed by the Commission of Delimitation.

4. It will be necessary to renew, as required, the thorn protection around the iron poles in order to guard them from shocks caused by cattle or wild animals.

The maintenance of the beacons is particularly important during the earlier years, before the natives have become perfectly familiarized with the position of the frontier. . . .

Done in duplicate in English and in French at London, the 19th February, 1910.

R. POER O'SHEE, Major, Royal Engineers,
British Commissioner

J. TILHO, Capitaine d'Infanterie coloniale,
Commissaire français

—Anglo-French Commission for the Delimitation of the Frontier East of
the Niger, Northern Nigeria.

Communiqué of the Nigeria-Niger Transborder Cooperation Workshop, Kano, July 2–8, 1989

The Workshop on Nigeria-Niger Transborder Cooperation was formally opened with a key-note address by Alhaji Mohammed Gambo, the Inspector-General of Police, Member of the Armed Forces Ruling Council representing Nigeria's Chief of General Staff, Vice Admiral Augustus Wikhomu in the presence of:

- Mr. Mouttari Moussa, President of the National Council on Development, Member of the Executive Bureau of the council for National Orientation.
- The Honourable Minister of Internal Affairs of Nigeria, Colonel John N. Shagaya.
- The Honourable Minister of Interior of Niger, Mr. Attaher Darkoye.
- The Military Governor of the Northern 'Gateway' States of Kano, Sokoto, Katsina, Borno and their Nigérien Counterparts, the Prefects of the Adjacent Departments of Zinder and Maradi as well as the Secretary-General of the Departments of Dosso, Diffa and Tahoua.
- Representatives of relevant Border Local Administrations.
- Staff of relevant State Ministries and Parastatals from both countries.
- Members of the Academic Community of appropriate research expertise drawn from such institutions as the Université de Niamey; Bayero University Kano; University of Maiduguri; Kano Polytechnique; Usman Danfodio University, Sokoto and Ahmadu Bello University, Zaria and Imo State University. . . .

Deserving of great mention is the presence of highly respected border traditional rulers of both Nigeria and Niger, whose presence was aimed at invoking the Nigeria-Niger borderland customary and ancestral blessing on the workshop. They included their Royal Highness, Alhaji Ibrahim

Dasuki, the Sultan of Sokoto; Alhaji Mustapha Umar El-Kanemi, Shehu of Borno; Alhaji Boubakar Amadou Sanda, the Sultan of Damagaram. Equally present were the Emirs of Katsina, Daura, Hadejia, Gumel and Kazaure as well as the Chefs de Province of Maradi and Gobir. Others are the District Head of Dambatta, Kano and the Chefs de Canton of Kantché, Sassambouroum, Chetimari, Dosso, Goudoumari, Koumi Madadina Dioundou and Tibiri all from Niger Republic. Playing host to this pageantry of traditional rulers was the Emir of Kano, Alhaji Ado Bayero.

Other eminent presences are Alhaji Maitama Sule, former permanent Representative of Nigeria at U.N.O.; and His Excellency Lt. Col. Tandja Mohammed, the Ambassador of Niger in Nigeria as well as His Excellency, Mr. Dus Mai Kassua, the Consul General of Niger in Kano.

The Objectives of the Workshop

The specific objectives of the workshop were:

1. To provide a forum for discussion of issues which ensure the consolidation of peaceful, cooperative and friendly relationship between the Federal Republic of Niger and the Republic of Niger at national and local levels.

2. To highlight the age-long socio-economic interlinks between the two countries and deliberate on how these linkages can be positively utilised to promote stronger transborder cooperation.

3. To broaden, systematize and consolidate existing relationship between the two countries by adopting specific resolutions and recommendations which will serve as models for improving transborder cooperation and safeguarding security in ECOWAS region and Africa in general.

Opening Statement

After mutual exchange of encomiums showered on the two countries by their various delegations in which they recognized the oneness of their peoples in both cultural institutions, the need to enhance these advantages in spite of their independent and sovereign status was made evident. They evoked ecological and other economic problems facing their border areas and wished that whatever policies emerged from this workshop must be directed towards enhancing not only the activities of the local inhabitants but also the overall law enforcement and State Security Programme of both countries. In this way, their political will shall guarantee flexibility in the appreciation of rules at the border and control over executing agents.

A. Identified Problems

The Workshop identified problems which had hitherto tended to limit the level of cooperation between Nigeria and the Republic of Niger. Among these were the following:

1. The use of two foreign languages which impedes the communication flow across the border.

2. Lack of sufficient policy-information on the border administration of both countries.

3. Porous nature of their borders.

4. Insufficient efforts in combatting common natural disasters such as drought and instances of willingness to extradition of suspected criminals and recovered goods.

5. Non-ratification of existing treaties, especially those that concern frequent livestock movement.

6. The economic situation in both countries brought about by low prices of uranium and oil; foreign debts and reduction in growth rate.

7. To ensure the application of cultural agreements concluded between the two countries.

B. Border Economy

1. To accelerate the economic integration of the two countries in conformity with the Lagos Plan of Action and the ECOWAS Protocol.

2. Harmonize and co-ordinate existing texts with the view to facilitating customs facilities.

3. To sensitize the populations on the need for better understanding of trade mechanism in order to increase border incomes of the State.

4. Formalise, modernise and ensure the expansion of border markets.

5. Comprehensive appraisal of live-stock census, traffic movement and the needed resources of the pastoralists, including the alarming increase in land cultivation, which takes up traditional grazing reserves, thus intensifying the migratory trend of transhumance. Consequently, there is need for a complete mapping of cattle routes in order to ensure effective control. There is also need to share information on animal health and diseases

as well as the development of vaccines and the establishment of properly manned control posts.

6. Acceleration of the economic integration process in the area of road, rail, inland waters, telephones and satellite. To this effect, the television authorities of both countries should immediately submit detailed plans; detailed plans should also be submitted in the area of resuscitating the direct air link between the capitals of the two countries.

C. Border Administration

1. All existing agreements and protocols under the O.A.U. and ECOWAS with relevance to joint border cooperation and other bilateral agreements should be promptly ratified and implemented.

2. Exchange of vital information concerning protection of life, property and good neighbourliness.

3. Establishment of a Joint Research Council for the study, preservation, documentation of the history, economy, culture of the people and for the award of scholarships for the exchange of and organization of conferences and seminars.

4. Establishment of Joint Security Patrols for the more effective control of crimes such as armed banditry, smuggling, drug-trafficking etc.

5. Both countries should make efforts to provide amenities such as schools, roads, clinics, water, electricity, telecommunications to their border communities.

D. Border Management and Security

1. That beacons established by the 1910 Treaty be replaced with more standard durable beacons in order to enhance the clarity of the boundary.

2. That the boundary as defined by the Komadougu-Yobe Rivers be precisely established and mapped as in previous treaties.

3. That the Boundary Commission of the two countries should meet to ensure strategies for implementing the above recommendations.

4. That the border areas on both sides be developed to serve as effective bridges for functional cooperation rather than barriers.

5. That security and border enforcement agencies should endeavour to cooperate in tackling their common problems through institutional, investigative and patrol measures.

E. Legal Aspects

1. That Nigeria and Niger are recognized as two sovereign and independent neighbouring States whose common boundary has separated peoples
of the same cultural descent, for historical reasons.

2. That both countries have through their membership of the Niger
Basin Authority, the Lake Chad Basin Commission and the ECOWAS,
established some legal basis for transborder cooperation. Both countries
are therefore called upon to ratify all outstanding relevant instruments
concluded under the auspices of these organisations.

3. Both countries have also concluded a number of bilateral arrangments
under the auspices of the Nigeria-Niger Joint Commission for cooperation; and negotiations are still going on for more agreements. The two
countries should take steps to renew expired agreements, sign those due
for signature and expedite action on those still being negotiated. Consequently, the draft instrument for the creation of Local Bilateral Committees should be completed as soon as possible in order to give legal backing
to existing transborder contacts. There is also need for an inter-State agreement on pollution control, in the area of toxic waste as well as in crime
control.

4. That because the European outline convention is unsuited to Africa's
conditions, the Nigeria-Niger Joint Commission for cooperation offer for
the moment a satisfactory alternative.

5. That the existence of parallel legal systems in both countries constitutes
obstacles to the realisation of effective transborder cooperation. Consequently, a programme for the harmonization of the legal system should be
established to take cognisance of their cultural conditions. To this effect
they should promote free flow of information and encourage comparative
legal research in their universities.

Made at Bagauda Lake Hotel, Kano
8th July, 1989

Glossary

Although standard Nigerian Hausa orthography is generally followed here, occasionally the Daura dialectical form is preferred. If the plural form is employed in the text, it is provided here in parentheses.

addini   religion
agogo   watch
al'ada   custom; market sales tax
albarka   prosperity, blessing; divine gift or grace
alhaji (alhazai)   one who has made the pilgrimage to Mecca; title for rich or important person
alƙali   judge, usually in Islamic context
alƙanin wasa   referee
allo   wooden slate on which Koranic students write
amaro   roasted peanuts
amfani   usefulness, advantage; profit
ana   third-person pronoun; form of address used for royalty
anasara   Christian; white person
arziki   wealth; good fortune
asali   ancestral home, pedigree; family regional origin
asken kwalaba   cutting people on the head with broken glass
attajiri (attajirai)   big-time trader
audita   auditor
aure   marriage
babban riga   formal, traditional male attire; *see* riga
babur   motorcycle
baƙin anasara   black white men
baƙo (baƙi)   visitor, guest; stranger
bante   strip of cloth that covers only the private parts
Banza Bakwai   the Illegitimate Seven; in Hausa mythology, illegitimate sons of Bawo
bara   alms-seeking; servant
barantaka   clientage
barawo (barayi)   thief
bariki   barracks; colonial commandant; administrative headquarters

bashi   loan
bature (turawa)   European; white person
beit-al-mal   native treasury
ɓira   to jump; used to describe a kind of torture
birni   city, urban settlement; walled town
birodi   bread
biyayya   obedience, loyalty; order
boko [book]   Western, secular education; fraud; false
bori   trance of possession
buga   beat, thrash, strike, hit
buhu   large sack often used for packaging grain
caca   gambling
cayaman   chairman
cediya   fig tree
cif organiza   head planner
cin hanci   bribery
dagaci (dagatai)   village area head
daji   countryside, "bush"
ɗan ('yan) doka   emirate policeman
ɗan ('yan) kauye   bushman (pejorative)
ɗan ('yan) sanda   policeman
ɗan ('yan) siyasa   politician
ɗara   fez
daraja   rank, standing; respect
dashi   resin-yielding shrub
daudu   transvestism
ɗauren aure   wedding ceremony
dawa   sorghum
deɓe   dirt road; beaten earth; floor
difatiman [département]   administrative unit in Niger, equivalent to county
dimokuradiyya   democracy
direba   driver
dodo   serpent, dragon
dogari (dogarai)   traditional palace guard
doka   rule; law; order
dole   obligation
dukiya   wealth
faɗa   fighting; quarreling; attack
Faransa, Faranshi   France/Niger
faskarawa   unruliness
fata   skin; leather
fatake   long-distance traders
fatauci   long-distance (caravan) trade
fito   exit, come out
fula   pillbox cap worn with traditional dress

fura   dish of cooked millet balls mixed with sour milk
gadi   bodyguard, watchman
gadon gida   inheritance; family guild
gaisuwa   greeting; gift to a patron
gaje   cloth currency
gardi (gardawa)   follower of or apprentice to Islamic teacher
gargajiya   tradition; old times
gari   town, large village; settlement
garin haihuwa   birthplace
gaskiya   truth
gayya   communal work effort, accompanied by festive drumming and a collective meal
giginya   deleb palm
girma   prestige, importance, greatness
giya   beer; wine; alcohol
godiya   thanks, gratitude
gona   farm
goro   kola nut
guda   joyful shrilling sound, ululation
gudun kare   making people run and bark like dogs
gujiya   peanuts
gunduma   administrative district
gwale-gwale   corporal punishment
gwamna   governor
gwamnoti   government
gwanjo   shirt; used clothes; auction
Gwaranci   poorly spoken Hausa (pejorative)
gyaran dunya   repairing of the world
Habe   Hausa person without Fulani blood or ancestry
hadan kai   collective unity (lit., joining heads)
ha'inci   corruption; fraud, deceit
hajj   Muslim pilgrimage
hakimi (hakimai)   district head
hali   character, personality, temperament
hamada   abundance; desert
hankali   good sense, intelligence; care
haraji   poll tax
haram   forbidden by Islamic law; activity so forbidden
hardo   chief (Fulani)
hatsi   millet
hauka   craziness, unruliness
Hausa Bakwai   Hausa Seven; the seven original families or nations from which the Hausa are derived
haya   renting out or hiring
horo   punishment; training; disciplinary action

humushi   one-fifth; 20 percent levy on war booty
hurumi   tax exemptions
iko   authority, power
ikon Allah   the will of God
ilmi   learning, knowledge
iyyaka   boundary, border, frontier
jakada (jakadu)   royal messenger; titled courier
jama'a   community, public
jandam   gendarme
jangali   cattle tax
jan gindi   making people drag their buttocks on the pavement with stones under
    them
jan kunne   making people hold their ears for hours at a time
jawon hankali   dispute arbitration
jiha   state
jihad   holy war to spread or purify Islam
jin kai   arrogance (lit., feeling [one's own] head)
ƙabila   tribe, language
ƙaɗaɓaɓai   a fearful insect; name of famine
kai   second-person pronoun; see ana
Kaƙalaba   famine of 1913–14
Kaƙuɗuɓa   Sahelian drought of the early 1970s
kanti   small shop
kantoma   local government administrator
karamci   generosity
ƙaramin hukuma   district (lit., small authority)
karangiya   prickly burrs from a grass
karạtu   (Koranic) study
ƙarfi   strength
ƙariya   lying; deceit
karo   see haraji
karuwa (karuwai)   prostitute, courtesan
karuwanci   prostitution
ƙasa   country, land
ƙasar Faranshi   Niger
ƙasar Inglishi   Nigeria
kashe   hit, thrash; kill
ƙasƙasta   lowering of status; humiliation
kasuwa (kasuwoyi)   market
ƙauye   "bush"; village
keta   maliciousness
kinciya   lily plant
kirki   arete; excellence of character; kindness
kishin ƙasa   nationalism
kiwo   livestock raising

koli   small wares
komandan   commandant
ƙose   bean cake
kuɗi   cowrie shells; money
kuɗin baƙi   postharvest tax on strangers
kuɗin ciyawa   grazing tax on migrant pastoralists
kuɗin garka   farm or garden plot tax
kuɗin kabari   cemetery tax
kulikuli   small, round fried cakes of groundnut oil extract
kulle   seclusion of women; purdah
kumya   shame; modesty; discretion
ƙungiya   association; club; organization
kuwa   shouting
kwajaja   thin person with pot belly; hay
kwatchewa   seize, take by force, plunder
ladabi   respect; politeness
laifi   crime, wrong; fault
lalata   spoil; bad conduct
langa-langa   long strings used for tying loads or bales; a tall, slender person
lardu   Nigérien Hausa term for *département*
lekol [*l'école*]   secular school
likita   doctor; paramedic
limam   officiating Muslim priest
lokaci(n)   time (of), era
lura da zaman jama'a   peace and welfare of community
ma'aji   treasurer
magajin gari   village comptroller
magatakarda   secretary
Maguzawa   non-Islamized Hausa
mahalbi   hunter
mahaukaci   mentally ill, crazy
mahaukacin gida   crazy house (gambling arena)
mai allura   needleman; village dispensary worker
mai gari (masu gari)   village chief (lit., holder of the village)
mai gida   head of household
mai gunduma   *see* dagaci
mai ilmi (masu ilmi)   *see* ilmi; modern-trained graduate; technician
mai kamfani (masu kamfi)   in Niger, the chief's emissary to a district
mairam   a tax on occupational specialists
mai sarauta (masu sarauta)   titleholder; nobleman, royalty
mai taimakon audita   assistant auditor
mai taimakon baƙi   assistant visitors' secretary
mai taimakon cayaman   vice chairman
mai taimakon ma'aji   assistant treasurer
mai taimakon mai bada shawara   assistant counselor

mai taimakon sakatare   assistant secretary
mai taimakon sakatare watsan labaru   assistant press secretary
mai tebur   petty merchant
mai unguwa   ward head
makaɗi (makaɗa)   drummer, musician
maƙami   see muƙami
makaranta   school
makaranta alkorani   Koranic school
makaranta boku   Western-style school
makaranta haoussa   Koranic school (in Nigeria)
mallam (mallamai)   scribe; Muslim scholar, teacher, or "priest"
mallamanci   Koranic teaching
mallam makaranta   schoolteacher
manufofin kungiya   charter
manya-manya   big shots; fat cats
Marisuwa   influenza epidemic of 1918
maroƙi (maroƙa)   praise singer
matsa   squeeze; harass; treat harshly
mesenja   messenger
miya   sauce made of local condiments (okra, pimento, dried baobab leaves, locust-
    bean seed, goat meat, etc.)
mugu   evil, bad
muhimmanci   importance; significance
muƙami   standing, status, influence
mulki   regime; rule; control; sovereignty
mulkin douane   rule by the customs service
mulkin kai   self-rule; independence
mulkin mallaka   colonial era, colonial rule; colonialism
mulkin Yardiar   rule of RDR; see Yardiar
mulkin zahi   "hot" or "fiery" rule
mutumci   dignity; manhood
mutumci sarauta   authority, respect for traditional rulers
naɗa   turbaning; ceremony of elevation within chiefly hierarchy
nasara   see anasara
nasaranci   Westernization (lit., Christianizing)
Na yafeka   traditional formula of forgiveness
noma   farming
nono   bowl of sour milk, usually served with millet balls
polis   sergeant at arms
ra'ayi   opinion; viewpoint
raba   cut, split, divide
rabon ƙasa   partition
rahoto   spy
rangaɗi   tour, especially of countryside
rarrafe   crawling; type of torture

rashin ladabi   disrespect, impoliteness
rawani   turban
rifi   conceal, shut
riga   cloth gown worn by men
rikici   deceit, corruption
rowa   miserliness
rumaci   senseless drivel
rumbu (rumbuna)   granary, storage bin
sai anjima   until next time, *au revoir*
sakatare   secretary
sakatare ayyuka   public works secretary
sakatare baki   visitors' secretary
sakatare watsan labaru   press secretary
sam   none at all
samari   youth
samariya   age-group association, youth movement
sana'a   secondary occupation
sanda   stick, baton, club; staff
sarauta   chieftaincy, traditional rulership
sarauta na gargajiya   traditional leadership
sardauna   royal title in Sokoto
sarki (sarakai, sarakuna)   ruler, high chief, emir, king
Sarkin Aiki   "King of Work" (nickname for Commandant Bordeaux)
sarkin di'a   seed king
sarkin noma   farm king
sarkin samari   youth king
sarkin yara   child king
sauki   ease, lightness
saurayi (samari)   young man, youth
sawaba   relief, ease
Sawaba   Freedom party (Niger)
shan giya   drinking alcoholic beverages
shari'a   Islamic religious law
sharo   Fulani whipping-cum-initiation
shege   bastard
shegentaka   mischievousness; unruliness; impudence
shi ke nan   that's it; so it is (was); the end
shinkafa   rice
shugaba   political head; leader; elected leader
shugaban kasa   president
simugal   smuggling
siyasa   politics
soja, soji (soji, sojoji)   soldier
son kudi   love of money
sulhu   accommodation; reconciliation, arbitration

surutu   chatter; idle talk
ta'a   accommodation; obedience
tabarya   long, thick, heavy wooden pestle
tafiyan agwagwa   "walking [like a] duck"; a kind of torture
Taƙaƙabwa   drought of mid-1980s
takarda   written paper
takin zamani   modern or industrial fertilizer
talaka (talakawa)   commoner; peasants; common folk
talauci   poverty
taliya   pasta
talla-talla   hawking of goods, often by young women carrying wares on their heads
tangaraho   iron pole; telegraph pole; boundary marker
tausayi   pity, compassion
teyatur   drama, theater
tireda   (trading in) commercial goods; trader, merchant
tiya   a measure for grain
tsaidau   kind of weed
tsanani   strict, stern person
tsiya   poverty, destitution
tsofaffi   elders
tsoho   old man
tsoro   fear; apprehension
tukurda   cloth currency
turanci   English or French language; way of Europeans
turawa   see bature
tururuwa   kind of black ant
tuwo   oval loaf of pounded millet cooked in boiling water
unguwa (unguwoyi)   administrative term for ward or quarter
wahalla   suffering
wake   beans
walki   leather loincloth
wanzami   barber
wayyo   cry in anguish
wewe   marijuana
wuya   suffering, trouble
yafe   forgive; see Na yafeka
yanburu   coarse flour gruel
'yan-ci-rani   eaters of the dry season; seasonal migrants
yanke   cut
yanken ƙasa   partition
yarda   agree; consent
Yardiar   RDR; Rassemblement Démocratique Africain
yare   language
yawo   wander; drift; stroll
yekuwa   oral, public proclamation

yunwa   hunger; starvation
zage   insult, abuse, curse
zahi   hot; heat, fire
zakka   10 percent grain tax ordained by Muslim law
zalumci   oppression
zama   time, condition of
zamanin da   olden days
zamanin turawa   time of the Europeans; colonial era
zaman lafiya   peaceful times
zance   talk, conversation; chat

Bibliography

Aborisade, Oladimeji, ed. 1985. *Local Government and the Traditional Rulers in Nigeria*. Ile-Ife: University of Ife Press.

———, ed. 1986. *Readings in Nigerian Local Government*. Ile-Ife: University of Ife Press.

Abraham, R. C. 1958. *Dictionary of the Hausa Language*. London: Hodder & Stoughton.

Abubakar, Sa'ad. 1974. "The Emirate-Type of Government in the Sokoto Caliphate." *Journal of the Historical Society of Nigeria* 7:211–29.

Adamu, Mahdi. 1978. *The Hausa Factor in West African History*. Zaria: Ahmadu Bello University.

Adefuye, Ade. 1985. "The Kakwa of Uganda and the Sudan: The Ethnic Factor in National and International Politics." In Asiwaju, ed., 1985.

Adeji, Niran. 1986. "Role of Traditional Rulers in Modern Nigeria." In Aborisade, ed., 1986.

Adejuyigbe, Omolade. 1976. "The Readjustment of Superimposed Boundaries in Africa." *Nigerian Journal of International Affairs* 2:68–84.

Adeleye, R. A. 1971. "Hausaland and Bornu, 1600–1800." In Ajayi & Crowder, eds., 1971–73, vol. 1.

———. 1973. "The Sokoto Caliphate in the Nineteenth Century." In Ajayi & Crowder, eds., 1971–73, vol. 2.

Afigbo, A. E. 1971. "West African Chiefs during Colonial Rule and After." *Odu* n.s. 5:99–110.

———. 1973. "The Establishment of Colonial Rule, 1900–1918." In Ajayi & Crowder, eds., 1971–73, vol. 2.

Ahmad, Syed Salahuddin. 1980. "Niger-Nigeria Relations, 1960–1975: A Survey of the Dynamics of Bilateral Relations between Neighbouring Countries." *Kano Studies* n.s. 2.

———. 1984. "Political and Diplomatic Interactions between Nigeria and Niger." *Pakistan Horizon* 4:54–67.

343

Ajayi, J. F. A., and Michael Crowder, eds. 1971–73. *History of West Africa*. 2 vols. Vol. 1, London: Longman; vol. 2, New York: Columbia University Press.

Alabi, Mac, ed. 1983. *Elections 1983*. Apapa, Nigeria: Daily Times.

Alexandre, Pierre. 1970a. "Chiefs, Commandants, and Clerks: Their Relationship from Conquest to Decolonisation in French West Africa." In Crowder & Ikime, eds., 1970.

———. 1970b. "The Problems of Chieftaincies in French-Speaking Africa." In Crowder & Ikime, eds., 1970.

Almond, Gabriel. 1956. "Comparative Political Systems." *Journal of Politics* 18:391–409.

Aluko, Olajide. 1973. "Politics of Decolonization in British West Africa, 1945–1960." In Ajayi & Crowder, eds., 1971–73, vol. 2.

Amosu, Akwe. 1987. "Riots in Kaduna State." *West Africa*, 3628 (23 March): 550–51.

Amuwo, 'Kunle. 1986. "Military-Inspired Anti-bureaucratic Corruption Campaigns: An Appraisal of Niger's Experience." *Journal of Modern African Studies* 24:285–301.

Anene, J. C. 1970. *The International Boundaries of Nigeria, 1885–1960: The Framework of an Emergent African Nation*. New York: Humanities Press.

Apter, David. 1961. *The Political Kingdom in Uganda*. Princeton: Princeton University Press.

———. 1970. "The Role of Traditionalism in the Political Modernization of Ghana and Uganda." In Crowder & Ikime, eds., 1970.

———. 1972. *Ghana in Transition*. Princeton: Princeton University Press.

Asiwaju, A. I. 1970. "The Alaketu of Ketu and the Onimeko of Meko: The Changing Status of Two Yoruba Rulers under French and British Rule." In Crowder & Ikime, eds., 1970.

———. 1974. "New Trends in Colonial African Historiography: France and Britain in Africa." *Journal of the Historical Society of Nigeria* 7:563–69.

———. 1976a. "Migrations as Revolt: The Example of the Ivory Coast and the Upper Volta before 1945." *Journal of African History* 17:577–94.

———. 1976b. *Western Yorubaland under European Rule, 1889–1945*. Atlantic Highlands, N.J.: Humanities Press.

———. 1985a. "The Conceptual Framework." In Asiwaju, ed., 1985.

———. 1985b. "The Global Perspective and Border Management Policy." In Asiwaju, ed., 1985.

———. 1990. *Artificial Boundaries*. New York: Civiletis International.

———, ed. 1985. *Partitioned Africans: Ethnic Relations across Africa's International Boundaries, 1884–1984*. New York: St. Martin's Press.

———, ed. 1989. *Borderlands in Africa: A Multidisciplinary and Comparative Focus on Nigeria and West Africa*. Lagos: University of Lagos Press.

Baier, Stephen. 1980. *An Economic History of Central Niger*. Oxford: Clarendon.

Balandier, Georges. 1955. *The Sociology of Black Africa*. Trans. Douglas Garman. London: André Deutsch.

Barkindo, Bawuro M. 1985. "The Mandara Astride the Nigeria-Cameroon Boundary." In Asiwaju, ed., 1985.

Barkow, Jerome. 1972. "Hausa Women and Islam." *Canadian Journal of African Studies* 6:317–28.

——. 1973. "Operationalizing the Concept Ethos." In *Survey Research in Africa: Its Applications and Limits*, ed. William M. O'Barr, David H. Spain, and Mark A. Tessler. Evanston, Ill.: Northwestern University Press.

——. 1974. "Evaluation of Character and Social Control among the Hausa." *Ethos* 2:1–14.

——. 1975. "Strategies for Self-esteem and Prestige in Maradi, Niger Republic." In *Psychological Anthropology*, ed. Thomas R. Williams. The Hague: Mouton.

——. 1976. "The Generation of an Incipient Ethnic Split: A Hausa case (Nigeria)." *Anthropos* 71:857–67.

——. 1977. "Conformity to Ethos and Reproductive Success in Two Hausa Communities." *Ethos* 5:409–25.

Barth, Fredrik, ed. 1969. *Ethnic Groups and Boundaries*. Boston: Little, Brown.

Baum, Edward. 1972. "Recent Administrative Reform in Local Government in Northern Nigeria." *Journal of Developing Areas* 7:75–88.

Beckett, Paul A. 1987. "Elections and Democracy in Nigeria." In *Elections in Independent Africa*, ed. Fred Hayward. Boulder, Colo.: Westview.

Beik, Janet. 1984. "National Development as Theme in Current Hausa Drama in Niger." *Research in Africa Literatures* 15:1–24.

Benmessaoud Tredano, Abdelmoughit. 1989. *Intangibilité des frontières coloniales et espace étatique en Afrique*. Paris: Librairie Générale de Droit et de Jurisprudence.

Besmer, Fremont E. 1983. *Horses, Musicians, and Gods: The Hausa Cult of Possession-Trance*. Zaria: Ahmadu Bello University Press.

Betts, Raymond. 1961. *Assimilation and Association in French Colonial Theory, 1890–1914*. New York: Columbia University Press.

Biaghere, Sunny. 1984. "Buhari Woos the Obas and Emirs." *Africa Now*, March, 65–66.

Bienen, Henry S. 1983. "Religion and Economic Change in Nigeria." In *Global Economics and Religion*, ed. James Finn. New Brunswick, N.J.: Transaction.

——. 1986. "Religion, Legitimacy, and Conflict in Nigeria." *Annals of the American Academy of Political and Social Science* 483:50–60.

Boahen, A. Adu. 1987. *African Perspectives on Colonialism*. Baltimore: Johns Hopkins University Press.

——, ed. 1985. *General History of Africa*. Vol. 7, *Africa under Colonial Domination, 1880–1935*. Paris: UNESCO; London: Heinemann Educational Books.

Boyd, J. Barron, Jr. 1970. "African Boundary Conflict: An Empirical Study." *African Studies Review* 22:1–14.

Briggs, Charles L. 1986. *Learning How to Ask: A Sociolinguistic Appraisal of the Role of the Interview in Social Science Research*. Cambridge: Cambridge University Press.

Brown, Peter G., and Henry Shue, eds. 1981. *Boundaries: National Autonomy and Its Limits*. Totowa, N.J.: Rowman & Littlefield.

Brunschwig, Henri. 1949. *La Colonisation française du pacte coloniale à l'union française*. Paris: Calmann-Levy.

Callaway, Barbara. 1984. "Ambiguous Consequences of the Socialisation and Seclusion of Hausa Women." *Journal of Modern African Studies* 22:429–50.

——. 1987a. *Muslim Hausa Women in Nigeria.* Syracuse: Syracuse University Press.

——. 1987b. "Women and Political Participation in Kano City." *Comparative Politics* 19:379–93.

Camara, Camille. 1982. *Le Nigéria.* Paris: Presses Universitaires de France.

Césaire, Aimé. 1971. *Return to My Native Land.* Trans. Emilie Snyder. Paris: Présence Africaine.

Challenor, Herschelle Sullivan. 1979. "Strangers as Colonial Intermediaries: The Dahomeyans in Francophone Africa." In Shack & Skinner, eds., 1979.

Charlick, Robert. 1972. "Participatory Development and Rural Modernization in Hausa Niger." *African Review* 2:499–524.

——. 1985. "Small Farmer Production in Western Niger—Lessons and Opportunities of Crisis and 'Conjoncture.'" Paper presented to the African Studies Association, New Orleans.

——. 1991. *Niger: Personal Rule and Survival in the Sahel.* Boulder, Colo.: Westview.

Clarke, Peter. 1979. "The Religious Factor in the Developmental Process in Nigeria: A Socio-Historical Analysis." *Genève-Afrique* 17:46–63.

——. 1982. *West Africa and Islam: A Study of Religious Development from the 8th to the 20th Century.* London: Edward Arnold.

——. 1988. "Islamic Reform in Contemporary Nigeria: Methods and Aims." *Third World Quarterly* 10:519–38.

Clarke, Peter, and Ian Linden. 1983. *Islam in Modern Nigeria: A Study of a Muslim Community in a Post-independence State, 1960–1980.* Mainz: Gruenewald.

Clarke, Thurston. 1978. *The Last Caravan.* New York: Putnam.

Clough, Paul. 1981. "Farmers and Traders in Hausaland." *Development and Change* 12:273–92.

——. 1985. "The Social Relations of Grain Marketing in Northern Nigeria." *Review of African Political Economy* 34:16–34.

Cohen, Abner. 1969. *Custom and Politics in Urban Africa: A Study of Hausa Migrants in Yoruba Towns.* Berkeley: California University Press.

Coleman, James. 1958. *Nigeria: Background to Nationalism.* Berkeley: University of California Press.

Coles, Catherine. 1991. "Hausa Women's Work in a Declining Urban Economy: Kaduna, Nigeria, 1980–1985." In Coles & Mack, eds., 1991.

Coles, Catherine, and Beverly Mack. 1991. "Women in Twentieth-Century Hausa Society." In Coles & Mack, eds., 1991.

——, eds. 1991. *Hausa Women in the Twentieth Century.* Madison: University of Wisconsin Press.

Colley, Linda. 1992. *Britons: Forging the Nation, 1707–1837.* New Haven: Yale University Press.

Collins, John Davison. 1974. "Government and Groundnut Marketing in Rural Hausa Niger: The 1930's to 1970's in Magaria." Ph.D. dissertation, Johns Hopkins University.

——. 1976. "The Clandestine Movement of Groundnuts across the Niger-Nigeria Boundary." *Canadian Journal of African Studies* 10:259–78.

——. 1985. "Partitioned Culture Areas and Smuggling: The Hausa and Groundnut Trade across the Nigeria-Niger Boundary up to the 1970s." In Asiwaju, ed., 1985.

Constitution of the Federal Republic of Nigeria, with the Amendments. 1979. Apapa: Daily Times.

Cook, Andy, Mani Yahaya, and Seydou Harouna. 1988. "Niger's Livestock Export Policy." Unpublished report, Integrated Livestock Production Project, Government of Niger, Tufts University, USAID.

Coulon, Christian. 1983. "Le Réseau Islamique." *Politique Africaine* 9:68–83.

Crowder, Michael. 1962. *A Short History of Nigeria.* New York: Praeger.

——. 1964. "Indirect Rule—French and British Style." *Africa* 34:197–205.

——. 1968. *West Africa under Colonial Rule.* Evanston, Ill.: Northwestern University Press.

——. 1973a. "The 1914–1918 European War and West Africa." In Ajayi & Crowder, eds., 1971–73, vol. 2.

——. 1973b. "The 1939–45 War and West Africa." In Ajayi & Crowder, eds., 1971–73, vol. 2.

Crowder, Michael, and J. F. A. Ajayi. 1973. "West Africa, 1919–1939: The Colonial Situation." In Ajayi & Crowder, eds., 1971–73, vol. 2.

Crowder, Michael, and Obaro Ikime, eds. 1970. *West African Chiefs: Their Changing Status under Colonial Rule and Independence.* New York: Africana.

Crowder, Michael, and D. Cruise O'Brien. 1973. "French West Africa, 1945–1960." In Ajayi & Crowder, eds., 1971–73, vol. 2.

Cummings, John, Hossein Askari, and Ahmad Mustafa. 1980. "Islam and Modern Economic Change." In *Islam and Development: Religion and Sociopolitical Change,* ed. John L. Esposito. Syracuse: Syracuse University Press.

Dalby, David. 1964. "The Noun Garii in Hausa: A Semantic Study." *Journal of African Languages* 3:273–305.

Davidson, Basil 1989. *Modern Africa: A Social and Political History.* 2d ed. London and New York: Longman.

Davies, A. E. 1990. "The Fluctuating Fortunes of Traditional Rulers in Nigeria." *Plural Societies* 19:133–44.

Decalo, Samuel. 1979. *Historical Dictionary of Niger.* Metuchen, N.J.: Scarecrow Press.

Delavignette, Robert. 1950. *Freedom and Authority in French West Africa.* Trans. International African Institute. London: Oxford University Press.

Derrick, Jonathan. 1986. "Nigeria Marketing Boards: Decline and Fall." *West Africa,* May 12.

Deschamps, Hubert. 1953. *Méthodes et doctrine coloniales de la France (du XVI siècle à nos jours).* Paris: Armand Colin.

——. 1963. "Et maintenant, Lord Lugard?" *Africa* 4:293–306.

Devereux, George. 1975. "Ethnic Identity: Its Logical Foundations and Its Dysfunctions." In *Ethnic Identity: Cultural Continuities and Change,* ed. George De Vos and Lola Romanucci-Ross. Palo Alto: Mayfield.

Diamond, Larry. 1983a. "Class, Ethnicity, and the Democratic State: Nigeria, 1950–1966." *Comparative Studies in Society and History* 25:457–89.

——. 1983b. "A Tarnished Victory for the NPN?" *Africa Report* 28, 6:18–23.

——. 1984a. "The Coup and the Future." *Africa Report* 29, 2:9–15.

——. 1984b. "Nigeria in Search of Democracy." *Foreign Affairs* 62:905–27.

——. 1987a. "Issues in the Constitutional Design of a Third Nigerian Republic." *African Affairs* 86:209–26.

——. 1987b. "Nigeria between Dictatorship and Democracy." *Current History* 86:201–4, 222–24.

——. 1988. "Nigeria: Pluralism, Statism, and the Struggle for Democracy." In *Democracy in Developing Nations,* ed. Larry Diamond, Juan Linz, and Seymour Martin Lipset. Boulder, Colo.: Lynne Rienner.

Donaint, Pierre, and François Lancrenon. 1976. *Le Niger.* 2d ed. Paris: Presses Universitaires de France.

Donohue, John, and John Esposito, eds. 1982. *Islam in Transition: Muslim Perspectives.* New York: Oxford University Press.

Drake, St. Clair. 1965. "Traditional Authority and Social Action in Former British West Africa." In *Africa: Social Problems of Change and Conflict,* ed. Pierre L. van den Berghe. San Francisco: Chandler.

Duchacek, Ivo D. 1986. "International Competence of Subnational Governments: Borderlands and Beyond." In *Across Boundaries: Transborder Interaction in Comparative Perspective,* ed. Oscar J. Martinez. El Paso: Texas Western Press.

Dudley, B. J. 1968. *Parties and Politics in Northern Nigeria.* London: Cass.

Duffield, Mark. 1983. "Change among West African Settlers in Northern Sudan." *Review of African Political Economy* 26:45–59.

Dunbar, Roberta Ann. 1991. "Islamic Values, the State, and the 'Development of Women': The Case of Niger." In Coles & Mack, eds., 1991.

Eliade, Mircea. 1963. *Myth and Reality.* Trans. Willard R. Trask. New York: Harper & Row.

Ezenwe, Uka. 1983. *ECOWAS and the Economic Integration of West West Africa.* New York: St. Martin's Press.

Fahrmeier, Edward D. 1975. "The Effect of School Attendance on Intellectual Development in Northern Nigeria." *Child Development* 46:281–85.

Fallers, Lloyd. 1955. "The Predicament of the Modern African Chief: An Instance from Uganda." *American Anthropologist* 57:299–305.

Falola, Toyin, and Julius Ihonvbere. 1985. *The Rise and Fall of Nigeria's Second Republic: 1979–84.* London: Zed.

Fanon, Frantz. 1967. *Black Skin, White Masks.* Trans. Charles Lam Markmann. New York: Grove.

Fanso, Verkijida G. 1986. "Traditional and Colonial African Boundaries: Concepts and Functions in Inter-group Relations." *Présence Africaine* 137–38:58–75.

Faulkingham, Ralph. 1970. "Political Support in a Hausa Village." Ph.D. dissertation, Michigan State University.

Fieldhouse, David. 1966. *The Colonial Empire.* London: Weidenfeld & Nicholson.

——. 1988. "Arrested Development in Anglophone Black Africa?" In Gifford and Louis, eds., 1988.

Fisher, H. J. 1977. "The Eastern Maghrib and the Central Sudan." In *The Cambridge History of Africa,* ed. Roland Oliver, vol. 3. Cambridge: Cambridge University Press.

Flegel, E. R. 1985. *The Biography of Madugu Mohamman Mai Gaishin Baki.* Trans. M. B. Duffill. Berkeley: University of California Press.

Fletcher, Roland S. 1912. *Hausa Sayings and Folklore*. London: Oxford University Press.

Flint, J. E. 1973. "Economic Change in West Africa in the Nineteenth Century." In Ajayi & Crowder, eds., 1971–73, vol. 2.

Frélastre, Georges. 1983. "Le Séminaire de Zinder (novembre 1982) et la nouvelle stratégie du Niger." *Le Mois en Afrique* 211–12:69–80, 97–106.

Frishman, Alan. 1991. "Hausa Women in the Urban Economy of Kano." In Coles & Mack, eds., 1991.

Fuglestad, Finn. 1973. "Djibo Bakary, the French, and the Referendum of 1958 in Niger." *Journal of African History* 14:313–30.

——. 1978a. "Archival Research in Niger—Some Practical Hints." *African Research and Documentation* 16–17:26–27.

——. 1978b. "A Reconsideration of Hausa History before the Jihad." *Journal of African History* 19:319–39.

——. 1980. "A Propos de travaux récents sur la mission Voulet-Chanoine." *Revue Française d'Histoire d'Outre-mer* 246–47:73–86.

——. 1983. *A History of Niger, 1850–1960*. Cambridge: Cambridge University Press.

Furniss, Graham. 1986. "Social Problems in Kano in the 1970s: A Poet's Eye View." Paper presented at the African Studies Association conference, Madison, Wis.

——. 1991. "Hausa Poetry on the Nigerian Civil War." *African Languages and Cultures* 4:21–28.

Gambari, Ibrahim. 1992. "The Role of Religion in National Life: Reflections on Recent Experiences in Nigeria." In Hunwick, ed., 1992.

Gifford, Prosser, and William Roger Louis, eds. 1988. *Decolonization and African Independence: The Transfers of Power, 1960–1980*. New Haven: Yale University Press.

Gilliland, Dean S. 1986. *African Religion Meets Islam: Religious Change in Northern Nigeria*. Lanham, Md.: University Press of America.

Given, James B. 1990. *State and Society in Medieval Europe: Gwynedd and Languedoc under Outside Rule*. Ithaca: Cornell University Press.

Goddard, A. D. 1973. "Changing Family Structures among the Rural Hausa." *Africa* 43:207–18.

Goldman, Minton. 1974. "Nigeria: Political Change in a Multinational Setting." In *Dynamics of the Third World: Political and Social Change*, ed. David Schmitt. Cambridge, Mass.: Winthrop.

Graf, William. 1986. "Nigerian 'Grassroots' Politics: Local Government, Traditional Rule and Class Domination." *Journal of Commonwealth and Comparative Politics* 24:99–130.

Gramont, Sanche de. 1977. *The Strong Brown God: The Story of the Niger River*. Boston: Houghton Mifflin.

Guillemin, Jacques. 1982. "Note sur l'évolution de l'organisation administrative territoriale de la République du Niger." *Le Mois en Afrique* 201–2:97–103.

——. 1983. "Chefferie traditionnelle et administration publique au Niger." *Le Mois en Afrique* 213–14:115–24.

Hama, Boubou, and M. Guilhem. 1975. *Histoire du Niger. L'Afrique. Le Monde. Cours Moyens*. 2d ed. Ligel: Paris.

——. 1977. *Récits historiques*. Paris: Ligel.

Hargreaves, J. D. 1973. "The European Partition of West Africa." In Ajayi & Crowder, eds., 1971–73, vol. 2.

———. 1985a. "The Making of the Boundaries: Focus on West Africa." In Asiwaju, ed., 1985.

———. 1985b. *West Africa Partitioned. Vol. 2, The Elephants and the Grass.* Madison: University of Wisconsin Press.

Henige, David P. 1970. *Colonial Governors from the Fifteenth Century to the Present.* Madison: University of Wisconsin Press.

Hentgen, E. F. 1974. "L'Organisation régionale et locale de la République du Niger." Niamey: Ecole Nationale d'Administration.

Herbst, Jeffrey. 1989. "The Creation and Maintenance of National Boundaries in Africa." *International Organizations* 43:673–92.

Heussler, Robert. 1968a. *The British in Northern Nigeria.* London: Oxford University Press.

———. 1968b. "Indirect Rule in Northern Nigeria." *South Atlantic Quarterly* 67.

Higgott, Richard, and Finn Fuglestad. 1975. "The 1974 Coup d'Etat in Niger: Towards an Explanation." *Journal of Modern African Studies* 13:383–98.

Hill, Polly. 1968. "The Myth of the Amorphous Peasantry: A Northern Nigerian Case Study." *Nigerian Journal of Economic and Social Studies* 10:239–60.

———. 1969. "Hidden Trade in Hausaland." *Man* n.s. 4:392–409.

———. 1972. *Rural Hausa: A Village and a Setting.* Cambridge: Cambridge University Press.

———. 1975. "The Relationship between Cities and Countryside in Kano Emirate in 1900." *West African Journal of Sociology and Political Science* 1:3–19.

———. 1977. *Population, Prosperity, and Poverty: Rural Kano, 1900 and 1970.* Cambridge: Cambridge University Press.

———. 1982. *Dry Grain Farming Families: Hausaland (Nigeria) and Karnataka (India) Compared.* Cambridge: Cambridge University Press.

Hiskett, Mervyn. 1973. *The Sword of Truth: The Life and Times of the Shehu Usuman Dan Fodio.* Oxford: Oxford University Press.

———. 1976. "The Nineteenth-Century Jihads in West Africa." In *The Cambridge History of Africa,* ed. John E. Flint, vol. 5. Cambridge: Cambridge University Press.

———. 1984. *The Development of Islam in West Africa.* London and New York: Longman.

———. 1987. "The Maitatsine Riots in Kano, 1980: An Assessment." *Journal of Religion in Africa* 17:209–23.

Hodder-Williams, Richard 1984. *An Introduction to the Politics of Tropical Africa.* London: George Allen & Unwin.

Hogben, S. J., and A. H. M. Kirk-Greene. 1966. *The Emirates of Northern Nigeria: A Preliminary Survey of Their Historical Traditions.* London: Oxford University Press.

Hogendorn, Jan S. 1980. "Slave Acquisition and Delivery in Precolonial Hausaland." In *West African Culture Dynamics: Archaeological and Historical Perspectives,* ed. B. K. Swartz, Jr., and Raymond Dumett. The Hague: Mouton.

Horowitz, Michael M. 1972. "Ethnic Boundary Maintenance among Pastoralists and Farmers in the Western Sudan (Niger)." *Journal of Asian and African Studies* 7:105–14.

——. 1974. "Barbers and Bearers: Ecology and Ethnicity in an Islamic Society." *Africa* 44:371–82.

——. 1983. *Niger: A Social and Institutional Profile*. Binghamton, N.Y.: Institute for Development Anthropology.

Hudson, Michael. 1980. "Islam and Political Development." In *Islam and Development: Religion and Sociopolitical Change*, ed. John L. Esposito. Syracuse: Syracuse University Press.

Hunwick, John. 1992. "An African Case Study of Political Islam: Nigeria." *Annals of the American Academy of Political and Social Science* 524:143–55.

——, ed. 1992. *Religion and National Integration in Africa: Islam, Christianity, and Politics in the Sudan and Nigeria*. Evanston, Ill.: Northwestern University Press.

Ibrahim, Jibrin. 1991. "Religion and Political Turbulence in Nigeria." *Journal of Modern African Studies* 29:115–36.

Idrissa, Kimba. 1986. "Le Territoire du Niger et al question de la 'mise en valeur': A propos des investissements de 1900 à 1940." Paper presented to Walter Rodney African Studies Center, Boston University.

Ikime, Obaro. 1968. "Reconsidering Indirect Rule: The Nigerian Example." *Journal of the Historical Society of Nigeria* 4:421–38.

Inkeles, Alex, and Daniel Levinson. 1954. "National Character: The Study of Modal Personality and Sociocultural Systems." In *Handbook of Social Psychology*, ed. Gardner Lindzey, vol. 4. Reading, Mass.: Addison-Wesley.

Isaacs, Harold. 1974. "Basic Group Identity." *Ethnicity* 1:15–42.

Johnson, G. Wesley. 1973. "African Political Activity in French West Africa, 1900–1940." In Ajayi & Crowder, eds., 1971–73, vol. 2.

Jones, G. I. 1974. "Social Anthropology in Nigeria during the Colonial Period." *Africa* 44:280–89.

Joseph, Richard. 1981. "The Ethnic Trap: Notes on the Nigerian Campaign and Elections, 1978–79." In Whitaker, ed., 1981.

——. 1983. "Class, State, and Prebendal Politics in Nigeria." *Journal of Commonwealth and Comparative Politics* 3:21–38.

——. 1984. "The Overthrow of Nigeria's Second Republic." *Current History* 83:122–24, 138.

Kaduna State Ministry of Economic Planning, Statistics Division. 1983. *Kaduna State Statistical Year Book, 1983*.

Kavanagh, Dennis. 1983. *Political Science and Political Behaviour*. London: George Allen & Unwin.

Khan, Z. M. 1982. "Islam in Subsaharan Africa." *Africa Quarterly* 21:62–68.

Kirk-Greene, A. H. M. 1963. "Neologisms in Hausa: A Sociological Approach." *Africa* 33:25–44.

——. 1965. "Bureaucratic Cadres in a Traditional Milieu." In *Education and Political Development*, ed. James Coleman. Princeton: Princeton University Press.

——. 1968. "The Merit Principle in an African Bureaucracy: Northern Nigeria." In *Nations by Design*, ed. Arnold Rivkin. Garden City, N.Y.: Anchor.

——. 1971. "Emiratism in Northern Nigeria." *Journal of African History* 12:663–65.

——. 1974. *Mutumin Kirkii: The Concept of the Good Man in Hausa.* Third Annual Hans Wolff Memorial Lecture. Bloomington: Indiana University Press.

——. 1976. "Zamanin Siyasa: Political Culture and Personalities in Modern Hausaland." *African Affairs* 75:532–35.

——. 1977. "The Other Hausas." *West Africa* 3130:1348–49.

——. 1980. "'Damnosa Hereditas': Ethnic Ranking and the Martial Races Imperative in Africa." *Ethnic and Racial Studies* 3:397–411.

——. 1986. "Colonial Administration and Race Relations: Some Research Reflections and Directions." *Ethnic and Racial Studies* 9:275–87.

——. 1988. "'A Sense of Belonging': The Nigerian Constitution of 1979 and the Promotion of National Loyalty." *Journal of Commonwealth and Comparative Politics* 26:158–72.

——. 1992. "A Hausa Half-Dozen" (review article). *West Africa* 3896 (18–24 May): 859–60.

——, ed. 1965. *The Principles of Native Administration in Nigeria: Selected Documents, 1900–1947.* London: Oxford University Press.

——, trans. 1966. *Hausa Ba Dabo Ba Ne: A Collection of 500 Proverbs.* Ibadan: Oxford University Press.

Kiwanuka, M. Semakula. 1970. "Colonial Policies and Administrations in Africa: The Myths of the Contrasts." *African Historical Studies* 3:295–313.

Kleis, Gerald W., and Salisu A. Abdullahi. 1983. "Masculine Power and Gender Ambiguity in Urban Hausa Society." *African Urban Studies* 16:39–53.

Kratochwil, Friedrich. 1986. "Of Systems, Boundaries, and Territoriality: An Inquiry into the Formation of the State System." *World Politics* 39:27–52.

Kraus, Jon. 1978. "Islamic Affinities and International Politics in Sub-Saharan Africa." *Current History* 456:154–58, 182–85.

Laitin, David. 1977. *Politics, Language, and Thought: The Somali Experience.* Chicago: University of Chicago Press.

——. 1982. "The Sharia Debate and the Origins of Nigeria's Second Republic." *Journal of Modern African Studies* 20:411–30.

——. 1991. "The National Uprisings in the Soviet Union." *World Politics* 44:139–77.

Lancaster, Thomas. 1987. "Comparative Nationalism: The Basques in Spain and France." *European Journal of Political Research* 15:561–90.

Lanne, Bernard. 1983. "Régime militaire et société de développement au Niger (1974–1983)." *Afrique Contemporaine* 125:38–44.

Larrat, R. 1955. *Problèmes de la Viande en A.O.F.: Zones de Production II, Niger.* Paris: Editions de l'Outre-mer.

Last, Murray. 1970. "Aspects of Administration and Dissent in Hausaland." *Africa* 40:345–57.

——. 1973. "Reform in West Africa: The Jihad Movements of the Nineteenth Century." In Ajayi & Crowder, eds., 1971–73, vol. 2.

Last, Murray, and M. A. Al-Hajj. 1965. "Attempts at Defining a Muslim in Nineteenth Century Hausaland and Bornu." *Journal of the Historical Society of Nigeria* 3:231–40.

Lebovics, Herman. 1992. *True France: The Wars over Cultural Identity, 1900–1945*. Ithaca: Cornell University Press.

Levine, Robert A. 1966. *Dreams and Deeds: Achievement Motivation in Nigeria*. Chicago: University of Chicago Press.

Levine, Robert A., and Douglass R. Price-Williams. 1974. "Children's Kinship Concepts: Cognitive Development and Early Experience among the Hausa." *Ethnology* 13:25–43.

Levtzion, Nehemiah. 1968. *Muslims and Chiefs in West Africa: A Study of Islam in the Middle Volta Basin in the Pre-Colonial Period*. Oxford: Clarendon.

——. 1979a. *International Islamic Solidarity and Its Limitations*. Jerusalem: Magnes.

——. 1979b. "Islam in West African Politics: Accommodation and Tension between the 'Ulama and the Political Authorities." *Cahiers d'Etudes Africaines* 18:337–45.

——. 1986. "Rural and Urban Islam in West Africa: An Introductory Essay." *Asian and African Studies* 20:7–26.

Lewis, I. M. 1980. *Islam in Tropical Africa*. 2d ed. Bloomington, Ind., and London: International African Institute.

Lewis, Martin Dening. 1962. "One Hundred Million Frenchmen: The 'Assimilation' Theory in French Colonial Policy." *Comparative Studies in Society and History* 4:129–53.

Longhurst, Richard. 1982. "Resource Allocation and the Sexual Division of Labor: A Case Study of a Moslem Hausa Village in Northern Nigeria." In *Women and Development: The Sexual Division of Labor in Rural Societies*, ed. Lourdes Beneria. New York: Praeger.

Low, Anthony. 1988. "The End of the British Empire in Africa." In Gifford & Louis, 1988.

Lubeck, Paul. 1979. "Islam and Resistance in Northern Nigeria." In *The World System of Capitalism*, ed. Walter Goldfrank. Beverly Hills, Calif.: Sage.

——. 1981. "Islamic Networks and Urban Capitalism: An Instance of Articulation from Northern Nigeria." *Cahiers d'Etudes Africaines* 21:67–78.

——. 1985. "Islamic Protest under Semi-industrial Capitalism: 'Yan Tatsine Explained." *Africa* 55:369–87.

Lugard, Frederick. 1906/1970. *Political Memoranda*. London: Frank Cass.

McIntyre, J. A. "The Language of Hausa Greetings: The Social Construction of Hierarchy." *Afrika und Ubersee* 63:39–67.

Mackintosh, John P. 1966. *Nigerian Government and Politics*. London: George Allen & Unwin.

Magari, Chamsou. 1989. "Clôture samedi à Bagaouda (Nigéria) des travaux du séminaire-atelier sur la coopération transfrontalière." *Sahel* (Niamey) 10:vii.

Mair, Lucy. 1958. "African Chiefs Today." *Africa* 28:195–206.

Mannoni, Dominique O. 1964. *Prospero and Caliban: The Psychology of Colonization*. Trans. Pamela Powesland. New York: Praeger.

Maqsud, Muhammad. 1980. "Relationships between Personal Control, Moral Reasoning, and Socioeconomic Status of Nigerian Hausa Adolescents." *Journal of Youth and Adolescence* 9:281–88.

Martin, Michael. 1974. "Understanding and Participant Observation in Cultural and Social Anthropology." In *Verstehen: Subjective Understanding in the Social Sciences,* ed. Marcello Truzzi. Reading, Mass.: Addison-Wesley.

Mazrui, Ali A. 1983. "Francophone Nations and English-Speaking States: Imperial Ethnicity and African Political Formations." In *State versus Ethnic Claims: African Policy Dilemmas,* ed. Donald Rothchild and Victor A. Olorunsola. Boulder, Colo.: Westview.

———. 1988. "African Islam and Competitive Religion: Between Revivalism and Expansion." *Third World Quarterly* 10:499–518. (Contains special reference to Nigeria).

———, ed. 1977. "The Warrior Tradition in Modern Africa." *Journal of Asian and African Studies* 12 (special issue).

Merrick, Captain G. 1905. *Hausa Proverbs.* London: Kegan Paul, Trench, Trubner.

Miles, William F. S. 1986a. *Elections and Ethnicity in French Martinique: A Paradox in Paradise.* New York: Praeger.

———. 1986b. "Islam and Development in the Western Sahel: Engine or Brake?" *Journal of the Institute of Muslim Minority Affairs* 7:439–63.

———. 1986c. "Self-identity, Ethnic Affinity, and National Consciousness: An Example from Rural Hausaland." *Ethnic and Racial Studies* 9:427–44.

———. 1987. "Partitioned Royalty: The Evolution of Hausa Chiefs in Niger and Nigeria." *Journal of Modern African Studies* 25:233–58.

———. 1988. *Elections in Nigeria: A Grassroots Perspective.* Boulder, Colo.: Lynne Rienner.

———. 1989a. "Motives, Morality, and Methodology in Third World Research." *PS: Political Science and Politics* 22:852–55.

———. 1989b. "The Rally as Ritual: Dramaturgical Politics in Nigerian Hausaland." *Comparative Politics* 21:323–38.

———. 1990. "Islam and Development in West Africa." In *West African Regional Cooperation and Development,* ed. Julius Emeka Okolo and Stephen Wright. Boulder, Colo.: Westview.

———. 1993. "Colonial Hausa Idioms: Towards a West African Ethno-Ethnohistory." *African Studies Review* 36.

Miles, William F. S., and David A. Rochefort. 1991. "Nationalism versus Ethnic Identity in Sub-Saharan Africa." *American Political Science Review* 85:393–403.

Miller, Norman. 1968. "The Political Survival of Traditional Leadership." *Journal of Modern African Studies* 6:183–201.

Miner, Horace. 1960. "Culture Change under Pressure: A Hausa Case." *Human Organization* 19:164–67.

———. 1965. "Urban Influences on the Rural Hausa." In *Urbanization and Migration in West Africa,* ed. Hilda Kuper. Berkeley: University of California Press.

Morton, R. F. 1985. "Chiefs and Ethnic Unity in Two Colonial Worlds: The Bakgatla baga Kgafela of the Bechuanaland Protectorate and the Transvaal, 1872–1966." In Asiwaju, ed., 1985.

Muffet, D. J. M. 1964. *Concerning Brave Captains: Being a History of the British Occupation of Kano and Sokoto and of the Last Stand of the Fulani Forces.* London: André Deutsch.

——. 1971. "Nigeria-Sokoto Caliphate." In *West African Resistance: The Military Response to Colonial Occupation,* ed. Michael Crowder. New York: Africana.

——. 1975. "Legitimacy and Deference in a Tradition Oriented Society: Observations Arising from an Examination of Some Aspects of a Case Study Associated with the Abdiction of the Emir of Kano in 1963." *African Studies Review* 18:101–15.

Muhammad, Akbar. 1980. "Islam and National Integration through Education in Nigeria." In *Islam and Development: Religion and Sociopolitical Change,* ed. John L. Esposito. Syracuse: Syracuse University Press.

Murch, Arvin. 1971. *Black Frenchmen: The Political Integration of the French Antilles.* Cambridge, Mass.: Schenkman.

Nandy, Ashis. 1983. *The Intimate Enemy: Loss and Recovery of Self under Colonialism.* Delhi: Oxford University Press.

Neuberger, Benyamin. 1991. "Irredentism and Politics in Africa." In *Irredentism and International Politics,* ed. Naomi Chazan. Boulder, Colo.: Lynne Rienner.

Newman, Roxana Ma. 1990. *An English-Hausa Dictionary.* New Haven: Yale University Press.

Nicolas, Guy. 1960. "Un Village haoussa de la République du Niger: Tassao haoussa." *Cahiers d'Outre-mer* 52:421–50.

——. 1975. "Les Catégories d'ethnie et de fraction ethnique au sein du système social hausa." *Cahiers d'Etudes Africaines* 15:399–441.

——. 1984. "Métamorphose de l'Islam nigérian." *Le Mois en Afrique* 223–24:118–44; 225–26:132–43.

Nwankwo, Onyekwere G. 1984. "Management Problems of the Proliferation of Local Government in Nigeria." *Public Administration and Development* 4:63–76.

Nwosu, H. N. 1986. "The Responsibility of Traditional Rulers in Local Administration: A Process for National Development." In Aborisade, ed., 1986.

Nyang, Sulayman S. 1988. "West Africa." In *The Politics of Islamic Revivalism: Diversity and Unity,* ed. Shireen Hunter. Bloomington: Indiana University Press. (Contains specific references to Niger and Nigeria.)

O'Brien, D. C. 1967. "Towards an 'Islamic Policy' in French West Africa, 1854–1914." *Journal of African History* 8:303–16.

——. 1981. "La Filière musulmane: Confréries soufies et politique en Afrique noire." *Politique Africaine* 1:7–30.

Ogionwo, W. 1980. "'We' and 'They': A Study of Ethnic Stereotypes in Nigeria." *Sociologus* 30:97–123.

Ohadike, Don. 1992. "Muslim-Christian Conflict and Political Instability in Nigeria." In Hunwick, ed., 1992.

Ojiako, James. 1981. *Nigeria: Yesterday, Today, And . . . ?* Onitsha: Africana Educational Publishers.

Ojigbo, Okion. 1980. *Nigeria Returns to Civilian Rule.* Lagos: Tokion.

Okoli, Enukora. 1982. "Revolution or Tradition in Kano?" *West Africa* 3361 (4 January): 5–7.

Ola, R. O. F., and C. A. Olowu. 1977. "Recent Administrative Developments in Nigeria, January 1975–April 1977." *Quarterly Journal of Administration* 11:299–307.

Olofson, Harold. 1975. "Cultural Values, Communication, and Urban Image in Hausaland." *Urban Anthropology* 4:145–60.

——. 1976. "Yawon Dandi: A Hausa Category of Migration." *Africa* 46:66–79.

——. 1980. "Children of the Bowed Lute: Social Organization and Expressive Culture of Hausa Urban Itinerant Entertainers." *Anthropos* 75:920–29.

——. 1981. "Hausa Kinship and Diaspora." *Ethnos* 1–2:80–91.

Oloruntimehin, B. Olatunji. 1973. "The Western Sudan and the Coming of the French, 1800–1893." In Ajayi & Crowder, eds., 1971–73, vol. 2.

Olusanya, G. O. 1967. "Political Awakening in the North: A Re-interpretation." *Journal of the Historical Society of Nigeria* 4:125–34.

Onibonoje, 'Biodun. 1977. *Living in Our State: Kaduna State.* Primary Social Studies, bk. 4. Ibadan: Onibonoje Press.

Orewa, G. O. 1978. "The Role of Traditional Rulers in Administration." *Quarterly Journal of Administration* 12:151–65.

Ortiz, Sutti. 1974. "Obstacle to Agricultural Growth in Hausaland Viewed through a Village Study." *Economic Development and Cultural Change* 23:163–68.

Osaji, Debe. 1977. "Language Imposition: Sociolinguistic Case Study of the Hausa Language in Nigeria." *African Languages* 3:117–29.

Osuntokun, Jide. 1975. "Nigeria's Colonial Government and the Islamic Insurgency in French West Africa, 1914–1918." *Cahiers d'Etudes Africaines* 15:85–93.

Owolabi, A. Olayiwola. 1990. "Nigeria's Boundaries: The Issue of Border Security." *Plural Societies* 20:69–79.

Oyediran, Oyeleye, ed. 1981. *The Nigerian 1979 Elections.* London: Macmillan.

Paden, John. 1967. "Situational Ethnicity in Urban Africa with Special Reference to the Hausa." Paper presented to the African Studies Association, New York.

——. 1970a. "Aspects of Emirship in Kano." In Crowder & Ikime, eds., 1970.

——. 1970b. "Urban Pluralism, Integration, and Adapatation of Communal Identity in Kano, Nigeria." In *From Tribe to Nation in Africa: Studies in Incorporation Processes,* ed. Ronald Cohen and John Middleton. Scranton: Chandler.

——. 1973. *Religion and Political Culture in Kano.* Berkeley: University of California Press.

——. 1981. "Islamic Political Culture and Constitutional Change in Nigeria." In Whitaker, ed., 1981.

——. 1986. *Ahmadu Bello: Sardauna of Sokoto.* Zaria: Hudahuda.

——. 1992. "Religious Identity and Political Values in Nigeria: The Transformation of the Muslim Community." Paper presented to the African Seminar series, Center for International Affairs, Harvard University.

Panter-Brick, Keith. 1988. "Independence, French Style." In Gifford & Louis, eds. 1988.

Peil, Margaret. 1975. "Interethnic Contacts in Nigerian Cities." *Africa* 45:107–21.

——. 1976. *Nigerian Politics: The People's View.* London: Cassell.

Pellow, Deborah. 1991a. "From Accra to Kano: One Woman's Experience." In Coles & Mack, eds., 1991.

——. 1991b. "The Power of Space in the Evolution of an Accra *Zongo.*" *Ethnohistory* 38:414–50.

Phiri, S. H. 1985. "National Integration, Rural Development, and Frontier Communities: The Case of the Chewa and the Ngoni Astride Zambian Boundaries with Malawi and Mozambique." In Asiwaju, ed., 1985.

Pitten, Renée. 1983. "Houses of Women: A Focus on Alternative Life-Styles in Katsina City." In *Female and Male in West Africa*, ed. Christine Oppong. London: George Allen & Unwin.

———. 1984. "Migration of Women in Nigeria: The Hausa Case." *International Migration Review* 18:1293–313.

Poitou, Danièle. 1981. "Délinquance juvénile et urbanisation au Niger et au Nigeria." *Cahiers d'Etudes Africaines* 21:111–27.

Post, Kenneth. 1963. *The Nigerian Federal Election of 1959: Politics and Administration in a Developing Political System*. London: Oxford University Press.

Post, Kenneth, and Michael Vickers. 1973. *Structure and Conflict in Nigeria, 1960–1966*. Madison: University of Wisconsin Press.

Potter, David C. 1986. *India's Political Administrators, 1919–1983*. Oxford: Oxford University Press.

Prescott, J. R. V. 1958. "The Evolution of Nigeria's Boundaries." *Nigerian Geographical Journal* 2:80–103.

———. 1971. *The Evolution of Nigeria's International and Regional Boundaries: 1861–1971*. Vancouver: Tantalus Research.

———. 1987. *Political Frontiers and Boundaries*. London: George Allen & Unwin.

Pye, Lucian. 1965. "Introduction: Political Culture and Political Development." In *Political Culture and Political Development*, ed. Lucian Pye and Sidney Verba. Princeton: Princeton University Press.

———. 1968. "Political Culture." In *International Encyclopedia of the Social Sciences*, vol. 12. New York: Free Press.

———. 1971. "Political Culture and National Character." In *Social Psychology and Political Behavior: Problems and Prospects*, ed. Gilbert Abcarian and John Soule. Columbus, Ohio: Merrill.

Ragab, Ibrahim A. 1980. "Islam and Development." *World Development* 8:513–21.

Raynal, Jean-Jacques. 1990. "De la démocratisation à la démocratie? La Constitution nigérienne du 24 septembre 1989." *Afrique Contemporaine* 155:68–79.

Raynaut, Claude. 1977. "Circulation monétaire et évolution des structures socio-économiques chez les haoussas du Niger." *Africa* 47:160–70.

Reed, Cyrus. 1982. "The Role of Traditional Rulers in Elective Politics in Nigeria." Fifth Annual Graduate Student Paper Competition, Indiana University.

Renner, F. A. 1985. "Ethnic Affinity: Partition and Political Integration in Senegambia." In Asiwaju, ed., 1985.

Republic of Niger, Ministry of Plan, and USAID, Evaluation Bureau. 1983. "Joint Program Assessment of Grain Marketing in Niger." Vol. 1. Niamey.

Rivières, Edmond Séré. 1952. *Le Niger*. Paris: Société d'Editions Géographiques Maritimes et Coloniales.

Roberts, T. W. 1972. "Railway Imperialism and French Advances toward Lake Chad, 1890–1900." Ph.D. dissertation, Cambridge University.

Robinson, Charles Henry. 1900/1967. *Nigeria, Our Latest Protectorate*. New York: Negro Universities Press.

Robinson, Pearl 1975. "African Traditional Rulers and the Modern State: The Linkage Role of Chiefs in the Republic of Niger." Ph.D. dissertation, Columbia University.

——. 1983. "Traditional Clientage and Political Change in a Hausa Community." In *Transformation and Resiliency in Africa as Seen by Afro-American Scholars*, ed. Pearl Robinson and Elliott P. Skinner. Washington, D.C.: Howard University Press.

——. 1991. "Niger: Anatomy of a Neotraditional Corporatist State." *Comparative Politics* 23:1–20.

——. 1991–92. "The National Conference Phenomenon in Francophone Africa." *Précis* 3 (Center for International Studies, MIT).

Rose, Dan. 1990. *Living the Ethnographic Life*. Newbury Park, Calif.: Sage.

Sahlins, Peter. 1989. *Boundaries: The Making of France and Spain in the Pyrenees*. Berkeley: University of California Press.

Salamone, Frank. 1969. "Further Notes on Hausa Culture and Personality." *International Journal of Social Psychiatry* 16:39–44.

——. 1971. "Some Aspects of Social Stratification among the Hausa." *International Journal of Group Tensions* 1:335–49.

——. 1973. "The Drug Problem in a Small Emirate in Northern Nigeria." *Human Organization* 32:322–25.

——. 1975. "Becoming Hausa: Ethnic Identity Change and Its Implications for the Study of Ethnic Pluralism and Stratification." *Africa* 45:410–23.

——. 1985a. "Colonialism and the Emergence of Fulani Identity." *Journal of Asian and African Studies* 20:194–201.

——. 1985b. "The Social Construction of Reality: Yauri Emirate." *Cahiers d'Etudes Africaines* 25:139–59.

——. 1987. "The Social Construction of Colonial Reality: Yauri Emirate." *Journal of Legal Pluralism and Unofficial Law* 25/26:47–70.

——. 1992. "Playing at Nationalism: Nigeria, a Nation of 'Ringers.'" *Genève-Afrique* 30:55–75.

Salamone, Virginia A. 1991. "*Kirki:* A Developmental Perspective on Hausa Ethos." *Third World Studies* 46:115–24.

Samatar, Said S. 1985. "The Somali Dilemma: Nation in Search of a State." In Asiwaju, ed., 1985.

Sani, Habibu A. 1977. "Traditional Rulers and Local Government." In *Issues in the Nigerian Draft Constitution*, ed. Suleimanu Kumo and Abubakar Aliyu. Zaria: Baraka Press.

——. 1980. "State-Local Relations: A Challenge for the Nigerian Presidential System." *Quarterly Journal of Administration* 14:231–41.

Sardar, Ziauddin. 1977. *Science, Technology, and Development in the Muslim World*. Atlantic Highlands, N.J.: Humanities Press.

Sardar, Ziauddin, and M. A. Zaki Badawi, eds. N.d. *Hajj Studies*. vol. 1. London: Croom Helm.

Schildkrout, Enid. 1983. "Dependence and Autonomy: The Economic Activities of Secluded Hausa Women in Kano." In *Female and Male in West Africa,* ed. Christine Oppong. London: George Allen & Unwin.

Scott, Earl P. 1978. "Subsistence, Markets, and Rural Development in Hausaland." *Journal of Developing Areas* 12:449–69.

Seibel, Dieter H. 1967. "Some Aspects of Inter-ethnic Relations in Nigeria." *Nigerian Journal of Economic and Social Studies* 9:217–28.

Shack, William A. 1979. "Open Systems and Closed Boundaries: The Ritual Process of Stranger Relations in New African States." In Shack & Skinner, eds., 1979.

Shack, William A., and Elliott P. Skinner, eds. 1979. *Strangers in African Societies.* Berkeley: University of California Press.

Shelley, Toby. 1989. "Towards a New Era." *West Africa* 3746 (5–11 June): 920–1. (Describes plan for Niger's Development Society.)

Shenton, R. W., and Louise Lennihan. 1981. "Capital and Class: Peasant Differentiation in Northern Nigeria." *Journal of Peasant Studies* 9:47–70.

Shweder, Robert, and Robert Levine. 1975. "Dream Concepts of Hausa Children: A Critique of the 'Doctrine of Invariant Sequence' in Cognitive Development." *Ethos* 3:209–30.

Skinner, Elliott P. 1963. "Strangers in West African Societies." *Africa* 33:307–20.

Skinner, Neil, ed. 1977. *Alhaji Mahmudu Koki, Kano Malam.* Zaria: Ahmadu Bello University Press.

Smith, Abdullahi. 1970. "Some Considerations Relating to the Formation of States in Hausaland." *Journal of the Historical Society of Nigeria* 5:329–46.

Smith, Brian. 1967. "The Evolution of Local Government in Nigeria." *Journal of Administration Overseas* 6:28–42.

Smith, Brian, and G. S. Owojaiye. 1981. "Constitutional, Legal, and Political Problems of Local Government in Nigeria." *Public Administration and Development* 1:211–24.

Smith, H. F. C. 1961. "A Neglected Theme of West African History: The Islamic Revolution of the 19th Century." *Journal of the Historical Society of Nigeria* 2:169–85.

Smith, John. 1968. *Colonial Cadet in Nigeria.* Durham, N.C.: Duke University Press.

——. 1970. "The Relationship of the British Political Officer to His Chief in Northern Nigeria." In Crowder & Ikime, eds., 1970.

Smith, M. G. 1957. "The Social Functions and Meaning of Hausa Praise-Singing." *Africa* 27:26–43.

——. 1959. "The Hausa System of Social Status." *Africa* 19:239–51.

——. 1960. *Government in Zazzau: 1800–1950.* New York: Oxford University Press.

——. 1961. "Kebbi and Hausa Stratification." *British Journal of Sociology* 12:52–64.

——. 1964. "Historical and Cultural Conditions of Political Corruption among the Hausa." *Comparative Studies in Society and History* 6:164–94.

——. 1965a. "The Hausa of Northern Nigeria." In *Peoples of Africa,* ed. James Gibbs. New York: Holt, Rinehart & Winston.

——. 1965b. "Slavery and Emancipation in Two Societies." In Smith, *The Plural Society in the British West Indies.* Berkeley: University of California Press.

——. 1978. *The Affairs of Daura: History and Change in a Hausa State, 1800–1958.* Berkeley: University of California Press.

Smith, Mary. 1954/1981. *Baba of Karo: A Woman of the Muslim Hausa.* New Haven: Yale University Press.

Smith, Tony. 1978. "A Comparative Study of French and British Decolonization." *Comparative Studies in Society and History* 20:70–102.

Smythe, Hugh, and Mabel Smythe. 1960. *The New Nigerian Elite.* Stanford: Stanford University Press.

Southall, Aidan. 1985. "Partitioned Alur." In Asiwaju, ed., 1985.

Stoller, Paul. 1984. "Horrific Comedy: Cultural Resistance and the *Hauka* Movement in Niger." *Ethos* 12:165–88.

Suret-Canale, Jean. 1958. *Afrique noire: Occidentale et centrale.* Paris: Editions Sociales.

——. 1964. *Afrique noire: L'Ere coloniale (1900–1945).* Paris: Editions Sociales.

Sutcliffe, Claud. 1975. "Is Islam an Obstacle to Development? Ideal Patterns of Belief versus Actual Patterns of Behavior." *Journal of Developing Areas* 10:77–82.

Sutton, J. E. G. 1979. "Towards a Less Orthodox History of Hausaland." *Journal of African History* 20:179–201.

Tangban, O. E. 1991. "The Hajj and the Nigerian Economy." *Journal of Religion in Africa* 23:241–55.

Temple, C. L. 1918. *Native Races and Their Rulers.* Cape Town.

Thom, Derrick J. 1970. "The Niger-Nigeria Borderlands: A Politico-Geographic Analysis of Boundary Influence upon the Hausa." Ph.D. dissertation, Michigan State University.

——. 1975. *The Niger-Nigeria Boundary, 1890–1906: A Study of Ethnic Frontiers and a Colonial Boundary.* Papers in International Studies, Africa Series no. 23. Athens: Ohio University Center for International Studies, Africa Program.

Tibenderana, Peter. 1988. "The Irony of Indirect Rule in Sokoto Emirate, Nigeria, 1903–1944." *African Studies Review* 31:67–92.

——. 1989. "British Administration and the Decline of the Patronage-Clientage System in Northwestern Nigeria, 1900–1934." *African Studies Review* 32:71–95.

Tilly, Charles. 1984. *Big Structures, Large Processes, Huge Comparisons.* New York: Russell Sage Foundation.

Touval, Saadia. 1969. "The Sources of Status Quo and Irredentist Policies." In *African Boundary Problems,* ed. Carl Gosta Widstrand. Uppsala: Scandinavian Institute of African Studies.

——. 1985. "Partitioned Groups and Inter-state Relations." In Asiwaju, ed., 1985.

Triaud, Jean-Louis. 1981–1982. "L'Islam et l'état en République du Niger." *Le Mois en Afrique* 192–93:9–26; 194–95:35–48.

Trimingham, J. Spencer. 1980. *The Influence of Islam upon Africa.* 2d ed. London and New York: Longman.

Uphoff, Norman. 1986. *Local Institutional Development: An Analytic Sourcebook with Cases.* West Hartford, Conn.: Kumarian Press.

Urvoy, Yves. 1934/1977. "L'Autorité du chef de famille, du chef de village et du prince chez les Hausa du nord-ouest." *Bulletin de l'I.F.A.N.,* ser. B, 39:202–21.

U.S. Agency for International Development/Niger. 1979. "Country Development Strategy Statement." Niamey.

Van Klaveren, J. J. 1964. "Comment" (on M. G. Smith 1964). *Comparative Studies in Society and History* 6:195–98.

Van Maanen, John. 1988. *Tales of the Field: On Writing Ethnography.* Chicago: University of Chicago Press.

Vansina, Jan. 1961. *Oral Tradition: A Study in Historical Methodology.* Chicago: Aldine.

Vaughn, Olufemi. 1989. "Les Chefs traditionnels face au pouvoir politique." *Politique Africaine* 32:44–56.

Vengroff, Richard. 1975. "Traditional Political Structures in the Contemporary Context: The Chieftaincy in Kwenema." *African Studies* 34:39–56.

Verba, Sidney. 1965. "Comparative Political Culture." In *Political Culture and Political Development,* ed. Lucian Pye and Sidney Verba. Princeton: Princeton University Press.

Voll, John O. 1992. "Religion and Politics in Islamic Africa." In *The Religious Challenge to the State,* ed. Matthew Moen and Lowell Gustafson. Philadelphia: Temple University Press. (Contains special reference to Nigeria.)

Watts, Michael John. 1983a. "The Political Economy of Climatic Hazards: A Village Perspective on Drought and Peasant Economy in a Semi-arid Region of West Africa." *Cahiers d'Etudes Africaines* 23:37–72.

———. 1983b. *Silent Violence: Food, Famine, and Peasantry in Northern Nigeria.* Berkeley: University of California Press.

Weber, Eugen. 1976. *Peasants into Frenchmen: The Modernization of Rural France, 1870–1914.* Stanford: Stanford University Press.

Webster, J. B. 1973. "Political Activity in British West Africa, 1900–1940." In Ajayi & Crowder, eds., 1971–73, vol. 2.

Weekes, Richard, ed. 1978. *Muslim Peoples: A World Ethnographic Survey.* Westport, Conn.: Greenwood.

Welch, Claude E. 1966. *Dream of Unity: Pan-Africanism and Political Unification in West Africa.* Ithaca: Cornell University Press.

West Africa. 1986. "Emirs Look to the Future." November 3–10, 2312–14.

———. 1989. "Big Chiefs and Rulers." March 20–26, 431–32.

Whitaker, C. S., Jr. 1965. "Three Perspectives on Hierarchy: Political Thought and Leadership in Northern Nigeria." *Journal of Commonwealth Political Studies* 3:1–19.

———. 1967. "A Dysrhythmic Process of Political Change." *World Politics* 19:190–217.

———. 1970. *The Politics of Tradition: Continuity and Change in Northern Nigeria, 1946–1966.* Princeton: Princeton University Press.

———. 1981. "Second Beginnings: The New Political Framework." In Whitaker, ed., 1981.

———, ed. 1981. *Perspectives on the Second Republic of Nigeria.* Waltham, Mass.: Crossroads.

Wiseman, John A. 1979. "Structural and Ideological Tensions in a Rural Hausa Village." *African Studies Review* 22:1–11.

Works, John. 1976. *Pilgrims in a Strange Land: Hausa Communities in Chad.* New York: Columbia University Press.

Yahaya, Ibrahim Yaro. 1979. "Oral Art and Socialisation Process." Ph.D. dissertation, Ahmadu Bello University.

Yanko, Jennifer J. 1983. "Language Attitudes and Bilingualism in Niamey, Niger." *Africana Journal* 14:1–9.

Yusuf, Ahmed Beitallah. 1974. "A Reconsideration of Urban Conceptions: Hausa Urbanization and the Hausa Rural-Urban Continuum." *Urban Anthropology* 3:201–21.

——. 1975. "Capital Formation and Management among the Muslim Hausa Traders of Kano, Nigeria." *Africa* 45:167–82.

Yusuf, Bilkisu. 1991. "Hausa-Fulani Women: The State of the Struggle." In Coles & Mack, eds., 1991.

Index

#28708467